SAMUEL TAYLOR COLERIDGE was born in Devon on 21 October 1772 and educated at Christ's Hospital, London, and Jesus College, Cambridge. In 1795 he married Sara Fricker, Robert Southey's sister-in-law, a match that proved unhappy. In 1798 he went to Germany to learn the language, and spent 1804-6 abroad, mainly in Italy and Malta, where he was secretary to the first British governor. On his return to England he maintained himself by lecturing and journalism, and passed his last years at Highgate, a noted conversationalist and controversial writer. He died on 25 July 1834.

Coleridge's literary life had already begun before he met Wordsworth in Bristol in the mid 1790s. But it was their intimate friendship, which lasted until their quarrel in 1810, that he always acknowledged as the chief event of his intellectual life; and Wordworth returned the tribute by addressing *The Prelude,* his verse autobiography, to Coleridge and to his own sister, Dorothy. In 1798 the two young poets, by then largely disillusioned of their revolutionary sentiments, joined in writing *Lyrical Ballads,* where Coleridge's 'Ancient Mariner' first appeared; and it was Coleridge who urged Wordsworth to write a preface for the second edition of 1800 that represented a manifesto of the new school of poets. By 1815, when most of the *Biographia* was written, Coleridge's critical mind had shifted towards disagreement with his old friend, though to the end of his life he regarded Wordsworth as the greatest poet of the age, and the book is at once a record of that shift and of that abiding admiration.

GEORGE WATSON, who is a Fellow of St John's College, Cambridge, is author of *Coleridge the Poet, Politics and Literature in Modern Britain,* and *Writing a Thesis,* and editor of the *New Cambridge Bibliography of English Literature.* He has been a visiting professor at the universities of Zurich, Minnesota, New York and Georgia, and is editor of the Unservile State Group.

SAMUEL TAYLOR COLERIDGE

Biographia Literaria

or Biographical Sketches of
My Literary Life and Opinions

Edited, with an introduction, by
George Watson
St John's College, Cambridge

J. M. Dent & Sons Ltd
London
Charles E. Tuttle Co., Inc.
Rutland, Vermont

EVERYMAN'S LIBRARY

Notes, additions and revisions,
© David Campbell Publishers Ltd, 1965, 1975
All rights reserved

Made in Great Britain by
The Guernsey Press Co. Ltd, Guernsey, C.I. for
J. M. Dent & Sons Ltd
91, Clapham High Street, London SW4 7TA
and
Charles E. Tuttle Co., Inc.
28, South Main Street, Rutland, Vermont
05701, U.S.A.

This edition was first published by J. M. Dent, 1906
Re-edited and reset 1956
Reprinted, with additions and corrections, 1965
First published in this edition 1975
Reprinted 1980, 1982, 1984, 1987
Reissued 1991

ISBN 0 460 87108 0

Everyman's Library
Reg. U.S. Patent Office

CONTENTS

BIOGRAPHIA LITERARIA

[VOLUME I]

INTRODUCTION

I. 1800–1815

THE story of the *Biographia Literaria* begins seventeen years
before it appeared as two volumes on the London bookstalls in
July 1817: it begins in a conversation between two friends.   In
the autumn of 1800 Wordsworth and Coleridge, both settled in
the Lake District after their return from Germany in the previous
year, were debating what form a second edition of the *Lyrical
Ballads* should take to replace the exhausted edition of 1798.
In the course of a walk the idea of replacing the brief Advertisement by a critical preface was conceived.   To the aged memory
of Wordsworth many years after, the idea, and indeed the very
substance of the Preface as he came to write it, were all Coleridge's.   'I never cared a straw about the theory,' he wrote
impatiently on the manuscript of Barron Field's biography of
himself, 'and the Preface was written at the request of Mr Coleridge out of sheer good nature.   I recollect the very spot, a
deserted quarry in the Vale of Grasmere, where he pressed the
thing upon me, and but for that it would never have been
thought of.'

This is the first recorded moment in the life of this book.   For
though it would be an exaggeration to call the Preface a first draft
of the *Biographia*, the exaggeration would be a rewarding one.
Coleridge himself said it was 'half a child of my own brain',[1]
and admitted to another friend at the same time that he had first
suggested writing the Preface himself, but had abandoned it and
turned over his notes to Wordsworth.[2]   By 1815, of course,
when he came to write the *Biographia*, the Preface was 'Wordsworth' and the *Biographia* Coleridge's reply to Wordsworth;
but the simplification is much too crude.   No doubt there were
already real if hidden differences between the two men in 1800,
but if so they were hidden from Coleridge himself.   It is easy to
detect the note of surprise in his letters of 1802–3 when he first
speaks of disagreements, and even then he was uncertain what
the disagreements were.   On the evidence it seems fair to

[1] Letter to Robert Southey, 29 July 1802.
[2] Letter to William Sotheby, 13 July 1802.   But the letter is torn and the
reading conjectural.   Cf. *Notebooks*, 787n.

suppose that the attacks upon the Preface in the *Biographia*, sharp as they are, are the sharpness of a middle-aged man disagreeing with his youth. No wonder if Wordsworth, who had written the Preface only under persuasion, resented these attacks; but it proves nothing about his part in composing the Preface that he constantly reprinted it. An author may feel as protective of the reputation of commissioned work as of any other.

The Preface of 1800 poses and tries to answer two closely connected questions: first, what relation should the language of poetry bear to that of ordinary life? And secondly, what relation should the subject of poetry bear to life itself? (The order in which the questions are put looks irrational, but it is Wordsworth's own order and there are good reasons for it.) The answers of the Preface are 'the real language of men in a state of vivid sensation' (restated in 1802 as 'a *selection* of the language really spoken by men'), and 'the incidents of common life.' These two questions, or rather Coleridge's attempt to modify and clarify the old answers to them, are together the central theme of the second half of the *Biographia*. It is conventional to call this part of the book (chs. 14–22) the 'critique of Wordsworth,' but the convention is highly misleading. Little or nothing purely Wordsworthian is here under arraignment, though Coleridge seizes the opportunity to use the poetry of Wordsworth, whom he considered the greatest poet of his age, to illustrate his mature views on the language and subject of poetry.

The Coleridge who had turned over to Wordsworth the task of writing a critical preface was a man who was nursing a similar project of his own. His plans for a biography of Lessing, which he had gone to Germany to prepare, were being pushed out of his thoughts by the more seductive idea of a treatise which would combine in some unspecified way his twin interests of philosophy and poetry. On 9 October 1800 he wrote to Humphry Davy: 'The works which I gird myself up to attack as soon as money concerns will permit me are the life of Lessing and the essay on poetry. The latter is still more at my heart than the former: its title would be *An Essay on the Elements of Poetry*—it would be in reality a disguised system of morals and politics.' Writing again to Davy four months later (3 February 1801) he complained that illness was preventing him from writing the treatise, which was now to be called *Concerning Poetry, and the Nature of the Pleasures Derived from it* and was to deal with 'the affinities of the feelings with words and ideas.' The more he thought about the Preface the less he agreed with it, and talking to Wordsworth only made matters worse: 'We have had lately some little controversy on this subject, and we begin to suspect that there is somewhere or other a radical difference [in our] opinions.'[1]

'Somewhere or other'—at the age of thirty Coleridge is very certain he wants to write a treatise on aesthetics but still uncertain what to put into it.   A fortnight later he decided on a pragmatic approach, a study of contemporary poetry, 'one volume essays, the second selections. . . .   The object is not to examine what is good in each writer, but what has *ipso facto* pleased and to what faculties, or passions, or habits of the mind they may be supposed to have given pleasure.'[2]   The final object, in fact, an aesthetic theory, is kept in view, but a new approach has been found to it. More importantly the Preface has already become 'Wordsworth's' and Coleridge is now talking of impartial mediation between the old and the new schools of poetry.   He goes on: 'Of course Darwin[3] and Wordsworth having given each a defence of their mode of poetry and a disquisition on the nature and essence of poetry in general, I shall necessarily be led rather deeper, and these I shall treat of either first or last.'   As for his disagreement with Wordsworth, 'this I shall endeavour to go to the bottom of, and acting the arbiter between the old school and the new school hope to lay down some plain and perspicuous, tho' not superficial, canons of criticism respecting poetry.' He had high hopes of writing the book quickly; he wrote to Tom Wedgwood (20 October 1802) promising that 'very shortly . . . I shall present you from the press with my opinions in full on the subject of style both in prose and verse,' about which he claimed to have 'thought much and patiently.'   By now he has moved so far from the Preface that he feels poetic diction to 'require a certain *aloofness* from [the la]nguage of real life, which I think deadly to poetry.'   But still the treatise was not written.

By the autumn of 1803 he had come to a fresh and utterly surprising decision on the form the book was to take: it was to be contained in an autobiographical frame and his views were to be stated in the context of the events that had made them.   In September he wrote in his notebook: 'Seem to have made up my mind to write my metaphysical works as *my* Life, & *in* my Life—

---

[1] Letter to Sotheby, op. cit.
[2] Letter to Southey, op. cit.
[3] Erasmus Darwin (1731–1802), who included a brief 'Apology' and 'Philosophical Notes' in his *Botanic Garden* (1789–91).

intermixed with all the other events or history of the mind & fortunes of S. T. Coleridge.'[1] This decision, at least, was irrevocable, but why he took it we shall never know. Perhaps it was an acknowledgement of failure, of some private incapacity ever to write a work of formal logical design however often he aspired to do so. Or it may have been a recognition of a distinctive talent, of an intense personalism that haunts everything he wrote down to the most crabbed and back-broken of his paragraphs, an inescapable I AM. No one can deny that the form of the *Biographia*, eccentric (indeed unique) as it is, is perfectly suited to what Coleridge has to offer, however easy it is to object that he has offered too much or too little. He had found a plan flexible enough to admit of the fragmentary and the inconclusive as the difficulties of his theme might demand. It was a good choice, in the circumstances. Not knowing all the answers he was in a position fairly and frankly to say why.

By the end of 1803 the distinction between imagination and fancy was already formulated,[2] an incisive restatement of an ancient value-judgment, and only health and leisure seemed wanting to write the book. But for twelve years little or nothing was done towards it. Instead ill health drove him to Malta and Italy (1804–6), indecision and money troubles diverted his energies, while his views on aesthetics were dissipated in public lectures which were never published in his lifetime. By March 1815, still without a permanent home, he had settled for a year with his friends the Morgans at Calne in Wiltshire. A group of friends, one of them J. M. Gutch, the Bristol printer, now advanced him money on the security of his manuscripts with the prospect of a collection of his verse, published and unpublished, to be issued later in the year. After fifteen years of hesitation and delay the *Biographia* was begun.

II. 1815

By September 1815 the manuscript was complete and in the hands of Gutch at Bristol[3] after six months or less of crowded work; but the story of its composition is confused and doubtful.

---

[1] Quoted by George Whalley, *The Integrity of 'Biographia Literaria*,' Essays and Studies, new series VI (1953). Cf. *Notebooks*, 1515. This is the first mention of the *Biographia* in the notebooks.
[2] Letter to Richard Sharp, 15 January 1804: 'Imagination, or the *modifying* power in the highest sense of the word, in which I have ventured to oppose it to Fancy, or the *aggregating* power.'
[3] Letter to John May, 27 September 1815.

The traditional story we may dismiss at the outset. On 20 August, Mary Lamb, writing to Sarah Hutchinson, spoke of a letter she had recently received from Mrs Morgan, Coleridge's hostess at Calne: 'Your old friend Coleridge is very hard at work on a preface to a new edition which he is going to publish in the same form as Mr Wordsworth's—at first the preface was not to exceed five or six pages, it has however grown into a work of great importance. I believe Morgan has already written nearly two hundred pages [i.e. as Coleridge's amanuensis]. The title is *Autobiographia Literaria*: to which are added *Sybilline Leaves* [*sic*], a collection of poems by the same author.'[1]

Mary Lamb's understanding of Mrs Morgan's notion of what Coleridge or her husband told her was, in fact, that Coleridge was collecting his verse for publication as Wordsworth had done for his two-volume collection of *Poems* of March 1815, that he set out to write a brief preface and was carried away into writing a work of hundreds of pages. This would be an astonishing story on any evidence, but as it happens there is no evidence for it beyond this letter of Mary Lamb's, and that is at second hand. It is one woman's report to another of what a third has told her of her husband's (or lodger's) conversation: evidence of a sort that is daily dismissed in courts of law. What did happen (and it is easy to see how the misunderstanding arose) is explained by Coleridge himself in a letter probably written within a few days of the events it describes and addressed to his friend Dr Brabant (29 July 1815): 'The necessity of extending, what I first intended as a preface, to an *Autobiographia Literaria, or Sketches of my Literary Life and Opinions*, as far as poetry and *poetical* criticism is concerned, has confined me to my study from 11 to 4 and from 6 to 10, since I last left you. I have just finished it, having only the correction of the MSS. to go thro'. I have given a full account (*raisonné*) of the controversy concerning Wordsworth's poems and theory, in which my name has been so constantly included. I have no doubt that Words- worth will be displeased—but I have done my duty to myself and to the public in (as I believe) compleatly subverting the theory & in proving that the poet himself has never acted on it except in particular stanzas which are the blots of his com- positions.'

The statement seems perfectly explicit and gives rise to two conclusions:

---

[1] *Letters of Charles Lamb*, etc., ed. E. V. Lucas (1935), II, 172. Coleridge dictated a good part of the book to John Morgan; cf. *Notebooks*, 4108n.

(i) That by July 1815 Coleridge had already written a work which he called *Autobiographia Literaria* which did *not* include the 'critique of Wordsworth.' This must have consisted, approximately, of vol. i of the first edition, or chapters 1–13, a work primarily philosophical and remarkably similar to his project of the years 1800–3 quoted above—'my metaphysical works as *my* Life, & *in* my Life.'

(ii) That in July, believing this work to be more or less complete, he sat down to write a preface to it which outgrew his intentions by developing into a long discussion of the theories of the 1800 Preface, i.e. vol. ii of the first edition, or chapters 14–22 at the least. It must have been this 'preface' which Mary Lamb, or Mrs Morgan, confused with the preface to his poems, *Sibylline Leaves*, which in the event appeared in August 1817 with nothing but a factual three-page preface. The confusion is the more understandable if we remember that Coleridge seems from the beginning to have regarded the *Biographia* as a whole, if not as a preface in the conventional sense, at least as a companion volume to his collection of verse.[1] In fact the sheets of *Sibylline Leaves*, printed for Gutch by John Evans of Bristol in 1815, appeared two years later with the then meaningless register 'Vol. ii' in their signatures. Apparently this volume was meant to follow upon a one-volume *Biographia*, the two to represent the author's literary achievement—a splendid reply to the repeated and deeply resented charge of idleness.

But a book, as the evidence proves, the *Biographia* was always intended to be, a prose work in its own right to be published alone between separate boards. It is important that the legend put about by Mary Lamb's letter should be silenced. It is not simply that it is untrue; it has also made it altogether too easy for those who have criticized the design of the book, the first of whom was Coleridge himself in the course of it, to dismiss it as nothing better than a series of digressions—'Biographical Sketches' indeed, as the concessive sub-title has it. But this will not do. The design of the work may be unorthodox and was certainly obscured by adventures in the press, but it does exist and demands to be understood.

One must approach with caution, however, since the most important decision of all has left no record. Coleridge now had

---

[1] On 30 March 1815 Coleridge had written to Byron: 'A general Preface will be pre-fixed [to the volume of verse], on the principles of philosophic and genial criticism relatively to the fine arts in general; but especially to poetry'—i.e. vol. i of the first edition of the *Biographia*. Cf. Note, p. xxii, below.

a philosophical work of some dozen chapters; he had an unpre-meditated essay embodying his ideas of fifteen years past con-cerning the theories of the 1800 Preface which was growing longer every day and which promised to become nearly as long as the work itself. It had been begun as a preface, but it must soon have seemed natural to stand the book on its feet and put philosophy before criticism, the two parts pivoted on the imagination theory. Philosophy could explain and establish this theory: a discussion of the language and subject of poetry could then apply it. It may well be that it was a lost note from Coleridge, written to his printer Gutch in the high summer of 1815 warning him to expect twice the prose he had bargained for, that led to a fateful miscalculation.

But for Coleridge the old plan stood, and material intended for two volumes, one of prose and one of verse, was delivered to Gutch in Bristol in September 1815. Coleridge was elated. In six months he had achieved more than in a dozen years and unexpectedly fulfilled an old ambition. He could hardly wait for the *Biographia* to see the light. Of the form of the book he felt uncertain, since it followed a plan neither narrative nor logical but a disconcerting combination of the two. So 'im-methodical a miscellany,' he called it disparagingly, and 'this semi-narrative.' [1] But about its substance he had no reserva-tions. It was definitive. In a letter to Sotheby (31 January 1816) he expressed impatience to see the book out, both because it would help his financial position by setting out plainly the achievements of his career and because it 'settled the controversy concerning the nature of poetic diction, as far as reasoning can settle it.' He had recorded his old achievements and added another.

III. 1815–1817

An unusual disappointment was in store for him. Early in 1816 Gutch told him he had miscalculated the size of the manu-script, paginated for two volumes of some three hundred pages each and exhausted the manuscript half-way through the second volume. The sheets were printed, and the cost of remaking would be prohibitive. It was not only a crippling disappoint-ment but an apparently insoluble dilemma as well. The only solution seemed to be to add a further set of chapters at the end

---

[1] pp. 52–3, 93 below.

to make up the second volume. But the book was already bigger than Coleridge had originally intended; he had said his say and he had other urgent tasks to hand. By April he had left Calne for his final home with Dr Gillman at Highgate and Gutch's sheets had been bought by the London firm of Gale & Fenner. In the circumstances the quickest solution was to use some of his published writings as a makeweight. He seems to have considered his rejected tragedy *Zapolya* for the purpose, and bought back the copyright from Murray, but sensibly decided it would be out of place. By September 1816 the task was urgent and had to be dismissed. On 22nd he wrote to Fenner that he planned to 'commence the next week with the matter which I have been forced by the blunder and false assurance of the printer to add to the *Literary Life* in order to render the volumes of something like the same size. I not only shall not, but I cannot think of or do anything till the three volumes complete [i.e. two of the *Biographia* and one of *Sibylline Leaves*] are in Mr Gale's house.' The problem was pressing, but it was complex.

To begin with, the printed sheets as they stood represented a completed work and presumably had a conclusion of their own. If he had to incorporate new material, this last would have to be scrapped, and the final chapter that remained (ch. 22) would have to be rewritten, at least at the latter end, so that the work could be extended without a premature conclusion. This surely explains why Fenner's printing begins in mid-chapter, at p. 145 of volume ii [1] and not at the beginning of 'Satyrane's Letters.' The old conclusion had to be replaced with connective tissue. There is no certain evidence that Coleridge rewrote the latter part of chapter 22 (ii. 145–82) or padded out his examination of Wordsworth's characteristic defects and excellences, but there is a natural presumption that he did so. He needed more material, he avails himself here even more liberally than usual of long quotations, and the Fenner section of the chapter is nearly three times as long as the Gutch, which surely suggests it more than replaces the original ending. The final note to the chapter was obviously added at this time and has misled Coleridge scholars ever since, though to interpret it as literally as they have done is to suggest a bibliographical impossibility: 'For more than eighteen months have . . . *Sibylline Leaves* and the present volumes, up to this page, been printed and ready for publication.' Something corresponding to 'this page' may well

---

[1] p. 254 below. For this discovery I am indebted to Mr Herbert Davis's examination of the copy in the Bodleian Library.

have been printed in Bristol, but for Coleridge to be able to add a note at this point proves that this page (ii. 182) must have been printed in London.[1]

Coleridge rewrote and probably expanded the latter part of chapter 22, the end of his critical section, adding to it an explanatory note to justify the insertion of three letters written home from Germany during his youthful visit there (1798–9) and already printed in *The Friend*. He revised them and entitled them 'Satyrane's Letters.' But he still had space to fill, and he needed more material in some sense autobiographical. He chose the review he had written with Morgan for the *Courier* damning Maturin's tragedy *Bertram*, which had been preferred by Drury Lane to his own *Zapolya*. And still his vexations were not quite over. The book needed a conclusion and he still had the old one to hand; it may well have been the last pages of the book we now have, an impassioned defence of his religious orthodoxy. We cannot be certain. But it is clear that Coleridge was in a hurry, that the conclusion would have followed strangely upon a most unchristian attack upon a successful rival and that some bridge-passage was necessary if it were to be used at all. There is an undated and uncollected letter to his printer Curtis which may belong to this moment of distraction: 'The introductory pages wanting for the *Life and Opinions* I am now employed on, and if I can finish it before I go to bed I will. The remainder, should there be any, I will endeavour to finish in town to-morrow after eleven o'clock; for from seven to eleven I shall be engaged in going to and having an interview with Mr Southey.' The only recorded visit of Southey to London from his Keswick home which would fit the terms of this letter was a visit made towards the end of April 1817, three months before the *Biographia* appeared and probably at the very time when the additions were going to press. Now the middle of the existing Conclusion, a complaint against Hazlitt for two reviews of the *Statesman's Manual* which had appeared in December 1816, can only have been written early in 1817. These are probably the 'introductory pages' referred to in this letter, introductory to the religious apologia. And this apologia was probably the conclusion of the *Biographia* of the 1815 manuscript, printed by Gutch, scrapped by Fenner, and reinstated now at the end of the

---

[1] Dykes Campbell in his *Narrative* (1894), and following him T. J. Wise in his *Bibliography* (1913), state that the Bristol printing ends at ii. 128. There is no evidence for this. They have apparently accepted Coleridge's figure of ii. 182 literally and then suffered a misprint.

extended work, its first pages rewritten to include the complaint against Hazlitt.

There were, then, four additions made to the original *Biographia* at the behest of the printer, three certain and one likely. The three certain additions are 'Satyrane's Letters,' the critique of *Bertram* ('Chapter XXIII'), and part of the Conclusion. The likely addition is the latter part of chapter 22, which may well have been padded. Only the last two additions are organic. The attack upon Hazlitt at the beginning of the Conclusion merely resumes the subject of Coleridge's mistreatment at the hands of reviewers, a recurring theme throughout the book. And the latter part of chapter 22, whether padded or not, cannot run beyond Coleridge's original intention in substance, since the argument at the head of the chapter was printed in Bristol and is observed throughout. But no defence can be made for 'Satyrane's Letters' or the critique of *Bertram*. They were no part of Coleridge's original intention; he added them when desperately in search of makeweights. and they add nothing to the substance of the book. For these reasons they are excluded from this edition, which is therefore the first to present the *Biographia* as nearly as possible according to the author's intentions.

IV. 1817 and After

In July 1817, after a delay of nearly two years, a desperate scramble and real financial injury to Coleridge himself, the *Biographia* appeared in two ill-printed demy octavo volumes from the house of Fenner. It must have been a dreary enough occasion. The delay had robbed Coleridge of his first joyful anticipation of the success of the book, the irrelevant additions had obscured his intentions, and there were many misprints. To end all the book was damned by *Blackwood's*, while the *Quarterly Review* ignored it altogether. It was never reprinted in Coleridge's lifetime. Even Wordsworth, the reader he most ardently respected, refused to do more than skim the book and found 'the praise extravagant and the censure inconsiderate.' [1] Failure must have seemed complete. But the leaves were being turned by two young men who were both strangers to Coleridge. In November 1817 John Keats wrote to Dilke for a copy of *Sibylline Leaves*, and a close echo of Coleridge's language in his

[1] Crabb Robinson, *Diary*, December 1817.

famous letter concerning 'negative capability' (21 December
1817) suggests that he read the *Biographia* at the same time.[1]
And Shelley, established at Marlow, read the book as soon as it
appeared and retained a key phrase which four years later he
appropriated for his *Defence of Poetry*.[2]   These small beginnings
were characteristic.   The book has always been seminal and
has always been recognized as such, a proper object for respect
and for plunder.   But its very existence as a book, with one
notable exception,[3] has been doubted and denied by those best
qualified to speak.   By the strangest of oversights no editor has
so far sought to rescue it from the undignified legend set about by
Mary Lamb's letter that the book is an extended afterthought,
an exercise in garrulity; or even from the extraneous matter that
Coleridge was forced by circumstances to insert.   Design and
purpose have been denied it, and yet its greatest originality is its
design.

Not that Coleridge's original plan for the book demands our
praise or even our attention.   Coleridge had such a plan, but he
broke it.   He set out to write a work of metaphysics to which he
hoped the events of his life would give a continuity: he ended by
producing a work of aesthetics to which such narrative as there is
has failed to give continuity.   But there is another unity, and it is
peculiarly Coleridgean.   He succeeds for the first and (so far)
for the last time in English criticism in marrying the twin
studies of philosophy and literature, not simply by writing about
both within the boards of a single book or by insisting that such a
marriage should be, but in discovering a causal link between the
two in the century-old preoccupation of English critics with the
theory of the poet's imagination.   Here at chapters 12 and 13,
mid-point in the *Biographia*, the theory finds it proper setting
and fulfils its just service, the link is forged.   The operation is
effected without modesty, with more than enough appeals to
authority and much heralding and hesitation, none of which is
defensible by strict standards.   Chapters 10 and 11, in particular, are a lamentable exhibition of cold feet.   But Coleridge
was right to appreciate the difficulty and importance of what he
was trying to do.   He was trying to solve with superior and
up-to-date intellectual tools a problem which his predecessors in
their detached and dilettante way had been considering ever
since Hobbes and Dryden had stated the difficulty in the 1650's

[1] p. 256 below.
[2] p. 169 below.
[3] George Whalley, *The Integrity of 'Biographia Literaria,'* op. cit.

and 1660's. Aesthetics, after all, were a well-established parlour-game in eighteenth-century England. When Edmund Burke, in defiance of the real bent of his genius, produced in his twenty-eighth year a treatise called *A Philosophical Enquiry into the Origin of our Ideas of the Sublime and Beautiful* (1757) he was doing what many young authors had done to attract attention to themselves. But all these early attempts to justify literary criticism by philosophic method fail to impress. Hobbes was too much of a professional philosopher to indulge his literary interests except as a hobby; Dryden too much of a professional man of letters to offer more than a brilliant aside on the subject; and the eighteenth-century aestheticians (Addison, Burke, Kames, Reynolds, Beattie and many others) were dilettanti in criticism, coiners of theories that never found currency. Johnson managed to write the critical masterpiece of the age, the *Lives of the Poets*, without once referring to the theories of any of them.

Vulgar and abrupt as it must have seemed, the Preface of 1800 had put them all to flight by asking two questions of practical interest to poets and readers alike, and Coleridge made one of the most important decisions of his life in deciding to follow up this *succès de scandale* by abandoning Lessing to write an elaborate treatise on the new aesthetic. His delay was unfortunate, the delay of his printers doubly frustrating. But all this need not prevent us now from understanding his intention. He was not writing an autobiography, not even an account of his literary life, and any sort of biographical approach to the book is certain to be disappointed.[1] Nor was he writing an essay in the history of ideas, a task for which he was peculiarly unfitted for two reasons: his memory, though capacious, was inaccurate and inventive, and he had no more than an occasional curiosity to know the provenance of ideas. 'I regard truth as a divine ventriloquist: I care not from whose mouth the sounds are supposed to proceed.'[2] A queer fish among English critics, his curiosity was all for ideas. He did not even care about being entertaining, and shrugged off the charge of obscurity with the retort that 'my severest critics have not pretended to have found in my compositions triviality, or traces of a mind that shrunk from the toil of thinking.'[3] There was a task to be done, and it is still undone: to convince that hasty evaluation is never much better than an arbitrary rule-of-thumb, however stimulating a game it

---

[1] p. 281n. below.   [2] p. 89 below.   [3] p. 124 below.

may be, and that 'the ultimate end of criticism is much more to establish principles of writing than to furnish rules how to pass judgement on what has been written by others.'[1] He wrote in the infancy of psychology, but he could see that the claims of poetry to respect all depended upon a study of those mental faculties common in their operation to poet and reader. To isolate and define these faculties would give the study of literature a security it had never had. His object, as he told Byron a few weeks after sending the *Biographia* to the press, was 'to reduce criticism to a system by the deduction of causes from principles involved in our faculties.'[2] Of course his success is debatable. The imagination-concept may be the wrong place to start; or, even if it is the right place, Coleridge's definitions and distinctions might be exposed as imprecise or question-begging. So much remains to be done, even as a beginning. To set out from the *Biographia* and go straight on in the same inquiring spirit could give the criticism of tomorrow a profundity and a range that it lacks to-day.

GEORGE WATSON.

NOTE (1965)

THE demand for a new edition has enabled me to make a few corrections. As for my introduction, which was written in 1955, the appearance in 1959 of the fourth volume of Professor Griggs's Oxford edition of the *Collected Letters*, containing a more accurate transcript of the letter to Dr Brabant (29 July 1815) from the manuscript in the possession of Lord Latymer, has restored to obscurity Coleridge's account of the composition of the *Biographia*—an account which, on p. xiii above, I once dared to call 'perfectly explicit.' Professor Griggs's view is that 'at no time did Coleridge propose a preface to his autobiography' (p. 578n.), and that his reference to 'what I first intended as a preface' can only, in view of the punctuation, refer to a preface to the poems (p. 579n.). The difficulty of interpreting the letter is not confined to this point: it is not even clear, so erratic is Coleridge's use of punctuation and capitalization, how much of the sentence refers to the title of the book he is engaged on.

My present view is that the letter to Brabant cannot be interpreted with certainty, but that the notion that 'preface' refers to a preface to a collection of poems is unnatural, given that no

---

[1] p. 217 below. [2] Letter to Byron, 17 October 1815.

reference to such a collection has so far been made in the letter. But whether it refers to some part of what is now the *Biographia*, as I supposed ten years ago, is equally a matter for doubt. A likelihood has been reduced to a possibility.

Professor Griggs has also collected, and for the first time, the letter to Thomas Curtis referred to on p. xvii, above, and on convincing grounds has dated it 29 April 1817. No textual problem is here involved, since the letter survives only in *Lippincott's Magazine* (June 1874); but Professor Griggs's conjecture that the phrase 'introductory pages wanting for the Life and Opinions' refers to preliminary matter to *Sibylline Leaves* (p. 727n.) seems to me inadmissible.

G. W.

St John's College, Cambridge.
March 1965.

SECOND NOTE (1974)

THE appearance of this new edition, nearly twenty years after its first making, has given me the opportunity to enter several corrections into the text and commentary, and to substitute a much enlarged Select Bibliography (p. xxiv). I am grateful to correspondents who have suggested improvements over the years.

Meanwhile Volume 3 of Coleridge's *Notebooks*, edited by Kathleen Coburn, has recently appeared (1973), covering the years 1808–19, including the period of the composition of the *Biographia* in 1815 and much of its long preparation over the previous dozen years. The total relationship between these notes and the *Biographia* remains to be explored in detail, and Miss Coburn offers convincing evidence that certain notes were 'in Coleridge's mind, possibly the notebook was in his hand, when *BL* was being dictated' to John Morgan in Calne in 1815 (no. 3285n.). I have added to my commentary a number of references to this new material.

Note to p. 100, l. 24ff.: *They will bear witness for me how opposite even then my principles were to those of Jacobinism or even of democracy* . . . John Thelwall, in recently published marginalia to the first edition of the *Biographia*, sharply accuses Coleridge of misrepresenting his youthful revolutionary views in this passage: 'That Mr C. was indeed far from Democracy, because he was far beyond it, I well remember—for he was a down right zealous leveller, & indeed in one of the worst senses of the word he was a Jacobin, a man of blood—Does he forget the letters he wrote to me (& which I believe I yet have) acknowledging the justice of my castigation of him for the violence and sanguinary tendency of some of his doctrines?' Cf. Burton R. Pollin, 'John Thelwall's Marginalia in a Copy of Coleridge's *Biographia Literaria*', *Bulletin of New York Public Library* (February 1970). Thelwall (1764–1832) did not meet Coleridge till 1797, after an extended correspondence with him; the earliest surviving letters to him from Coleridge date from April to June 1796 (*Letters* I. 204f.). Coleridge speaks there of still being a 'necessitarian' in moral questions, and announces he has only just ceased to be an infidel, having been recently prejudiced against atheism by the example of William Godwin (I. 221). It seems probable that Coleridge in the *Biographia* substantially underrates his revolutionary sympathies in the early and mid-1790s, though they seem to have been in retreat by 1796.

St John's College, Cambridge.   G. W.
   February 1974.

SELECT BIBLIOGRAPHY

COLERIDGE'S WRITINGS

Poems on various subjects, 1796; *The watchman*, 1796 (periodical); *Lyrical ballads*, 1798 (with 'Ancient Mariner'), 2 vols., 1800 (enlarged, with Wordsworth's Preface); *Wallenstein*, 1800 (translated from Schiller); *The friend: a weekly paper*, 1809–10, 1812 (collected); *Remorse: a tragedy*, 1813; *Christabel, Kubla Khan, The pains of sleep*, 1816; *Lay sermons*, 1816–17; *Biographia literaria*, 2 vols., 1817; *Zapolya*, 1817; *Sibylline leaves: a collection of poems*, 1817; *Aids to reflection*, 1825.

Table-talk (ed. H. N. Coleridge), 2 vols., 1835; *Literary remains* (ed. H. N. Coleridge), 4 vols., 1836–9; *Animae poetae* (ed. E. H. Coleridge), 1895 (from notebooks); *Shakespearean criticism* (ed. T. M. Raysor), 2 vols., 1930; *Miscellaneous criticism* (ed. Raysor), 1936; *Philosophical lectures* (ed. Kathleen Coburn), 1949; *Inquiring spirit* (ed. Coburn), 1951 (from Notebooks etc.); *Notebooks* (ed. Coburn), 11 vols., 1957– ; *Collected letters* (ed. E. L. Griggs), 6 vols., 1956–71.

The *Collected works* of Coleridge, edited by Kathleen Coburn and others, began to appear in 1969. The poetical works have been edited by E. H. Coleridge, 2 vols., 1912, and selected writings by Stephen Potter in the Nonesuch Library 1933, 1950 (enlarged).

BIOGRAPHY AND CRITICISM

John Stuart Mill, 'Coleridge' (1840) in *Bentham and Coleridge* (ed. F. R. Leavis, 1950); James Dykes Campbell, *Coleridge: a narrative of his life*, 1894; J. L. Lowes, *The road to Xanadu*, 1927, 1930 (enlarged); I. A. Richards, *Coleridge on imagination*, 1934, 1960 (revised); E. K. Chambers, *Coleridge: a biographical study*, 1938; Humphry House, *Coleridge*, 1953; J. B Beer, *Coleridge the visionary*, 1959; George Watson, *Coleridge the poet*, 1966; J. A. Appleyard, *Coleridge's philosophy of literature*, 1965; W. J. Bate, *Coleridge*, 1969; Basil Willey, *Coleridge*, 1972; Owen Barfield, *What Coleridge thought*, 1972. For early criticism see *Coleridge: the critical heritage*, ed. J. R. de J. Jackson, 1970; and for recent studies, *Coleridge*, ed. R. L. Brett, 1971; K. M. Wheeler, *Sources, Processes and Methods in Coleridge's Biographia Literaria*, 1980.

NOTE ON THE TEXT

THE text of this edition is based wholly upon the first edition of 1817, the only one published in England in Coleridge's lifetime. No attempt has been made to modernize the text, but obvious misprints have been silently corrected, spelling of names regularized, and an attempt made to rationalize the use of italics and capitalization, both of which have been much reduced. The editor's footnotes are distinguished from Coleridge's by square brackets.

This is the fourth annotated edition of the *Biographia Literaria* to appear, and it is deeply indebted to its predecessors. The pioneer edition was that by the poet's nephew and son-in-law Henry Nelson Coleridge, which was completed after his death by his widow Sara and appeared in three volumes in 1847. Its text, which is amended and slightly expurgated, has no authority, but the annotation betrays careful if unprofessional scholarship, while the long introduction includes a fervent defence by Sara Coleridge of her father's religious orthodoxy and of the innocent nature of his plagiarism. The second, by John Shawcross (the Oxford edition) appeared in two volumes in 1907, its text based on *1817* and its notes on *1847*. The third, being chapters 1–4 and 14–22 only, together with the 1800 Preface and other related texts, was edited by George Sampson and appeared in Cambridge in 1920.

So wenig er auch bestimmt seyn mag, andere zu belehren, so wünscht er doch sich denen mitzutheilen, die er sich gleichgesinnt weiss, oder hofft, deren Anzahl aber in der Breite der Welt zerstreut ist: er wünscht sein Verhältniss zu den ältesten Freunden dadurch wieder anzuknüpfen, mit neuen es fortzusetzen, und in der letzen Generation sich wieder andere für seine übrige Lebenszeit zu gewinnen. Er wünscht der Jugend die Umwege zu ersparen, auf denen er sich selbst verirrte.

GOETHE.[1]

Translation. Little call as he may have to instruct others, he wishes nevertheless to open out his heart to such as he either knows or hopes to be of like mind with himself, but who are widely scattered in the world: he wishes to knit anew his connections with his oldest friends, to continue those recently formed, and to win other friends among the rising generation for the remaining course of his life. He wishes to spare the young those circuitous paths on which he himself had lost his way.

[1] [From the introduction to *Die Propyläen*, 1798–1800.]

CHAPTER I

The motives of the present work—Reception of the author's first publication
—The discipline of his taste at school—The effect of contemporary writers
on youthful minds—Bowles's Sonnets—Comparison between the poets
before and since Mr Pope.

It has been my lot to have had my name introduced, both in conversation and in print, more frequently than I find it easy to
explain, whether I consider the fewness, unimportance and
limited circulation of my writings, or the retirement and distance
in which I have lived, both from the literary and political world.
Most often it has been connected with some charge which I could
not acknowledge, or some principle which I had never entertained. Nevertheless, had I had no other motive or incitement,
the reader would not have been troubled with this exculpation.
What my additional purposes were will be seen in the following
pages. It will be found that the least of what I have written
concerns myself personally. I have used the narration chiefly
for the purpose of giving a continuity to the work, in part for the
sake of the miscellaneous reflections suggested to me by particular events; but still more as introductory to the statement of
my principles in politics, religion and philosophy, and the
application of the rules deduced from philosophical principles to
poetry and criticism. But of the objects which I proposed to
myself, it was not the least important to effect, as far as possible,
a settlement of the long-continued controversy concerning the
true nature of poetic diction, and at the same time to define with
the utmost impartiality the real poetic character of the poet by
whose writings this controversy was first kindled and has been
since fuelled and fanned.

In 1794, when I had barely passed the verge of manhood, I
published a small volume of juvenile poems.[1] They were
received with a degree of favor which, young as I was, I well
knew was bestowed on them not so much for any positive merit
as because they were considered buds of hope and promises of
better works to come. The critics of that day, the most flattering equally with the severest, concurred in objecting to them

[1] [*Poems on Various Subjects*, actually published in April 1796, when
Coleridge was twenty-three.]

1

obscurity, a general turgidness of diction and a profusion of new-coined double epithets.[1] The first is the fault which a writer is the least able to detect in his own compositions; and my mind was not then sufficiently disciplined to receive the authority of others as a substitute for my own conviction. Satisfied that the thoughts, such as they were, could not have been expressed otherwise, or at least more perspicuously, I forgot to inquire whether the thoughts themselves did not demand a degree of attention unsuitable to the nature and objects of poetry. This remark, however, applies chiefly, though not exclusively, to the 'Religious Musings.' The remainder of the charge I admitted to its full extent, and not without sincere acknowledgements to both my private and public censors for their friendly admonitions. In the after editions I pruned the double epithets with no sparing hand, and used my best efforts to tame the swell and glitter both of thought and diction; though, in truth, these parasite plants of youthful poetry had insinuated themselves into my longer poems with such intricacy of union, that I was often obliged to omit disentangling the weed from the fear of snapping the flower. From that period to the date of the present work I have published nothing with my name which could by any possibility have come before the board of anonymous criticism.[2] Even the three or four poems, printed with the works of a friend, as far as they were censured at all, were charged with the same or similar defects, though I am

---

[1] The authority of Milton and Shakespeare may be usefully pointed out to young authors. In the 'Comus' and earlier poems of Milton there is a super-fluity of double epithets; while in the *Paradise Lost* we find very few, in the *Paradise Regained* scarce any. The same remark holds almost equally true of the *Love's Labour's Lost, Romeo and Juliet, Venus and Adonis,* and *Lucrece,* compared with the *Lear, Macbeth, Othello,* and *Hamlet* of our great drama-tist. The rule for the admission of double epithets seems to be this: either that they should be already denizens of our language, such as *blood-stained, terror-stricken, self-applauding;* or when a new epithet, or one found in books only, is hazarded, that it at least be one word, not two words made one by mere virtue of the printer's hyphen. A language which, like the English, is almost without cases, is indeed in its very genius unfitted for compounds. If a writer, every time a compounded word suggests itself to him, would seek for some other mode of expressing the same sense, the chances are always greatly in favour of his finding a better word. '*Tanquam scopulum sic vites insolens verbum,*' is the wise advice of Caesar to the Roman orators, and the precept applies with double force to the writers in our own language. But it must not be forgotten that the same Caesar wrote a gram-matical treatise for the purpose of reforming the ordinary language by bringing it to a greater accordance with the principles of logic or universal grammar.

[2] [i.e. since the third edition of the *Poems* in 1803. Evidently written in 1815—but even so Coleridge has forgotten his tragedy *Remorse*, 1813.]

persuaded not with equal justice: with an excess of ornament, in addition to strained and elaborate diction.[1]   May I be permitted to add that, even at the early period of my juvenile poems, I saw and admitted the superiority of an austerer and more natural style, with an insight not less clear than I at present possess.   My judgement was stronger than were my powers of realizing its dictates; and the faults of my language, though indeed partly owing to a wrong choice of subjects and the desire of giving a poetic colouring to abstract and metaphysical truths in which a new world then seemed to open upon me, did yet, in part likewise, originate in unfeigned diffidence of my own comparative talent.   During several years of my youth and early manhood I reverenced those who had reintroduced the manly simplicity of the Grecian and of our own elder poets, with such enthusiasm as made the hope seem presumptuous of writing successfully in the same style.   Perhaps a similar process has happened to others; but my earliest poems were marked by an ease and simplicity which I have studied, perhaps with inferior success, to impress on my later compositions.

At school I enjoyed the inestimable advantage of a very sensible, though at the same time a very severe master.   He [2] early moulded my taste to the preference of Demosthenes to Cicero, of Homer and Theocritus to Virgil, and again of Virgil to Ovid.   He habituated me to compare Lucretius (in such extracts as I then read), Terence and, above all, the chaster poems of Catullus not only with the Roman poets of the so-called silver and brazen ages but with even those of the Augustan era; and, on grounds of plain sense and universal logic, to see and assert the superiority of the former in the truth and nativeness both of their thoughts and diction.   At the same time that we were studying the Greek tragic poets he made us read Shakespeare and Milton as lessons; and they were the lessons, too, which required most time and trouble to *bring up*, so as to escape his censure.   I learnt from him that poetry, even that of the loftiest and, seemingly, that of the wildest odes, had a logic of its own as severe as that of science; and more difficult, because more subtle, more complex, and dependent on more and more fugitive causes. In the truly great poets, he would say, there is a reason assignable, not only for every word, but for the position of every word;

[1] Vide the criticisms on the 'Ancient Mariner' in the *Monthly* and *Critical Reviews* of the first volume of the *Lyrical Ballads*.
[2] The Rev. James Bowyer, many years Head Master of the Grammar School, Christ's Hospital.

and I well remember that, availing himself of the synonimes to the Homer of Didymus, he made us attempt to show, with regard to each, why it would not have answered the same purpose, and wherein consisted the peculiar fitness of the word in the original text.

In our own English compositions (at least for the last three years of our school education) he showed no mercy to phrase, metaphor or image unsupported by a sound sense, or where the same sense might have been conveyed with equal force and dignity in plainer words. Lute, harp and lyre, muse, muses and inspirations, Pegasus, Parnassus and Hippocrene were all an abomination to him. In fancy I can almost hear him now, exclaiming, 'Harp? Harp? Lyre? Pen and ink, boy, you mean! Muse, boy, muse? Your nurse's daughter, you mean! Pierian spring? Oh, aye! the cloister-pump, I suppose!' Nay, certain introductions, similes and examples were placed by name on a list of interdiction. Among the similes there was, I remember, that of the manchineel fruit, as suiting equally well with too many subjects, in which, however, it yielded the palm at once to the example of Alexander and Clytus, which was equally good and apt whatever might be the theme. Was it ambition? Alexander and Clytus! Flattery? Alexander and Clytus! Anger? Drunkenness? Pride? Friendship? Ingratitude? Late repentance? Still, still Alexander and Clytus! At length the praises of agriculture having been exemplified in the sagacious observation that, had Alexander been holding the plough, he would not have run his friend Clytus through with a spear, this tried and serviceable old friend was banished by public edict *in secula seculorum*. I have sometimes ventured to think that a list of this kind or an *index expurgatorius* of certain well known and ever returning phrases, both introductory and transitional, including the large assortment of modest egotisms and flattering illeisms, etc. etc., might be hung up in our law courts and both Houses of Parliament with great advantage to the public as an important saving of national time, an incalculable relief to his Majesty's ministers; but, above all, as insuring the thanks of country attorneys and their clients, who have private bills to carry through the House.

Be this as it may, there was one custom of our master's which I cannot pass over in silence, because I think it imitable and worthy of imitation. He would often permit our theme exercises, under some pretext of want of time, to accumulate till each lad had four or five to be looked over. Then placing the whole

number abreast on his desk, he would ask the writer why this or
that sentence might not have found as appropriate a place under
this or that other thesis; and if no satisfying answer could be
returned and two faults of the same kind were found in one
exercise, the irrevocable verdict followed, the exercise was torn
up and another on the same subject to be produced, in addition
to the tasks of the day.   The reader will, I trust, excuse this
tribute of recollection to a man whose activities, even now, not
seldom furnish the dreams by which the blind fancy would fain
interpret to the mind the painful sensations of distempered sleep;
but neither lessen nor dim the deep sense of my moral and intellectual obligations.   He sent us to the University excellent Latin
and Greek scholars and tolerable Hebraists.   Yet our classical
knowledge was the least of the good gifts which we derived from
his zealous and conscientous tutorage.   He is now gone to his
final reward, full of years and full of honors, even of those honors
which were dearest to his heart as gratefully bestowed by that
school, and still binding him to the interests of that school in
which he had been himself educated and to which during his
whole life he was a dedicated thing.

From causes which this is not the place to investigate, no
models of past times, however perfect, can have the same vivid
effect on the youthful mind as the productions of contemporary
genius.   The discipline my mind had undergone, 'Ne falleretur
rotundo sono et versuum cursu, cincinnis et floribus; sed ut
inspiceret quidnam subesset, quae sedes, quod firmamentum,
quis fundus verbis; an figurae essent mera ornatura et orationis
fucus: vel sanguinis e materiae ipsius corde effluentis rubor
quidam nativus et incalescentia genuina,' [1] removed all obstacles
to the appreciation of excellence in style without diminishing my
delight.   That I was thus prepared for the perusal of Mr
Bowles's sonnets and earlier poems at once increased their
influence and my enthusiasm.   The great works of past ages
seem to a young man things of another race in respect to which
his faculties must remain passive and submiss, even as to the
stars and mountains.   But the writings of a contemporary,
perhaps not many years older than himself, surrounded by the

[1] ['Let him not be deceived by the smooth sound and flow of the verse, by
ornaments and flowers; but let him look down to the foundations, to the very
essence of the words, and see if the figures are mere ornament and the falsity
of rhetoric or if indeed they are the native redness of the blood, the meaning
itself, flowing from the heart as a genuine passion.'   Quotation untraced—
apparently from a Renaissance treatise, perhaps a comment on Cicero, De
oratore, III. xxv. 100.]

same circumstances and disciplined by the same manners, possess a *reality* for him and inspire an actual friendship as of a man for a man. His very admiration is the wind which fans and feeds his hope. The poems themselves assume the properties of flesh and blood. To recite, to extol, to contend for them is but the payment of a debt due to one who exists to receive it.

There are indeed modes of teaching which have produced, and are producing, youths of a very different stamp; modes of teaching in comparison with which we have been called on to despise our great public schools and universities

> in whose halls are hung
> Armoury of the invincible knights of old [1]—

modes by which children are to be metamorphosed into prodigies. And prodigies with a vengeance have I known thus produced! Prodigies of self-conceit, shallowness, arrogance and infidelity! Instead of storing the memory during the period when the memory is the predominant faculty with facts for the after exercise of the judgement; and instead of awakening by the noblest models the fond and unmixed love and admiration which is the natural and graceful temper of early youth, *these* nurslings of improved pedagogy are taught to dispute and decide; to suspect all but their own and their lecturer's wisdom; and to hold nothing sacred from their contempt but their own contemptible arrogance: boy-graduates in all the technicals and in all the dirty passions and impudence of anonymous criticism. To such dispositions alone can the admonition of Pliny be requisite, 'Neque enim debet operibus ejus obesse quod vivit. an si inter eos quos nunquam vidimus floruisset, non solum libros ejus verum etiam imagines conquireremus; ejusdem nunc honor praesentis et gratia quasi satietate languescet? at hoc pravum malignumque est, non admirari hominem admiratione dignissimum, quia videre, complecti, nec laudare tantum verum etiam amare contingit.' Plin. Epist., Lib. I.[2]

---

[1] [From Wordsworth's Sonnet xvi in his *Poems Dedicated to National Independence*:
> 'In our halls is hung
> Armoury of the invincible Knights of old.']

[2] ['For the works of the living should not suffer. If he had flourished among men we had never seen we should seek out not only his books but even portraits of him; should we now let his fame and favour languish as though we were tired of him? It is false and unkind not to admire someone so worthy of admiration because we can see and embrace him, because we can praise and even love him.']

I had just entered on my seventeenth year when the sonnets of Mr Bowles,[1] twenty in number, and just then published in a quarto pamphlet, were first made known and presented to me by a schoolfellow who had quitted us for the University and who, during the whole time that he was in our first form (or in our school language a Grecian), had been my patron and protector. I refer to Dr Middleton, the truly learned and every way excellent Bishop of Calcutta:

> Qui laudibus amplis
> Ingenium celebrare meum, calamumque solebat,
> Calcar agens animo validum.   Non omnia terrae
> Obruta!   Vivit amor, vivit dolor!   Ora negatur
> Dulcia conspicere; at flere et meminisse [2] relictum est.
>   Petr. Ep., Lib. I, Ep. I.[3]

It was a double pleasure to me, and still remains a tender recollection, that I should have received from a friend so revered the first knowledge of a poet by whose works, year after year, I was so enthusiastically delighted and inspired.   My earliest acquaintances will not have forgotten the undisciplined eagerness and impetuous zeal with which I laboured to make proselytes, not only of my companions, but of all with whom I conversed, of whatever rank and in whatever place.   As my school finances did not permit me to purchase copies I made, within less than a year and a half, more than forty transcriptions, as the best presents I could offer to those who had in any way won my regard.   And with almost equal delight did I receive the three or four following publications of the same author.

Though I have seen and known enough of mankind to be well aware that I shall perhaps stand alone in my creed, and that it will be well if I subject myself to no worse charge than that of singularity; I am not therefore deterred from avowing that I regard and ever have regarded the obligations of intellect among the most sacred of the claims of gratitude.   A valuable thought,

---

[1] [Apparently the second and enlarged edition of the *Sonnets* of William Lisle Bowles (1762–1850), which like the first was published at Bath in 1789. It contained 21 sonnets.]

[2] I am most happy to have the necessity of informing the reader that, since this passage was written, the report of Dr Middleton's death on his voyage to India has been proved erroneous.   He lives and long may he live; for I dare prophecy that with his life only will his exertions for the temporal and spiritual welfare of his fellow men be limited.

[3] [Petrarch (1304–74): 'who used to honour my talent and song with generous praises, a strong spur upon my spirit.   Everything is not hidden in the earth.   Love, grief live on.   We may not see their sweet faces; but it is left to us to weep and remember.']

or a particular train of thoughts, gives me additional pleasure when I can safely refer and attribute it to the conversation or correspondence of another.   My obligations to Mr Bowles were indeed important and for radical good.   At a very premature age, even before my fifteenth year, I had bewildered myself in metaphysicks and in theological controversy.   Nothing else pleased me.   History and particular facts lost all interest in my mind.   Poetry (though for a school-boy of that age I was above par in English versification and had already produced two or three compositions which, I may venture to say without reference to my age, were somewhat above mediocrity, and which had gained me more credit than the sound good sense of my old master was at all pleased with), poetry itself, yea novels and romances, became insipid to me.   In my friendless wanderings on our leave-days [1] (for I was an orphan, and had scarce any connections in London), highly was I delighted if any passenger, especially if he were dressed in black, would enter into conversation with me.   For I soon found the means of directing it to my favorite subjects

> Of providence, fore-knowledge, will, and fate,
> Fixed fate, free will, fore-knowledge absolute,
> And found no end in wandring mazes lost.[2]

This preposterous pursuit was, beyond doubt, injurious both to my natural powers and to the progress of my education.   It would perhaps have been destructive had it been continued; but from this I was auspiciously withdrawn, partly indeed by an accidental introduction to an amiable family,[3] chiefly however by the genial influence of a style of poetry so tender and yet so manly, so natural and real, and yet so dignified and harmonious, as the sonnets, etc., of Mr Bowles!   Well were it for me, perhaps, had I never relapsed into the same mental disease; if I had continued to pluck the flower and reap the harvest from the cultivated surface, instead of delving in the unwholesome quicksilver mines of metaphysic depths.   But if in after time I have sought a refuge from bodily pain and mismanaged sensibility in abstruse researches which exercised the strength and subtlety of the understanding without awakening the feelings of the heart; still

[1] The Christ's Hospital phrase, not for holidays altogether, but for those on which the boys are permitted to go beyond the precincts of the school.
[2] [*Paradise Lost*, II. 559–61.]
[3] [The family of Mary Evans, his first love, whom Coleridge first met in 1788.]

there was a long and blessed interval, during which my natural faculties were allowed to expand and my original tendencies to develop themselves; my fancy, and the love of nature, and the sense of beauty in forms and sounds.

The second advantage which I owe to my early perusal and ad-miration of these poems (to which let me add, though known to me at a somewhat later period, the *Lewesdon Hill* of Mr Crow) [1] bears more immediately on my present subject. Among those with whom I conversed there were, of course, very many who had formed their taste and their notions of poetry from the writings of Mr Pope and his followers: or to speak more gener-ally, in that school of French poetry condensed and invigorated by English understanding which had predominated from the last century. I was not blind to the merits of this school, yet as from inexperience of the world and consequent want of sym-pathy with the general subjects of these poems they gave me little pleasure, I doubtless undervalued the *kind*, and with the pre-sumption of youth withheld from its masters the legitimate name of poets. I saw that the excellence of this kind consisted in just and acute observations on men and manners in an artificial state of society as its matter and substance—and in the logic of wit conveyed in smooth and strong epigrammatic couplets as its form. Even when the subject was addressed to the fancy or the intellect, as in the *Rape of the Lock* or the *Essay on Man*; nay, when it was a consecutive narration, as in that astonishing product of matchless talent and ingenuity, Pope's translation of the Iliad; still a *point* was looked for at the end of each second line, and the whole was as it were a sorites or, if I may exchange a logical for a grammatical metaphor, a *conjunction disjunctive* of epigrams. Meantime the matter and diction seemed to me characterized not so much by poetic thoughts as by thoughts *translated* into the language of poetry. On this last point I had occasion to render my own thoughts gradually more and more plain to myself by frequent amicable disputes concerning Darwin's *Botanic Garden*,[2] which for some years was greatly extolled, not only by the reading public in general, but even by those whose genius and natural robustness of understanding enabled them afterwards to act foremost in dissipating these 'painted mists' that occasionally rise from the marshes at the

---

[1] [William Crowe (1745–1829), whose *Lewesdon Hill*, a moral-descriptive poem in a manner similar to that of Bowles, was published at Oxford in 1788.]

[2] [Appeared in two parts, 1789–90, by Erasmus Darwin (1731–1802), a long botanical allegory in heroic couplets.]

foot of Parnassus. During my first Cambridge vacation I
assisted a friend in a contribution [1] for a literary society in
Devonshire, and in this I remember to have compared Darwin's
work to the Russian palace of ice, glittering, cold and transitory.
In the same essay too I assigned sundry reasons, chiefly drawn
from a comparison of passages in the Latin poets with the
original Greek from which they were borrowed, for the preference of Collins's odes to those of Gray, and of the simile in
Shakespeare:

> How like a younker or a prodigal
> The scarfed bark puts from her native bay,
> Hugg'd and embraced by the strumpet wind!
> How like the prodigal doth she return,
> With over-weather'd ribs and ragged sails,
> Lean, rent and beggar'd by the strumpet wind! [2]

to the imitation in the *Bard*:

> Fair laughs the Morn, and soft the Zephyr blows
> While proudly riding o'er the azure realm
> In gallant trim the gilded Vessel goes;
> YOUTH on the prow, and Pleasure at the helm;
> Regardless of the sweeping Whirlwind's sway,
> That, hush'd in grim repose, expects its evening-prey. [3]

(In which, by the bye, the words 'realm' and 'sway' are rhymes
dearly purchased.) I preferred the original, on the ground that
in the imitation it depended wholly in the compositor's putting,
or not putting, a small capital both in this and in many other
passages of the same poet whether the words should be personi-
fications or mere abstracts. I mention this because, in referring
various lines in Gray to their original in Shakespeare and Milton,
and in the clear perception how completely all the propriety was
lost in the transfer, I was at that early period led to a conjecture
which, many years afterwards, was recalled to me from the same
thought having been started in conversation, but far more ably,
and developed more fully, by Mr Wordsworth; namely, that this
style of poetry which I have characterized above as translations
of prose thoughts into poetic language had been kept up by, if it
did not wholly arise from, the custom of writing Latin verses and
the great importance attached to these exercises in our public

---

[1] [This essay was never published and is now lost.]
[2] [*Merchant of Venice*, II. vi. 14–19.]
[3] [Gray, *The Bard* (1757), II. 2.]

schools. Whatever might have been the case in the fifteenth
century, when the use of the Latin tongue was so general among
learned men that Erasmus is said to have forgotten his native
language; yet in the present day it is not to be supposed that a
youth can think in Latin, or that he can have any other reliance
on the force or fitness of his phrases but the authority of the
author from whence he had adopted them. Consequently he
must first prepare his thoughts and then pick out from Virgil,
Horace, Ovid, or perhaps more compendiously, from his
Gradus,[1] halves and quarters of lines in which to embody them.

I never object to a certain degree of disputatiousness in a
young man from the age of seventeen to that of four or five and
twenty, provided I find him always arguing on one side of the
question. The controversies occasioned by my unfeigned zeal
for the honor of a favorite contemporary, then known to me
only by his works, were of great advantage in the formation and
establishment of my taste and critical opinions. In my defence
of the lines running into each other instead of closing at each
couplet, and of natural language, neither bookish nor vulgar,
neither redolent of the lamp nor of the kennel, such as *I will
remember thee*; instead of the same thought tricked up in the
rag-fair finery of

> ———Thy image on her wing
> Before my Fancy's eye shall Memory bring,

I had continually to adduce the metre and diction of the Greek
poets from Homer to Theocritus inclusive; and still more of our
elder English poets from Chaucer to Milton. Nor was this all.
But as it was my constant reply to authorities brought against
me from later poets of great name that no authority could avail
in opposition to Truth, Nature, Logic, and the Laws of Universal Grammar; actuated too by my former passion for metaphysical investigations, I labored at a solid foundation on which
permanently to ground my opinions in the component faculties
of the human mind itself and their comparative dignity and

---

[1] In the *Nutricia* of Politian there occurs this line:
'Pura coloratos interstrepit unda lapillos.'
Casting my eye on a University prize-poem, I met this line:
'Lactea purpureos interstrepit unda lapillos.'

Now look out in the Gradus for *purus*, and you find as the first synonime,
lacteus; for *coloratus*, and the first synonime is *purpureus*. I mention this by
way of elucidating one of the most ordinary processes in the *ferrumination*
of these centos.

importance.   According to the faculty or source from which the
pleasure given by any poem or passage was derived I estimated
the merit of such poem or passage.   As the result of all my
reading and meditation, I abstracted two critical aphorisms,
deeming them to comprise the conditions and criteria of poetic
style: first, that not the poem which we have *read*, but that to
which we *return* with the greatest pleasure, possesses the genuine
power and claims the name of essential poetry.   Second, that
whatever lines can be translated into other words of the same
language without diminution of their significance, either in
sense of association or in any worthy feeling, are so far vicious
in their diction.   Be it however observed, that I excluded from
the list of worthy feelings the pleasure derived from mere novelty
in the reader, and the desire of exciting wonderment at his
powers in the author.   Oftentimes since then, in perusing
French tragedies, I have fancied two marks of admiration at the
end of each line, as hieroglyphics of the author's own admiration
at his own cleverness.   Our genuine admiration of a great poet is
a continuous under-current of feeling; it is everywhere present,
but seldom anywhere as a separate excitement.   I was wont
boldly to affirm that it would be scarcely more difficult to push a
stone out from the pyramids with the bare hand than to alter a
word, or the position of a word, in Milton or Shakespeare (in
their most important works at least), without making the author
say something else, or something worse, than he does say.   One
great distinction I appeared to myself to see plainly, between
even the characteristic faults of our elder poets and the false
beauties of the moderns.   In the former, from Donne to Cowley,
we find the most fantastic out-of-the-way thoughts, but in the
most pure and genuine mother English; in the latter, the most
obvious thoughts, in language the most fantastic and arbitrary.
Our faulty elder poets sacrificed the passion and passionate flow
of poetry to the subtleties of intellect and to the starts of wit; the
moderns to the glare and glitter of a perpetual yet broken and
heterogeneous imagery, or rather to an amphibious something,
made up half of image and half of abstract [1] meaning.   The one
sacrificed the heart to the head, the other both heart and head to
point and drapery.

The reader must make himself acquainted with the general
style of composition that was at that time deemed poetry in order

[1] I remember a ludicrous instance in the poem of a young tradesman:
'No more will I endure love's pleasing pain,
    Or round my *heart's leg* tie his galling chain.'

to understand and account for the effect produced on me by the *Sonnets*, the *Monody at Matlock* and the *Hope* of Mr Bowles; for it is peculiar to original genius to become less and less striking in proportion to its success in improving the taste and judgement of its contemporaries. The poems of West,[1] indeed, had the merit of chaste and manly diction, but they were cold and, if I may so express it, only dead-coloured; while in the best of Warton's [2] there is a stiffness which too often gives them the appearance of imitations from the Greek. Whatever relation therefore of cause or impulse Percy's collection of Ballads may bear to the most popular poems of the present day; yet in the more sustained and elevated style, of the then living poets Bowles and Cowper [3] were, to the best of my knowledge, the first who combined natural thoughts with natural diction; the first who reconciled the heart with the head.

It is true, as I have before mentioned, that from diffidence in my own powers I for a short time adopted a laborious and florid diction which I myself deemed, if not absolutely vicious, yet of very inferior worth. Gradually, however, my practice conformed to my better judgement, and the compositions of my twenty-fourth and twenty-fifth years (ex. gr., the shorter blank verse poems, the lines which are now adopted in the introductory part of the *Vision* in the present collection in Mr Southey's *Joan of Arc*, 2nd book, 1st edition, and the tragedy of *Remorse*) are not more below my present ideal in respect of the general tissue of the style than those of the latest date. Their faults were at least a remnant of the former leaven, and among the many who have done me the honor of putting my poems in the same class with those of my betters, the one or two who have pretended to

---

[1] [Gilbert West (1703–56), the author of imitations of Spenser and a verse translation of Pindar.]

[2] [It is not certain which of the three Wartons is here intended. The other reference to 'Warton' in the *Biographia* (p. 33 below) links his name with a preference for ballads, which suggests the antiquarian Thomas Warton the younger (1728–90). But the verse of Joseph Warton (1722–1800), being composed largely of Pindaric odes, is a good deal more 'Greek' than his brother's.]

[3] Cowper's *Task* was published some time before the Sonnets of Mr Bowles; but I was not familiar with it till many years afterwards. The vein of satire which runs through that excellent poem, together with the sombre hue of its religious opinions, would probably, at that time, have prevented its laying any strong hold on my affections. The love of nature seems to have led Thomson to a chearful religion; and a gloomy religion to have led Cowper to a love of nature. The one would carry his fellow-men along with him into nature: the other flies to nature from his fellow-men. In chastity of diction however, and the harmony of blank verse, Cowper leaves Thomson unmeasurably below him; yet still I feel the latter to have been the born poet.

bring examples of affected simplicity from my volume have been able to adduce but one instance, and that out of a copy of verses half ludicrous, half splenetic, which I intended, and had myself characterized, as *sermoni propiora*.[1]

Every reform, however necessary, will by weak minds be carried to an excess that itself will need reforming. The reader will excuse me for noticing that I myself was the first to expose *risu honesto* the three sins of poetry, one or the other of which is the most likely to beset a young writer. So long ago as the publication of the second number of the *Monthly Magazine*, under the name of Nehemiah Higginbottom I contributed three sonnets, the first of which had for its object to excite a good-natured laugh at the spirit of doleful egotism, and at the recurrence of favorite phrases, with the double defect of being at once trite and licentious. The second, on low, creeping language and thoughts, under the pretence of simplicity. And the third, the phrases of which were borrowed entirely from my own poems, on the indiscriminate use of elaborate and swelling language and imagery. The reader will find them in the note [2] below, and

---

[1] ['The Address to a Young Jackass' (*Morning Chronicle*, 30 December 1794). The motto was in fact prefixed to the 'Reflexions on Having Left a Place of Retirement.']

[2] SONNET I

Pensive at eve, on the *hard* world I mused,
And *my poor* heart was sad; so at the Moon
I gazed, and sighed, and sighed: for ah how soon
Eve saddens into night! mine eyes perused
With tearful vacancy the *dampy* grass
That wept and glittered in the *paly* ray:
And I *did pause me* on my lonely way
And *mused me* on the *wretched ones* that pass
O'er the bleak heath of sorrow. But alas!
Most of *myself* I thought! when it befel,
That the *soothe* spirit of the *breezy* wood
Breath'd in mine ear: 'All this is very well,
But much of *one* thing is for *no* thing good.'
Oh *my poor heart's* Inexplicable Swell!

SONNET II

Oh I do love thee, meek Simplicity!
For of thy lays the lulling simpleness
Goes to my heart and soothes each small distress,
Distress tho' small, yet haply great to me.
'Tis true on Lady Fortune's gentlest pad
I amble on; and yet I know not why
So sad I am! but should a friend and I
Frown, pout and part, then I am *very* sad,
And then with sonnets and with sympathy
My dreamy bosom's mystic woes I pall;

will I trust regard them as reprinted for biographical purposes, and not for their poetic merits.   So general at that time and so decided was the opinion concerning the characteristic vices of my style, that a celebrated physician[1] (now, alas! no more), speaking of me in other respects with his usual kindness to a gentleman who was about to meet me at a dinner party, could not, however, resist giving him a hint not to mention the 'House that Jack built' in my presence, for 'that I was as sore as a boil about that sonnet;' he not knowing that I was myself the author of it.

Now of my false friend plaining plaintively,
Now raving at mankind in general;
But whether sad or fierce, 'tis simple all,
All very simple, meek Simplicity!

SONNET III

And this reft house is that, the which he built,
Lamented Jack! and here his malt he piled,
Cautious in vain! these rats that squeak so wild,
Squeak not unconscious of their father's guilt.
Did he not see her gleaming thro' the glade!
Belike 'twas she, the maiden all forlorn.
What though she milk no cow with crumpled horn,
Yet, *aye* she haunts the dale where *erst* she strayed:
And *aye* beside her stalks her amorous knight!
Still on his thighs their wonted brogues are worn,
And thro' those brogues, still tattered and betorn,
His hindward charms gleam an unearthly white.
Ah! thus thro' broken clouds at night's high Noon
Peeps in fair fragments forth the full-orb'd harvest-moon!

[First published in the *Monthly Magazine*, November 1797.]

The following anecdote will not be wholly out of place here, and may perhaps amuse the reader.   An amateur performer in verse expressed to a common friend a strong desire to be introduced to me, but hesitated in accepting my friend's immediate offer on the score that 'he was, he must acknowledge, the author of a confounded severe epigram on my *Ancient Mariner* which had given me great pain.'   I assured my friend that if the epigram was a good one, it would only increase my desire to become acquainted with the author, and begg'd to hear it recited: when, to my no less surprise than amusement, it proved to be one which I had myself some time before written and inserted in the *Morning Post*:

To the author of the 'Ancient Mariner':

Your poem must eternal be,
Dear sir! it cannot fail,
For 'tis incomprehensible
And without head or tail.

[1] [Thomas Beddoes of Bristol (1760–1808), father of the poet Thomas Lovell Beddoes.]

CHAPTER II

Supposed irritability of men of genius—Brought to the test of facts—Causes and occasions of the charge—Its injustice.

I HAVE often thought that it would be neither uninstructive nor unamusing to analyse, and bring forward into distinct consciousness, that complex feeling with which readers in general take part against the author in favor of the critic; and the readiness with which they apply to *all* poets the old sarcasm of Horace upon the scribblers of his time: 'Genus irritabile vatum.' [1] A debility and dimness of the imaginative power, and a consequent necessity of reliance on the immediate impressions of the senses, do, we well know, render the mind liable to superstition and fanaticism. Having a deficient portion of internal and proper warmth, minds of this class seek in the crowd *circum fana* for a warmth in common which they do not possess singly. Cold and phlegmatic in their own nature, like damp hay, they heat and inflame by co-acervation; or like bees they become restless and irritable through the increased temperature of collected multitudes. Hence the German word for fanaticism (such at least was its original import) is derived from the swarming of bees, namely, *schwärmen*, *Schwärmerey*. The passion being in an inverse proportion to the insight, that the more vivid as this the less distinct, anger is the inevitable consequence. The absence of all foundation within their own minds for that which they yet believe both true and indispensable for their safety and happiness cannot but produce an uneasy state of feeling, an involuntary sense of fear from which nature has no means of rescuing herself but by anger. Experience informs us that the first defence of weak minds is to recriminate.

> There's no philosopher but sees,
> That rage and fear are one disease,
> Tho' that may burn, and this may freeze,
> They're both alike the ague.
>
> MAD OX.[2]

[1] [Horace, *Epistles*, II. ii. 102: 'the touchy race of poets.']
[2] [Coleridge, 'Recantation,' *ll.* 63–6.]

But where the ideas are vivid and there exists an endless power of combining and modifying them, the feelings and affections blend more easily and intimately with these ideal creations than with the objects of the senses; the mind is affected by thoughts rather than by things; and only then feels the requisite interest even for the most important events and accidents, when by means of meditation they have passed into *thoughts*. The sanity of the mind is between superstition with fanaticism on the one hand, and enthusiasm with indifference and a diseased slowness to action on the other. For the conceptions of the mind may be so vivid and adequate as to preclude that impulse to the realizing of them, which is strongest and most restless in those who possess more than mere talent (or the faculty of appropriating and applying the knowledge of others) yet still want something of the creative and self-sufficing power of absolute genius. For this reason, therefore, they are men of commanding genius. While the former rest content between thought and reality, as it were in an intermundium of which their own living spirit supplies the substance, and their imagination the ever-varying form; the latter must impress their preconceptions on the world without in order to present them back to their own view with the satisfying degree of clearness, distinctness and individuality. These in tranquil times are formed to exhibit a perfect poem in palace or temple or landscape-garden; or a tale of romance in canals that join sea with sea, or in walls of rock which, shouldering back the billows, imitate the power and supply the benevolence of nature to sheltered navies; or in aqueducts that, arching the wide vale from mountain to mountain, give a Palmyra to the desert. But alas! in times of tumult they are the men destined to come forth as the shaping spirit of Ruin, to destroy the wisdom of ages in order to substitute the fancies of a day, and to change kings and kingdoms, as the wind shifts and shapes the clouds.[1] The records of biography seem to confirm this theory. The men of the greatest genius, as far as we can judge from their own works or from the accounts of their contemporaries, appear to have

---

[1] 'Of old things all are over old,
    Of good things none are good enough:—
We'll show that we can help to frame
    A world of other stuff.

'I too will have my kings, that take
    From me the sign of life and death:
Kingdoms shall shift about, like clouds,
    Obedient to my breath.'
                     Wordsworth's 'Rob Roy.'

been of calm and tranquil temper in all that related to themselves.   In the inward assurance of permanent fame, they seem
to have been either indifferent or resigned with regard to immediate reputation.   Through all the words of Chaucer there
reigns a chearfulness, a manly hilarity, which makes it almost
impossible to doubt a correspondent habit of feeling in the
author himself.   Shakespeare's evenness and sweetness of
temper were almost proverbial in his own age.   That this did
not arise from ignorance of his own comparative greatness
we have abundant proof in his Sonnets, which could scarcely
have been known to Mr Pope [1] when he asserted that our
great bard 'grew immortal in his own despite.' [2]   Speaking
of one whom he had celebrated, and contrasting the duration
of his works with that of his personal existence, Shakespeare
adds:

> Your name from hence immortal life shall have,
> Though I, once gone, to all the world must die;
> The earth can yield me but a common grave,
> When you entombed in men's eyes shall lie,
> Your monument shall be my gentle verse,
> Which eyes not yet created shall o'er-read;
> And *tongues to be* your being shall rehearse,
> When all the breathers of this world are dead:
>> You still shall live, such virtue hath my pen,
>> Where breath most breathes, e'en in the mouths of men.
>
> SONNET 81ST.

[1] Mr Pope was under the common error of his age, an error far from being
sufficiently exploded even at the present day.   It consists (as I explained at
large, and proved in detail in my public lectures) in mistaking for the *essentials*
of the Greek stage certain rules which the wise poets imposed upon themselves in order to render all the remaining parts of the drama consistent with
those that had been forced upon them by circumstances independent of their
will; out of which circumstances the drama itself arose.   The circumstances
in the time of Shakespeare, which it was equally out of his power to alter,
were different and such as in my opinion allowed a far wider sphere, and a
deeper and more human interest.   Critics are too apt to forget that *rules*
are but means to an end; consequently where the ends are different the rules
must be likewise so.   We must have ascertained what the end *is*, before we
can determine what the rules *ought* to be.   Judging under this impression, I
did not hesitate to declare my full conviction that the consummate judgement
of Shakespeare, not only in the general construction but in all the *detail*
of his dramas, impressed me with greater wonder than even the might of his
genius or the depth of his philosophy.   The substance of these lectures I
hope soon to publish; and it is but a debt of justice to myself and my friends
to notice that the first course of lectures, which differed from the following
courses only by occasionally varying the illustrations of the same thoughts,
was addressed to very numerous and I need not add, respectable audiences
at the Royal Institution before Mr Schlegel gave his lectures on the same
subjects at Vienna.
[2] [*First Epistle of the Second Book of Horace Imitated*, i. 72.]

I have taken the first that occurred; but Shakespeare's readiness to praise his rivals, *ore pleno*, and the confidence of his own equality with those whom he deemed most worthy of his praise, are alike manifested in the 86th Sonnet:

> Was it the proud full sail of his great verse
> Bound for the prize of all-too-precious you,
> That did my ripe thoughts in my brain inhearse,
> Making their tomb the womb wherein they grew?
> Was it his spirit, by spirits taught to write
> Above a mortal pitch, that struck me dead?
> No, neither he, nor his compeers by night
> Giving him aid, my verse astonished.
> He, nor that affable familiar ghost
> Which nightly gulls him with intelligence,
> As victors of my silence cannot boast;
> I was not sick of any fear from thence!
> But when your countenance filled up his line,
> Then lacked I matter; that enfeebled mine.

In Spenser, indeed, we trace a mind constitutionally tender, delicate and, in comparison with his three great compeers, I had almost said *effeminate*; and this additionally saddened by the unjust persecution of Burleigh, and the severe calamities which overwhelmed his latter days.[1]   These causes have diffused over all his compositions 'a melancholy grace' and have drawn forth occasional strains, the more pathetic from their gentleness.   But nowhere do we find the least trace of irritability, and still less of quarrelsome or affected contempt of his censurers.

The same calmness and even greater self-possession may be affirmed of Milton, as far as his poems and poetic character are concerned.   He reserved his anger for the enemies of religion, freedom and his country.   My mind is not capable of forming a more august conception than arises from the contemplation of this great man in his latter days: poor, sick, old, blind, slandered, persecuted:

> Darkness before, and danger's voice behind,[2]

---

[1] [This legend of Spenser's persecution by Burghley is apparently based upon a misinterpretation of *Mother Hubberds Tale* (1591).   Even less substantial is Coleridge's assertion that the final disaster of Spenser's life, the destruction of his home Kilcolman in County Cork by fire three months before his death in 1599, was responsible for the melancholy of some of his verse.]

[2] [Wordsworth, *The Prelude*, III. 286.   This poem was then still in manuscript and was not published till 1850.]

in an age in which he was as little understood by the party for whom, as by that against whom, he had contended, and among men before whom he strode so far as to dwarf himself by the distance; yet still listening to the music of his own thoughts, or, if additionally cheered, yet cheered only by the prophetic faith of two or three solitary individuals, he did nevertheless

> argue not
> Against Heaven's hand or will, nor bate a jot
> Of heart or hope; but still bore up and steer'd
> Right onward.[1]

From others only do we derive our knowledge that Milton, in his latter day, had his scorners and detractors; and even in his day of youth and hope, that he had enemies would have been unknown to us had they not been likewise the enemies of his country.

I am well aware that in advanced stages of literature when there exist many and excellent models, a high degree of talent, combined with taste and judgement and employed in works of imagination, will acquire for a man the name of a great genius; though even that analogon of genius which in certain states of society may even render his writings more popular than the absolute reality could have done would be sought for in vain in the mind and temper of the author himself. Yet even in instances of this kind, a close examination will often detect that the irritability which has been attributed to the author's genius as its cause did really originate in an ill conformation of body, obtuse pain or constitutional defect of pleasurable sensation. What is charged to the author belongs to the man, who would probably have been still more impatient but for the humanizing influences of the very pursuit which yet bears the blame of his irritability.

How then are we to explain the easy credence generally given to this charge, if the charge itself be not, as we have endeavoured to show, supported by experience? This seems to me of no very difficult solution. In whatever country literature is widely diffused there will be many who mistake an intense desire to possess the reputation of poetic genius for the actual powers and original tendencies which constitute it. But men whose dearest wishes are fixed on objects wholly out of their own power become in all cases more or less impatient and prone to anger. Besides, though it may be paradoxical to assert that a man can know one thing and believe the opposite, yet assuredly a vain person may

[1] [Milton, Sonnet 'To Mr Cyriack Skinner.']

have so habitually indulged the wish and persevered in the attempt to appear what he is not as to become himself one of his own proselytes. Still, as this counterfeit and artificial persuasion must differ, even in the person's own feelings, from a real sense of inward power, what can be more natural than that this difference should betray itself in suspicious and jealous irritability? Even as the flowery sod which covers a hollow may be often detected by its shaking and trembling.

But alas! the multitude of books and the general diffusion of literature have produced other and more lamentable effects in the world of letters and such as are abundant to explain, tho' by no means to justify, the contempt with which the best-grounded complaints of injured genius are rejected as frivolous or entertained as matter of merriment. In the days of Chaucer and Gower our language might (with due allowance for the imperfections of a simile) be compared to a wilderness of vocal reeds, from which the favorites only of Pan or Apollo could construct even the rude Syrinx; and from this the constructors alone could elicit strains of music. But now, partly by the labours of successive poets and in part by the more artificial state of society and social intercourse, language, mechanized as it were into a barrel-organ, supplies at once both instrument and tune.[1] Thus even the deaf may play so as to delight the many. Sometimes (for it is with similes as it is with jests at a wine-table, one is sure to suggest another) I have attempted to illustrate the present state of our language in its relation to literature by a press-room of larger and smaller stereotype pieces which, in the present Anglo-Gallican fashion of unconnected epigrammatic periods, it requires but an ordinary portion of ingenuity to vary indefinitely and yet still produce something which, if not sense, will be so like it as to do as well. Perhaps better: for it spares the reader the trouble of thinking; prevents vacancy while it indulges indolence; and secures the memory from all danger of an intellectual plethora. Hence of all trades literature at present demands the least talent or information; and of all modes of literature, the manufacturing of poems. The difference indeed between these and the works of genius is not less than between an egg and an egg-shell; yet at a distance they both look alike. Now it is no less remarkable than true with how little examination works of polite literature are commonly perused, not only by the mass of readers, but by men of first-rate ability, till some

[1] [Cf. *Notebooks*, 470 (September–October 1799): 'Of the harm that bad poets do in stealing & making unnovel beautiful images.']

accident or chance [1] discussion have roused their attention and
put them on their guard. And hence individuals below
mediocrity, not less in natural power than in acquired know-

[1] In the course of my lectures I had occasion to point out the almost faultless position and choice of words in Mr Pope's *original* compositions, particularly in his satires and moral essays, for the purpose of comparing them
with his translation of Homer, which I do not stand alone in regarding as the
main source of our pseudo-poetic diction. And this, by the bye, is an
additional confirmation of a remark made, I believe, by Sir Joshua Reynolds,
that next to the man who formed and elevated the taste of the public, he that
corrupted it is commonly the greatest genius. Among other passages I
analysed sentence by sentence, and almost word by word, the popular lines,

'As when the moon, resplendent lamp of night,' etc.,

[Pope's *Iliad*, VIII. 555.]

much in the same way as has been since done in an excellent article on
Chalmers's British Poets in the *Quarterly Review*. The impression on the
audience in general was sudden and evident; and a number of enlightened
and highly educated individuals, who at different times afterwards addressed
me on the subject, expressed their wonder that truth so obvious should not
have struck them before; but at the same time acknowledged (so much had
they been accustomed, in reading poetry, to receive pleasure from the
separate images and phrases successively, without asking themselves whether
the collective meaning was sense or nonsense) that they might in all probability have read the same passage again twenty times with undiminished
admiration, and without once reflecting, that 'ἄστρα φαεινὴν ἀμφὶ σελήνην
Φαίνετ' ἀμπρεπέα' ' (i.e. the stars around, or near the full moon, shine pre-
eminently bright) conveys a just and happy image of a moonlight sky: while
it is difficult to determine whether in the lines,

Around her *throne* the vivid planets *roll*,
And stars *unnumber'd gild* the *glowing pole*,'

the sense or the diction be the more absurd. My answer was: that tho' I had
derived peculiar advantages from my school discipline, and tho' my general
theory of poetry was the same then as now, I had yet experienced the same
sensations myself, and felt almost as if I had been newly couched, when by
Mr Wordsworth's conversation I had been induced to re-examine with
impartial strictness Gray's celebrated elegy. I had long before detected the
defects in the *Bard*; but the *Elegy* I had considered as proof against all fair
attacks; and to this day I cannot read either without delight and a portion of
enthusiasm. At all events, whatever pleasure I may have lost by the clearer
perception of the faults in certain passages has been more than repaid to me
by the additional delight with which I read the remainder.

An instance in confirmation of the note, p. 39, occurs to me as I am
correcting this sheet, with the *Faithful Shepherdess* open before me. Mr
Seward first traces Fletcher's lines:

'More foul diseases than e'er yet the hot
Sun bred thro' his burnings, while the dog
Pursues the raging lion, throwing the fog
And deadly vapor from his angry breath,
Filling the lower world with plague and death,'

[I. ii. 134-8.]

to Spenser's *Shepherd's Calendar*:

'The rampant lion hunts he fast
With dogs of noisome breath;
Whose baleful barking brings, in haste,
Pyne, plagues, and dreary death!'

[July, 21-4.]

ledge; nay, bunglers that have failed in the lowest mechanical crafts and whose presumption is in due proportion to their want of sense and sensibility; men who, being first scribblers from idleness and ignorance, next become libellers from envy and malevolence, have been able to drive a successful trade in the employment of the booksellers; nay, have raised themselves into temporary name and reputation with the public at large by that most powerful of all adulation, the appeal to the bad and malignant passions of mankind.[1]   But as it is the nature of scorn,

---

He then takes occasion to introduce Homer's simile of the sight of Achilles' shield to Priam compared with the Dog Star, literally thus:
   'For this indeed is most splendid, but it was made an evil sign, and brings many a consuming disease to wretched mortals.'   Nothing can be more simple as a description, or more accurate as a simile: which (says Mr S.) is thus finely translated by Mr Pope:

     'Terrific Glory! for his burning breath
     Taints the red air with fevers, plagues, and death!'
                                                    [XXII. 30-1.]

Now here (not to mention the tremendous bombast) the Dog Star, so called, is turned into a real dog, a very odd dog, a fire, fever, plague, and death-breathing, red-air-tainting dog: and the whole visual likeness is lost, while the likeness in the effects is rendered absurd by the exaggeration.   In Spenser and Fletcher the thought is justifiable; for the images are at least consistent, and it was the intention of the writers to mark the seasons by this allegory of visualized *puns*.
   [Beaumont and Fletcher, *Works*, ed. Theobald, Seward, and Sympson (1750), vol. iii, p. 113.   The afterthought was originally printed at the end of the chapter.]

   [1] Especially 'in this age of personality, this age of literary and political gossiping, when the meanest insects are worshipped with a sort of Egyptian superstition, if only the brainless head be atoned for by the sting of personal malignity in the tail!   When the most vapid satires have become the objects of a keen public interest, purely from the number of contemporary characters named in the patchwork notes (which possess, however, the comparative merit of being more poetical than the text) and because to increase the stimulus the author has sagaciously left his own name for whispers and conjectures!   In an age when even sermons are published with a double appendix stuffed with names—in a generation so transformed from the characteristic reserve of Britons, that from the ephemeral sheet of a London newspaper to the everlasting Scotch Professorial Quarto, almost every publication exhibits or flatters the epidemic distemper; that the very "last year's rebuses" in the Ladies Diary, are answered in a serious elegy "on my father's death" with the name and habitat of the elegiac Oedipus subscribed; and "other ingenious solutions were likewise given" to the said rebuses—not as heretofore by Crito, Philander, A. B. Y., etc., but by fifty or sixty plain English sirnames at full length with their several places of abode!   In an age, when a bashful Philalethes, or Phileleutheros is as rare on the title-pages, and among the signatures of our magazines, as a real name used to be in the days of our shy and notice-shunning grandfathers!   When (more exquisite than all) I see an Epic Poem (spirits of Maro and Maeonides make ready to welcome your new compeer!) advertised with the special recommendation, that the said Epic Poem contains more than an hundred names of living persons.'
                                        Friend, No. 10 [19 October 1809].

envy and all malignant propensities to require a quick change of
objects, such writers are sure sooner or later to awake from their
dream of vanity to disappointment and neglect with embittered
and envenomed feelings. Even during their short-lived success,
sensible in spite of themselves on what a shifting foundation it
rested, they resent the mere refusal of praise as a robbery, and at
the justest censures kindle at once into violent and undisciplined
abuse; till the acute disease changing into chronical, the more
deadly as the less violent, they become the fit instruments of
literary detraction and moral slander. They are then no longer
to be questioned without exposing the complainant to ridicule
because, forsooth, they are anonymous critics and authorized
as 'synodical individuals'[1] to speak of themselves *plurali
majestatico*! As if literature formed a cast, like that of the
paras[2] in Hindostan who, however maltreated, must not dare to
deem themselves wronged! As if that which, in all other cases,
adds a deeper dye to slander, the circumstance of its being
anonymous, here acted only to make the slanderer inviolable!
Thus, in part, from the accidental tempers of individuals (men
of undoubted talent, but not men of genius) tempers rendered
yet more irritable by their desire to appear men of genius; but
still more effectively by the excesses of the mere counterfeits both
of talent and genius; the number too being so incomparably
greater of those who are thought to be, than those who really are,
men of real genius; and in part from the natural, but not therefore the less partial and unjust distinction, made by the public
itself between literary and all other property; I believe the prejudice to have arisen which considers an unusual irascibility concerning the reception of its products as characteristic of genius.
It might correct the moral feelings of a numerous class of readers
to suppose a review set on foot, the object of which was to
criticize all the chief works presented to the public by our ribbon-
weavers, calico-printers, cabinet-makers and china-manu-
facturers; a review conducted in the same spirit, and which
should take the same freedom with personal character, as our
literary journals. They would scarcely, I think, deny their

---

[1] A phrase of Andrew Marvel's. [Andrew Marvell (1621–78), *The
Rehearsal Transpros'd* (1672), p. 43, attacking Samuel Parker, Bishop of
Oxford: 'But I wonder how he comes to be Prolocutor of the Church of
England! For he talks at that rate as if he were a *Synodical Individuum*; nay
if he had a fifth Council in his belly he could not dictate more dogmatically.']
[2] [i.e. *pariahs*, Indian untouchables. This attack upon reviewers is aimed
principally at Francis Jeffrey (1773–1850), a chief contributor to the *Edinburgh Review* since its foundation in 1802 and by this date its editor.]

belief, not only that the 'genus irritabile' would be found to include many other species besides that of bards; but that the irritability of trade would soon reduce the resentments of poets into mere shadow-fights (σκιομαχίας) in the comparison.   Or is wealth the only rational object of human interest?   Or even if this were admitted, has the poet no property in his works?   Or is it a rare or culpable case, that he who serves at the altar of the muses should be compelled to derive his maintenance from the altar when too he has perhaps deliberately abandoned the fairest prospects of rank and opulence in order to devote himself, an entire and undistracted man, to the instruction or refinement of his fellow-citizens?   Or should we pass by all higher objects and motives, all disinterested benevolence and even that ambition of lasting praise which is at once the crutch and ornament, which at once supports and betrays the infirmity of human virtue; is the character and property of the individual who labours for our intellectual pleasures less entitled to a share of our fellow-feeling than that of the wine-merchant or milliner?   Sensibility, indeed, both quick and deep, is not only a characteristic feature, but may be deemed a component part, of genius.   But it is no less an essential mark of true genius that its sensibility is excited by any other cause more powerfully than by its own personal interests; for this plain reason, that the man of genius lives most in the ideal world, in which the present is still constituted by the future or the past; and because his feelings have been habitually associated with thoughts and images, to the number, clearness and vivacity of which the sensation of self is always in an inverse proportion.   And yet, should he perchance have occasion to repel some false charge or to rectify some erroneous censure, nothing is more common than for the many to mistake the general liveliness of his manner and language, whatever is the subject, for the effects of peculiar irritation from its accidental relation to himself.[1]

---

[1] This is one instance among many of deception by the telling the half of a fact and omitting the other half, when it is from their mutual counteraction and neutralization that the whole truth arises, as a *tertium aliquid* different from either.   Thus in Dryden's famous line 'Great wit' (which here means genius) 'to madness sure is near allied.'   Now as far as the profound sensibility, which is doubtless one of the components of genius, were alone considered, single and unbalanced, it might be fairly described as exposing the individual to a greater chance of mental derangement; but then a more than usual rapidity of association, a more than usual power of passing from thought to thought and image to image, is a component equally essential; and in the due modification of each by the other the genius itself consists; so that it would be just as fair to describe the earth as in imminent danger of exorbitating, or of falling into the sun, according as the assertor of the absurdity confined his attention either to the projectile or to the attractive force exclusively.

For myself, if from my own feelings or from the less suspicious test of the observations of others, I had been made aware of any literary testiness or jealousy, I trust that I should have been however neither silly or arrogant enough to have burthened the imperfection on genius. But an experience (and I should not need documents in abundance to prove my words if I added) a tried experience of twenty years has taught me that the original sin of my character consists in a careless indifference to public opinion and to the attacks of those who influence it; that praise and admiration have become yearly less and less desirable, except as marks of sympathy; nay, that it is difficult and distressing to me to think with any interest even about the sale and profit of my works, important as in my present circumstances such considerations must needs be. Yet it never occurred to me to believe or fancy that the quantum of intellectual power bestowed on me by nature or education was in any way connected with this habit of my feelings, or that it needed any other parents or fosterers than constitutional indolence, aggravated into languor by ill-health; the accumulating embarrassments of procrastination; the mental cowardice, which is the inseparable companion of procrastination, and which makes us anxious to think and converse on anything rather than on what concerns ourselves: in fine, all those close vexations, whether chargeable on my faults or my fortunes, which leave me but little grief to spare for evils comparatively distant and alien.

Indignation at literary wrongs I leave to men born under happier stars. I cannot afford it. But so far from condemning those who can, I deem it a writer's duty, and think it creditable to his heart, to feel and express a resentment proportioned to the grossness of the provocation and the importance of the object. There is no profession on earth which requires an attention so early, so long or so unintermitting as that of poetry; and indeed as that of literary composition in general, if it be such as at all satisfies the demands both of taste and of sound logic. How difficult and delicate a task even the mere mechanism of verse is may be conjectured from the failure of those who have attempted poetry late in life. Where then a man has, from his earliest youth, devoted his whole being to an object which by the admission of all civilized nations in all ages is honorable as a pursuit and glorious as an attainment; what of all that relates to himself and his family, if only we except his moral character, can have fairer claims to his protection, or more authorize acts of self-defence, than the elaborate products of his intellect and intellectual industry? Prudence itself would command us to show, even if defect or diversion of natural sensibility had prevented us from feeling, a due interest and qualified anxiety for the offspring and representatives of our nobler being. I know it, alas! by woeful experience! I have laid too many eggs in the hot sands of this wilderness, the world, with ostrich carelessness and ostrich oblivion. The greater part indeed have been trod under foot, and are forgotten; but yet no small number have crept forth into life, some to furnish feathers for the caps of others, and still more to plume the shafts in the quivers of my enemies, of them that unprovoked have lain in wait against my soul.

'Sic vos, non vobis mellificatis, apes!'[1]

[1] [Virgil (fragment): 'So you bees make honey, but not for yourselves.']

CHAPTER III

The author's obligations to critics, and the probable occasion—Principles of modern criticism—Mr Southey's works and character.

To anonymous critics in reviews, magazines and news-journals of various name and rank, and to satirists with or without a name, in verse or prose, or in verse-text aided by prose-comment, I do seriously believe and profess that I owe full two-thirds of whatever reputation and publicity I happen to possess. For when the name of an individual has occurred so frequently in so many works for so great a length of time, the readers of these works (which with a shelf or two of Beauties, Elegant Extracts and Anas,[1] form nine-tenths of the reading of the reading public [2]) cannot but be familiar with the name without distinctly remembering whether it was introduced for eulogy or for censure. And this becomes the more likely if (as I believe) the habit of perusing periodical works may be properly added to Averroes'[3] catalogue of Anti-Mnemonics, or weakeners of the

[1] [i.e. collections of sayings.]

[2] For as to the devotees of the circulating libraries, I dare not compliment their pass-time, or rather kill-time, with the name of reading. Call it rather a sort of beggarly day-dreaming during which the mind of the dreamer furnishes for itself nothing but laziness and a little mawkish sensibility; while the whole *materiel* and imagery of the doze is supplied *ab extra* by a sort of mental *camera obscura* manufactured at the printing office, which *pro tempore* fixes, reflects and transmits the moving phantasms of one man's delirium, so as to people the barrenness of an hundred other brains afflicted with the same trance or suspension of all common sense and all definite purpose. We should therefore transfer this species of amusement (if indeed those can be said to retire *a musis*, who were never in their company, or relaxation be attributable to those whose bows are never bent) from the genus, reading, to that comprehensive class characterized by the power of reconciling the two contrary yet co-existing propensities of human nature, namely indulgence of sloth and hatred of vacancy. In addition to novels and tales of chivalry in prose or rhyme, (by which last I mean neither rhythm nor metre) this genus comprises as its species, gaming, swinging or swaying on a chair or gate; spitting over a bridge; smoking; snuff-taking: tête-à-tête quarrels after dinner between husband and wife; conning word by word all the advertisements of the *Daily Advertiser* in a public house on a rainy day, etc. etc. etc.

[3] Ex. gr. *Pediculos e capillis excerptos in arenam jacere incontusos*; eating of unripe fruit; gazing on the clouds and (*in genere*) on moveable things suspended in the air; riding among a multitude of camels; frequent laughter; listening to a series of jests and humourous anecdotes, as when (so to modernize the learned Saracen's meaning) one man's droll story of an Irishman inevitably occasions another's droll story of a Scotchman, which again by the same sort of conjunction disjunctive leads to some *étourderie* of a Welchman, and that again to some sly hit of a Yorkshireman; the habit of reading tombstones in church-yards, etc. By the bye this catalogue, strange as it may appear, is not insusceptible of a sound psychological commentary. [The quotation (which is not from Averroes) is untraced.]

memory.   But where this has not been the case, yet the reader
will be apt to suspect that there must be something more than
usually strong and extensive in a reputation that could either
require or stand so merciless and long continued a cannonading.
Without any feeling of anger therefore (for which indeed, on my
own account, I have no pretext) I may yet be allowed to express
some degree of surprize that after having run the critical
gauntlet for a certain class of faults which I *had*, nothing having
come before the judgement-seat in the interim, I should, year
after year, quarter after quarter, month after month (not to
mention sundry petty periodicals of still quicker revolution, 'or
weekly or diurnal') have been for at least seventeen years
consecutively dragged forth by them into the foremost ranks of
the *proscribed* and forced to abide the brunt of abuse for faults
directly opposite, and which I certainly had not.   How shall I
explain this?

Whatever may have been the case with others, I certainly
cannot attribute this persecution to personal dislike, or to envy,
or to feelings of vindictive animosity.   Not to the former, for,
with the exception of a very few who are my intimate friends
and were so before they were known as authors, I have had little
other acquaintance with literary characters than what may be
implied in an accidental introduction or casual meeting in a
mixed company.   And, as far as words and looks can be trusted,
I must believe that even in these instances I had excited no
unfriendly disposition.[1]   Neither by letter or in conversation

---

[1] Some years ago a gentleman, the chief writer and conductor of a celebrated review distinguished by its hostility to Mr Southey, spent a day or two
at Keswick.   That he was, without diminution on this account, treated with
every hospitable attention by Mr Southey and myself I trust I need not say.
But one thing I may venture to notice: that at no period of my life do I
remember to have received so many, and such high coloured compliments,
in so short a space of time.   He was likewise circumstantially informed by
what series of accidents it had happened that Mr Wordsworth, Mr Southey
and I had become neighbours; and how utterly unfounded was the supposition, that we considered ourselves as belonging to any common school
but that of good sense confirmed by the long-established models of the best
times of Greece, Rome, Italy and England; and still more groundless the
notion that Mr Southey (for as to myself I have published so little, and that
little of so little importance, as to make it almost ludicrous to mention my
name at all) could have been concerned in the formation of a poetic sect with
Mr Wordsworth, when so many of his works had been published not only
previously to any acquaintance between them, but before Mr Wordsworth
himself had written any thing but in a diction ornate and uniformly sustained; when too the slightest examination will make it evident that between
those and the after writings of Mr Southey there exists no other difference
than that of a progressive degree of excellence from progressive development
of power, and progressive facility from habit and increase of experience.

have I ever had dispute or controversy beyond the common social interchange of opinions. Nay, where I had reason to suppose my convictions fundamentally different it has been my habit and, I may add, the impulse of my nature to assign the grounds of my belief rather than the belief itself; and not to express dissent till I could establish some points of complete sympathy, some grounds common to both sides, from which to commence its explanation.

Still less can I place these attacks to the charge of envy. The few pages which I have published are of too distant a date, and the extent of their sale a proof too conclusive against their having been popular at any time, to render probable, I had almost said possible, the excitement of envy on their account; and the man

---

Yet among the first articles which this man wrote after his return from Keswick we were characterized as 'the School of whining and hypochondriacal poets that haunt the Lakes.' In reply to a letter from the same gentleman, in which he had asked me whether I was in earnest in preferring the style of Hooker to that of Dr Johnson and Jeremy Taylor to Burke, I stated, somewhat at large, the comparative excellences and defects which characterized our best prose writers from the Reformation to the first half of Charles II: and that of those who had flourished during the present reign and the preceding one. About twelve months afterwards a review appeared on the same subject, in the concluding paragraph of which the reviewer asserts that his chief motive for entering into the discussion was to separate a rational and qualified admiration of our elder writers from the indiscriminate enthusiasm of a recent school who praised what they did not understand, and caricatured what they were unable to imitate. And, that no doubt might be left concerning the persons alluded to, the writer annexes the names of Miss Baillie, Southey, Wordsworth and Coleridge. For that which follows I have only hearsay evidence, but yet such as demands my belief: viz. that on being questioned concerning this apparently wanton attack, more especially with reference to Miss Baillie, the writer had stated as his motives that this lady when at Edinburgh had declined a proposal of introducing him to her; that Mr Southey had written against him; and Mr Wordsworth had talked contemptuously of him; but that as to Coleridge he had noticed him merely because the names of Southey and Wordsworth and Coleridge always went together. But if it were worth while to mix together, as ingredients, half the anecdotes which I either myself know to be true, or which I have received from men incapable of intentional falsehood, concerning the characters, qualifications and motives of our anonymous critics whose decisions are oracles for our reading public, I might safely borrow the words of the apocryphal Daniel: 'Give me leave, O SOVEREIGN PUBLIC, and I shall slay this dragon without sword or staff.' For the compound would be as the 'pitch, and fat, and hair, which Daniel took, and did seethe them together, and made lumps thereof, and put into the dragon's mouth, and so the dragon burst in sunder: and Daniel said LO; THESE ARE THE GODS YE WORSHIP.'

[The reviewer in question is again Jeffrey, who had visited the Lakes in 1810 and who defended himself against these charges in a review of the *Biographia* in the *Edinburgh Review* (August 1817) by charging Coleridge with inaccuracy. There is no evidence that Jeffrey ever made the remarks here quoted. H. N. Coleridge, the poet's nephew and son-in-law, suppressed this footnote in the second edition of 1847.]

who should envy me on any other, verily he must be envy-mad!

Lastly, with as little semblance of reason, could I suspect any animosity towards me from vindictive feelings as the cause.   I have before said, that my acquaintance with literary men has been limited and distant and that I have had neither dispute nor controversy.   From my first entrance into life I have, with few and short intervals, lived either abroad or in retirement.   My different essays on subjects of national interest published at different times, first in the *Morning Post* and then in the *Courier*, with my courses of lectures on the principles of criticism as applied to Shakespeare and Milton, constitute my whole publicity; [1] the only occasions on which I could offend any member of the republic of letters.   With one solitary exception in which my words were first mis-stated and then wantonly applied to an individual, I could never learn that I had excited the displeasure of any among my literary contemporaries. Having announced my intention to give a course of lectures on the characteristic merits and defects of English poetry in its different eras: first, from Chaucer to Milton; second, from Dryden inclusive to Thomson; and third, from Cowper to the present day; I changed my plan, and confined my disquisition to the two former æras, that I might furnish no possible pretext for the unthinking to misconstrue, or the malignant to misapply my words, and having stampt their own meaning on them to pass them as current coin in the marts of garrulity or detraction.[2]

Praises of the unworthy are felt by ardent minds as robberies of the deserving; and it is too true, and too frequent, that Bacon, Harrington, Machiavel and Spinoza are not read, because Hume, Condillac and Voltaire are.   But in promiscuous company no prudent man will oppugn the merits of a contemporary in his own supposed department; contenting himself with praising in his turn those whom he deems excellent.   If I should ever deem it my duty at all to oppose the pretensions of individuals, I would oppose them in books which could be weighed and answered, in which I could evolve the whole of my reasons and feelings, with their requisite limits and modifications; not in irrecoverable conversation where, however strong the reasons might be, the feelings that prompted them would assuredly be attributed by

[1] [Coleridge has forgotten his several political pamphlets, as well as his periodicals *The Watchman* (Bristol, 1796) and *The Friend* (Penrith, 1809–10).]
[2] [Coleridge lectured several times in London and Bristol from 1808, and certainly included criticism of living authors in his earlier lectures.]

some one or other to envy and discontent. Besides, I well know, and I trust have acted on that knowledge, that it must be the ignorant and injudicious who extol the unworthy; and the eulogies of critics without taste or judgement are the natural reward of authors without feeling or genius. 'Sint unicuique sua premia.'

How then, dismissing as I do these three causes, am I to account for attacks, the long continuance and inveteracy of which it would require all three to explain? The solution may seem to have been given, or at least suggested, in a note to a preceding page. *I was in habits of intimacy with Mr Wordsworth and Mr Southey!* This, however, transfers rather than removes the difficulty. Be it, that by an unconscionable extention of the old adage 'noscitur a socio' my literary friends are never under the water-fall of criticism but I must be wet through with the spray; yet how came the torrent to descend upon them?

First, then, with regard to Mr Southey. I well remember the general reception of his earlier publications: viz. the poems published with Mr Lovell under the names of Moschus and Bion, the two volumes of poems under his own name and the *Joan of Arc*.[1] The censures of the critics by profession are extant, and may be easily referred to:—careless lines, inequality in the merit of the different poems, and (in the lighter works) a predilection for the strange and whimsical; in short, such faults as might have been anticipated in a young and rapid writer were indeed sufficiently enforced. Nor was there at that time wanting a party spirit to aggravate the defects of a poet who with all the courage of uncorrupted youth had avowed his zeal for a cause which he deemed that of liberty and his abhorrence of oppression by whatever name consecrated. But it was as little objected by others as dreamt of by the poet himself that he *preferred* careless and prosaic lines on rule and of forethought, or indeed that he pretended to any other art or theory of poetic diction besides that which we may all learn from Horace, Quintilian, the admirable dialogue *De causis corruptae eloquentiae*[2] or Strada's Prolusions;[3] if indeed natural good sense and the early study

---

[1] [*Poems* by Robert Lovell and Robert Southey (Bath, 1795), *Joan of Arc, an Epic Poem* (Bristol, 1796), and *Poems* (2 vols., 1797–9). The 1795 volume was published with the authors' names on the title-page, Southey's poems being distinguished by the name 'Bion,' Lovell's by 'Moschus.']

[2] [The *Dialogus de oratoribus* of Tacitus, probably his first work and written *c.* A.D. 80.]

[3] [Famiano Strada (1572–1649), an Italian Jesuit, whose treatise on poetics *Prolusiones* appeared in Rome in 1617.]

of the best models in his own language had not infused the same maxims more securely and, if I may venture the expression, more vitally.   All that could have been fairly deduced was that in his taste and estimation of writers Mr Southey agreed far more with Warton than with Johnson.   Nor do I mean to deny that at all times Mr Southey was of the same mind with Sir Philip Sidney [1] in preferring an excellent ballad in the *humblest* style of poetry to twenty indifferent poems that strutted in the *highest*.   And by what have his works published since then [2] been characterized, each more strikingly than the preceding, but by greater splendor, a deeper pathos, profounder reflections and a more sustained dignity of language and of metre?   Distant may the period be, but whenever the time shall come when all his works shall be collected by some editor worthy to be his biographer, I trust that an excerpta of all the passages in which his writings, name and character have been attacked, from the pamphlets and periodical works of the last twenty years, may be an accompaniment.   Yet that it would prove medicinal in after times I dare not hope; for as long as there are readers to be delighted with calumny there will be found reviewers to calumniate.   And such readers will become in all probability more numerous in proportion as a still greater diffusion of literature shall produce an increase of sciolists; and sciolism bring with it petulance and presumption.   In times of old, books were as religious oracles; as literature advanced, they next became venerable preceptors; they then descended to the rank of instructive friends; and as their numbers increased they sank still lower to that of entertaining companions; and at present they seem degraded into culprits to hold up their hands at the bar of every self-elected yet not the less peremptory judge who chooses to write from humour or interest, from enmity or arrogance, and to abide the decision (in the words of Jeremy Taylor) 'of him that reads in malice, or him that reads after dinner.' [3]

The same gradual retrograde movement may be traced in the relation which the authors themselves have assumed towards their readers, from the lofty address of Bacon: 'These are the

---

[1] [*Apologie for Poetrie* (1595): 'I never heard the old song of Percy and Douglas that I found not my heart moved more than with a trumpet. . . . What would it work, trimmed in the gorgeous eloquence of Pindar?']

[2] [Principally *Thalaba* (1801), *Madoc* (1805), *Kehama* (1810), and *Roderick* (1815), all verse romances.]

[3] [Probably a vague recollection of a proverb quoted by Taylor in his *Rules and Advice to the Clergy of Down and Connor* (Dublin, 1661), xlix: 'After a good dinner let us sit down and backbite our neighbours.']

meditations of Francis of Verulam which, that posterity should
be possessed of, he deemed their interest'; [1] or from dedication
to Monarch or Pontiff, in which the honor given was asserted in
equipoise to the patronage acknowledged from Pindar's

$$\text{———— } ἐν' ἄλλοι-$$
$$\text{-σι δ'ἄλλοι μεγάλοι : τὸ δ'ἔσχατον κορυ-}$$
$$\text{-φοῦται βασιλεῦσι: μηκέτι}$$
$$\text{πάπταινε πόρσιον.}$$
$$\text{εἴη σέ τε τοῦτον}$$
$$\text{ὑψοῦ χρόνον πατεῖν, ἐμέ}$$
$$\text{τε τοσσάδε νικαφόροις}$$
$$\text{ὁμιλεῖν, πρόφαντον σορίᾳ καθ' Ἑλ-}$$
$$\text{-λανας ἐόντα παντᾷ.}$$

Olymp. Od. 1.[2]

Poets and philosophers, rendered diffident by their very
number, addressed themselves to 'learned readers'; then, aimed
to conciliate the graces of 'the candid reader'; till, the critic still
rising as the author sunk, the amateurs of literature collectively
were erected into a municipality of judges, and addressed as the
Town!   And now finally, all men being supposed able to read,
and all readers able to judge, the multitudinous public, shaped
into personal unity by the magic of abstraction, sits nominal
despot on the throne of criticism.   But, alas! as in other des-
potisms, it but echoes the decision of its invisible ministers,
whose intellectual claims to the guardianship of the Muses seem,
for the greater part, analogous to the physical qualifications
which adapt their oriental brethren for the superintendence of
the harem.   Thus it is said that St Nepomuc was installed the
guardian of bridges because he had fallen over one and sunk out of
sight.   Thus, too, St Cecilia is said to have been first propitiated
by musicians, because, having failed in her own attempts, she had
taken a dislike to the art and all its successful professors.   But I
shall probably have occasion hereafter to deliver my convictions
more at large concerning this state of things, and its influences on
taste, genius and morality.

In the *Thalaba*, the *Madoc*, and still more evidently, in the

---

[1] [From the Latin preface to his *Novum Organum* (1620).]

[2] [*ll.* 113–16: 'Some men are great in one thing, others in another—but the
crowning summit is for kings.   Do not look too far.   May you plant your
feet on high as long as you live, and may I live with the victors all my life and
be the first poet among the Greeks of every land.']

unique[1] *Cid,* the *Kehama* and as last, so best, the *Don Roderick,* Southey has given abundant proof: 'Se cogitasse quam sit
magnum dare aliquid in manus hominum: nec persuadere sibi
posse, non saepe tractandum quod placere et semper et omnibus
cupiat.'—Plin. Ep. Lib. 7, Ep. 17.[2] But on the other hand I
guess that Mr Southey was quite unable to comprehend wherein
could consist the crime or mischief of printing half a dozen or
more playful poems; or, to speak more generally, compositions
which would be enjoyed or passed over, according as the taste
and humour of the reader might chance to be, provided they
contained nothing immoral. In the present age 'periturae
parcere chartae'[3] is emphatically an unreasonable demand.
The merest trifle he ever sent abroad had tenfold better claims to
its ink and paper than all the silly criticisms which prove no
more than that the critic was not one of those for whom the
trifle was written, and than all the grave exhortations to a greater
reverence for the public. As if the passive page of a book, by
having an epigram or doggrel tale impressed on it, instantly
assumed at once locomotive power and a sort of ubiquity, so as to
flutter and buz in the ear of the public to the sore annoyance of
the said mysterious personage. But what gives an additional
and more ludicrous absurdity to these lamentations is the curious
fact that if, in a volume of poetry, the critic should find poem or
passage which he deems more especially worthless, he is sure to
select and reprint it in the review; by which, on his own grounds,
he wastes as much more paper than the author as the copies of a
fashionable review are more numerous than those of the original
book; in some, and those the most prominent instances, as ten
thousand to five hundred. I know nothing that surpasses the
vileness of deciding on the merits of a poet or painter (not by
characteristic defects; for where there is genius, these always

---

[1] I have ventured to call it 'unique'; not only because I know no work of
the kind in our language (if we except a few chapters of the old translation of
Froissart), none which uniting the charms of romance and history keeps the
imagination so constantly on the wing, and yet leaves so much for after
reflection; but likewise, and chiefly, because it is a compilation, which in the
various excellencies of translation, selection and arrangement, required and
proves greater genius in the compiler as living in the present state of society
than in the original composers. [Southey's *Chronicle of the Cid* (1808) was a
version of the thirteenth-century Spanish epic compounded with passages
from other Spanish Cid poems.]

[2] ['That he reflects upon the importance of publishing and cannot be
persuaded that what he wishes to please everyone forever ought not to be
constantly revised.']

[3] [Juvenal, *Satires,* I. 18: '(It is foolishly merciful, when you meet so many
poets on all sides) to spare the work which is bound to perish.']

point to his characteristic beauties; but) by accidental failures or
faulty passages; except the imprudence of defending it, as the
proper duty and most instructive part of criticism. Omit, or
pass slightly over, the expression, grace and grouping of
Raphael's figures; but ridicule in detail the knitting-needles and
broom-twigs that are to represent trees in his back grounds, and
never let him hear the last of his gallipots! Admit that the
Allegro and *Penseroso* of Milton are not without merit; but repay
yourself for this concession by reprinting at length the two poems
on the University Carrier! As a fair specimen of his Sonnets,
quote:

> A Book was writ of late call'd *Tetrachordon*;

and as characteristic of his rhythm and metre cite his literal
translation of the first and second psalm! In order to justify
yourself, you need only assert that, had you dwelt chiefly
on the beauties and excellencies of the poet, the admiration
of these might seduce the attention of future writers from
the objects of their love and wonder to an imitation of the
few poems and passages in which the poet was most unlike
himself.

But till reviews are conducted on far other principles and with
far other motives; till in the place of arbitrary dictation and
petulant sneers the reviewers support their decisions by reference to fixed canons of criticism, previously established and
deduced from the of nature man; reflecting minds will pronounce
it arrogance in them thus to announce themselves to men of
letters as the guides of their taste and judgement. To the
purchaser and mere reader it is, at all events, an injustice. He
who tells me that there are defects in a new work, tells me
nothing which I should not have taken for granted without his
information. But he who points out and elucidates the beauties
of an original work, does indeed give me interesting information,
such as experience would not have authorized me in anticipating.
And as to compositions which the authors themselves announce
with 'Haec ipsi novimus esse nihil,' [1] why should we judge by a
different rule two printed works, only because the one author is
alive and the other in his grave? What literary man has not
regretted the prudery of Spratt in refusing to let his friend

---

[1] ['We ourselves know these things to be nothing.' At Coleridge's suggestion Southey had actually prefixed this motto to his collection *Minor
Poems* (3 vols., 1815).]

Cowley appear in his slippers and dressing-gown? [1] I am not perhaps the only one who has derived an innocent amusement from the riddles, conundrums, trisyllable lines, etc. etc., of Swift and his correspondents in hours of languor, when to have read his more finished works would have been useless to myself and in some sort an act of injustice to the author. But I am at a loss to conceive by what perversity of judgement these relaxations of his genius could be employed to diminish his fame as the writer of *Gulliver's Travels* and the *Tale of a Tub*. Had Mr Southey written twice as many poems of inferior merit or partial interest as have enlivened the journals of the day, they would have added to his honour with good and wise men, not merely or principally as proving the versatility of his talents but as evidences of the purity of that mind, which even in its levities never wrote a line which it need regret on any moral account.

I have in imagination transferred to the future biographer the duty of contrasting Southey's fixed and well-earned fame with the abuse and indefatigable hostility of his anonymous critics from his early youth to his ripest manhood. But I cannot think so ill of human nature as not to believe that these critics have already taken shame to themselves, whether they consider the object of their abuse in his moral or his literary character. For reflect but on the variety and extent of his acquirements! He stands second to no man, either as an historian or as a bibliographer; and when I regard him as a popular essayist (for the articles of his compositions in the reviews are for the greater part essays on subjects of deep or curious interest rather than criticisms on particular works [2] I look in vain for any writer who has conveyed so much information, from so many and such recondite sources, with so many just and original reflections, in a style so lively and poignant, yet so uniformly classical and perspicuous; no one in short who has combined so much wisdom with so much wit; so much truth and knowledge with so much life and fancy. His prose is always intelligible and always entertaining. In poetry he has attempted almost every species of composition known before, and he has added new ones; and if we except the highest lyric (in which how few, how very few even of the

---

[1] [Thomas Sprat (1635–1713), in the biography of his friend Abraham Cowley which he wrote after Cowley's death in 1667 and published in his edition of Cowley's *English Works* (1668), declined to include Cowley's letters as too private for publication.   Johnson in his *Life* of Cowley condemned the biography as 'confused and enlarged through the mist of panegyrick.']

[2] See the articles on Methodism in the *Quarterly Review*; the small volume on the *New System of Education*, etc. [an anonymous treatise (1812), probably by Southey].

greatest minds have been fortunate), he has attempted every species successfully: from the political song of the day, thrown off in the playful overflow of honest joy and patriotic exultation, to the wild ballad;[1] from epistolary ease and graceful narrative, to the austere and impetuous moral declamation; from the pastoral charms and wild streaming lights of the *Thalaba*, in which sentiment and imagery have given permanence even to the excitement of curiosity; and from the full blaze of the *Kehama* (a gallery of finished pictures in one splendid fancy piece in which, notwithstanding, the moral grandeur rises gradually above the brilliance of the colouring and the boldness and novelty of the machinery) to the more sober beauties of the *Madoc*; and lastly, from the *Madoc* to his *Roderick* in which, retaining all his former excellencies of a poet eminently inventive and picturesque, he has surpassed himself in language and metre, in the construction of the whole and in the splendor of particular passages.

Here then shall I conclude? No! The characters of the deceased, like the encomia on tombstones, as they are described with religious tenderness so are they read, with allowing sympathy indeed, but yet with rational deduction. There are men who deserve a higher record; men with whose characters it is the interest of their contemporaries, no less than that of posterity, to be made acquainted; while it is yet possible for impartial censure, and even for quick-sighted envy, to cross-examine the tale without offence to the courtesies of humanity; and while the eulogist detected in exaggeration or falsehood must pay the full penalty of his baseness in the contempt which brands the convicted flatterer. Publicly has Mr Southey been reviled by men who (I would fain hope for the honor of human nature) hurled fire-brands against a figure of their own imagination, publicly have his talents been depreciated, his principles denounced; as publicly do I therefore, who have known him intimately, deem it my duty to leave recorded that it is Southey's almost unexampled felicity to possess the best gifts of talent and genius free from all their characteristic defects.[2] To those who remember the state of our public schools and universities some twenty years past it will appear no ordinary praise in any man to have passed from innocence into virtue, not only free from

[1] See the incomparable 'Return to Moscow' and the 'Old Women of Berkeley.'

[2] [Coleridge is evidently trying to restore a balance. His private view of Southey was much less favourable. According to Crabb Robinson he considered that 'neither Southey nor Scott were poets.']

all vicious habit but unstained by one act of intemperance or the degradations akin to intemperance. That scheme of head, heart and habitual demeanour, which in his early manhood and first controversial writings Milton, claiming the privilege of self-defence, asserts of himself and challenges his calumniators to disprove; this will his school-mates, his fellow-collegians and his maturer friends, with a confidence proportioned to the intimacy of their knowledge, bear witness to as again realized in the life of Robert Southey. But still more striking to those who by biography or by their own experience are familiar with the general habits of genius will appear the poet's matchless industry and perseverance in his pursuits; the worthiness and dignity of those pursuits; his generous submission to tasks of transitory interest, or such as his genius alone could make otherwise; and that having thus more than satisfied the claims of affection or prudence, he should yet have made for himself time and power to achieve more, and in more various departments, than almost any other writer has done, though employed wholly on subjects of his own choice and ambition. But as Southey possesses and is not possessed by his genius, even so is he the master even of his virtues. The regular and methodical tenor of his daily labours, which would be deemed rare in the most mechanical pursuits, and might be envied by the mere man of business, loses all semblance of formality in the dignified simplicity of his manners in the spring and healthful chearfulness of his spirits. Always employed, his friends find him always at leisure. No less punctual in trifles, than stedfast in the performance of highest duties, he inflicts none of those small pains and discomforts which irregular men scatter about them, and which in the aggregate so often become formidable obstacles both to happiness and utility; while on the contrary he bestows all the pleasures and inspires all that ease of mind on those around him or connected with him which perfect consistency and (if such a word might be framed) absolute *reliability*, equally in small as in great concerns, cannot but inspire and bestow: when this too is softened without being weakened by kindness and gentleness. I know few men who so well deserve the character which an ancient attributes to Marcus Cato, namely that he was likest virtue, inasmuch as he seemed to act aright, not in obedience to any law or outward motive, but by the necessity of a happy nature which could not act otherwise.[1] As son, brother, husband,

---

[1] [From Vellius Paterculus (*c.* 19 B.C.–*c.* A.D. 31), *Historiae Romanae*, II. 35.]

father, master, friend, he moves with firm yet light steps, alike unostentatious and alike exemplary. As a writer, he has uniformly made his talents subservient to the best interests of humanity, of public virtue and domestic piety; his cause has ever been the cause of pure religion and of liberty, of national independence and of national illumination. When future critics shall weigh out his guerdon of praise and censure, it will be Southey the poet only that will supply them with the scanty materials for the latter. They will likewise not fail to record that as no man was ever a more constant friend, never had poet more friends and honorers among the good of all parties; and that quacks in education, quacks in politics, and quacks in criticism were his only enemies.[1]

---

[1] It is not easy to estimate the effects which the example of a young man as highly distinguished for strict purity of disposition and conduct as for intellectual power and literary acquirements may produce on those of the same age with himself, especially on those of similar pursuits and congenial minds. For many years my opportunities of intercourse with Mr Southey have been rare and at long intervals; but I dwell with unabated pleasure on the strong and sudden, yet I trust not fleeting influence, which my moral being underwent on my acquaintance with him at Oxford, whither I had gone at the commencement of our Cambridge vacation on a visit to an old school-fellow. Not indeed on my moral or religious principles, for *they* had never been contaminated; but in awakening the sense of the duty and dignity of making my actions accord with those principles, both in word and deed. The irregularities only not universal among the young men of my standing, which I always knew to be wrong, I then learnt to feel as degrading; learnt to know that an opposite conduct, which was at that time considered by us as the easy virtue of cold and selfish prudence, might originate in the noblest emotions, in views the most disinterested and imaginative. It is now however from grateful recollections only that I have been impelled thus to leave these my deliberate sentiments on record; but in some sense as a debt of justice to the man whose name has been so often connected with mine, for evil to which he is a stranger. As a specimen I subjoin part of a note from *The Beauties of the Anti-Jacobin*, in which having previously informed the public that I had been dishonor'd at Cambridge for preaching Deism, at a time when for my youthful ardour in defence of Christianity I was decried as a bigot by the proselytes of French Phi- (or to speak more truly, Psi-) losophy, the writer concludes with these words: 'Since this time he has left his native country, commenced citizen of the world, *left his poor children fatherless, and his wife destitute.   Ex his disce, his friends* LAMB *and* SOUTHEY.' With severest truth it may be asserted that it would not be easy to select two men more exemplary in their domestic affections than those whose names were thus printed at full length as in the same rank of morals with a denounced infidel and fugitive, who had left his children *fatherless and his wife destitute*! Is it surprising that many good men remained longer than perhaps they otherwise would have done, adverse to a party which encouraged and openly rewarded the authors of such atrocious calumnies? Qualis es, nescio: sed per quales agis, scio et doleo. [*Anti-Jacobin*, 8 July 1798; on 'psilosophy', or slender wisdom, cf. *Notebooks*, 3244 and n., and p. 101 below.]

CHAPTER IV

The *Lyrical Ballads* with the Preface—Mr Wordsworth's earlier poems—On fancy and imagination—The investigation of the distinction important to the fine arts.

I HAVE wandered far from the object in view, but as I fancied to myself readers who would respect the feelings that had tempted me from the main road; so I dare calculate on not a few who will warmly sympathize with them. At present it will be sufficient for my purpose if I have proved that Mr Southey's writings no more than my own furnished the original occasion to this fiction of a new school of poetry, and of clamors against its supposed founders and proselytes.

As little do I believe that 'Mr Wordsworth's *Lyrical Ballads*' [1] were in themselves the cause. I speak exclusively of the two volumes so entitled. A careful and repeated examination of these confirms me in the belief that the omission of less than a hundred lines would have precluded nine-tenths of the criticism on this work. I hazard this declaration, however, on the supposition that the reader had taken it up, as he would have done any other collection of poems purporting to derive their subjects or interests from the incidents of domestic or ordinary life, intermingled with higher strains of meditation which the poet utters in his own person and character; with the proviso that they were perused without knowledge of, or reference to, the author's peculiar opinions, and that the reader had not had his attention previously directed to those peculiarities. In these, as was actually the case with Mr Southey's earlier works, the lines and passages which might have offended the general taste would have been considered as mere inequalities, and attributed to inattention, not to perversity of judgement. The men of business who had passed their lives chiefly in cities and who might therefore be expected to derive the highest pleasure from acute notices of men and manners conveyed in easy, yet correct

[1] [This collection appeared anonymously in one volume in 1798, followed in 1800 by the second edition enlarged into two volumes and with the addition of the famous Preface written by Wordsworth at Coleridge's suggestion. This second edition, to which Coleridge here refers, appeared as by Wordsworth only. but like the first it included several poems by Coleridge, notably the 'Ancient Mariner.']

41

and pointed language; and all those who, reading but little poetry, are most stimulated with that species of it which seems most distant from prose, would probably have passed by the volumes altogether.   Others more catholic in their taste, and yet habituated to be most pleased when most excited, would have contented themselves with deciding that the author had been successful in proportion to the elevation of his style and subject. Not a few, perhaps, might by their admiration of the 'Lines written near Tintern Abbey,' those 'Left upon a Seat under a Yew-tree,' the 'Old Cumberland Beggar' and 'Ruth,' have been gradually led to peruse with kindred feeling 'The Brothers,' the 'Hart-leap Well' and whatever other poems in that collection may be described as holding a middle place between those written in the highest and those in the humblest style; as for instance between the 'Tintern Abbey' and 'The Thorn,' or the 'Simon Lee.'   Should their taste submit to no further change and still remain unreconciled to the colloquial phrases, or the imitations of them, that are more or less scattered through the class last mentioned; yet even from the small number of the latter, they would have deemed them but an inconsiderable subtraction from the merit of the whole work; or, what is sometimes not unpleasing in the publication of a new writer, as serving to ascertain the natural tendency and consequently the proper direction of the author's genius.

In the critical remarks, therefore, prefixed and annexed to the *Lyrical Ballads*, I believe that we may safely rest as the true origin of the unexampled opposition which Mr Wordsworth's writings have been since doomed to encounter.   The humbler passages in the poems themselves were dwelt on and cited to justify the rejection of the theory.   What in and for themselves would have been either forgotten or forgiven as imperfections, or at least comparative failures, provoked direct hostility when announced as intentional, as the result of choice after full deliberation.   Thus the poems, admitted by all as excellent, joined with those which had pleased the far greater number, though they formed two-thirds of the whole work, instead of being deemed (as in all right they should have been, even if we take for granted that the reader judged aright) an atonement for the few exceptions, gave wind and fuel to the animosity against both the poems and the poet.   In all perplexity there is a portion of fear which predisposes the mind to anger.   Not able to deny that the author possessed both genius and a powerful intellect, they felt very positive, but were not quite certain, that he might not be in the right and they themselves in the wrong; an unquiet state of mind, which seeks alleviation by quarrelling with the occasion of it, and by wondering at the perverseness of the man who had written a long and argumentative essay to persuade them that

Fair is foul, and foul is fair;

in other words, that they had been all their lives admiring without judgement, and were now about to censure without reason.[1]

That this conjecture is not wide from the mark I am induced to believe from the noticeable fact, which I can state on my own knowledge, that the same general censure should have been grounded almost by each different person on some different poem.   Among those whose candour and judgement I estimate highly, I distinctly remember six who expressed their objections to the *Lyrical Ballads* almost in the same words and altogether to the same purport, at the same time admitting that several of

---

[1] In opinions of long continuance, and in which we had never before been molested by a single doubt, to be suddenly convinced of an error is almost like being convicted of a fault.   There is a state of mind which is the direct antithesis of that, which takes place when we *make a bull*.   The bull namely consists in the bringing together two incompatible thoughts, with the sensation, but without the sense, of their connection.   The psychological condition, or that which constitutes the possibility of this state, being such disproportionate vividness of two distant thoughts, as extinguishes or obscures the consciousness of the intermediate images or conceptions, or wholly abstracts the attention from them.   Thus in the well-known bull, 'I was a fine child, but they changed me'; the first conception expressed in the word 'I,' is that of personal identity—Ego contemplans: the second expressed in the word 'me,' is the visual image or object by which the mind represents to itself its past condition, or rather, its personal identity under the form in which it imagined itself previously to have existed,—Ego contemplatus. Now the change of one visual image for another involves in itself no absurdity, and becomes absurd only by its immediate juxta-position with the first thought, which is rendered possible by the whole attention being successively absorbed in each singly, so as not to notice the interjacent notion, 'changed,' which by its incongruity with the first thought, 'I,' constitutes the bull. Add only, that this process is facilitated by the circumstance of the words 'I' and 'me,' being sometimes equivalent, and sometimes having a distinct meaning; sometimes, namely, signifying the act of self-consciousness, sometimes the external image in and by which the mind represents that act to itself, the result and symbol of its individuality.   Now suppose the direct contrary state, and you will have a distinct sense of the connection between two conceptions, without that sensation of such connection which is supplied by habit.   The man feels as if he were standing on his head, though he cannot but see that he is truly standing on his feet.   This, as a painful sensation, will of course have a tendency to associate itself with the person who occasions it; even as persons, who have been by painful means restored from derangement, are known to feel an involuntary dislike towards their physician.

the poems had given them great pleasure; and, strange as it might seem, the composition which one had cited as execrable, another had quoted as his favorite. I am indeed convinced in my own mind that could the same experiment have been tried with these volumes as was made in the well-known story of the picture, the result would have been the same; the parts which had been covered by the number of the black spots on the one day, would be found equally *albo lapide notatae* on the succeeding.

However this may be, it is assuredly hard and unjust to fix the attention on a few separate and insulated poems with as much aversion as if they had been so many plague-spots on the whole work, instead of passing them over in silence as so much blank paper or leaves of a bookseller's catalogue; especially as no one pretends to have found immorality or indelicacy; and the poems, therefore, at the worst, could only be regarded as so many light or inferior coins in a rouleau of gold, not as so much alloy in a weight of bullion. A friend whose talents I hold in the highest respect, but whose judgement and strong sound sense I have had almost continued occasion to revere, making the usual complaints to me concerning both the style and subjects of Mr Wordsworth's minor poems; I admitted that there were some few of the tales and incidents in which I could not myself find a sufficient cause for their having been recorded in metre. I mentioned the 'Alice Fell' as an instance; 'nay,' replied my friend, with more than usual quickness of manner, 'I cannot agree with you *there*! that I own *does* seem to me a remarkably pleasing poem.' In the *Lyrical Ballads* (for my experience does not enable me to extend the remark equally unqualified to the two subsequent volumes [1]) I have heard at different times and from different individuals every single poem extolled and reprobated, with the exception of those of loftier kinds, which as was before observed seem to have won universal praise. This fact of itself would have made me diffident in my censures, had not a still stronger ground been furnished by the strange contrast of the heat and long continuance of the opposition with the nature of the faults stated as justifying it. The seductive faults, the *dulcia vitia* of Cowley, Marini or Darwin, might reasonably be thought capable of corrupting the public judgement for half a century and require a twenty years' war, campaign after campaign, in order to dethrone the usurper and re-establish the legitimate taste. But that a downright simpleness, under the

[1] [*Poems in Two Volumes*, 1807.]

affectation of simplicity, prosaic words in feeble metre, silly
thoughts in childish phrases, and a preference of mean, degrading
or at best trivial associations and characters, should succeed in
forming a school of imitators, a company of almost *religious*
admirers, and this too among young men of ardent minds, liberal
education and not

> with academic laurels unbestowed;

and that this bare and bald counterfeit of poetry, which is characterized as below criticism, should for nearly twenty years have
well-nigh engrossed criticism, as the main, if not the only butt of
review, magazine, pamphlet, poem and paragraph; this is indeed
matter of wonder!   Of yet greater is it, that the contest should
still continue as undecided [1] as that between Bacchus and the
frogs in Aristophanes, when the former descended to the realms
of the departed to bring back the spirit of old and genuine
poesy:

> X.   βρεκεκεκὲξ κοὰξ, κοὰξ!
>
> Δ.   ἀλλ᾽ ἐξόλοισθ᾽ αὐτῷ κοάξ.
>   οὐδὲν γὰρ ἔστ᾽ ἀλλ᾽ ἢ κοάξ.
>   οἰμώζετ᾽ : οὐ γάρ μοι μέλει.
>
> X.   ἀλλὰ μὴν κεκραξόμεσθά γ᾽
>   ὁπόσον ἡ φάρυγξ ἂν ἡμῶν
>   χανδάνῃ δι᾽ ἡμέρας,
>   βρεκεκεκὲξ κοὰξ, κοὰξ!

[1] Without however the apprehensions attributed to the pagan reformer of
the poetic republic.   If we may judge from the preface to the recent collection
of his poems, Mr W. would have answered with Xanthias—

> Σὺ δ᾽ οὐκ ἔδεισας τὸν ψόφον τῶν ῥημάτων,
> Καὶ τάς ἀπειλάς; ΞΑΝ. οὐ μὰ Δι᾽, οὐδ᾽ ἐφρόντισα.

And here let me dare hint to the authors of the numerous parodies, and
pretended imitations of Mr Wordsworth's style, that at once to conceal and
convey wit and wisdom in the semblance of folly and dullness, as is done in
the clowns and fools, nay even in the Dogberry of our Shakespeare, is
doubtless a proof of genius, or at all events of satiric talent; but that the
attempt to ridicule a silly and childish poem by writing another still sillier
and still more childish can only prove (if it prove any thing at all) that the
parodist is a still greater blockhead than the original writer, and what is far
worse, a malignant coxcomb to boot.   The talent for mimicry seems strongest
where the human race are most degraded.   The poor, naked, half human
savages of New Holland were found excellent mimics: and in civilized
society, minds of the very lowest stamp alone satirize by copying.   At least
the difference, which must blend with and balance the likeness in order to
constitute a just imitation, existing here merely in caricature, detracts from
the libeller's heart without adding an iota to the credit of his understanding.

Δ.   τούτῳ γὰρ οὐ νικήσετε.

Χ.   οὐδὲ μὴν ἡμᾶς σὺ πάντως.

Δ.   οὐδὲ μὴν ὑμεῖς γ' ἐμέ.
οὐδέποτε· κεκράξομαι γάρ
κᾳν με δέῃ δι' ἡμέρας,
ἕως ἄν ὑμῶν ἐπικρατήσω τοῦ κοάξ!

Χ.   βρεκεκεκὲξ ΚΟΑΞ ΚΟΑΞ![1]

During the last year of my residence at Cambridge I became
acquainted with Mr Wordsworth's first publication, entitled
Descriptive Sketches;[2] and seldom, if ever, was the emergence of
an original poetic genius above the literary horizon more
evidently announced. In the form, style and manner of the
whole poem, and in the structure of the particular lines and
periods, there is a harshness and acerbity connected and combined with words and images all a-glow which might recall those
products of the vegetable world, where gorgeous blossoms rise
out of the hard and thorny rind and shell within which the rich
fruit was elaborating. The language was not only peculiar and
strong, but at times knotty and contorted, as by its own impatient
strength; while the novelty and struggling crowd of images
acting in conjunction with the difficulties of the style demanded
always a greater closeness of attention than poetry (at all events
than descriptive poetry) has a right to claim. It not seldom
therefore justified the complaint of obscurity. In the following
extract I have sometimes fancied that I saw an emblem of the
poem itself and of the author's genius as it was then displayed:

> 'Tis storm; and hid in mist from hour to hour,
> All day the floods a deepening murmur pour,
> The sky is veiled, and every cheerful sight;
> Dark is the region as with coming night;
> And yet what frequent bursts of overpowering light!

---

[1] [*The Frogs*, 226–7 and 257–66:
'FROGS: Brekekekex, ko-ax, ko-ax.
BACCHUS: Hang you and your ko-axing. You do nothing but ko-ax. . . .
Be damned to you—what is it to me?
FROGS: Still we shout and cry, stretching our throats the whole day with our
song. Brekekekex, ko-ax, ko-ax.
BACCHUS: You shan't win this fight.
FROGS: You shan't beat us.
BACCHUS: No, nor you me. Never. I'll shout all day, if I must, till I've
mastered your ko-ax.
FROGS: Brekekekex ko-ax ko-ax.']

[2] [Published in 1793. Coleridge left Cambridge in 1794.]

Triumphant on the bosom of the storm,
Glances the fire-clad eagle's wheeling form;
Eastward, in long perspective glittering, shine
The wood-crowned cliffs that o'er the lake recline;
Wide o'er the Alps a hundred streams unfold,
At once to pillars turn'd that flame with gold;
Behind his sail the peasant strives to shun
The West, that burns like one dilated sun,
Where in a mighty crucible expire
The mountains, glowing hot, like coals of fire.[1]

The poetic Psyche, in its process to full development, under-
goes as many changes as its Greek namesake, the butterfly.[2]
And it is remarkable how soon genius clears and purifies itself
from the faults and errors of its earliest products; faults which, in
its earliest compositions, are the more obtrusive and confluent
because, as heterogeneous elements which had only a temporary
use, they constitute the very ferment by which themselves are
carried off. Or we may compare them to some diseases, which
must work on the humours and be thrown out on the surface in
order to secure the patient from their future recurrence. I was
in my twenty-fourth year when I had the happiness of knowing
Mr Wordsworth personally; [3] and, while memory lasts, I shall
hardly forget the sudden effect produced on my mind by his
recitation of a manuscript poem [4] which still remains unpublished, but of which the stanza and tone of style were the same as
those of 'The Female Vagrant' as originally printed in the first
volume of the *Lyrical Ballads*. There was here no mark of
strained thought or forced diction, no crowd or turbulence of

---

[1] [*Descriptive Sketches, ll.* 332–47, 1815 text.]
[2] The fact that in Greek Psyche is the common name for the soul and the
butterfly, is thus alluded to in the following stanza from an unpublished
poem of the author:

'The butterfly the ancient Grecians made
The soul's fair emblem, and its only name—
But of the soul, escaped the slavish trade
Of mortal life! For in this earthly frame
Our's is the reptile's lot, much toil, much blame,
Manifold motions making little speed,
And to deform and kill the things whereon we feed.'

S. T. C.

[Verses here published for the first time and probably composed in the
winter of 1806–7.]
[3] [Their first meeting was in Bristol in 1795, probably in September, in
Coleridge's twenty-third year.]
[4] ['Guilt and Sorrow,' composed by Wordsworth between 1791 and 1794
but not published till 1842.   One-third of the poem was abstracted, revised
by Wordsworth and published as 'The Female Vagrant' in the *Lyrical
Ballads*, 1798.]

imagery, and, as the poet hath himself well described in his lines
on re-visiting the Wye,[1] manly reflection and human associations
had given both variety and an additional interest to natural
objects which in the passion and appetite of the first love they
had seemed to him neither to need or permit.   The occasional
obscurities which had risen from an imperfect controul over the
resources of his native language had almost wholly disappeared,
together with that worse defect of arbitrary and illogical phrases,
at once hackneyed and fantastic, which hold so distinguished a
place in the *technique* of ordinary poetry and will, more or less,
alloy the earlier poems of the truest genius, unless the attention
has been specifically directed to their worthlessness and incongruity.[2]   I did not perceive anything particular in the mere style
of the poem alluded to during its recitation, except indeed such
difference as was not separable from the thought and manner;
and the Spenserian stanza which always, more or less, recalls to
the reader's mind Spenser's own style, would doubtless have
authorized in my then opinion a more frequent descent to the
phrases of ordinary life than could, without an ill effect, have
been hazarded in the heroic couplet.   It was not however the
freedom from false taste, whether as to common defects or to
those more properly his own, which made so unusual an impression on my feelings immediately, and subsequently on my
judgement.   It was the union of deep feeling with profound
thought; the fine balance of truth in observing with the imaginative faculty in modifying the objects observed; and above all the
original gift of spreading the tone, the *atmosphere* and with it the
depth and height of the ideal world, around forms, incidents

---

[1] [i.e. 'Lines Composed above Tintern Abbey' (1798).   The reference is
to *ll*. 22 ff.]

[2] Mr Wordsworth, even in his two earliest, *The Evening Walk* and the
Descriptive Sketches, is more free from this latter defect than most of the
young poets his contemporaries.   It may however be exemplified, together
with the harsh and obscure construction in which he more often offended, in
the following lines:

> 'Mid stormy vapours ever driving by,
> Where ospreys, cormorants, and herons cry;
> Where hardly given the hopeless waste to cheer,
> Denied the bread of life the foodful ear,
> Dwindles the pear on autumn's latest spray,
> And *apple sickens* pale in summer's ray;
> *Ev'n here content has fixed her smiling reign*
> *With independence, child of high disdain.*

[*Descriptive Sketches*, 317–24.]

I hope, I need not say, that I have quoted these lines for no other purpose
than to make my meaning fully understood.   It is to be regretted that Mr
Wordsworth has not republished these two poems entire.

and situations of which, for the common view, custom had bedimmed all the lustre, had dried up the sparkle and the dew-drops. 'To find no contradiction in the union of old and new, to contemplate the Ancient of Days and all his works with feelings as fresh as if all had then sprang forth at the first creative fiat, characterizes the mind that feels the riddle of the world and may help to unravel it. To carry on the feelings of childhood into the powers of manhood; to combine the child's sense of wonder and novelty with the appearances which every day for perhaps forty years had rendered familiar:

> With sun and moon and stars throughout the year
> And man and woman;[1]

this is the character and privilege of genius, and one of the marks which distinguish genius from talents. And therefore it is the prime merit of genius, and its most unequivocal mode of mani-festation, so to represent familiar objects as to awaken in the minds of others a kindred feeling concerning them, and that freshness of sensation which is the constant accompaniment of mental no less than of bodily convalescence. Who has not a thousand times seen snow fall on water? Who has not watched it with a new feeling from the time that he has read Burns' comparison of sensual pleasure:

> To snow that falls upon a river
> A moment white—then gone for ever![2]

In poems, equally as in philosophic disquisitions, genius pro-duces the strongest impressions of novelty while it rescues the most admitted truths from the impotence caused by the very circumstance of their universal admission. Truths of all others the most awful and mysterious, yet being at the same time of universal interest, are too often considered as *so* true, that they lose all the life and efficiency of truth and lie bed-ridden in the dormitory of the soul side by side with the most despised and exploded errors.' *The Friend*,[3] p. 76, No. 5.

This excellence, which in all Mr Wordsworth's writings is more or less predominant and which constitutes the character of his mind, I no sooner felt than I sought to understand. Repeated

---

[1] [From Milton, 'To Mr Cyriack Skinner upon his Blindness.']

[2] [From 'Tam O'Shanter,' *ll.* 61–2.]

[3] As *The Friend* was printed on stamped sheets, and sent only by the post to a very limited number of subscribers, the author has felt less objection to quote from it, though a work of his own. To the public at large indeed it is the same as a volume in manuscript.

meditations led me first to suspect (and a more intimate analysis of the human faculties, their appropriate marks, functions and effects, matured my conjecture into full conviction), that fancy and imagination were two distinct and widely different faculties, instead of being, according to the general belief, either two names with one meaning, or at furthest the lower and higher degree of one and the same power. It is not, I own, easy to conceive a more apposite translation of the Greek *phantasia* than the Latin *imaginatio*; but it is equally true that in all societies there exists an instinct of growth, a certain collective unconscious good sense working progressively to desynonymize [1] those words originally of the same meaning which the conflux of dialects had supplied to the more homogeneous languages, as the Greek and German, and which the same cause, joined with accidents of translation from original works of different countries, occasion in mixt languages like our own. The first and most important point to be proved is that two conceptions perfectly distinct are confused under one and the same word, and (this done) to appropriate that word exclusively to one meaning, and the synonyme (should there be one) to the other. But if (as will be often the case in the arts and sciences) no synonyme exists, we must either invent or borrow a word. In the present instance the appropriation had already begun and been legitimated in the derivative adjective: Milton had a highly *imaginative*, Cowley a very *fanciful*, mind. If therefore I should succeed in establishing the actual existence of two faculties generally different, the nomenclature would be at

---

[1] This is effected either by giving to the one word a general, and to the other an exclusive use; as 'to put on the back' and 'to indorse'; or by an actual distinction of meanings as 'naturalist,' and 'physician'; or by difference of relation as 'I,' and 'Me'; (each of which the rustics of our different provinces still use in all the cases singular of the first personal pronoun). Even the mere difference or corruption in the pronunciation of the same word, if it have become general, will produce a new word with a distinct signification; thus 'property' and 'propriety,' the latter of which even to the time of Charles II was the written word for all the senses of both. Thus too 'mister' and 'master' both hasty pronunciations of the same word 'magister,' 'mistress,' and 'miss,' 'if,' and 'give,' etc. etc. There is a sort of minim immortal among the *animalcula infusoria* which has not naturally either birth, or death, absolute beginning or absolute end: for at a certain period a small point appears on its back, which deepens and lengthens till the creature divides in two and the same process recommences in each of the halves now become integral. This may be a fanciful but it is by no means a bad emblem of the formation of words, and may facilitate the conception how immense a nomenclature may be organized from a few simple sounds by rational beings in a social state. For each new application or excitement of the same sound will call forth a different sensation, which cannot but affect the pronunciation. The after recollection of the sound without the same vivid sensation will modify it still further; till at length all trace of the original likeness is worn away.

once determined.   To the faculty by which I had characterized Milton we should confine the term *imagination*; while the other would be contra-distinguished as *fancy*.   Now were it once fully ascertained that this division is no less grounded in nature than that of delirium from mania, or Otway's

> Lutes, laurels, seas of milk and ships of amber,[1]

from Shakespeare's

> What! have his daughters brought him to this pass?[2]

or from the preceding apostrophe to the elements, the theory of the fine arts and of poetry in particular could not, I thought, but derive some additional and important light.   It would in its immediate effects furnish a torch of guidance to the philosophical critic, and ultimately to the poet himself.   In energetic minds truth soon changes by domestication into power; and from directing in the discrimination and appraisal of the product becomes influencive in the production.   To admire on principle is the only way to imitate without loss of originality.

It has been already hinted that metaphysics and psychology have long been my hobby-horse.   But to have a hobby-horse, and to be vain of it, are so commonly found together that they pass almost for the same.   I trust therefore that there will be more good humour than contempt in the smile with which the reader chastises my self-complacency, if I confess myself uncertain whether the satisfaction for the perception of a truth new to myself may not have been rendered more poignant by the conceit that it would be equally so to the public.   There was a time, certainly, in which I took some little credit to myself in the belief that I had been the first of my countrymen who had pointed out the diverse meaning of which the two terms were capable, and analysed the faculties to which they should be appropriated.   Mr W. Taylor's recent volume of synonimes I have not yet seen;[3] but his specification of the terms in question

---

[1] [*Venice Preserv'd*, v. i. 369.   The 1817 edition of the *Biographia* has 'lobsters' for 'laurels.']

[2] [*King Lear*, III. iv. 63.]

[3] [*British Synonymes Discriminated*, 1813.]   I ought to have added, with the exception of a single sheet which I accidentally met with at the printer's. Even with this scanty specimen, I found it impossible to doubt the talent or not to admire the ingenuity of the author.   That his distinctions were for the greater part unsatisfactory to *my* mind, proves nothing against their accuracy; but it may possibly be serviceable to him in case of a second edition if I take this opportunity of suggesting the query: whether he may not have been

has been clearly shown to be both insufficient and erroneous by Mr Wordsworth in the preface added to the late collection of his *Lyrical Ballads* and other poems. The explanation which Mr Wordsworth has himself given will be found to differ from mine chiefly, perhaps, as our objects are different. It could scarcely indeed happen otherwise, from the advantage I have enjoyed of frequent conversation with him on a subject to which a poem of his own[1] first directed my attention, and my conclusions concerning which he had made more lucid to myself by many happy instances drawn from the operation of natural objects on the mind. But it was Mr Wordsworth's purpose to consider the influences of fancy and imagination as they are manifested in poetry, and from the different effects to conclude their diversity in kind; while it is my object to investigate the seminal principle, and then from the kind to deduce the degree. My friend has drawn a masterly sketch of the branches with their *poetic* fruitage. I wish to add the trunk, and even the roots, as far as they lift themselves above ground and are visible to the naked eye of our common consciousness.

Yet even in this attempt I am aware that I shall be obliged to draw more largely on the reader's attention than so immethodical

---

occasionally misled by having assumed, as to me he appeared to have done, the non-existence of any absolute synonimes in our language? Now I cannot but think, that there are many which remain for our posterity to distinguish and appropriate and which I regard as so much reversionary wealth in our mother-tongue. When two distinct meanings are confounded under one or more words (and such must be the case, as sure as our knowledge is progressive and of course imperfect), erroneous consequences will be drawn, and what is true in the sense of the word will be affirmed as true *in toto*. Men of research, startled by the consequences, seek in the things themselves (whether in or out of the mind) for a knowledge of the fact, and having discovered the difference remove the equivocation either by the substitution of a new word or by the appropriation of one of the two or more words that had before been used promiscuously. When this distinction has been so naturalized and of such general currency that the language itself does as it were *think* for us (like the sliding rule which is the mechanic's safe substitute for arithmetical knowledge) we then say, that it is evident to *common sense*. Common sense, therefore, differs in different ages. What was born and christened in the schools passes by degrees into the world at large and becomes the property of the market and the tea-table. At least I can discover no other meaning of the term, *common sense*, if it is to convey any specific difference from sense and judgment *in genere*, and where it is not used scholastically for the *universal reason*. Thus in the reign of Charles II the philosophic world was called to arms by the moral sophisms of Hobbes, and the ablest writers exerted themselves in the detection of an error which a schoolboy would now be able to confute by the mere recollection that *compulsion* and *obligation* conveyed two ideas perfectly disparate, and that what appertained to the one had been falsely transferred to the other by a mere confusion of terms.

[1] [Probably 'Ruth' (comp. 1799, pub. 1800).]

a miscellany can authorize, when in such a work (*the Ecclesiastical Polity*) of such a mind as Hooker's the judicious author, though no less admirable for the perspicuity than for the port and dignity of his language and though he wrote for men of learning in a learned age, saw nevertheless occasion to anticipate and guard against 'complaints of obscurity' as often as he was to trace his subject 'to the highest well-spring and fountain.' Which (continues he), 'because men are not accustomed to, the pains we take are more needful a great deal than acceptable; and the matters we handle seem by reason of newness (till the mind grow better acquainted with them) dark and intricate.' I would gladly therefore spare both myself and others this labour, if I knew how without it to present an intelligible statement of my poetic creed; not as my *opinions*, which weigh for nothing, but as deductions from established premises conveyed in such a form as is calculated either to effect a fundamental conviction or to receive a fundamental confutation. If I may dare once more adopt the words of Hooker, 'they unto whom we shall seem tedious are in no wise injured by us, because it is in their own hands to spare that labour which they are not willing to endure.' [1] Those at least, let me be permitted to add, who have taken so much pains to render me ridiculous for a perversion of taste, and have supported the charge by attributing strange notions to me on no other authority than their own conjectures, owe it to themselves as well as to me not to refuse their attention to my own statement of the theory, which I *do* acknowledge; or shrink from the trouble of examining the grounds on which I rest it, or the arguments which I offer in its justification.

[1] [Bk. I, ch. i, § 2.]

CHAPTER V

On the law of association—Its history traced from Aristotle to Hartley.

THERE have been men in all ages who have been impelled as by an instinct to propose their own nature as a problem, and who devote their attempts to its solution. The first step was to construct a table of distinctions, which they seem to have formed on the principle of the absence or presence of the Will. Our various sensations, perceptions and movements were classed as active or passive, or as media partaking of both. A still finer distinction was soon established between the voluntary and the spontaneous. In our perceptions we seem to ourselves merely passive to an external power, whether as a mirror reflecting the landscape or as a blank canvas on which some unknown hand paints it. For it is worthy of notice that the latter, or the system of idealism, may be traced to sources equally remote with the former, or materialism; and Berkeley can boast an ancestry at least as venerable as Gassendi or Hobbes. These conjectures, however, concerning the mode in which our perceptions originated, could not alter the natural difference of things and thoughts. In the former the cause appeared wholly external, while in the latter sometimes our will interfered as the producing or determining cause, and sometimes our nature seemed to act by a mechanism of its own, without any conscious effort of the will, or even against it. Our inward experiences were thus arranged in three separate classes: the passive sense, or what the school-men call the merely receptive quality of the mind; the voluntary; and the spontaneous, which holds the middle place between both. But it is not in human nature to meditate on any mode of action without inquiring after the law that governs it; and in the explanation of the spontaneous movements of our being the metaphysician took the lead of the anatomist and natural philosopher. In Egypt, Palestine, Greece and India the analysis of the mind had reached its noon and manhood, while experimental research was still in its dawn and infancy. For many, very many centuries, it has been difficult to advance a new truth, or even a new error, in the philosophy of the intellect or morals. With regard however to the laws that direct the spontaneous movements of thought and the principle of their intellectual

54

mechanism there exists, it has been asserted, an important exception most honorable to the moderns, and in the merit of which our own country claims the largest share. Sir James Mackintosh (who amid the variety of his talents and attainments is not of less repute for the depth and accuracy of his philosophical inquiries than for the eloquence with which he is said to render their most difficult results perspicuous, and the driest attractive) affirmed in the lectures [1] delivered by him at Lincoln's Inn Hall that the law of association as established in the contemporaneity of the original impressions formed the basis of all true psychology; and any ontological or metaphysical science not contained in such (i.e. empirical) psychology was but a web of abstractions and generalizations. Of this prolific truth, of this great fundamental law, he declared Hobbes to have been the original discoverer, while its full application to the whole intellectual system we owe to David Hartley; who stood in the same relation to Hobbes as Newton to Kepler; the law of association being that to the mind, which gravitation is to matter.

Of the former clause in this assertion, as it respects the comparative merits of the ancient metaphysicians, including their commentators the school-men, and of the modern French and British philosophers from Hobbes to Hume, Hartley and Condillac, this is not the place to speak. So wide indeed is the chasm between this gentleman's philosophical creed and mine, that so far from being able to join hands we could scarce make our voices intelligible to each other; and to bridge it over would require more time, skill and power than I believe myself to possess. But the latter clause involves for the greater part a mere question of fact and history, and the accuracy of the statement is to be tried by documents rather than reasoning.

First, then, I deny Hobbes's claim *in toto*: for he had been anticipated by Des Cartes, whose work *De methodo* preceded Hobbes's *De natura humana* by more than a year.[2] But what is of much more importance, Hobbes builds nothing on the principle which he had announced. He does not even announce it as differing in any respect from the general laws of material motion and impact: nor was it indeed possible for him so to do compatibly with his system, which was exclusively material and mechanical. Far otherwise is it with Des Cartes; greatly as he

---

[1] [Delivered in 1799. The first of these lectures was published as *The Law of Nature and of Nations* (1799).]

[2] [By thirteen years, in fact. Hobbes's *Humane Nature* appeared in 1650, Descartes's *Discours de la méthode* in 1637.]

too in his after writings (and still more egregiously his followers, De la Forge and others) obscured the truth by their attempts to explain it on the theory of nervous fluids and material configurations. But in his interesting work *De methodo* [1] Des Cartes relates the circumstance which first led him to meditate on this subject, and which since then has been often noticed and employed as an instance and illustration of the law. A child who with its eyes bandaged had lost several of his fingers by amputation continued to complain for many days successively of pains, now in this joint and now in that, of the very fingers which had been cut off. Des Cartes was led by this incident to reflect on the uncertainty with which we attribute any particular place to any inward pain or uneasiness, and proceeded after long consideration to establish it as a general law that contemporaneous impressions, whether images or sensations, recall each other mechanically. On this principle, as a ground work, he built up the whole system of human language as one continued process of association. He showed in what sense not only general terms, but generic images (under the name of abstract ideas) actually existed, and in what consists their nature and power. As one word may become the general exponent of many, so by association a simple image may represent a whole class. But in truth Hobbes himself makes no claims to any discovery, and introduces this law of association or (in his own language) *discursus mentalis*, as an admitted fact, in the *solution* alone of which, this by causes purely physiological, he arrogates any originality. His system is briefly this: whenever the senses are impinged on by external objects, whether by the rays of light reflected from them, or by effluxes of their finer particles, there results a correspondent motion of the innermost and subtlest organs. This motion constitutes a representation, and there remains an impression of the same, or a certain disposition to repeat the same motion. Whenever we feel several objects at the same time, the impressions that are left (or in the language of Mr Hume, the *ideas*) are linked together. Whether therefore any one of the movements which constitute a complex impression is renewed through the senses, the others succeed mechanically. It follows of necessity therefore that Hobbes, as well as Hartley and all others who derive association from the connection and interdependence of the supposed matter, the movements of which constitute our thoughts, must have reduced all its forms

---

[1] [This story is actually recounted in the *Principia*, pt iv, where it is adduced as evidence for the soul's relation to the body.]

to the one law of time.   But even the merit of announcing this
law with philosophic precision cannot be fairly conceded to him.
For the objects of any two ideas [1] need not have co-existed in the
same sensation in order to become mutually associable.   The
same result will follow when one only of the two ideas has been
represented by the senses and the other by the memory.

Long however before either Hobbes or Des Cartes the law of
association had been defined and its important functions set
forth by Melanchthon, Ammerbach and Ludovicus Vives; [2] more
especially by the last.   *Phantasia*, it is to be noticed, is employed
by Vives to express the mental power of comprehension, or the
active function of the mind; and *imaginatio* for the receptivity
(*vis receptiva*) of impressions, or for the passive perception.

---

[1] I here use the word 'idea' in Mr Hume's sense on account of its general
currency among the English metaphysicians; though against my own judgment, for I believe that the vague use of this word has been the cause of much
error and much confusion.   The word, ἰδέα, in its original sense as used by
Pindar, Aristophanes and in the Gospel of Matthew, represented the visual
abstraction of a distant object when we see the whole without distinguishing
its parts.   Plato adopted it as a technical term, and as the antithesis to εἴδωλα,
or sensuous images; the transient and perishable emblems, or mental words,
of ideas.   The ideas themselves he considered as mysterious powers, living,
seminal, formative and exempt from time.   In this sense the word became
the property of the Platonic school; and it seldom occurs in Aristotle, without
some such phrase annexed to it as according to Plato, or as Plato says.   Our
English writers to the end of Charles 2nd's reign, or somewhat later, employed
it either in the original sense, or platonically, or in a sense nearly correspondent to our present use of the substantive *ideal*, always however opposing
it more or less to image, whether of present or absent objects.   The reader
will not be displeased with the following interesting exemplification from
Bishop Jeremy Taylor: 'St Lewis the King sent Ivo Bishop of Chartres on
an embassy, and he told that he met a grave and stately matron on the way
with a censer of fire in one hand, and a vessel of water in the other; and
observing her to have a melancholy, religious and phantastic deportment
and look, he asked her what those symbols meant, and what she meant to do
with her fire and water; she answered, my purpose is with the fire to burn
paradise and with my water to quench the flames of hell, that men may serve
God purely for the love of God.   But we rarely meet with such spirits which
love virtue so metaphysically as *to abstract her from all sensible compositions,
and love the purity of the idea.*'   Des Cartes having introduced into his
philosophy the fanciful hypothesis of *material idea*, or certain configurations
of the brain, which were as so many moulds to the influxes of the external
world; Mr Locke adopted the term, but extended its signification to whatever
is the immediate object of the mind's attention or consciousness.   Mr Hume
distinguishing those representations which are accompanied with a sense of a
present object, from those reproduced by the mind itself, designated the
former by *impressions*, and confined the word *idea* to the latter.

[Jeremy Taylor, *Golden Grove* (1651), Sermon xii; John Locke, *Essay
Concerning Humane Understanding* (1690), Introduction, § 8; David Hume,
A Treatise of Human Nature (1739–40), vol. i, p. 1.]

[2] [Coleridge took the substance of this paragraph, including the Vives
quotations, from J. G. E. Maass (1766–1832), *Versuch über die Einbildungs-
kraft* (1797), pp. 343–6).   His annotated copy of this book is now in the

The power of combination he appropriates to the former: 'quae singula et simplicia acceperat imaginatio, ea conjungit et disjungit phantasia.' And the law by which the thoughts are spontaneously presented follows thus: 'quae simul sunt a phantasia comprehensa, si alterutrum occurrat, solet secum alterum representare.' To time therefore he subordinates all the other exciting causes of association. The soul proceeds 'a causa ad effectum, ab hoc ad instrumentum, a parte ad totum'; thence to the place, from place to person, and from this to whatever preceded or followed, all as being parts of a total impression, each of which may recall the other. The apparent springs, 'saltus vel transitus etiam longissimos,' he explains by the same thought having been a component part of two or more total impressions. Thus 'ex Scipione venio in cogitationem potentiae Turcicae, propter victorias ejus in eâ parte Asiae in qua regnabat Antiochus.'

But from Vives I pass at once to the source of his doctrines and (as far as we can judge from the remains yet extant of Greek philosophy) as to the first, so to the fullest and most perfect enunciation of the associative principle, viz. to the writings of Aristotle; and of these principally to the books *De anima, De memoria* and that which is entitled in the old translations *Parva naturalia.*[1] In as much as later writers have either deviated from or added to his doctrines, they appear to me to have introduced either error or groundless supposition.

In the first place it is to be observed that Aristotle's positions on this subject are unmixed with fiction. The wise Stagyrite speaks of no successive particles propagating motion like billiard balls (as Hobbes [2]); nor of nervous or animal spirits, where

---

British Museum. Vives (1492–1540) completed in 1538 a psychological treatise entitled *De anima et vita*, which was followed by two works under the title *De anima* by the German theologicans Veit Amerbach (1504–57) and Philipp Melanchthon (1497–1560). The three works were eventually published together in Zürich in 1563, and from this edition (pp. 35 and 63–4) Maass quoted from Vives: 'The *phantasia* joins and disjoins what the *imaginatio* receives as single units.' 'What the *phantasia* brings together, if one comes to mind so too does the other.' '[The mind moves] from cause to effect, from this to the original object, from the part to the whole. . . . There may even be long jumps and gaps. For example, from Scipio the power of the Turks comes into my mind because of their victories in the part of Asia where Antiochus once ruled.']

[1] [A collection of psychological and physiological treatises (so called since the fifteenth century) of which the *De memoria* is in fact one.]

[2] [There is no such passage in Hobbes. Coleridge may have confused it with Hume, *Enquiry concerning Human Understanding* (1748), vol. iv, ch. i, p. 24: 'We fancy that were we brought on a sudden into this world we could at first have inferred that one Billiard-ball would communicate motion to another upon impulse.']

inanimate and irrational solids are thawed down and distilled, or filtrated by ascension, into living and intelligent fluids that etch and re-etch engravings on the brain (as the followers of Des Cartes and the humoral pathologists in general); nor of an oscillating ether which was to effect the same service for the nerves of the brain considered as solid fibres, as the animal spirits perform for them under the notion of hollow tubes (as Hartley teaches)—nor finally (with yet more recent dreamers) of chemical compositions by elective affinity, or of an electric light at once the immediate object and the ultimate organ of inward vision, which rises to the brain like an Aurora Borealis, and there disporting in various shapes (as the balance of plus and minus, or negative and positive, is destroyed or re-established) images out both past and present.   Aristotle delivers a just *theory* without pretending to an *hypothesis*; or in other words a comprehensive survey of the different facts, and of their relations to each other without *supposition*, i.e. a fact *placed under* a number of facts as their common support and explanation; though in the majority of instances these hypotheses or suppositions better deserve the name of ὑποποιησεῖς, or suffictions.   He uses indeed the word κινησεῖς, to express what we call representations or ideas, but he carefully distinguishes them from material motion, designating the latter always by annexing the words ἐν τόπῳ, or κατὰ τόπον.[1] On the contrary, in his treatise *De anima* he excludes place and motion from all the operations of thought, whether representations or volitions, as attributes utterly and absurdly heterogeneous.

The general law of association or, more accurately, the common condition under which all exciting causes act and in which they may be generalized, according to Aristotle is this.   Ideas by having been together acquire a power of recalling each other; or every partial representation awakes the total representation of which it had been a part.   In the practical determination of this common principle to particular recollections he admits five agents or occasioning causes: 1st, connection in time, whether simultaneous, preceding or successive; 2nd, vicinity or connection in space; 3rd, interdependence or necessary connection, as cause and effect; 4th, likeness; and 5th, contrast.[2]   As an

---

[1] [*De anima*, II. iii: 'movement in space.']
[2] [*De memoria*, 2.451b *et passim*.   In fact Aristotle distinguishes only four such agents, the third (causation) being Coleridge's addition.   The 'additional solution' which follows does not occur in Aristotle but in Maass (see above, p. 58n.]

additional solution of the occasional seeming chasms in the
continuity of reproduction he proves that movements or ideas
possessing one or the other of these five characters had passed
through the mind as intermediate links, sufficiently clear to recall
other parts of the same total impressions with which they had
co-existed, though not vivid enough to excite that degree of
attention which is requisite for distinct recollection, or as we may
aptly express it, *after-consciousness*.   In association then consists
the whole mechanism of the reproduction of impressions in the
Aristotelian psychology.   It is the universal law of the passive
fancy and mechanical memory; that which supplies to all other
faculties their objects, to all thought the elements of its
materials.

In consulting the excellent commentary of St Thomas Aquinas
on the *Parva naturalia* of Aristotle I was struck at once with its
close resemblance to Hume's essay on association.[1]   The main
thoughts were the same in both, the order of the thoughts was
the same, and even the illustrations differed only by Hume's
occasional substitution of more modern examples.   I mentioned
the circumstances to several of my literary acquaintances, who
admitted the closeness of the resemblance and that it seemed too
great to be explained by mere coincidence; but they thought it
improbable that Hume should have held the pages of the angelic
Doctor worth turning over.   But some time after Mr Payne, of
the King's Mews, shewed Sir James Mackintosh some odd
volumes of St Thomas Aquinas, partly perhaps from having
heard that Sir James (then Mr) Mackintosh had in his lectures
passed a high encomium on this canonized philosopher, but
chiefly from the fact that the volumes had belonged to Mr Hume
and had here and there marginal marks and notes of reference in
his own handwriting.   Among these volumes was that which
contains the *Parva naturalia*, in the old Latin version, swathed
and swaddled in the commentary afore mentioned!

It remains then for me first to state wherein Hartley differs
from Aristotle; then to exhibit the grounds of my conviction that
he differed only to err; and next, as the result, to shew by what
influences of the choice and judgement the associative power
becomes either memory or fancy; and, in conclusion, to appro-

[1] [Presumably the *Treatise of Human Nature* (1739–40).   But the theory of
association pervades Hume's writings.   Later, in the *Enquiry Concerning
Human Understanding* (1748), Hume described himself as the first to have
'attempted to enumerate or class all the principles of association' (E. 24), in
spite of Aristotle's attempt in the *De memoria*.   Cf. *Notebooks*, 973A.]

priate the remaining offices of the mind to the reason and the imagination. With my best efforts to be as perspicuous as the nature of language will permit on such a subject I earnestly solicit the good wishes and friendly patience of my readers, while I thus go 'sounding on my dim and perilous way.' [1]

[1] [Wordsworth, *The Excursion* (1814), III. 701.]

CHAPTER VI

That Hartley's system, as far as it differs from that of Aristotle, is neither tenable in theory nor founded in facts.

OF Hartley's hypothetical vibrations in his hypothetical oscillating ether of the nerves,[1] which is the first and most obvious distinction between his system and that of Aristotle, I shall say little. This, with all other similar attempts to render that an object of the sight which has no relation to sight, has been already sufficiently exposed by the younger Reimarus,[2] Maass, etc., as outraging the very axioms of mechanics in a scheme, the merit of which consists in its being mechanical. Whether any other philosophy be possible but the mechanical, and again, whether the mechanical system can have any claim to be called philosophy, are questions for another place. It is, however, certain that as long as we deny the former and affirm the latter, we must bewilder ourselves, whenever we would pierce into the adyta[3] of causations; and all that laborious conjecture can do is to fill up the gaps of fancy. Under that despotism of the eye (the emancipation from which Pythagoras by his numeral, and Plato by his musical, symbols, and both by geometric discipline, aimed at, as the first προπαιδευτικον[4] of the mind)—under this strong sensuous influence we are restless because invisible things are not the objects of vision; and metaphysical systems, for the most part, become popular not for their truth but in proportion as they attribute to causes a susceptibility of being seen, if only our visual organs were sufficiently powerful.

From a hundred possible confutations let one suffice.[5] According to this system the idea or vibration *a* from the external object A becomes associable with the idea or vibration *m* from the external object M, because the oscillation *a* propagated itself so as to reproduce the oscillation *m*. But the original impression from M was essentially different from the impression [from] A:

---

[1] [David Hartley (1705–57), *Observations on Man* (2 vols., 1749), I. i.]

[2] [J. A. Reimarus (1729–1814), a German rationalist philosopher.]

[3] [i.e. shrines. This passage is an expansion, 'imagination' being significantly changed to 'fancy,' of Coleridge's note to his addition to Southey's *Joan of Arc* (1796), p. 42n.]

[4] [i.e. preparatory instruction.]

[5] [This passage is based upon Maass, *Versuch*, pp. 32–3.]

unless therefore different causes may produce the same effect, the vibration *a* could never produce the vibration *m*: and this therefore could never be the means by which *a* and *m* are associated. To understand this, the attentive reader need only be reminded that the ideas are themselves, in Hartley's system, nothing more than their appropriate configurative vibrations. It is a mere delusion of the fancy to conceive the pre-existence of the ideas in any chain of association as so many differently colored billiard-balls in contact, so that when an object, the billiard-stick, strikes the first or white ball, the same motion propagates itself through the red, green, blue, black, etc., and sets the whole in motion. No! we must suppose the very same force which constitutes the white ball to constitute the red or black; or the idea of a circle to constitute the idea of a triangle; which is impossible.

But it may be said that, by the sensations from the objects A and M, the nerves have acquired a disposition to the vibrations *a* and *m*, and therefore *a* need only be repeated in order to re-produce *m*. Now we will grant, for a moment, the possibility of such a disposition in a material nerve, which yet seems scarcely less absurd than to say that a weather-cock has acquired a habit of turning to the east, from the wind having been so long in that quarter: for if it be replied, that we must take in the circumstance of life, what then becomes of the mechanical philosophy? And what is the nerve but the flint which the wag placed in the pot as the first ingredient of his stone-broth, requiring only salt, turnips, and mutton for the remainder! But if we waive this, and presuppose the actual existence of such a disposition, two cases are possible. Either every idea has its own nerve and correspondent oscillation, or this is not the case. If the latter be the truth, we should gain nothing by these dispositions; for then, every nerve having several dispositions when the motion of any other nerve is propagated into it, there will be no ground or cause present why exactly the oscillation *m* should arise, rather than any other to which it was equally pre-disposed. But if we take the former, and let every idea have a nerve of its own, then every nerve must be capable of propagating its motion into many other nerves; and again, there is no reason assignable why the vibration *m* should arise, rather than any other *ad libitum*.

It is fashionable to smile at Hartley's vibrations and vibratiuncles; and his work has been re-edited by Priestley,[1] with the

---

[1] [*Hartley's Theory of the Human Mind*, ed. Joseph Priestley, 1775. Priestley omitted these 'astronomical disquisitions,' including the vibration theory, from his edition.]

omission of the material hypothesis.   But Hartley was too great a man, too coherent a thinker, for this to have been done either consistently or to any wise purpose.   For all other parts of his system, as far as they are peculiar to that system, once removed from their mechanical basis not only lose their main support but the very motive which led to their adoption.   Thus the principle of contemporaneity, which Aristotle had made the common condition of all the laws of association, Hartley was constrained to represent as being itself the sole law.   For to what law can the action of material atoms be subject, but that of proximity in place?   And to what law can their motions be subjected, but that of time?   Again, from this results inevitably that the will, the reason, the judgement and the understanding, instead of being the determining causes of association, must needs be represented as its creatures, and among its mechanical effects.   Conceive, for instance, a broad stream, winding through a mountainous country with an indefinite number of currents, varying and running into each other according as the gusts chance to blow from the opening of the mountains.   The temporary union of several currents in one, so as to form the main current of the moment, would present an accurate image of Hartley's theory of the will.

Had this been really the case, the consequence would have been that our whole life would be divided between the despotism of outward impressions and that of senseless and passive memory.   Take his law in its highest abstraction and most philosophical form, viz. that every partial representation recalls the total representation of which it was a part; and the law becomes nugatory, were it only from its universality.   In practice it would indeed be mere lawlessness.   Consider how immense must be the sphere of a total impression from the top of St Paul's church; and how rapid and continuous the series of such total impressions.   If therefore we suppose the absence of all interference of the will, reason and judgement, one or other of two consequences must result.   Either the ideas (or relicts of such impression) will exactly imitate the order of the impression itself, which would be absolute delirium: or any one part of that impression might recall any other part, and (as from the law of continuity there must exist in every total impression some one or more parts which are components of some other following total impression, and so on *ad infinitum*) any part of any impression might recall any part of any other, without a cause present to determine what it should be.   For to bring in the will, or reason, as causes of their own cause, that is, as at once causes and effects, can satisfy those only who in their pretended evidences of a God having first demanded organization as the sole cause and ground of intellect, will then coolly demand the pre-existence of intellect as the cause and ground-work of organization.   There is in truth but one state to which this theory applies at all, namely that of complete light-headedness; and even to this it applies but partially, because the will and reason are perhaps never wholly suspended.

A case of this kind occurred in a Catholic town in Germany a year or two before my arrival at Göttingen,[1] and had not then ceased to be a frequent subject of conversation. A young woman of four or five and twenty, who could neither read nor write, was seized with a nervous fever; during which, according to the asseverations of all the priests and monks of the neighbourhood, she became possessed and, as it appeared, by a very learned devil.   She continued incessantly talking Latin, Greek and Hebrew, in very pompous tones and with most distinct enuncia-tion.   This possession was rendered more probable by the known fact that she was or had been an heretic.   Voltaire humorously advises the devil to decline all acquaintance with medical men; and it would have been more to his reputation if he had taken this advice in the present instance.   The case had attracted the particular attention of a young physician, and by his statement many eminent physiologists and psychologists visited the town and cross-examined the case on the spot.   Sheets full of her ravings were taken down from her own mouth, and were found to consist of sentences, coherent and intelligible each for itself, but with little or no connection with each other.   Of the Hebrew, a small portion only could be traced to the Bible; the remainder seemed to be in the rabbinical dialect.   All trick or conspiracy was out of the question.   Not only had the young woman ever been a harmless, simple creature; but she was evidently labouring under a nervous fever.   In the town, in which she had been resident for many years as a servant in different families, no solution presented itself.   The young physician, however, determined to trace her past life step by step; for the patient herself was incapable of returning a rational answer.   He at length succeeded in discovering the place where her parents had lived: travelled thither, found them dead, but an uncle surviving; and from him learnt that the patient had been

---

[1] [In February 1799.]

charitably taken by an old Protestant pastor at nine years old, and had remained with him some years, even till the old man's death. Of this pastor the uncle knew nothing but that he was a very good man. With great difficulty, and after much search, our young medical philosopher discovered a niece of the pastor's who had lived with him as his house-keeper, and had inherited his effects. She remembered the girl; related that her venerable uncle had been too indulgent, and could not bear to hear the girl scolded; that she was willing to have kept her, but that after her patron's death the girl herself refused to stay. Anxious inquiries were then, of course, made concerning the pastor's habits; and the solution of the phenomenon was soon obtained. For it appeared that it had been the old man's custom for years to walk up and down a passage of his house into which the kitchen door opened, and to read to himself with a loud voice out of his favorite books. A considerable number of these were still in the niece's possession. She added that he was a very learned man and a great Hebraist. Among the books were found a collection of rabbinical writings, together with several of the Greek and Latin Fathers; and the physician succeeded in identifying so many passages with those taken down at the young woman's bedside that no doubt could remain in any rational mind concerning the true origin of the impressions made on her nervous system.

This authenticated case furnishes both proof and instance that reliques of sensation may exist for an indefinite time in a latent state, in the very same order in which they were originally impressed; and as we cannot rationally suppose the feverish state of the brain to act in any other way than as a stimulus, this fact (and it would not be difficult to adduce several of the same kind) contributes to make it even probable that all thoughts are in themselves imperishable; and that if the intelligent faculty should be rendered more comprehensive, it would require only a different and apportioned organization, the body celestial instead of the body terrestrial, to bring before every human soul the collective experience of its whole past existence. And this, this, perchance, is the dread book of judgement in whose mysterious hieroglyphics every idle word is recorded! Yea, in the very nature of a living spirit, it may be more possible that heaven and earth should pass away than that a single act, a single thought, should be loosened or lost from that living chain of causes, to all whose links, conscious or unconscious, the free-will, our only absolute self, is co-extensive and co-present. But not now dare

I longer discourse of this, waiting for a loftier mood and a nobler
subject, warned from within and from without, that it is a pro-
fanation to speak of these mysteries τοῖς μηδὲ φαντασθεῖσιν
ὡς καλὸν τὸ τῆς δικαιοσύνης καὶ σωφροσύνης πρόσωπον, καὶ ὡς
οὔτε ἕσπερος οὔτε ἕως οὕτω καλά. . . Τὸ γὰρ ὁρῶν πρὸς τὸ
ὁρώμενον συγγενὲς καὶ ὅμοιον ποιησάμενον δεῖ ἐπιβάλλειν τῇ
θέᾳ· οὐ γὰρ ἄν πώποτε εἶδεν ᾿ὀφθαλμὸς ἥλιον ἡλιοείδης μὴ
γεγενημένος, οὐδὲ τὸ καλὸν ἄν ἴδοι ψυχὴ μὴ καλὴ γενομένη.
PLOTINUS.[1]

[1] 'To those to whose imagination it has never been presented how beautiful
is the countenance of justice and wisdom; and that neither the morning nor
the evening star are so fair. . . . For in order to direct the view aright, it
behoves that the beholder should have made himself congenerous and similar
to the object beheld. Never could the eye have beheld the sun, had not its
own essence been soliform,' (i.e. *pre-configured to light by a similarity of
essence with that of light*) 'neither can a soul not beautiful attain to an intuition
of beauty.' [*Ennead*, I. vi. 4 and 9.]

CHAPTER VII

Of the necessary consequences of the Hartleian theory—Of the original
mistake or equivocation which procured admission for the theory—Memoria
technica.

WE will pass by the utter incompatibility of such a law (if law it
may be called, which would itself be the slave of chances) with
even that appearance of rationality forced upon us by the outward phenomena of human conduct abstracted from our own
consciousness. We will agree to forget this for the moment, in
order to fix our attention on that subordination of final to efficient
causes in the human being which flows of necessity from the
assumption that the will, and with the will all acts of thought and
attention, are parts and products of this blind mechanism,
instead of being distinct powers whose function it is to controul,
determine and modify the phantasmal chaos of association.
The soul becomes a mere *ens logicum*; for as a real separable
being, it would be more worthless and ludicrous than the
grimalkins in the cat-harpsichord described in the *Spectator*.[1]
For these did form a part of the process; but in Hartley's scheme
the soul is present only to be pinched or stroked, while the very
squeals or purring are produced by an agency wholly independent and alien. It involves all the difficulties, all the incom-
prehensibility (if it be not indeed, ὡς ἔμοιγε δοκεῖ, the absurdity)
of intercommunion between substances that have no one
property in common, without any of the convenient consequences that bribed the judgement to the admission of the
dualistic hypothesis. Accordingly, this *caput mortuum* of the
Hartleian process has been rejected by his followers, and the
consciousness considered as a result, as a tune, the common
product of the breeze and the harp: tho' this again is the mere
remotion of one absurdity to make way for another equally
preposterous. For what is harmony but a mode of relation, the
very *esse* of which is *percipi*? an *ens rationale*, which pre-supposes
the power that by perceiving creates it? The razor's edge
becomes a saw to the armed vision; and the delicious melodies of
Purcell or Cimarosa might be disjointed stammerings to a hearer

---

[1] [Addison, *Spectator*, No. 361 (24 April 1712): 'Give some account of this
strange Instrument called a Cat-call . . .']

whose partition of time should be a thousand times subtler than ours. But this obstacle too let us imagine ourselves to have surmounted, and 'at one bound high overleap all bound!' Yet according to this hypothesis, the disquisition to which I am at present soliciting the reader's attention may be as truly said to be written by Saint Paul's church as by *me*: for it is the mere motion of my muscles and nerves; and these again are set in motion from external causes equally passive, which external causes stand themselves in interdependent connection with every thing that exists or has existed. Thus the whole universe co-operates to produce the minutest stroke of every letter, save only that I myself, and I alone, have nothing to do with it, but merely the causeless and effectless beholding of it when it is done. Yet scarcely can it be called a beholding; for it is neither an act nor an effect; but an impossible creation of a *something-nothing* out of its very contrary! It is the mere quick-silver plating behind a looking-glass; and in this alone consists the poor worthless I! The sum total of my moral and intellectual intercourse dissolved into its elements is reduced to extension, motion, degrees of velocity and those diminished copies of configurative motion which form what we call notions, and notions of notions. Of such philosophy well might Butler say

> The metaphysics but a puppet motion
> That goes with screws, the notion of a notion,
> The copy of a copy and lame draught
> Unnaturally taken from a thought;
> That counterfeits all pantomimic tricks,
> And turns the eyes like an old crucifix;
> That counterchanges whatsoe'er it calls
> B' another name, and makes it true or false,
> Turns truth to falsehood, falsehood into truth,
> By virtue of the Babylonian's tooth.[1]
>
> 'Miscellaneous Thoughts.'

The inventor of the watch did not in reality invent it; he only look'd on, while the blind causes, the only true artists, were unfolding themselves. So must it have been too with my friend Allston,[2] when he sketched his picture of the dead man revived by the bones of the prophet Elijah. So must it have been with Mr Southey and Lord Byron, when the one fancied himself composing his *Roderick*, and the other his *Childe Harold*. The same

---

[1] [Samuel Butler (1613–80), *Genuine Remains* (2 vols., 1759), vol. i, p. 233; *Satires, etc.*, ed. René Lamar (Cambridge, 1928), p. 160.]

[2] [Washington Allston (1779–1843), the American painter of historical and religious subjects, whom Coleridge first met in Rome in 1805.]

must hold good of all systems of philosophy; of all arts, govern-
ments, wars by sea and by land; in short, of all things that ever
have been or that ever will be produced.   For according to this
system it is not the affections and passions that are at work, in as
far as they are *sensations* or *thoughts*.   We only *fancy* that we act
from rational resolves, or prudent motives, or from impulses
of anger, love or generosity.   In all these cases the real agent is
a *something-nothing-every-thing*, which does all of which we know,
and knows nothing of all that itself does.

The existence of an infinite spirit, of an intelligent and holy
will, must on this system be mere articulated motions of the air.
For as the function of the human understanding is no other than
merely (to appear to itself) to combine and to apply the phaenomena of the association; and as these derive all their reality from
the primary sensations; and the sensations again all their reality
from the impressions *ab extra*; a God not visible, audible or
tangible can exist only in the sounds and letters that form his
name and attributes.   If in ourselves there be no such faculties
as those of the will and the scientific reason, we must either have
an innate idea of them, which would overthrow the whole system,
or we can have no idea at all.   The process by which Hume
degraded the notion of cause and effect into a blind product of
delusion and habit, into the mere sensation of proceeding life
(*nisus vitalis*) associated with the images of the memory; this
same process must be repeated to the equal degradation of every
fundamental idea in ethics or theology.

Far, very far am I from burthening with the odium of these
consequences the moral characters of those who first formed or
have since adopted the system!   It is most noticeable of the
excellent and pious Hartley that in the proofs of the existence
and attributes of God with which his second volume commences
he makes no reference to the principles or results of the first.
Nay, he assumes as his foundations ideas which, if we embrace
the doctrines of his first volume, can exist nowhere but in the
vibrations of the ethereal medium common to the nerves and to
the atmosphere.   Indeed the whole of the second volume is,
with the fewest possible exceptions, independent of his peculiar
system.   So true is it that the faith which saves and sanctifies is a
collective energy, a total act of the whole moral being; that its
living sensorium is in the heart; and that no errors of the understanding can be morally arraigned unless they have proceeded
from the heart.   But whether they be such, no man can be
certain in the case of another, scarcely perhaps even in his own.

Hence it follows by inevitable consequence that man may per-chance determine what is a heresy; but God only can know who is a heretic. It does not, however, by any means follow that opinions fundamentally false are harmless. A hundred causes may co-exist to form one complex antidote. Yet the sting of the adder remains venomous, though there are many who have taken up the evil thing, and it hurted them not! Some indeed there seem to have been, in an unfortunate neighbour-nation at least, who have embraced this system with a full view of all its moral and religious consequences; some

> ——who deem themselves most free,
> When they within this gross and visible sphere
> Chain down the winged thought, scoffing ascent,
> Proud in their meanness; and themselves they cheat
> With noisy emptiness of learned phrase,
> Their subtle fluids, impacts, essences,
> Self-working tools, uncaus'd effects, and all
> Those blind omniscients, those almighty slaves,
> Untenanting creation of its God! [1]

Such men need discipline, not argument; they must be made better men before they can become wiser.

The attention will be more profitably employed in attempting to discover and expose the paralogisms by the magic of which such a faith could find admission into minds framed for a nobler creed. These, it appears to me, may be all reduced to one sophism as their common genus: the mistaking the conditions of a thing for its causes and essence; and the process by which we arrive at the knowledge of a faculty, for the faculty itself. The air I breathe is the condition of my life, not its cause. We could never have learnt that we had eyes but by the process of seeing; yet having seen we know that the eyes must have pre-existed in order to render the process of sight possible. Let us cross-examine Hartley's scheme under the guidance of this distinction; and we shall discover that contemporaneity (Leibnitz's *Lex Continui* [2]) is the limit and condition of the laws of mind, itself being rather a law of matter, at least of phaenomena considered as material. At the utmost, it is to thought the same as the law of gravitation is to locomotion. In every voluntary movement we first counteract gravitation, in order to avail ourselves of it. It

---

[1] [Coleridge, *The Destiny of Nations*, *ll.* 26–34. These lines first appeared in his contribution to Southey's *Joan of Arc*, 1796.]
[2] [First propounded in his *Lettre à M. Bayle* (1687).]

must exist, that there may be a something to be counteracted, and
which by its reaction aids the force that is exerted to resist it.
Let us consider what we do when we leap. We first resist the
gravitating power by an act purely voluntary, and then by
another act, voluntary in part, we yield to it in order to light on
the spot which we had previously proposed to ourselves. Now
let a man watch his mind while he is composing; or, to take a still
more common case, while he is trying to recollect a name; and he
will find the process completely analogous. Most of my readers
will have observed a small water-insect on the surface of rivulets
which throws a cinque-spotted shadow fringed with prismatic
colours on the sunny bottom of the brook; and will have noticed
how the little animal wins its way up against the stream, by
alternate pulses of active and passive motion, now resisting the
current, and now yielding to it in order to gather strength and a
momentary fulcrum for a further propulsion. This is no unapt
emblem of the mind's self-experience in the act of thinking.
There are evidently two powers at work which relatively to each
other are active and passive; and this is not possible without an
intermediate faculty, which is at once both active and passive.
(In philosophical language we must denominate this intermediate faculty in all its degrees and determinations the
imagination. But in common language, and especially on
the subject of poetry, we appropriate the name to a superior
degree of the faculty, joined to a superior voluntary controul
over it.)

Contemporaneity then, being the common condition of all the
laws of association, and a component element in all the *materia
subjecta*, the parts of which are to be associated, must needs be
co-present with all. Nothing, therefore, can be more easy than
to pass off on an incautious mind this constant companion of
each for the essential substance of all. But if we appeal to our
own consciousness, we shall find that even time itself, as the
cause of a particular act of association, is distinct from contemporaneity, as the condition of all association. Seeing a mackerel
it may happen that I immediately think of gooseberries, because
I at the same time ate mackerel with gooseberries as the sauce.
The first syllable of the latter word being that which had
co-existed with the image of the bird so called, I may then think
of a goose. In the next moment the image of a swan may arise
before me, though I had never seen the two birds together. In
the two former instances, I am conscious that their co-existence
in time was the circumstance that enabled me to recollect them;

and equally conscious am I, that the latter was recalled to me by the joint operation of likeness and contrast.   So it is with cause and effect; so too with order.   So am I able to distinguish whether it was proximity in time, or continuity in space, that occasioned me to recall B on the mention of A.   They cannot be indeed separated from contemporaneity; for that would be to separate them from the mind itself.   The act of consciousness is indeed identical with time considered in its essence.   (I mean time *per se*, as contra-distinguished from our notion of time; for this is always blended with the idea of space, which as the contrary of time is therefore its measure.)   Nevertheless the accident of seeing two objects at the same moment acts as a distinguishable cause from that of having seen them in the same place: and the true practical general law of association is this, that whatever makes certain parts of a total impression more vivid or distinct than the rest will determine the mind to recall these in preference to others equally linked together by the common condition of contemporaneity or (what I deem a more appropriate and philosophical term) of continuity.   But the will itself by confining and intensifying [1] the attention may arbitrarily give vividness or distinctness to any object whatsoever; and from hence we may deduce the uselessness, if not the absurdity, of certain recent schemes which promise an artificial memory, but which in reality can only produce a confusion and debasement of the fancy.   Sound logic, as the habitual subordination of the individual to the species, and of the species to the genus; philosophical knowledge of facts under the relation of cause and effect; a chearful and communicative temper that disposes us to notice the similarities and contrasts of things, that we may be able to illustrate the one by the other; a quiet conscience; a condition free from anxieties: a sound health, and above all (as far as relates to passive remembrance) a healthy digestion; these are the best, these are the only Arts of Memory.

---

[1] I am aware that this word occurs neither in Johnson's Dictionary nor in any classical writer.   But the word 'to intend,' which Newton and others before him employ in this sense, is now so completely appropriated to another meaning that I could not use it without ambiguity: while to paraphrase the sense, as by *render intense*, would often break up the sentence and destroy that harmony of the position of the words with the logical position of the thoughts, which is a beauty in all composition, and more especially desirable in a close philosophical investigation.   I have therefore hazarded the word *intensify*; though, I confess, it sound uncouth to my own ear.

CHAPTER VIII

The system of Dualism introduced by Des Cartes—Refined first by Spinoza and afterwards by Leibnitz into the doctrine of Harmonia praestabilita—Hylozoism—Materialism—Neither of these systems, on any possible theory of association, supplies or supersedes a theory of perception or explains the formation of the associable.

To the best of my knowledge Des Cartes [1] was the first philosopher who introduced the absolute and essential heterogeneity of the soul as intelligence and the body as matter. The assumption and the form of speaking have remained, though the denial of all other properties to matter but that of extension on which denial the whole system of dualism is grounded has been long exploded. [2] For since impenetrability is intelligible only as a mode of resistance, its admission places the essence of matter in an act or power which it possesses in common with spirit, and body and spirit are therefore no longer absolutely heterogeneous but may, without any absurdity, be supposed to be different modes or degrees in perfection of a common substratum. To this possibility, however, it was not the fashion to advert. The soul was a thinking substance, and the body a space-filling substance. Yet the apparent action of each on the other pressed heavy on the philosopher on the one hand, and no less heavily on the other hand pressed the evident truth that the law of causality holds only between homogeneous things, i.e. things having some common property, and cannot extend from one world into another, its opposite. A close analysis evinced it to be no less absurd than the question whether a man's affection for his wife lay north-east or south-west of the love he bore towards his child? Leibnitz's doctrine of a pre-established harmony, [3] which he certainly borrowed from Spinoza, who had himself taken the hint from Des Cartes's animal machines, was, in its common interpretation, too strange to survive the inventor, too repugnant to our common sense (which is not indeed entitled to a

[1] [*Principia philosophiae* (Amsterdam, 1644), pt ii.]
[2] [By Leibniz in his *Lettre sur la question si l'essence du corps consiste dans l'étendue* (Paris, 1691), in which he attributed resistance as well as extension to matter.]
[3] [i.e. between body and soul. Coleridge is mistaken in supposing that Spinoza was the source of this theory.]

judicial voice in the courts of scientific philosophy, but whose whispers still exert a strong secret influence). Even Wolf, the admirer and illustrious systematizer of the Leibnitzian doctrine, contents himself with defending the possibility of the idea but does not adopt it as a part of the edifice.

The hypothesis of Hylozoism,[1] on the other side, is the death of all rational physiology and indeed of all physical science; for that requires a limitation of terms and cannot consist with the arbitrary power of multiplying attributes by occult qualities. Besides, it answers no purpose; unless indeed a difficulty can be solved by multiplying it, or that we can acquire a clearer notion of our soul by being told that we have a million souls, and that every atom of our bodies has a soul of its own. Far more prudent is it to admit the difficulty once for all, and then let it lie at rest. There is a sediment indeed at the bottom of the vessel, but all the water above it is clear and transparent. The Hylozoist only shakes it up and renders the whole turbid.

But it is not either the nature of man or the duty of the philosopher to despair concerning any important problem until, as in the squaring of the circle, the impossibility of a solution has been demonstrated.[2] How the *esse* assumed as originally distinct from the *scire* can ever unite itself with it, how *being* can transform itself into a *knowing*, becomes conceivable on one only condition: namely, if it can be shown that the *vis representativa*, or the Sentient, is itself a species of being, i.e. either as a property or attribute, or as an hypostasis or self-subsistence. The former is indeed the assumption of materialism; a system which could not but be patronized by the philosopher, if only it actually performed what it promises. But how any affection from without can metamorphose itself into perception or will, the materialist has hitherto left not only as incomprehensible as he found it but has aggravated it into a comprehensible absurdity. For, grant that an object from without could act upon the conscious self as on a consubstantial object; yet such an affection could only engender something homogeneous with itself. Motion could only propagate motion. Matter has no Inward. We remove one surface, but to meet with another. We can but divide a particle into particles; and each atom comprehends in itself the properties of the material universe. Let any reflecting mind make the experiment of explaining to itself the evidence of

---

[1] [The ancient theory that matter and life are one.]
[2] [This paragraph bears a resemblance to Schelling, *System des transcendentalen Idealismus* (1800), III. B.]

our sensuous intuitions, from the hypothesis that in any given perception there is a something which has been communicated to it by an impact or an impression *ab extra*.   In the first place, by the impact on the percipient or *ens representans*, not the object itself but only its action or effect will pass into the same. Not the iron tongue, but its vibrations, pass into the metal of the bell.   Now in our immediate perception it is not the mere power or act of the object, but the object itself, which is immediately present.   We might indeed attempt to explain this result by a chain of deductions and conclusions; but that, first, the very faculty of deducing and concluding would equally demand an explanation; and, secondly, that there exists in fact no such intermediation by logical notions, such as those of cause and effect.   It is the object itself, not the product of a syllogism which is present to our consciousness.   Or would we explain this supervention of the object to the sensation by a productive faculty set in motion by an impulse; still the transition into the percipient of the object itself, from which the impulse proceeded, assumes a power that can permeate and wholly possess the soul,

> And like a God by spiritual art,
> Be all in all, and all in every part.
>
>   Cowley.[1]

And how came the percipient here?   And what is become of the wonder-promising Matter, that was to perform all these marvels by force of mere figure, weight and motion?   The most consistent proceeding of the dogmatic materialist is to fall back into the common rank of *soul-and-bodyists*; to affect the mysterious, and declare the whole process a revelation given and not to be understood, which it would be profane to examine too closely. Datur non intelligitur.   But a revelation unconfirmed by miracles and a faith not commanded by the conscience a philosopher may venture to pass by without suspecting himself of any irreligious tendency.

   Thus as materialism has been generally taught it is utterly unintelligible, and owes all its proselytes to the propensity so common among men to mistake distinct images for clear conceptions; and vice versa, to reject as inconceivable whatever from its own nature is unimaginable.   But as soon as it becomes intelligible it ceases to be materialism.   In order to explain

---

[1] [From Cowley, *All-over, Love*, *ll*. 9–10:
         'But like a God by pow'rful Art,
         'Twas all in all, and all in every Part.']

thinking, as a material phenomenon, it is necessary to refine matter into a mere modification of intelligence, with the twofold function of appearing and perceiving. Even so did Priestley in his controversy with Price.[1] He stript matter of all its material properties; substituted spiritual powers; and when we expected to find a body, behold! we had nothing but its ghost! the apparition of a defunct substance!

I shall not dilate further on this subject, because it will (if God grant health and permission) be treated of at large and systematically in a work which I have many years been preparing, on the Productive Logos human and divine; with, and as an introduction to, a full commentary on the Gospel of St John.[2] To make myself intelligible, as far as my present subject requires, it will be sufficient briefly to observe—1. That all association demands and presupposes the existence of the thoughts and images to be associated.   2. The hypothesis of an external world exactly correspondent to those images or modifications of our own being which alone (according to this system) we actually behold, is as thorough idealism as Berkeley's, inasmuch as it equally (perhaps in a more perfect degree) removes all reality and immediateness of perception and places us in a dream-world of phantoms and spectres, the inexplicable swarm and equivocal generation of motions in our own brains.   3. That this hypothesis neither involves the explanation, nor precludes the necessity, of a mechanism and co-adequate forces in the percipient, which at the more than magic touch of the impulse from without is to create anew for itself the correspondent object. The formation of a copy is not solved by the mere pre-existence of an original; the copyist of Raphael's Transfiguration must repeat more or less perfectly the process of Raphael.   It would be easy to explain a thought from the image on the retina, and that from the geometry of light, if this very light did not present the very same difficulty. We might as rationally chant the Brahmin creed of the tortoise that supported the bear that supported the elephant that supported the world, to the tune of 'This is the house that Jack built.'   The *sic Deo placitum est* we all admit as the sufficient cause, and the divine goodness as the sufficient reason; but an answer to the whence? and why? is no answer to the how? which alone is the physiologist's

[1] [*A Free Discussion of the Doctrines of Materialism and Philosophical Necessity* (1778–80).]

[2] [Coleridge conceived the idea of a philosophical defence of the Articles of the Church as early as 1814, but he never completed it.]

concern.   It is a mere *sophisma pigrum*,[1] and (as Bacon hath said)
the arrogance of pusillanimity, which lifts up the idol of a
mortal's fancy and commands us to fall down and worship it as a
work of divine wisdom, an ancile or palladium fallen from
heaven.   By the very same argument the supporters of the
Ptolemaic system might have rebuffed the Newtonian, and
pointing to the sky with self-complacent grin [2] have appealed to
common sense whether the sun did not move and the earth stand
still.

---

[1] [*Novum Organum* (1620), I. 88: 'Knowledge has suffered from littleness
of spirit (*pusillanimitas*) and the triviality of the tasks which human industry
has set itself.   And worst of all this very littleness of spirit is accompanied by
arrogance and superiority.'   Quoted below, p. 159.]

[2] 'And coxcombs vanquish Berkeley by a grin.'   Pope.   [Actually by
John Brown (1715–66), *Essay Occasion'd by the Death of Mr Pope* (Dodsley's
Collection, 1748, iii. 124).]

CHAPTER IX

AFTER I had successively studied in the schools of Locke, Berkeley, Leibnitz and Hartley, and could find in neither of them an abiding place for my reason, I began to ask myself: is a system of philosophy, as different from mere history and historic classification, possible? If possible, what are its necessary conditions? I was for a while disposed to answer the first question in the negative, and to admit that the sole practicable employment for the human mind was to observe, to collect and to classify. But I soon felt that human nature itself fought up against this wilful resignation of intellect; and as soon did I find that the scheme taken with all its consequences and cleared of all inconsistencies was not less impracticable than contranatural. Assume in its full extent the position, *nihil in intellectu quod non prius in sensu*, without Leibnitz's qualifying *praeter ipsum intellectum*,[1] and in the same sense in which it was understood by Hartley and Condillac: and what Hume had demonstratively deduced from this concession concerning cause and effect will apply with equal and crushing force to all the other eleven categorical forms,[2] and the logical functions corresponding to them. How can we make bricks without straw? Or build without cement? We learn all things indeed by occasion of experience; but the very facts so learnt force us inward on the antecedents, that must be pre-supposed in order to render experience itself possible. The first book of Locke's Essays (if the supposed error which it labours to subvert be not

[1] [*Nouveaux essais sur l'entendement humain* (comp. 1703), liv: 'Nihil est in intellectu quod non fuerit in sensu, excipe: nisi ipse intellectus.' ('There is nothing in the intellect which has not been in the senses—except the intellect itself.')]

[2] Videlicet: quantity, quality, relation and mode, each consisting of three subdivisions. Vide *Kritik der reinen Vernunft*, pp. 95 and 106. See too the judicious remarks in Locke and Hume.

a mere thing of straw, an absurdity which no man ever did or indeed ever could believe) is formed on a σόφισμα ἑτεροξητήσεως,[1] and involves the old mistake of *cum hoc: ergo, propter hoc.*

The term *philosophy* defines itself as an affectionate seeking after the truth; but Truth is the correlative of Being. This again is no way conceivable but by assuming as a postulate that both are *ab initio* identical and co-inherent; that intelligence and being are reciprocally each other's substrate. I presumed that this was a possible conception (i.e. that it involved no logical inconsonance) from the length of time during which the scholastic definition of the *Supreme Being*, as *actus purissimus sine ullâ potentialitate*, was received in the schools of Theology, both by the Pontification and the Reformed divines. The early study of Plato and Plotinus, with the commentaries and the *Theologia platonica* of the illustrious Florentine;[2] of Proclus and Gemistius Pletho; and at a later period of the *De immenso et innumerabili*, and the *De la causa, principio et uno* of the philosopher of Nola,[3] who could boast of a Sir Philip Sidney and Fulke Greville among his patrons, and whom the idolators of Rome burnt as an atheist in the year 1600; had all contributed to prepare my mind for the reception and welcoming of the *Cogito quia sum, et sum quia cogito*;[4] a philosophy of seeming hardihood, but certainly the most ancient and therefore presumptively the most natural.

Why need I be afraid? Say rather how dare I be ashamed of the Teutonic theosophist, Jacob Behmen? Many, indeed, and gross were his delusions; and such as furnish frequent and ample occasion for the triumph of the learned over the poor ignorant shoemaker who had dared think for himself. But while we remember that these delusions were such as might be anticipated from his utter want of all intellectual discipline and from his ignorance of rational psychology, let it not be forgotten that the latter defect he had in common with the most learned theologians of his age. Neither with books nor with book-learned men was he conversant. A meek and shy quietist, his intellectual powers were never stimulated into fev'rous energy by crowds of proselytes or by the ambition of proselyting. Jacob Behmen was an

---

[1] [i.e. a red herring. Bk I of the *Essay concerning Human Understanding* (1690) is entitled 'Of Innate Notions.']

[2] [Marsilio Ficino (1433–99), *Theologia platonica de animorum immortalitate* (1482).]

[3] [Giordano Bruno (1548–1600), whose above-mentioned works appeared in 1591 and 1584. Bruno visited England in 1583–4 and met Sidney and Fulke Greville there.]

[4] [Descartes, *Discours de la méthode* (1637).]

enthusiast in the strictest sense, as not merely distinguished, but as contra-distinguished, from a fanatic.   While I in part translate the following observations from a contemporary writer of the Continent,[1] let me be permitted to premise that I might have transcribed the substance from memoranda of my own, which were written many years before his pamphlet was given to the world; and that I prefer another's words to my own, partly as a tribute due to priority of publication; but still more from the pleasure of sympathy in a case where coincidence only was possible.

Whoever is acquainted with the history of philosophy during the two or three last centuries cannot but admit that there appears to have existed a sort of secret and tacit compact among the learned not to pass beyond a certain limit in speculative science.   The privilege of free thought, so highly extolled, has at no time been held valid in actual practice except within this limit; and not a single stride beyond it has ever been ventured without bringing obloquy on the transgressor.   The few men of genius among the learned class who actually did overstep this boundary anxiously avoided the appearance of having so done. Therefore the true depth of science, and the penetration to the inmost centre, from which all the lines of knowledge diverge to their ever distant circumference, was abandoned to the illiterate and the simple, whom unstilled yearning and an original ebulliency of spirit had urged to the investigation of the indwelling and living ground of all things.   These then, because their names had never been inrolled in the guilds of the learned, were persecuted by the registered livery-men as interlopers on their rights and privileges.   All without distinction were branded as fanatics and phantasts; not only those whose wild and exorbitant imaginations had actually engendered only extravagant and grotesque phantasms and whose productions were, for the most part, poor copies and gross caricatures of genuine inspiration; but the truly inspired likewise, the originals themselves!   And this for no other reason but because they were the *unlearned*, men of humble and obscure occupations.   When, and from whom among the literati by profession, have we ever heard the divine doxology repeated, 'I thank Thee O Father, Lord of heaven and earth, because Thou hast hid these things from the wise and prudent, and hast revealed them unto babes'?[2]   No!

---

[1] [Schelling, whose *Natur-Philosophie* contributed much to the two following paragraphs.]

[2] [From Luke x. 21.]

the haughty priests of learning not only banished from the schools and marts of science all who had dared draw living waters from the fountain, but drove them out of the very Temple, which meantime 'the buyers, and sellers and money-changers' were suffered to make 'a den of thieves.'

And yet it would not be easy to discover any substantial ground for this contemptuous pride in those literati who have most distinguished themselves by their scorn of Behmen, De Thoyras,[1] George Fox, etc.; unless it be that they could write orthographically, make smooth periods, and had the fashions of authorship almost literally at their fingers' ends, while the latter, in simplicity of soul, made their words immediate echoes of their feelings. Hence the frequency of those phrases among them which have been mistaken for pretences to immediate inspiration; as for instance, '*It was delivered unto me*'; '*I strove not to speak*'; '*I said, I will be silent*'; '*but the word was in my heart as a burning fire*'; '*and I could not forbear.*' Hence too the unwillingness to give offence; hence the foresight, and the dread of the clamours which would be raised against them, so frequently avowed in the writings of these men and expressed, as was natural, in the words of the only book with which they were familiar. 'Woe is me that I am become a man of strife, and a man of contention; I love peace: the souls of men are dear unto me: yet because I seek for light every one of them doth curse me!'[2] O! it requires deeper feeling and a stronger imagination than belong to most of those to whom reasoning and fluent expression have been as a trade learnt in boyhood to conceive with what might, with what inward strivings and commotion, the conception of a new and vital truth takes possession of an uneducated man of genius. His meditations are almost inevitably employed on the eternal or the everlasting; for 'the world is not his friend, nor the world's law.' Need we then be surprised that under an excitement at once so strong and so unusual the man's body should sympathize with the struggles of his mind; or that he should at times be so far deluded as to mistake the tumultuous sensations of his nerves, and the co-existing spectres of his fancy, as parts or symbols of the truths which were opening on him? It has indeed been plausibly observed that in order to

---

[1] [Probably 'Thaulerus.' Johannes Tauler (*c.* 1300–61) was a Dominican mystic of Strasbourg.]

[2] [This passage, like the phrases quoted above, is thoroughly Boehmenistic in tone and full of biblical echoes (Jeremiah xx. 9, etc.). But it appears to be an impression by Coleridge of Boehme's writings rather than a direct quotation from them.]

derive any advantage, or to collect any intelligible meaning, from the writings of these ignorant mystics, the reader must bring with him a spirit and judgement superior to that of the writers themselves:

> And what he brings, what needs he elsewhere seek?
> *Paradise Regained.*[1]

—a sophism which, I fully agree with Warburton, is unworthy of Milton; how much more so of the awful person in whose mouth he has placed it? One assertion I will venture to make, as suggested by my own experience, that there exist folios on the human understanding and the nature of man which would have a far juster claim to their high rank and celebrity, if in the whole huge volume there could be found as much fulness of heart and intellect as burst forth in many a simple page of George Fox, Jacob Behmen, and even of Behmen's commentator, the pious and fervid William Law.[2]

The feeling of gratitude which I cherish towards these men has caused me to digress further than I had foreseen or proposed; but to have passed them over in an historical sketch of my literary life and opinions would have seemed to me like the denial of a debt, the concealment of a boon. For the writings of these mystics acted in no slight degree to prevent my mind from being imprisoned within the outline of any single dogmatic system. They contributed to keep alive the heart in the head; gave me an indistinct, yet stirring and working presentment, that all the products of the mere reflective faculty partook of death, and were as the rattling twigs and sprays in winter into which a sap was yet to be propelled from some root to which I had not penetrated, if they were to afford my soul either food or shelter. If they were too often a moving cloud of smoke to me by day, yet they were always a pillar of fire throughout the night, during my wanderings through the wilderness of doubt, and enabled me to skirt, without crossing, the sandy deserts of utter unbelief. That the system is capable of being converted into an irreligious Pantheism I well know. The *Ethics* of Spinoza may, or may not, be an instance. But at no time could I believe that in

---

[1] [*Paradise Regain'd*, IV. 325. William Warburton (1698–1779), in a footnote to this line contributed to Thomas Newton's edition of the poem (1752), remarks: 'The poet makes the old sophister the Devil always busy in his trade. 'Tis pity he should make Jesus (as he does here) use the same arms.']
[2] [William Law (1686–1761), whose 'Figures illustrating his Principles' were posthumously issued in the work known as 'Law's edition of Boehme' by Ward and Langcake (1764–81).]

itself and essentially it is incompatible with religion, natural or
revealed: and now I am most thoroughly persuaded of the contrary. The writings of the illustrious sage of Königsberg, the
founder of the Critical Philosophy, more than any other work
at once invigorated and disciplined my understanding. The
originality, the depth and the compression of the thoughts; the
novelty and subtlety, yet solidity and importance, of the dis-
distinctions; the adamantine chain of the logic; and I will
venture to add (paradox as it will appear to those who have taken
their notion of Immanuel Kant from reviewers and Frenchmen)
the clearness and evidence of the *Critique of the Pure Reason*;
of the *Judgement*; of the *Metaphysical Elements of Natural
Philosophy*, and of his *Religion within the Bounds of Pure Reason*,
took possession of me as with a giant's hand. After fifteen
years'[1] familiarity with them, I still read these and all his other
productions with undiminished delight and increasing admiration. The few passages that remained obscure to me after due
efforts of thought (as the chapter on original apperception [2]),
and the apparent contradictions which occur, I soon found were
hints and insinuations referring to ideas which Kant either did
not think it prudent to avow, or which he considered as consistently left behind in a pure analysis, not of human nature *in toto*,
but of the speculative intellect alone. Here therefore he was
constrained to commence at the point of reflection, or natural
consciousness: while in his moral system he was permitted to
assume a higher ground (the autonomy of the will) as a postulate
deducible from the unconditional command, or (in the technical
language of his school) the categorical imperative of the conscience. He had been in imminent danger of persecution
during the reign of the late king of Prussia, that strange compound of lawless debauchery and priest-ridden superstition:
and it is probable that he had little inclination, in his old age,
to act over again the fortunes and hair-breadth escapes of
Wolf.[3] The expulsion of the first among Kant's disciples [4] who

---

[1] [i.e. since 1800. It is probable Coleridge began to read Kant during his
nine months in Germany (September 1798 to July 1799). But his final
conversion to Kantian ideas is not apparent until two years later in a letter
to Poole (16 March 1801): 'I have not only completely extricated the notions
of time and space; but have overthrown the doctrine of association as taught
by Hartley . . .' Cf. *Notebooks*, 1517n.]

[2] [*Kritik der reinen Vernunft* (Elementarlehre, II. i. 1).]

[3] [Christian von Wolf (1679–1754), who was expelled from Prussia in 1723
for his theological views. In 1792 Kant was forbidden to publish his
religious views in the Prussia of Friedrich Wilhelm II.]

[4] [Fichte (1762–1814), who was expelled from Jena in 1799 on a charge of
atheism.]

attempted to complete his system from the university of Jena, with the confiscation and prohibition of the obnoxious work by the joint efforts of the courts of Saxony and Hanover, supplied experimental proof that the venerable old man's caution was not groundless. In spite therefore of his own declarations, I could never believe it was possible for him to have meant no more by his *Noumenon,* or Thing in Itself, than his mere words express; or that in his own conception he confined the whole plastic power to the forms of the intellect, leaving for the external cause, for the *materiale* of our sensations, a matter without form, which is doubtless inconceivable. I entertained doubts likewise whether in his own mind he even laid all the stress which he appears to do on the moral postulates.

An idea, in the highest sense of that word, cannot be conveyed but by a symbol; and, except in geometry, all symbols of necessity involve an apparent contradiction. *Φώνησε εὐνετοῖσιν:* [1] and for those who could not pierce through this symbolic husk his writings were not intended. Questions which can not be fully answered without exposing the respondent to personal danger are not entitled to a fair answer; and yet to say this openly would in many cases furnish the very advantage which the adversary is insidiously seeking after. Veracity does not consist in saying, but in the intention of communicating truth; and the philosopher who can not utter the whole truth without conveying falsehood and at the same time, perhaps, exciting the most malignant passions, is constrained to express himself either mythically or equivocally. When Kant therefore was importuned to settle the disputes of his commentators himself by declaring what he meant, how could he decline the honours of martyrdom with less offence than by simply replying, 'I meant what I said, and at the age of near four score I have something else and more important to do than to write a commentary on my own works.'

Fichte's *Wissenschaftslehre,* or Lore of Ultimate Science, was to add the key-stone of the arch: and by commencing with an act, instead of a thing or substance, Fichte assuredly gave the first mortal blow to Spinozism, as taught by Spinoza himself; and supplied the idea of a system truly metaphysical, and of a *metaphysique* truly systematic: (i.e. having its spring and principle within itself). But this fundamental idea he overbuilt with a heavy mass of mere notions and psychological acts of arbitrary

[1] [From Pindar, Olympian II. 152: 'He spoke to those with understanding.']

reflection.   Thus his theory degenerated into a crude *Egoismus*,[1] a boastful and hyperstoic hostility to Nature as lifeless, godless and altogether unholy: while his religion consisted in the assumption of a mere *ordo ordinans*, which we were permitted *exotericé* to call God; and his ethics in an ascetic and almost monkish mortification of the natural passions and desires.

In Schelling's *Natur-Philosophie*, and the *System des transcendentalen Idealismus*, I first found a genial coincidence with much that I had toiled out for myself, and a powerful assistance in what I had yet to do.

I have introduced this statement as appropriate to the narrative nature of this sketch; yet rather in reference to the work which I have announced in a preceding page than to my present subject.   It would be but a mere act of justice to myself were I to

---

[1] The following burlesque on the Fichtean Egoismus may, perhaps, be amusing to the few who have studied the system, and to those who are unacquainted with it may convey as tolerable a likeness of Fichte's idealism as can be expected from an avowed caricature:

The categorical imperative, or the annunciation of the new Teutonic God, 'ΕΓΩΕΝΚΑΙ-ΠΑΝ: a dithyrambic Ode, by QUERKOPF VON KLUBSTICK, Grammarian, and Subrector in Gymnasio.****

> Eu!   Dei vices gerens, ipse Divus,
> (*Speak English, Friend!*) the God Imperativus,
> Here on this market-cross aloud I cry:
> I, I, I! itself I!
> The form and the substance, the what and the why,
> The when and the where, and the low and the high,
> The inside and outside, the earth and the sky,
> I, you and he, and he, you and I,
> All souls and all bodies are I itself I!
>   All I itself I!
>   (Fools! a truce with this starting!)
>   All my I! all my I!
> He's a heretic dog who but adds Betty Martin!
> Thus cried the God with high imperial tone:
> In robe of stiffest state, that scoff'd at beauty,
> A pronoun-verb imperative he shone—
> Then substantive and plural-singular grown
> He thus spake on!   Behold in I alone
> (For ethics boast a syntax of their own)
> Or if in ye, yet as I doth depute ye,
> In O!   I, you, the vocative of duty!
> I of the world's whole Lexicon the root!
> Of the whole universe of touch, sound, sight
> The genitive and ablative to boot:
> The accusative of wrong, the nom'native of right,
> And in all cases the case absolute!
> Self-construed, I all other moods decline:
> Imperative, from nothing we derive us;
> Yet as a super-postulate of mine,
> Unconstrued antecedence I assign
> To X, Y, Z, the God Infinitivus!

warn my future readers that an identity of thought, or even similarity of phrase, will not be at all times a certain proof that the passage has been borrowed from Schelling, or that the conceptions were originally learnt from him. In this instance, as in the dramatic lectures of Schlegel to which I have before alluded, from the same motive of self-defence against the charge of plagiarism, many of the most striking resemblances, indeed all the main and fundamental ideas, were born and matured in my mind before I had ever seen a single page of the German philosopher; and I might indeed affirm with truth, before the more important works of Schelling had been written, or at least made public. Nor is this coincidence at all to be wondered at. We had studied in the same school; been disciplined by the same preparatory philosophy, namely, the writings of Kant; we had both equal obligations to the polar logic and dynamic philosophy of Giordano Bruno; and Schelling has lately and, as of recent acquisition, avowed that same affectionate reverence for the labours of Behmen and other mystics which I had formed at a much earlier period.[1] The coincidence of Schelling's system with certain general ideas of Behmen he declares to have been mere coincidence; while my obligations have been more direct. He needs give to Behmen only feelings of sympathy; while I owe him a debt of gratitude. God forbid! that I should be suspected of a wish to enter into a rivalry with Schelling for the honors so unequivocally his right, not only as a great and original genius, but as the founder of the Philosophy of Nature, and as the most successful improver of the Dynamic [2] System which,

---

[1] [*Darlegung des wahren Verhältnisses der Naturphilosophie mit der verbesserten Fichte'schen Lehre* (1806), pp. 156–7: 'I am not ashamed of the name of so many so-called enthusiasts but shall acclaim them and boast of having learnt from them, as Leibniz did, as soon as I can properly do so. . . . If I have not seriously studied their writings till now this is not in the least because of any contempt for them but through blameworthy negligence.']

[2] It would be an act of high and almost criminal injustice to pass over in silence the name of Mr Richard Saumarez, a gentleman equally well known as a medical man and as a philanthropist, but who demands notice on the present occasion as the author of *A New System of Physiology* in two volumes octavo, published 1797; and in 1812 of 'an examination of the natural and artificial systems of philosophy which now prevail' in one volume octavo, entitled *The Principles of Physiological and Physical Science*. The latter work is not quite equal to the former in style or arrangement; and there is a greater necessity of distinguishing the principles of the author's philosophy from his conjectures concerning colour, the atmospheric matter, comets, etc., which whether just or erroneous are by no means necessary consequences of that philosophy. Yet even in this department of this volume, which I regard as comparatively the inferior work, the reasonings by which Mr Saumarez invalidates the immanence of an infinite power in any finite substance are the offspring of no common mind; and the experiment on the expansibility of

begun by Bruno, was reintroduced (in a more philosophical
form, and freed from all its impurities and visionary accompaniments) by Kant; in whom it was the native and necessary growth
of his own system. Kant's followers, however, on whom (for
the greater part) their master's cloak had fallen without, or with
a very scanty portion of, his spirit, had adopted his dynamic
ideas only as a more refined species of mechanics. With exception of one or two fundamental ideas which cannot be withheld
from Fichte, to Schelling we owe the completion, and the most
important victories, of this revolution in philosophy. To me it
will be happiness and honor enough should I succeed in rendering the system itself intelligible to my countrymen, and in the
application of it to the most awful of subjects for the most
important of purposes. Whether a work is the offspring of a
man's own spirit and the product of original thinking will be
discovered by those who are its sole legitimate judges by better
tests than the mere reference to dates. For readers in general,
let whatever shall be found in this or any future work of mine
that resembles or coincides with the doctrines of my German
predecessor, though contemporary, be wholly attributed to him:
provided that the absence of distinct references to his books,
which I could not at all times make with truth as designating
citations or thoughts actually derived from him and which, I
trust, would after this general acknowledgement be superfluous, be not charged on me as an ungenerous concealment or
intentional plagiarism. I have not indeed (eheu! res angusta
domi!) been hitherto able to procure more than two of his

---

the air is at least plausible and highly ingenious. But the merit, which will
secure both to the book and to the writer a high and honorable name with
posterity, consists in the masterly force of reasoning, and the copiousness of
induction, with which he has assailed, and (in my opinion) subverted the
tyranny of the mechanic system in physiology; established not only the
existence of final causes, but their necessity and efficiency in every system
that merits the name of philosophical; and substituting life and progressive
power, for the contradictory inert force, has a right to be known and remembered as the first instaurator of the dynamic philosophy in England. The
author's views, as far as concerns himself, are unborrowed and completely
his own, as he neither possessed, nor do his writings discover, the least
acquaintance with the works of Kant, in which the germs of the philosophy
exist; and his volumes were published many years before the full development
of these germs by Schelling. Mr Saumarez's detection of the Braunonian
system was no light or ordinary service at the time; and I scarcely remember
in any work on any subject a confutation so thoroughly satisfactory. It is
sufficient at this time to have stated the fact; as in the preface to the work
which I have already announced on the Logos I have exhibited in detail the
merits of this writer and genuine philosopher, who needed only have taken
his foundations somewhat deeper and wider to have superseded a considerable
part of my labours.

books, viz. the 1st volume of his collected Tracts, and his *System of Transcendental Idealism*; to which, however, I must add a small pamphlet against Fichte,[1] the spirit of which was to *my* feelings painfully incongruous with the principles and which (with the usual allowance afforded to an antithesis) displayed the love of wisdom rather than the wisdom of love.   I regard truth as a divine ventriloquist: I care not from whose mouth the sounds are supposed to proceed, if only the words are audible and intelligible.   'Albeit, I must confess to be half in doubt whether I should bring it forth or no, it being so contrary to the eye of the world, and the world so potent in most men's hearts, that I shall endanger either not to be regarded or not to be understood.'—Milton: *Reason of Church Government*, [II. i].

And to conclude the subject of citation with a cluster of citations which, as taken from books not in common use, may contribute to the reader's amusement as a voluntary before a sermon: 'Dolet mihi quidem, deliciis literarum inescatos subito jam homines adeo esse, praesertim qui Christianos se profitentur, ut legere nisi quod ad delectationem facit, sustineant nihil; unde et disciplinae severiores et philosophia ipsa jam fere prorsus etiam a doctis negliguntur. Quod quidem propositum studiorum nisi mature corrigitur, tam magnum rebus incommodum dabit, quam dedit barbaries olim.   Pertinax res barbaries est fateor, sed minus potest tamen quam illa mollities et persuasa prudentia literarum, quae si ratione caret, sapientiae virtutisque specie misere mortales circumducens.   Succedet igitur, ut arbitror, haud ita multo post, pro rusticana seculi nostri ruditate captatrix illa communiloquentia robur animi virilis omne, omnem virtutem masculam profligatura, nisi cavetur.'[2]   A too prophetic remark, which has been in fulfilment from the year 1680 to the present 1815. N.B. By 'persuasa prudentia' Grynaeus means self-complacent common sense as opposed to science and philosophic reason.

[1] [The *Darlegung* (1806), op. cit.]
[2] Simon Grynaeus, *candido lectori*, prefixed to the Latin translation of Plato by Marsilius Ficinus, Lugduni, 1557. ['Indeed it saddens me that people (especially such as call themselves Christians) should nowadays be so misled by the attractions of literature as to read only for greedy delight and not for sustenance, so that the sciences and philosophy itself are now almost entirely neglected even by the learned. In fact the purpose of study, unless it is corrected in time, may do as much harm as ignorance did before it. I admit ignorance is an obstinate thing, but it can hurt less than the effeminacy and conceited cleverness of education, which if deficient in sense is most deceiving in its appearance of wisdom and value. . . . And so, I think, the rustic simplicity of our times is soon to give way to a pervasive flattery, which unless it is avoided will debase all the vigour of a man's spirit, all masculine virtue.']

'Est medius ordo, et velut equestris, ingeniorum quidem sagacium, et commodorum rebus humanis, non tamen in primam magnitudinem patentium. Eorum hominum, ut ita dicam, major annona est. Sedulum esse, nihil temere loqui, assuescere labori, et imagini prudentiae et modestiae tegere angustiores partes captus, dum exercitationem et usum quo isti in civilibus rebus pollent, pro natura et magnitudine ingenii accipiunt'—Barclaii, *Argenis*, p. 71.[1]

'As therefore physicians are many times forced to leave such methods of curing as themselves know to be fittest, and being overruled by the sick man's inpatience are fain to try the best they can; in like sort, considering how the case doth stand with this present age full of tongue and weak of brain, behold we would (*if our subject permitted it*) yield to the stream thereof. That way we are contented to prove our thesis, which being the worse in itself, is notwithstanding now by reason of common imbecility the fitter and likelier to be brooked.'—Hooker.[2]

If this fear could be rationally entertained in the controversial age of Hooker under the then robust discipline of the scholastic logic, pardonably may a writer of the present times anticipate a scanty audience for abstrusest themes and truths that can neither be communicated or received without effort of thought, as well as patience of attention.

> Che s'io non erro al calcolar de' punti,
> Par ch'Asinina stella a noi predomini,
> E'l Somaro e'l Castron si sian congiunti.
> Il tempo d'Apuleio più non si nomini:
> Che se allora un sol uom sembrava un asino,
> Molti asini a' miei dì rassembran uomini!
>
> Di Salvator Rosa Satir. I. i. 10.[3]

---

[1] [John Barclay (1582–1621), *Argenis* (1621), pp. 112–13: 'There is a middle order, like that of knights, of the talented and the wise, useful in human affairs but not of the first order of greatness. Of these men there is, as I might say, a more plentiful store. . . . To be diligent, to say nothing rashly, to be used to work and to the show of wisdom . . . to hide the weaker parts of the intelligence . . . while custom and experience, which advance them in public affairs, many receive by virtue of the nature and scale of their talents.']

[2] [*Ecclesiastical Polity*, I. viii.]

[3] [Salvator Rosa (1615–73): 'If I am not mistaken in my calculation, it is the Ass constellation that dominates us, and the Donkey and the Dolt are conjoined. The age of Apuleius is now past: for if one man then seemed an ass, in my day many asses look like men!']

CHAPTER X

A chapter of digression and anecdotes, as an interlude preceding that on the nature and genesis of the imagination or plastic power—On pedantry and pedantic expressions—Advice to young authors respecting publication—Various anecdotes of the author's literary life, and the progress of his opinions in religion and politics.

'*Esemplastic.*[1] The word is not in Johnson, nor have I met with it elsewhere.' Neither have I! I constructed it myself from the Greek words, εἰς ἕν πλάττειν, i.e. to shape into one; because, having to convey a new sense, I thought that a new term would both aid the recollection of my meaning, and prevent its being confounded with the usual import of the word *imagination*. 'But this is pedantry!' Not necessarily so, I hope. If I am not misinformed, pedantry consists in the use of words unsuitable to the time, place and company. The language of the market would be in the schools as pedantic, though it might not be reprobated by that name, as the language of the schools in the market. The mere man of the world who insists that no other terms but such as occur in common conversation should be employed in a scientific disquisition, and with no greater precision, is as truly a pedant as the man of letters who either over-rating the acquirements of his auditors, or misled by his own familiarity with technical or scholastic terms, converses at the wine-table with his mind fixed on his museum or laboratory; even though the latter pedant instead of desiring his wife to make the tea, should bid her add to the quant. suff. of thea sinensis the oxyd of hydrogen saturated with caloric. To use the colloquial (and in truth somewhat vulgar) metaphor, if the pedant of the cloyster, and the pedant of the lobby, both smell equally of the shop, yet the odour from the Russian binding of good old authentic-looking folios and quartos is less annoying than the steams from the tavern or bagnio. Nay, though the pedantry of the scholar should betray a little ostentation, yet a well-conditioned mind would more easily, methinks, tolerate the fox brush of learned vanity, than the *sans culotterie* of a

[1] Cf. *Notebooks*, 4176 and n., where Coleridge spells his coinage 'esenoplastic' (1813).

contemptuous ignorance that assumes a merit from mutilation in the self-consoling sneer at the pompous incumbrance of tails.

The first lesson of philosophic discipline is to wean the student's attention from the degrees of things which alone form the vocabulary of common life, and to direct it to the kind abstracted from degree. Thus the chemical student is taught not to be startled at disquisitions on the heat in ice, or on latent and fixible light. In such discourse the instructor has no other alternative than either to use old words with new meanings (the plan adopted by Darwin in his *Zoonomia*); or to introduce new terms, after the example of Linnaeus and the framers of the present chemical nomenclature. The latter mode is evidently preferable, were it only that the former demands a twofold exertion of thought in one and the same act. For the reader (or hearer) is required not only to learn and bear in mind the new definition; but to unlearn, and keep out of his view, the old and habitual meaning: a far more difficult and perplexing task, and for which the mere semblance of eschewing pedantry seems to me an inadequate compensation. Where indeed it is in our power to recall an appropriate term that had without sufficient reason become obsolete, it is doubtless a less evil to restore than to coin anew. Thus to express in one word all that appertains to the perception considered as passive and merely recipient, I have adopted from our elder classics the word *sensuous*;[1] because *sensual* is not at present used, except in a bad sense, or at least as a moral distinction, while *sensitive* and *sensible* would each convey a different meaning. Thus too I have followed Hooker, Sanderson, Milton, etc., in designating the immediateness of any act or object of knowledge by the word *intuition*, used sometimes subjectively, sometimes objectively, even as we use the word *thought*; now as *the* thought, or act of thinking, and now as *a* thought, or the object of our reflection; and we do this without confusion or obscurity. The very words *objective* and *subjective*, of such constant recurrence in the schools of yore, I have ventured to re-introduce, because I could not so briefly or conveniently, by any more familiar terms, distinguish the *percipere* from the *percipi*. Lastly, I have cautiously discriminated the terms, the *reason* and the *understanding*, encouraged and confirmed by the authority of our genuine divines and philosophers before the revolution:

[1] [The word was apparently invented by Milton as an alternative to *sensual*; but Coleridge is mistaken in thinking the word had been used by any other English writer before his own day.]

> both life and sense,
> Fansie and understanding, whence the Soule
> Reason receives, and reason is her being,
> Discursive, or Intuitive; discourse [1]
> Is oftest yours, the latter most is ours,
> Differing but in degree, of kind the same.
>
> *Paradise Lost*, Bk v [*ll.* 485–90].

I say, that I was confirmed by authority so venerable: for I had previous and higher motives in my own conviction of the importance, nay, of the necessity of the distinction, as both an indispensable condition and a vital part of all sound speculation in metaphysics, ethical or theological. To establish this distinction was one main object of *The Friend*; if even in a biography of my own literary life I can with propriety refer to a work which was printed rather than published, or so published that it had been well for the unfortunate author if it had remained in manuscript! I have even at this time bitter cause for remembering that which a number of my subscribers have but a trifling motive for forgetting. This effusion might have been spared; but I would feign flatter myself that the reader will be less austere than an oriental professor of the bastinado, who, during an attempt to extort *per argumentum baculinum* a full confession from a culprit, interrupted his outcry of pain by reminding him that it was 'a mere digression'! 'All this noise, Sir! is nothing to the point, and no sort of answer to my questions!' 'Ah! but' (replied the sufferer) 'it is the most pertinent reply in nature to your blows.'

An imprudent man of common goodness of heart cannot but wish to turn even his imprudences to the benefit of others, as far as this is possible. If therefore any one of the readers of this semi-narrative should be preparing or intending a periodical work, I warn him, in the first place, against trusting in the number of names on his subscription list. For he cannot be certain that the names were put down by sufficient authority; or should that be ascertained, it still remains to be known whether they were not extorted by some over zealous friend's importunity; whether the subscriber had not yielded his name merely from want of courage to answer, no! and with the intention of

---

[1] But for sundry notes on Shakespeare, etc., which have fallen my way, I should have deemed it unnecessary to observe that *discourse* here, or elsewhere, does not mean what we now call *discoursing*; but the discursion of the mind, the process of generalization and subsumption, of deduction and conclusion. Thus philosophy has hitherto been *discursive*; while geometry is always and essentially *intuitive*.

dropping the work as soon as possible. One gentleman procured me nearly a hundred names for *The Friend*, and not only took frequent opportunity to remind me of his success in his canvass, but laboured to impress my mind with the sense of the obligation I was under to the subscribers; for (as he very pertinently admonished me) 'fifty-two shillings a year was a large sum to be bestowed on one individual where there were so many objects of charity with strong claims to the assistance of the benevolent.' Of these hundred patrons ninety threw up the publication before the fourth number, without any notice; though it was well known to them that in consequence of the distance, and the slowness and irregularity of the conveyance, I was compelled to lay in a stock of stamped paper for at least eight weeks beforehand; each sheet of which stood me in five pence previous to its arrival at my printer's; though the subscription money was not to be received till the twenty-first week after the commencement of the work; and lastly, though it was in nine cases out of ten impracticable for me to receive the money for two or three numbers without paying an equal sum for the postage.

In confirmation of my first caveat, I will select one fact among many. On my list of subscribers, among a considerable number of names equally flattering, was that of an Earl of Cork, with his address. He might as well have been an Earl of Bottle for aught I knew of him, who had been content to reverence the peerage *in abstracto*, rather than *in concretis*. Of course *The Friend* was regularly sent as far, if I remember right, as the eighteenth number: i.e. till a fortnight before the subscription was to be paid. And lo! just at this time I received a letter from his Lordship, reproving me in language far more lordly than courteous for my impudence in directing my pamphlets to him, who knew nothing of me or my work! Seventeen or eighteen numbers of which, however, his Lordship was pleased to retain, probably for the culinary or the post-culinary conveniences of his servants.

Secondly, I warn all others from the attempt to deviate from the ordinary mode of publishing a work by the trade. I thought, indeed, that to the purchaser it was indifferent whether thirty per cent of the purchase-money went to the booksellers or to the government; and that the convenience of receiving the work by the post at his own door would give the preference to the latter. It is hard, I own, to have been labouring for years in collecting and arranging the materials; to have spent every shilling that

could be spared after the necessaries of life had been furnished
in buying books, or in journies for the purpose of consulting
them, or of acquiring facts at the fountain head; then to buy the
paper, pay for the printing, etc., all at least fifteen per cent
beyond what the trade would have paid; and then after all to
give thirty per cent, not of the net profits, but of the gross results
of the sale, to a man who has merely to give the books shelf or
warehouse room, and permit his apprentice to hand them over
the counter to those who may ask for them; and this too copy by
copy, although if the work be on any philosophical or scientific
subject it may be years before the edition is sold off.   All this, I
confess, must seem a hardship, and one to which the products of
industry in no other mode of exertion are subject.   Yet even this
is better, far better, than to attempt in any way to unite the
functions of author and publisher.   But the most prudent mode
is to sell the copyright, at least of one or more editions, for the
most that the trade will offer.   By few only can a large remuneration be expected; but fifty pounds and ease of mind are of more
real advantage to a literary man than the chance of five hundred
with the certainty of insult and degrading anxieties.   I shall have
been grievously misunderstood if this statement should be interpreted as written with the desire of detracting from the character
of booksellers or publishers.   The individuals did not make the
laws and customs of their trade but as in every other trade take
them as they find them.   Till the evil can be proved to be
removeable and without the substitution of an equal or greater
inconvenience, it were neither wise or manly even to complain
of it.   But to use it as a pretext for speaking, or even for thinking or feeling, unkindly or opprobriously of the tradesmen as
individuals, would be something worse than unwise or even than
unmanly; it would be immoral and calumnious!   My motives
point in a far different direction and to far other objects, as will
be seen in the conclusion of the chapter.

A learned and exemplary old clergyman, who many years ago
went to his reward followed by the regrets and blessings of his
flock, published at his own expense two volumes octavo, entitled
A New Theory of Redemption.   The work was most severely
handled in the *Monthly* or *Critical Review*, I forget which, and
this unprovoked hostility became the good old man's favorite
topic of conversation among his friends.   Well! (he used to
exclaim) in the second edition I shall have an opportunity of
exposing both the ignorance and the malignity of the anonymous
critic.   Two or three years however passed by without any

tidings from the bookseller, who had undertaken the printing and publication of the work, and who was perfectly at his ease, as the author was known to be a man of large property. At length the accounts were written for; and in the course of a few weeks they were presented by the rider for the house, in person. My old friend put on his spectacles, and holding the scroll with no very firm hand, began '*Paper, so much :* Oh, moderate enough —not at all beyond my expectation! *Printing, so much :* well! moderate enough! *Stitching, covers, advertisements, carriage, etc., so much.*' Still nothing amiss. *Selleridge* (for orthography is no necessary part of a bookseller's literary acquirements), £3 3s. 'Bless me! only three guineas for the what d'ye call it? the *selleridge*?' 'No more, Sir,' replied the rider. 'Nay, but that is too moderate,' rejoined my old friend. 'Only three guineas for selling a thousand copies of a work in two volumes?' 'Oh, sir!' cries the young traveller, 'you have mistaken the word. There have been none of them *sold*; they have been sent back from London long ago; and this £3 3s. is the the *cellaridge*, or warehouse-room in our book cellar.' The work was in consequence preferred from the ominous cellar of the publisher's to the author's garret; and on presenting a copy to an acquaintance, the old gentleman used to tell the anecdote with great humour and still greater good nature.

With equal lack of worldly knowledge, I was a far more than equal sufferer for it at the very outset of my authorship. Toward the close of the first year from the time that in an inauspicious hour I left the friendly cloysters and the happy grove of quiet, ever honored Jesus College, Cambridge, I was persuaded by sundry philanthropists and anti-polemists to set on foot a periodical work, entitled *The Watchman*, that (according to the general motto of the work) 'all might know the truth, and that the truth might make us free!' In order to exempt it from the stamp-tax, and likewise to contribute as little as possible to the supposed guilt of a war against freedom, it was to be published on every eighth day, thirty-two pages, large octavo, closely printed, and price only four-pence. Accordingly with a flaming prospectus, 'Knowledge is Power,' etc., 'to cry the state of the political atmosphere,' and so forth, I set off on a tour to the north, from Bristol to Sheffield, for the purpose of procuring customers, preaching by the way in most of the great towns as an hireless volunteer, in a blue coat and white waistcoat, that not a rag of the woman of Babylon might be seen on me. For I was at that time and long after, though a Trinitarian (i.e. *ad normam Platonis*) in philosophy, yet a zealous Unitarian [1] in religion; more accurately, I was a *psilanthropist*, one of those who believe our Lord to have been the real son of Joseph, and who lay the main stress on the resurrection rather than on the crucifixion. O! never can I remember those days with either shame or regret. For I was most sincere, most disinterested! My opinions were indeed in many and most important points erroneous; but my heart was single. Wealth, rank, life itself, then seemed cheap to me, compared with the interests of (what I believed to be) the truth, and the will of my maker. I cannot even accuse myself of having been actuated by vanity; for in the expansion of my enthusiasm I did not think of myself at all.

My campaign commenced at Birmingham; and my first attack was on a rigid Calvinist, a tallow-chandler by trade. He was a tall dingy man, in whom length was so predominant over breadth that he might almost have been borrowed for a foundry poker. O that face! a face $\kappa\alpha\tau$ ' $\check{\epsilon}\mu\phi\alpha\sigma\iota\nu$! I have it before me at this moment. The lank, black, twine-like hair, *pingui-nitescent*, cut in a straight line along the black stubble of his thin gunpowder eyebrows, that looked like a scorched after-math from a last week's shaving. His coat collar behind in perfect unison, both of colour and lustre, with the coarse yet glib cordage that I suppose he called his hair, and which with a bend inward at the nape of the neck (the only approach to flexure in his whole figure) slunk in behind his waistcoat; while the countenance lank, dark, very hard, and with strong, perpendicular furrows, gave me a dim notion of someone looking at me through a used gridiron, all soot, grease and iron! But he was one of the thorough-bred, a true lover of liberty, and (I was informed) had proved to the satisfaction of many that Mr Pitt was one of the horns of the second beast in the Revelations, *that spoke like a dragon*. A person to whom one of my letters of recommendation had been addressed was my introducer. It was a new event in my life, my first stroke in the new business I had undertaken of an author, yea, and of an author trading on his own account. My companion, after some imperfect sentences and a multitude of hums and haas, abandoned the cause to his client; and I commenced an harangue of half an hour to Phileleutheros, the tallow-chandler, varying my notes through the whole gamut of eloquence from the ratiocinative to the declamatory, and in the latter from the pathetic to the indignant. I argued, I described,

---

[1] [Coleridge had become a Unitarian at Cambridge in 1793 and did not finally accept Trinitarianism until his return from Italy in 1806.]

I promised, I prophesied, and beginning with the captivity of
nations I ended with the near approach of the millennium,
finishing the whole with some of my own verses describing that
glorious state out of the *Religious Musings*:

> —————————— Such delights
> As float to earth, permitted visitants!
> When in some hour of solemn jubilee
> The massive gates of Paradise are thrown
> Wide open, and forth come in fragments wild
> Sweet echoes of unearthly melodies,
> And odours snatched from beds of Amaranth,
> And they that from the crystal river of life
> Spring up on freshen'd wing, ambrosial gales!
>
> Religious Musings, i. 356.[1]

My taper man of lights listened with perseverant and praise-
worthy patience, though (as I was afterwards told on complaining
of certain gales that were not altogether ambrosial) it was a
melting day with him. 'And what, Sir,' he said, after a short
pause, 'might the cost be?' 'Only four-pence,' (O! how I felt
the anti-climax, the abysmal bathos of that *four-pence*)! 'Only
four-pence, Sir, each number, to be published on every eighth
day.' 'That comes to a deal of money at the end of a year. And
how much did you say there was to be for the money?' 'Thirty-
two pages, sir! large octavo, closely printed.' 'Thirty and two
pages? Bless me, why except what I does in a family way on the
Sabbath, that's more than I ever reads, Sir! all the year round.
I am as great a one as any man in Brummagem, sir! for liberty
and truth and all them sort of things, but as to this (no offence, I
hope, Sir) I must beg to be excused.'

So ended my first canvass. From causes that I shall presently
mention, I made but one other application in person. This took
place at Manchester, to a stately and opulent wholesale dealer in
cottons. He took my letter of introduction, and having perused
it measured me from head to foot, and again from foot to head,
and then asked if I had any bill or invoice of the thing. I
presented my prospectus to him; he rapidly skimmed and
hummed over the first side, and still more rapidly the second and
concluding page; crushed it within his fingers and the palm of
his hand; then most deliberately and significantly rubbed and

[1] [*ll.* 343–51. These lines first appeared in *The Watchman*, No. 11 (1796)
and were then included in 'Religious Musings,' which appeared in the same
year.]

smoothed one part against the other; and, lastly, putting it into his pocket, turned his back upon me with an 'over-run with these articles!' and so, without another syllable, retired into his counting-house; and, I can truly say, to my unspeakable amusement.

This I have said was my second and last attempt. On returning baffled from the first, in which I had vainly essayed to repeat the miracle of Orpheus with the Brummagem patriot, I dined with the tradesman who had introduced me to him. After dinner he importuned me to smoke a pipe with him and two or three other illuminati of the same rank. I objected, both because I was engaged to spend the evening with a minister and his friends, and because I had never smoked except once or twice in my lifetime, and then it was herb tobacco mixed with Oronooko. On the assurance however that the tobacco was equally mild, and seeing too that it was of a yellow colour (not forgetting the lamentable difficulty I have always experienced in saying no! and in abstaining from what the people about me were doing), I took half a pipe, filling the lower half of the bole with salt. I was soon, however, compelled to resign it, in consequence of a giddiness and distressful feeling in my eyes, which, as I had drank but a single glass of ale, must I knew have been the effect of the tobacco. Soon after, deeming myself recovered, I sallied forth to my engagement; but the walk and the fresh air brought on all the symptoms again, and I had scarcely entered the minister's drawing-room, and opened a small paquet of letters which he had received from Bristol for me, ere I sank back on the sofa in a sort of swoon rather than sleep. Fortunately, I had found just time enough to inform him of the confused state of my feelings and of the occasion. For here and thus I lay, my face like a wall that is whitewashing, deathy pale and with the cold drops of perspiration running down it from my forehead, while one after another there dropped in the different gentlemen who had been invited to meet and spend the evening with me, to the number of from fifteen to twenty. As the poison of tobacco acts but for a short time, I at length awoke from insensibility, and looked round on the party, my eyes dazzled by the candles which had been lighted in the interim. By way of relieving my embarrassment one of the gentlemen began the conversation with, 'Have you seen a paper to-day, Mr Coleridge?' 'Sir,' I replied, rubbing my eyes, 'I am far from convinced that a Christian is permitted to read either newspapers or any other works of merely political and temporary interest.' This remark, so ludicrously inapposite to, or rather incongruous with, the purpose for which I was known to have visited Birmingham, and to assist me in which they were all then met, produced an involuntary and general burst of laughter; and seldom indeed have I passed so many delightful hours as I enjoyed in that room from the moment of that laugh till an early hour the next morning. Never, perhaps, in so mixed and numerous a party, have I since heard conversation sustained with such animation, enriched with such variety of information and enlivened with such a flow of anecdote. Both then and afterwards they all joined in dissuading me from proceeding with my scheme; assured me in the most friendly and yet most flattering expressions that the employment was neither fit for me, nor I fit for the employment. Yet, if I had determined on persevering in it, they promised to exert themselves to the utmost to procure subscribers, and insisted that I should make no more applications in person, but carry on the canvass by proxy. The same hospitable reception, the same dissuasion, and (that failing) the same kind exertions in my behalf, I met with at Manchester, Derby, Nottingham, Sheffield, indeed at every place in which I took up my sojourn. I often recall with affectionate pleasure the many respectable men who interested themselves for me, a perfect stranger to them, not a few of whom I can still name among my friends. They will bear witness for me how opposite even then my principles were to those of Jacobinism or even of democracy, and can attest the strict accuracy of the statement which I have left on record in the 10th and 11th numbers of *The Friend*.

From this rememberable tour I returned with nearly a thousand names on the subscription list of *The Watchman*; yet more than half convinced that prudence dictated the abandonment of the scheme. But for this very reason I persevered in it; for I was at that period of my life so compleatly hag-ridden by the fear of being influenced by selfish motives, that to know a mode of conduct to be the dictate of prudence was a sort of presumptive proof to my feelings that the contrary was the dictate of duty. Accordingly I commenced the work, which was announced in London by long bills in letters larger than had ever been seen before, and which (I have been informed, for I did not see them myself) eclipsed the glories even of the lottery puffs. But, alas! the publication of the very first number was delayed beyond the day announced for its appearance. In the second number an essay against fast days, with a most censurable

application of a text from Isaiah [1] for its motto, lost me near five
hundred of my subscribers at one blow. In the two following
numbers I made enemies of all my Jacobin and democratic
patrons; for disgusted by their infidelity and their adoption of
French morals with French *psilosophy*; and perhaps thinking
that charity ought to begin nearest home, instead of abusing the
government and the aristocrats chiefly or entirely, as had been
expected of me, I levelled my attacks at 'modern patriotism,'
and even ventured to declare my belief that whatever the
motives of ministers might have been for the sedition (or as it
was then the fashion to call them, the *gagging*) bills; yet the bills
themselves would produce an effect to be desired by all the true
friends of freedom, as far as they should contribute to deter men
from openly declaiming on subjects the principles of which they
had never bottomed, and from 'pleading to the poor and
ignorant, instead of pleading *for* them.' At the same time I
avowed my conviction that national education and a concurring
spread of the gospel were the indispensable conditions of any
true political amelioration. Thus, by the time the seventh
number was published, I had the mortification (but why should
I say this, when in truth I cared too little for anything that
concerned my worldly interests to be at all mortified about it?)
of seeing the preceding numbers exposed in sundry old iron
shops for a penny a piece. At the ninth number I dropt the
work.[2] But from the London publisher I could not obtain a
shilling. He was a ―― and set me at defiance. From other
places I procured but little, and after such delays as rendered
that little worth nothing; and I should have been inevitably
thrown into jail by my Bristol printer, who refused to wait even
for a month for a sum between eighty and ninety pounds, if the
money had not been paid for me by a man by no means affluent,[3]
a dear friend who attached himself to me from my first arrival in
Bristol, who has continued my friend with a fidelity unconquered

---

[1] ['Wherefore my bowels shall sound like a harp.'—Isaiah xvi. 11. In
fact *The Watchman* contained no defence of Pitt's repressive legislation. The
article 'Modern Patriotism' (pp. 73-4) is an attack upon the hypocrisy of
English supporters of the French revolution.]

[2] [*The Watchman* ran to ten numbers (1 March-13 May 1796). The
reasons offered by Coleridge in the last number for its failure were that 'part
of my subscribers have relinquished it because it did not contain sufficient
original composition, and a still larger because it contained too much'
(p. 324).]

[3] [Thomas Poole (1765-1837), a tanner of Nether Stowey in Somerset who
raised a small subscription for Coleridge in 1796 and found him a small
cottage at Stowey in December. In 1809 he advanced money for *The
Friend*.]

by time or even by my own apparent neglect; a friend from whom I never received an advice that was not wise, or a remonstrance that was not gentle and affectionate.

Conscientiously an opponent of the first revolutionary war, yet with my eyes thoroughly opened to the true character and impotence of the favorers of revolutionary principles in England, principles which I held in abhorrence (for it was part of my political creed that whoever ceased to act as an individual by making himself a member of any society not sanctioned by his government forfeited the rights of a citizen), a vehement anti-ministerialist, but after the invasion of Switzerland a more vehement anti-Gallican, and still more intensely an anti-Jacobin, I retired to a cottage at Stowey, and provided for my scanty maintenance by writing verses for a London morning paper.[1] I saw plainly that literature was not a profession by which I could expect to live; for I could not disguise from myself that, whatever my talents might or might not be in other respects, yet they were not of the sort that could enable me to become a popular writer; and that whatever my opinions might be in themselves, they were almost equidistant from all the three prominent parties, the Pittites, the Foxites, and the Democrats. Of the unsaleable nature of my writings I had an amusing memento one morning from our own servant girl. For, happening to rise at an earlier hour than usual, I observed her putting an extravagant quantity of paper into the grate in order to light the fire, and mildly checked her for her wastefulness: 'La, Sir!' (replied poor Nanny), 'why, it is only *Watchmen*.'

I now devoted myself to poetry and the study of ethics and psychology; and so profound was my admiration at this time of Hartley's essay on man [2] that I gave his name to my first born. In addition to the gentleman, my neighbour, whose garden joined on to my little orchard, and the cultivation of whose friendship had been my sole motive in choosing Stowey for my residence, I was so fortunate as to acquire, shortly after my settlement there, an invaluable blessing in the society and neighbourhood of one to whom I could look up with equal reverence, whether I regarded him as a poet, a philosopher or a man.[3] His conversation extended to almost all subjects, except physics and politics; with the latter he never troubled himself.

---

[1] [The *Morning Post*.]
[2] [*Observations on Man*, 1748.]
[3] [Wordsworth settled with his sister Dorothy at Alfoxden, three miles from Stowey, in July 1797.]

Yet neither my retirement nor my utter abstraction from all the disputes of the day could secure me in those jealous times from suspicion and obloquy, which did not stop at me but extended to my excellent friend, whose perfect innocence was even adduced as a proof of his guilt. One of the many busy sycophants [1] of that day (I here use the word sycophant in its original sense, as a wretch who flatters the prevailing party by informing against his neighbours, under pretence that they are exporters of prohibited figs or fancies! for the moral application of the term it matters not which)—one of these sycophantic law-mongrels, discoursing on the politics of the neighbourhood, uttered the following deep remark: 'As to Coleridge, there is not so much harm in him, for he is a whirl-brain that talks whatever comes uppermost; but that ——! he is the dark traitor. You never hear him say a syllable on the subject.'

Now that the hand of providence has disciplined all Europe into sobriety, as men tame wild elephants, by alternate blows and caresses, now that Englishmen of all classes are restored to their old English notions and feelings, it will with difficulty be credited how great an influence was at that time possessed and exerted by the spirit of secret defamation (the too constant attendant on party zeal!) during the restless interim from 1793 to the commencement of the Addington administration, or the year before the truce of Amiens. For by the latter period the minds of the partizans, exhausted by excess of stimulation and humbled by mutual disappointment, had become languid. The same causes that inclined the nation to peace disposed the individuals to reconciliation. Both parties had found themselves in the wrong. The one had confessedly mistaken the moral character of the revolution, and the other had miscalculated both its moral and its physical resources. The experiment was made at the price of great, almost, we may say, of humiliating sacrifices; and wise men foresaw that it would fail, at least in its direct and ostensible object. Yet it was purchased cheaply, and realized an object of equal value and, if possible, of still more vital importance. For it brought about a national unanimity unexampled in our history since the reign of Elizabeth: and providence, never wanting to a good work when men have done their parts, soon provided a common focus in the cause of Spain, which made us all once more Englishmen by at once gratifying

---

[1] Σύκους φαίνειν, to shew or detect figs, the exportation of which from Attica was forbidden by the laws. [The true origin of the word is obscure, but this traditional explanation is rejected by O.E.D.]

and correcting the predilections of both parties. The sincere
reverers of the throne felt the cause of loyalty ennobled by its
alliance with that of freedom; while the honest zealots of the
people could not but admit that freedom itself assumed a more
winning form, humanized by loyalty and consecrated by religious principle. The youthful enthusiasts who, flattered by
the morning rainbow of the French revolution, had made a boast
of expatriating their hopes and fears, now disciplined by the
succeeding storms, and sobered by increase of years, had been
taught to prize and honor the spirit of nationality as the best
safeguard of national independence, and this again as the
absolute pre-requisite and necessary basis of popular rights.

If in Spain too disappointment has nipt our too forward
expectations, yet all is not destroyed that is checked. The crop
was perhaps springing up too rank in the stalk to *kern* [1] well; and
there were, doubtless, symptoms of the Gallican blight on it. If
superstition and despotism have been suffered to let in their
wolvish sheep to trample and eat it down even to the surface, yet
the roots remain alive, and the second growth may prove all the
stronger and healthier for the temporary interruption. At all
events, to *us* heaven has been just and gracious. The people of
England did their best, and have received their rewards. Long
may we continue to deserve it! Causes which it had been too
generally the habit of former statesmen to regard as belonging to
another world are now admitted by all ranks to have been the
main agents of our success. 'We fought from heaven; the stars
in their courses fought against Sisera.' [2] If then unanimity
grounded on moral feelings has been among the least equivocal
sources of our national glory, that man deserves the esteem of his
countrymen, even as patriots, who devotes his life and the utmost
efforts of his intellect to the preservation and continuance of that
unanimity by the disclosure and establishment of principles.
For by these all opinions must be ultimately tried; and (as the
feelings of men are worthy of regard only as far as they are the
representatives of their fixed opinions) on the knowledge of these
all unanimity, not accidental and fleeting, must be grounded.
Let the scholar who doubts this assertion refer only to the
speeches and writings of Edmund Burke at the commencement
of the American war, and compare them with his speeches and

---

[1] [To turn to seed. Ferdinand VII on returning to Spain as king in 1814
had refused to recognize the liberal constitution of 1812 and was ferociously
persecuting its adherents.]
[2] ['They fought from heaven . . .'—Judges v. 20.]

writings at the commencement of the French revolution. He
will find the principles exactly the same and the deductions the
same; but the practical inferences almost opposite in the one
case from those drawn in the other; yet in both equally legitimate
and in both equally confirmed by the results. Whence gained
he this superiority of foresight? Whence arose the striking
difference, and in most instances even the discrepancy between
the grounds assigned by him, and by those who voted with him,
on the same questions? How are we to explain the notorious
fact that the speeches and writings of Edmund Burke are more
interesting at the present day than they were found at the time
of their first publication; while those of his illustrious confeder-
ates are either forgotten, or exist only to furnish proofs that the
same conclusion which one man had deduced scientifically *may*
be brought out by another in consequence of errors that luckily
chanced to neutralize each other. It would be unhandsome as a
conjecture, even were it not, as it actually is, false in point of
fact, to attribute this difference to deficiency of talent on the part
of Burke's friends, or of experience, or of historical knowledge.
The satisfactory solution is that Edmund Burke possessed and
had sedulously sharpened that eye which sees all things, actions
and events in relation to the laws that determine their existence
and circumscribe their possibility. He referred habitually to
principles. He was a scientific statesman; and therefore a seer.
For every principle contains in itself the germs of a prophecy;
and as the prophetic power is the essential privilege of science, so
the fulfilment of its oracles supplies the outward and (to men in
general) the only test of its claim to the title. Wearisome as
Burke's refinements appeared to his parliamentary auditors, yet
the cultivated classes throughout Europe have reason to be
thankful that

> ——————————he went on refining,
> And thought of convincing, while they thought of dining.[1]

Our very sign-boards (said an illustrious friend to me) give
evidence that there has been a Titian in the world. In like
manner not only the debates in parliament, not only our pro-
clamations and state papers, but the essays and leading paragraphs of our journals are so many remembrancers of Edmund
Burke. Of this the reader may easily convince himself, if
either by recollection or reference he will compare the opposition

---

[1] [Oliver Goldsmith, *The Retaliation* (1774), *ll.* 35–6.]

newspapers at the commencement and during the five or six following years of the French revolution with the sentiments and grounds of argument assumed in the same class of journals at present, and for some years past.

Whether the spirit of Jacobinism, which the writings of Burke exorcised from the higher and from the literary classes, may not like the ghost in Hamlet be heard moving and mining in the underground chambers with an activity the more dangerous because less noisy, may admit of a question. I have given my opinions on this point, and the grounds of them, in my letters to Judge Fletcher, occasioned by his charge to the Wexford grand jury, and published in the *Courier*.[1] Be this as it may, the evil spirit of jealousy, and with it the Cerberean whelps of feud and slander, no longer walk their rounds in cultivated society.

Far different were the days to which these anecdotes have carried me back. The dark guesses of some zealous quidnunc met with so congenial a soil in the grave alarm of a titled Dogberry of our neighbourhood that a spy was actually sent down from the government *pour surveillance* of myself and friend. There must have been not only abundance, but variety of these 'honorable men' at the disposal of ministers: for this proved a very honest fellow. After three weeks' truly Indian perseverance in tracking us (for we were commonly together), during all which time seldom were we out of doors but we contrived to be within hearing (and all the while utterly unsuspected; how, indeed, could such a suspicion enter our fancies?), he not only rejected Sir Dogberry's request that he would try yet a little longer, but declared to him his belief that both my friend and myself were as good subjects, for aught he could discover to the contrary, as any in His Majesty's dominions. He had repeatedly hid himself, he said, for hours together, behind a bank at the sea-side (our favorite seat), and overheard our conversation. At first he fancied that we were aware of our danger; for he often heard me talk of one *Spy Nozy*, which he was inclined to interpret of himself, and of a remarkable feature belonging to him; but he was speedily convinced that it was the name of a man who had made a book and lived long ago. Our talk ran most upon books, and we were perpetually desiring each other to look at *this*, and to listen to *that*; but he could not catch a word about politics. Once he had joined me on the road (this occurred as I was returning home alone from my friend's house which was

---

[1] [In September–December 1814, on the subject of Catholic emancipation.]

about three miles from my own cottage), and passing himself off as a traveller, he had entered into conversation with me, and talked of purpose in a democrat way in order to draw me out. The result, it appears, not only convinced him that I was no friend of Jacobinism; but (he added) I had 'plainly made it out to be such a silly as well as wicked thing, that he felt ashamed, though he had only put it on.' I distinctly remembered the occurrence, and had mentioned it immediately on my return, repeating what the traveller with his Bardolph nose had said, with my own answer; and so little did I suspect the true object of my 'tempter ere accuser' that I expressed with no small pleasure my hope and belief that the conversation had been of some service to the poor misled malcontent. This incident therefore prevented all doubt as to the truth of the report which, through a friendly medium, came to me from the master of the village inn, who had been ordered to entertain the *government gentleman* in his best manner, but above all to be silent concerning such a person being in his house. At length he received Sir Dogberry's commands to accompany his guest at the final interview; and after the absolving suffrage of the gentleman honored with the confidence of ministers, answered as follows to the following queries:—D. Well, landlord! what do you know of the person in question? L. I see him often pass by with maister ————, my landlord (i.e. the owner of the house), and sometimes with the new-comers at Holford; but I never said a word to him, or he to me. D. But do you not know that he has distributed papers and handbills of a seditious nature among the common people? L. No, your honor! I never heard of such a thing. D. Have you not seen this Mr Coleridge, or heard of his haranguing and talking to knots and clusters of the inhabitants?—What are you grinning at, Sir? L. Beg your honor's pardon! but I was only thinking how they'd have stared at him. If what I have heard be true, your honor! they would not have understood a word he said. When our vicar was here, Dr L., the master of the great school and Canon of Windsor, there was a great dinner party at maister ————'s; and one of the farmers that was there told us that he and the Doctor talked real Hebrew Greek at each other for an hour together after dinner. D. Answer the question, Sir! Does he ever harangue the people? L. I hope your honor an't angry with me. I can say no more than I know. I never saw him talking with anyone, but my landlord, and our curate, and the strange gentleman. D. Has he not been seen wandering on the hills towards the

Channel, and along the shore, with books and papers in his hand, taking charts and maps of the country? L. Why, as to that, your honor! I own, I have heard; I am sure I would not wish to say ill of any body; but it is certain that I have heard—— D. Speak out, man! don't be afraid; you are doing your duty to your King and government. What have you heard? L. Why, folks do say, your honor! as how that he is a *Poet*, and that he is going to put Quantock and all about here in print; and as they be so much together, I suppose that the strange gentleman has some consarn in the business.—So ended this formidable inquisition, the latter part of which alone requires explanation, and at the same time entitles the anecdote to a place in my literary life. I had considered it as a defect in the admirable poem of the *Task* that the subject which gives the title to the work was not, and indeed could not be, carried on beyond the three or four first pages, and that throughout the poem the connections are frequently awkward, and the transitions abrupt and arbitrary. I sought for a subject that should give equal room and freedom for description, incident and impassioned reflections on men, nature and society, yet supply in itself a natural connection to the parts, and unity to the whole. Such a subject I conceived myself to have found in a stream, traced from its source in the hills among the yellow-red moss and conical glass-shaped tufts of bent, to the first break or fall, where its drops became audible, and it begins to form a channel; thence to the peat and turf barn, itself built of the same dark squares as it sheltered; to the sheepfold; to the first cultivated plot of ground; to the lonely cottage and its bleak garden won from the heath; to the hamlet, the villages, the market-town, the manufactories and the sea-port. My walks, therefore, were almost daily on the top of Quantock and among its sloping coombs. With my pencil and memorandum-book in my hand I was *making studies*, as the artists call them, and often moulding my thoughts into verse, with the objects and imagery immediately before my senses. Many circumstances, evil and good, intervened to prevent the completion of the poem, which was to have been titled 'The Brook.' Had I finished the work, it was my purpose in the heat of the moment to have dedicated it to our then committee of public safety as containing the charts and maps with which I was to have supplied the French government in aid of their plans of invasion. And these too for a tract of coast that from Clevedon to Minehead scarcely permits the approach of a fishing-boat!

All my experience from my first entrance into life to the present hour is in favor of the warning maxim that the man who opposes *in toto* the political or religious zealots of his age is safer from their obloquy than he who differs from them in one or two points, or perhaps only in degree. By that transfer of the feelings of private life into the discussion of public questions, which is the queen bee in the hive of party fanaticism, the partizan has more sympathy with an intemperate opposite than with a moderate friend. We now enjoy an intermission, and long may it continue! In addition to far higher and more important merits, our present bible societies and other numerous associations for national or charitable objects may serve perhaps to carry off the superfluous activity and fervor of stirring minds in innocent hyperboles and the bustle of management. But the poison-tree is not dead, though the sap may for a season have subsided to its roots. At least let us not be lulled into such a notion of our entire security as not to keep watch and ward, even on our best feelings. I have seen gross intolerance shown in support of toleration; sectarian antipathy most obtrusively displayed in the promotion of an undistinguishing comprehension of sects; and acts of cruelty (I had almost said, of treachery) committed in furtherance of an object vitally important to the cause of humanity; and all this by men too of naturally kind dispositions and exemplary conduct.

The magic rod of fanaticism is preserved in the very adyta of human nature; and needs only the re-exciting warmth of a master hand to bud forth afresh and produce the old fruits. The horror of the peasants' war in Germany, and the direful effects of the Anabaptists' tenets (which differed only from those of Jacobinism by the substitution of theological for philosophical jargon), struck all Europe for a time with affright. Yet little more than a century was sufficient to obliterate all effective memory of these events. The same principles, with similar though less dreadful consequences, were again at work from the imprisonment of the first Charles to the restoration of his son. The fanatic maxim of extirpating fanaticism by persecution produced a civil war. The war ended in the victory of the insurgents; but the temper survived, and Milton had abundant grounds for asserting that '*Presbyter* was but *Old Priest* writ large!' One good result, thank heaven! of this zealotry was the re-establishment of the Church. And now it might have been hoped that the mischievous spirit would have been bound for a season, 'and a seal set upon him that he might deceive the nation no more.'[1]   But no!   The ball of persecution was taken up with undiminished vigor by the persecuted. The same fanatic principle that under the solemn oath and covenant had turned cathedrals into stables, destroyed the rarest trophies of art and ancestral piety and hunted the brightest ornaments of learning and religion into holes and corners, now marched under episcopal banners, and having first crowded the prisons of England emptied its whole vial of wrath on the miserable covenanters of Scotland.[2]   A merciful providence at length constrained both parties to join against a common enemy. A wise government followed; and the established church became, and now is, not only the brightest example but our best and only sure bulwark of toleration!   The true and indispensable bank against a new inundation of persecuting zeal—*Esto perpetua!*

A long interval of quiet succeeded; or rather, the exhaustion had produced a cold fit of the ague which was symptomatized by indifference among the many, and a tendency to infidelity or scepticism in the educated classes.   At length those feelings of disgust and hatred which for a brief while the multitude had attached to the crimes and absurdities of sectarian and democratic fanaticism were transferred to the oppressive privileges of the noblesse and the luxury, intrigues and favoritism of the continental courts.   The same principles dressed in the ostentatious garb of a fashionable philosophy once more rose triumphant and effected the French revolution.   And have we not within the last three or four years had reason to apprehend that the detestable maxims and correspondent measures of the late French despotism had already bedimmed the public recollections of democratic phrensy; had drawn off to other objects the electric force of the feelings which had massed and upheld those recollections; and that a favorable concurrence of occasions was alone wanting to awaken the thunder and precipitate the lightning from the opposite quarter of the political heaven?[3]

In part from constitutional indolence, which in the very heyday of hope had kept my enthusiasm in check, but still more from the habits and influences of a classical education and academic pursuits, scarcely had a year elapsed from the commencement of my literary and political adventures before my mind sank into a state of thorough disgust and despondency,

---

[1] [From Revelation xx. 3.]
[2] [Malcolm] Laing's *History of Scotland* [1800], Walter Scott's bards, ballads, etc.
[3] See *The Friend*, p. 110 [Essay iii, 1809].

both with regard to the disputes and the parties disputant.
With more than *poetic* feeling I exclaimed:

> The sensual and the dark rebel in vain,
> Slaves by their own compulsion! In mad game
> They break their manacles, to wear the name
> Of freedom, graven on an heavier chain!
> O liberty! with profitless endeavor
> Have I pursued thee many a weary hour;
> But thou nor swell'st the victor's pomp, nor ever
> Didst breathe thy soul in forms of human power!
>   Alike from all, howe'er they praise thee
>   (Nor prayer nor boastful name delays thee)
>   From superstition's harpy minions
>   And factious blasphemy's obscener slaves,
>   Thou speedest on thy cherub pinions,
> The guide of homeless winds and playmate of the waves!
>
> *France, a Palinodia.*[1]

I retired to a cottage in Somersetshire at the foot of Quantock, and devoted my thoughts and studies to the foundations of religion and morals. Here I found myself all afloat. Doubts rushed in; broke upon me 'from the fountains of the great deep' and fell 'from the windows of heaven.' The fontal truths of natural religion and the books of Revelation alike contributed to the flood; and it was long ere my ark touched on an Ararat, and rested. The idea of the Supreme Being appeared to me to be as necessarily implied in all particular modes of being, as the idea of infinite space in all the geometrical figures by which space is limited. I was pleased with the Cartesian opinion that the idea of God is distinguished from all other ideas by involving its reality; but I was not wholly satisfied. I began then to ask myself, what proof I had of the outward existence of any thing? Of this sheet of paper for instance, as a thing in itself, separate from the phaenomenon or image in my perception. I saw that in the nature of things such proof is impossible; and that of all modes of being that are not objects of the senses, the existence is assumed by a logical necessity arising from the constitution of the mind itself, by the absence of all motive to doubt it, not from any absolute contradiction in the supposition of the contrary. Still the existence of a being, the ground of all existence, was not yet the existence of a moral creator and governor. 'In the position that all reality is either contained in the necessary being as an attribute or exists through him as its ground, it remains undecided whether the properties of intelligence and will are to

[1] [*ll.* 85–98. The ode was first published in the *Morning Post* (16 April 1798).]

be referred to the Supreme Being in the former or only in the latter sense; as inherent attributes, or only as consequences that have existence in other things through him.   Thus organization and motion are regarded as from God, not in God.   Were the latter the truth, then notwithstanding all the pre-eminence which must be assigned to the ETERNAL FIRST from the sufficiency, unity and independence of his being as the dread ground of the universe, his nature would yet fall far short of that which we are bound to comprehend in the idea of GOD.   For without any knowledge or determining resolve of its own it would only be a blind necessary ground of other things and other spirits; and thus would be distinguished from the FATE of certain ancient philosophers in no respect but that of being more definitely and intelligibly described.' [1]

For a very long time indeed I could not reconcile personality with infinity; and my head was with Spinoza, though my whole heart remained with Paul and John.   Yet there had dawned upon me, even before I had met with the *Critique of the Pure Reason*, a certain guiding light.   If the mere intellect could make no certain discovery of a holy and intelligent first cause, it might yet supply a demonstration that no legitimate argument could be drawn from the intellect *against* its truth.   And what is this more than St Paul's assertion that by wisdom (more properly translated by the powers of reasoning), no man ever arrived at the knowledge of God? [2]   What more than the sublimest, and probably the oldest, book on earth has taught us,

> Silver and gold man searcheth out:
> Bringeth the ore out of the earth, and darkness into light.
>
> But where findeth he wisdom?
> Where is the place of understanding?
>
> The abyss crieth; it is not in me!
> Ocean echoeth back; not in me!
>
> Whence then cometh wisdom?
> Where dwelleth understanding?
>
> Hidden from the eyes of the living:
> Kept secret from the fowls of heaven!
>
> Hell and death answer;
> We have heard the rumour thereof from afar!
>
> GOD marketh out the road to it;
> GOD knoweth its abiding place!

[1] Kant's [*Der*] *einzig mögliche Beweisgrund: vermischte Schriften, Zweiter Band*, §§ 102 and 103.   [From the *Beweisgrund* (1763), I. iv. 3.]
[2] ['For the wisdom of this world is foolishness with God.'—I Corinthians iii. 19.]

He beholdeth the ends of the earth;
He surveyeth what is beneath the heavens!

And as he weighed out the winds, and measured the sea,
And appointed laws to the rain,
And a path to the thunder,
A path to the flashes of the lightning!

Then did he see it,
And he counted it;
He searched into the depth thereof,
And with a line did he compass it round!

But to man he said,
The fear of the Lord is wisdom for THEE!
And to avoid evil,
That is *thy* understanding.

                              Job, Chap. 28th.[1]

I became convinced that religion, as both the corner-stone and the key-stone of morality, must have a moral origin; so far at least, that the evidence of its doctrines could not, like the truths of abstract science, be wholly independent of the will.   It were therefore to be expected that its fundamental truth would be such as *might* be denied; though only by the fool, and even by the fool from the madness of the heart alone!

The question then concerning our faith in the existence of a God, not only as the ground of the universe by his essence, but as its maker and judge by his wisdom and holy will, appeared to stand thus.   The sciential reason, whose objects are purely theoretical, remains neutral as long as its name and semblance are not usurped by the opponents of the doctrine.   But it then becomes an effective ally by exposing the false shew of demonstration, or by evincing the equal demonstrability of the contrary from premises equally logical.   The understanding meantime suggests, the analogy of experience facilitates, the belief. Nature excites and recalls it as by a perpetual revelation.   Our feelings almost necessitate it; and the law of conscience peremptorily commands it.   The arguments that at all apply to it are in its favor; and there is nothing against it but its own sublimity. It could not be intellectually more evident without becoming morally less effective; without counteracting its own end by sacrificing the life of faith to the cold mechanism of a worthless because compulsory assent.   The belief of a God and a future state (if a passive acquiescence may be flattered with the name of belief) does not indeed always beget a good heart; but a good

---

[1] [A literal translation of the German paraphrase in F. H. Jacobi (1743–1819), *Über die Lehre des Spinoza* (1785), where it occurs in a similar context.   It interprets only verses 1–3, 12, 14, and 20–8.]

heart so naturally begets the belief, that the very few exceptions must be regarded as strange anomalies from strange and unfortunate circumstances.

From these premisses I proceeded to draw the following conclusions. First, that having once fully admitted the existence of an infinite yet self-conscious Creator, we are not allowed to ground the irrationality of any other article of faith on arguments which would equally prove that to be irrational which we had allowed to be real. Secondly, that whatever is deducible from the admission of a self-comprehending and creative spirit may be legitimately used in proof of the possibility of any further mystery concerning the divine nature. 'Possibilitatem mysteriorum (*Trinitatis, etc.*) contra insultus infidelium et haereticorum a contradictionibus vindico; haud quidem veritatem, quae revelatione solâ stabiliri possit,' says Leibnitz in a letter to his Duke. He then adds the following just and important remark: 'In vain will tradition or texts of scripture be adduced in support of a doctrine, donec clava impossibilitatis et contradictionis e manibus horum Herculum extorta fuerit. For the heretic will still reply that texts, the literal sense of which is not so much above as directly against all reason, must be understood figuratively, as Herod is a fox, etc.' [1]

These principles I held, philosophically, while in respect of revealed religion I remained a zealous Unitarian. I considered the idea of the Trinity a fair scholastic inference from the being of God as a creative intelligence; and that it was therefore entitled to the rank of an esoteric doctrine of natural religion. But seeing in the same no practical or moral bearing, I confined it to the schools of philosophy. The admission of the logos as hypostasized (i.e. neither a mere attribute or a personification) in no respect removed my doubts concerning the incarnation and the redemption by the cross; which I could neither reconcile in reason with the impassiveness of the Divine Being, nor in my moral feelings with the sacred distinction between things and persons, the vicarious payment of a debt and the vicarious

---

[1] [From his letter to Duke Johann Friedrich of Hanover (1763?), which is in a mixture of German and Latin. Coleridge quotes from the letter with minor inaccuracies, translating some of the German into Latin, some into English: 'I am trying to establish not the truth, which derives from revelation, but the possibility of mysteries [the Trinity, etc.] against the attacks of unbelievers and atheists. . . . But it will all be in vain [to adduce ancient texts], just as the club cannot be seized from the hands of Hercules. For they will insist it is an impossible thing, self-contradictory and offensive to all reason, and necessarily to be understood figuratively, as with 'Herod is a fox.']

expiation of guilt.   A more thorough revolution in my philosophic principles, and a deeper insight into my own heart, were
yet wanting.   Nevertheless I cannot doubt that the difference
of my metaphysical notions from those of Unitarians in general
contributed to my final re-conversion to the whole truth in Christ;
even as according to his own confession the books of certain
Platonic philosophers (*libri quorundam Platonicorum*[1]) commenced
the rescue of St Augustine's faith from the same error aggravated
by the far darker accompaniment of the Manichaean heresy.

While my mind was thus perplexed, by a gracious providence
for which I can never be sufficiently grateful the generous and
munificent patronage of Mr Josiah and Mr Thomas Wedgwood
enabled me to finish my education in Germany.   Instead of
troubling others with my own crude notions and juvenile compositions, I was thenceforward better employed in attempting to
store my own head with the wisdom of others.   I made the best
use of my time and means; and there is therefore no period of my
life on which I can look back with such unmingled satisfaction.
After acquiring a tolerable sufficiency in the German language[2] at

[1] [*Confessions*, VII. ix: Procurasti mihi . . . quosdam Platonicorum libros
ex graeca lingua in latinum versos'—'Thou, my God, didst obtain for me
certain books of the Platonists translated from Greek into Latin.   Cf. *Notebooks*, 385.]

[2] To those who design to acquire the language of a country in the country
itself, it may be useful if I mention the incalculable advantage which I derived
from learning all the words that could possibly be so learnt with the objects
before me, and without the intermediation of the English terms.   It was a
regular part of my morning studies for the first six weeks of my residence at
Ratzeburg, to accompany the good and kind old pastor with whom I lived
from the cellar to the roof, through gardens, farm-yard, etc., and to call every,
the minutest, thing by its German name.   Advertisements, farces, jest books
and the conversation of children while I was at play with them, contributed
their share to a more home-like acquaintance with the language than I could
have acquired from works of polite literature alone, or even from polite
society.   There is a passage of hearty sound sense in Luther's German letter
on interpretation, to the translation of which I shall prefix, for the sake of
those who read the German, yet are not likely to have dipt often in the massive
folios of this heroic reformer, the simple, sinewy, idiomatic words of the
original.   'Denn man muss nicht die Buchstaben in der lateinischen
Sprache fragen, wie man soll deutsch reden; sondern man muss die Mutter
im Hause, die Kinder auf den Gassen, den gemeinen Mann auf dem Markte
darum fragen, und denselbigen auf das Maul sehen, wie sie reden, und
darnach dolmetschen.   So verstehen sie es denn, und merken, dass man
deutsch mit ihnen redet.'

TRANSLATION

For one must not ask the letters in the Latin tongue how one ought to speak
German; but one must ask the mother in the house, the children in the lanes
and alleys, the common man in the market, concerning this; yea, and look
at the moves of their mouths while they are talking, and thereafter interpret.
They understand you then, and mark that one talks German with them.
[*Sendbrief von Dolmetschen* (1530).   Cf. *Notebooks*, 385.]

Ratzeburg, which with my voyage and journey thither I have described in *The Friend*, I proceeded through Hanover to Göttingen.

Here I regularly attended the lectures on physiology in the morning, and on natural history in the evening, under Blumenbach, a name as dear to every Englishman who has studied at that university as it is venerable to men of science throughout Europe! Eichhorn's lectures on the New Testament were repeated to me from notes by a student from Ratzeburg, a young man of sound learning and indefatigable industry who is now, I believe, a professor of the oriental languages at Heidelberg. But my chief efforts were directed towards a grounded knowledge of the German language and literature. From Professor Tychsen I received as many lessons in the Gothic of Ulphilas as sufficed to make me acquainted with its grammar and the radical words of most frequent occurrence; and with the occasional assistance of the same philosophical linguist I read through Ottfried's metrical paraphrase of the gospel,[1] and the most important

---

[1] This paraphrase, written about the time of Charlemagne, is by no means deficient in occasional passages of considerable poetic merit. There is a flow and a tender enthusiasm in the following lines (at the conclusion of Chapter V) which even in the translation will not, I flatter myself, fail to interest the reader. Ottfried is describing the circumstances immediately following the birth of our Lord:

> 'She gave with joy her virgin breast;
> She hid it not, she bared the breast,
> Which suckled that divinest babe!
> Blessed, blessed were the breasts
> Which the Saviour infant kiss'd;
> And blessed, blessed was the mother
> Who wrapp'd his limbs in swaddling clothes,
> Singing placed him on her lap,
> Hung o'er him with her looks of love,
> And soothed him with a lulling motion.
> Blessed! for she shelter'd him
> From the damp and chilling air;
> Blessed, blessed! for she lay
> With such a babe in one blest bed,
> Close as babes and mothers lie!
> Blessed, blessed evermore,
> With her virgin lips she kiss'd,
> With her arms, and to her breast
> She embraced the babe divine,
> Her babe divine the virgin mother!
> There lives not on this ring of earth
> A mortal that can sing her praise.
> Mighty mother, virgin pure,
> In the darkness and the night
> For us she bore the heavenly Lord!'

Most interesting is it to consider the effect when the feelings are wrought above the natural pitch by the belief of something mysterious while all the images are purely natural. Then it is that religion and poetry strike deepest.

remains of the Theotiscan, or the transitional state of the Teutonic language from the Gothic to the old German of the Swabian period. Of this period (the polished dialect of which is analogous to that of our Chaucer, and which leaves the philosophic student in doubt whether the language has not since then lost more in sweetness and flexibility than it has gained in condensation and copiousness) I read with sedulous accuracy the Minnesinger (or singers of love, the Provençal poets of the Swabian court) and the metrical romances; and then laboured through sufficient specimens of the master singers, their degenerate successors; not however without occasional pleasure from the rude yet interesting strains of Hans Sachs, the cobbler of Nuremberg. Of this man's genius five folio volumes with double columns are extant in print, and nearly an equal number in manuscript; yet the indefatigable bard takes care to inform his readers that he never made a shoe the less, but had virtuously reared a large family by the labor of his hands.

In Pindar, Chaucer, Dante, Milton, etc. etc., we have instances of the close connection of poetic genius with the love of liberty and of genuine reformation. The moral sense at least will not be outraged, if I add to the list the name of this honest shoemaker (a trade, by the bye, remarkable for the production of philosophers and poets). His poem intitled the *Morning Star* [1] was the very first publication that appeared in praise and support of Luther; and an excellent hymn of Hans Sachs, which has been deservedly translated into almost all the European languages, was commonly sung in the Protestant churches whenever the heroic reformer visited them.

In Luther's own German writings, and eminently in his translation of the Bible, the German language commenced. I mean the language as it is at present *written*; that which is called the High German, as contra-distinguished from the Platt-Teutsch, the dialect of the flat or northern countries, and from the Ober-Teutsch, the language of the Middle and Southern Germany. The High German is indeed a *lingua communis*, not actually the native language of any province, but the choice and fragrancy of all the dialects. From this cause it is at once the most copious and the most grammatical of all the European tongues.

Within less than a century after Luther's death the German

---

[1] [Hans Sachs (1494–1576), the most celebrated of the Meistersinger, was not the author of 'Wie schön leuchtet der Morgenstern,' which was by Philipp Nicolai (1556–1608). The 'excellent hymn' is Sachs's 'Warum betrübst du dich, mein Herz.']

was inundated with pedantic barbarisms.   A few volumes of this period I read through from motives of curiosity; for it is not easy to imagine any thing more fantastic than the very appearance of their pages.   Almost every third word is a Latin word with a Germanized ending, the Latin portion being always printed in Roman letters, while in the last syllable the German character is retained.

At length, about the year 1620, Opitz [1] arose, whose genius more nearly resembled that of Dryden than any other poet who at present occurs to my recollection.   In the opinion of Lessing, the most acute of critics, and of Adelung, the first of lexicographers, Opitz and the Silesian poets, his followers, not only restored the language but still remain the models of pure diction. A stranger has no vote on such a question; but after repeated perusal of the work my feelings justified the verdict, and I seemed to have acquired from them a sort of tact for what is genuine in the style of later writers.

Of the splendid era which commenced with Gellert, Klopstock, Ramler, Lessing and their compeers I need not speak. With the opportunities which I enjoyed it would have been disgraceful not to have been familiar with their writings; and I have already said as much as the present biographical sketch requires concerning the German philosophers whose works, for the greater part, I became acquainted with at a far later period.

Soon after my return from Germany I was solicited to undertake the literary and political department in the *Morning Post*; [2] and I acceded to the proposal on the condition that the paper should thenceforwards be conducted on certain fixed and announced principles, and that I should be neither obliged or requested to deviate from them in favor of any party or any event.   In consequence, that journal became and for many years continued anti-ministerial indeed, yet with a very qualified approbation of the opposition, and with far greater earnestness and zeal both anti-Jacobin and anti-Gallican.   To this hour I cannot find reason to approve of the first war either in its commencement or its conduct.   Nor can I understand with what reason either Mr Perceval [3] (whom I am singular enough to

[1] [Martin Opitz (1597–1639).   His poems and the treatise *Buch von der deutschen Poeterey* appeared in 1624.]

[2] [Coleridge had accepted this invitation before leaving Germany in July 1799.   But he did not begin to contribute till January 1800.]

[3] [Spencer Perceval (1762–1812), who was assassinated in 1812 after three years as Prime Minister.]

regard as the best and wisest minister of this reign), or the present administration, can be said to have pursued the plans of Mr Pitt. The love of their country and perseverant hostility to French principles and French ambition are indeed honourable qualities common to them and to their predecessor. But it appears to me as clear as the evidence of facts can render any question of history that the successes of the Perceval and of the existing ministry have been owing to their having pursued measures the direct contrary to Mr Pitt's. Such for instance are the concentration of the national force to one object; the abandonment of the subsidizing policy, so far at least as neither to goad or bribe the continental courts into war till the convictions of their subjects had rendered it a war of their own seeking; and above all, in their manly and generous reliance on the good sense of the English people, and on that loyalty which is linked to the very heart of the nation by the system of credit and the interdependence of property.[1]

Be this as it may, I am persuaded that the *Morning Post* proved a far more useful ally to the Government in its most important objects, in consequence of its being generally considered as moderately anti-ministerial, than if it had been the avowed

---

[1] Lord Grenville has lately re-asserted (in the House of Lords) the imminent danger of a revolution in the earlier part of the war against France. I doubt not that his Lordship is sincere; and it must be flattering to his feelings to believe it. But where are the evidences of the danger to which a future historian can appeal? Or must he rest on an assertion? Let me be permitted to extract a passage on the subject from *The Friend*: 'I have said that to withstand the arguments of the lawless, the Anti-Jacobins proposed to suspend the law, and by the interposition of a particular statute to eclipse the blessed light of the universal sun, that spies and informers might tyrannize and escape in the ominous darkness. Oh! if these mistaken men, intoxicated and bewildered with the panic of property which they themselves were the chief agents in exciting, had ever lived in a country where there really existed a general disposition to change and rebellion! Had they ever travelled through Sicily; or through France at the first coming on of the revolution; or even alas! through too many of the provinces of a sister island; they could not but have shrunk from their own declarations concerning the state of feeling, and opinion at that time predominant throughout Great Britain. There was a time (heaven grant! that that time may have passed by) when by crossing a narrow strait they might have learnt the true symptoms of approaching danger, and have secured themselves from mistaking the meetings and idle rant of such sedition as shrunk appalled from the sight of a constable, for the dire murmuring and strange consternation which precedes the storm or earthquake of national discord. Not only in coffee-houses and public theatres, but even at the tables of the wealthy, they would have heard the advocates of existing Government defend their cause in the language and with the tone of men who are conscious that they are in a minority. But in England, when the alarm was at its highest, there was not a city, no not a town or village, in which a man suspected of holding democratic principles could move abroad without receiving some unpleasant proof of the hatred in

eulogist of Mr Pitt. (The few whose curiosity or fancy should lead them to turn over the journals of that date may find a small proof of this in the frequent charges made by the *Morning Chronicle* that such and such essays or leading paragraphs had been sent from the Treasury.) The rapid and unusual increase in the sale of the *Morning Post* is a sufficient pledge that genuine impartiality, with a respectable portion of literary talent, will secure the success of a newspaper without the aid of party or ministerial patronage. But by impartiality I mean an honest and enlightened adherence to a code of intelligible principles previously announced and faithfully referred to in support of every judgement on men and events; not indiscriminate abuse, not the indulgence of an editor's own malignant passions, and still less, if that be possible, a determination to make money by flattering the envy and cupidity, the vindictive restlessness and self-conceit of the half-witted vulgar; a determination almost fiendish, but which, I have been informed, has been boastfully avowed by one man, the most notorious of these mob-syco-phants! From the commencement of the Addington adminis-tration to the present day, whatever I have written in the *Morning Post* or (after that paper was transferred to other

---

which his supposed opinions were held by the great majority of the people; and the only instances of popular excess and indignation were in favor of the Government and the Established Church. But why need I appeal to these invidious facts? Turn over the pages of history and seek for a single instance of a revolution having been effected without the concurrence of either the nobles, or the ecclesiastics, or the monied classes, in any country in which the influences of property had ever been predominant, and where the interests of the proprietors were interlinked! Examine the revolution of the Belgic provinces under Philip 2nd; the civil wars of France in the preceding genera-tion; the history of the American revolution, or the yet more recent events in Sweden and in Spain; and it will be scarcely possible not to perceive that in England, from 1791 to the peace of Amiens, there were neither tendencies to confederacy nor actual confederacies, against which the existing laws had not provided sufficient safeguards and an ample punishment. But alas! the panic of property had been struck in the first instance for party purposes; and when it became general, its propagators caught it themselves and ended in believing their own lie; even as our bulls in Borrowdale sometimes run mad with the echo of their own bellowing. The consequences were most injurious. Our attention was concentrated on a monster which could not survive the convulsions in which it had been brought forth: even the en-lightened Burke himself too often talking and reasoning as if a perpetual and organized anarchy had been a possible thing! Thus while we were warring against French doctrines, we took little heed whether the means by which we attempted to overthrow them were not likely to aid and augment the far more formidable evil of French ambition. Like children we ran away from the yelping of a cur, and took shelter at the heels of a vicious war-horse.' [No. 10, 1809.]

proprietors) in the *Courier*, has been in defence or furtherance of the measures of government.[1]

> Things of this nature scarce survive that night
> That gives them birth; they perish in the sight;
> Cast by so far from after-life, that there
> Can scarcely aught be said, but that they were.
>
> > Cartwright's *Prol. to the Royal Slave.*[2]

Yet in these labors I employed, and in the belief of partial friends wasted, the prime and manhood of my intellect. Most assuredly they added nothing to my fortune or my reputation. The industry of the week supplied the necessities of the week. From government or the friends of government I not only never received remuneration, or ever expected it; but I was never honoured with a single acknowledgement or expression of satisfaction. Yet the retrospect is far from painful or matter of regret. I am not indeed silly enough to take as any thing more than a violent hyperbole of party debate Mr Fox's assertion that the *late* war (I trust that the epithet is not prematurely applied) was a war produced by the *Morning Post*; or I should be proud to have the words inscribed on my tomb. As little do I regard the circumstance that I was a specified object of Buonaparte's resentment during my residence in Italy in consequence of those essays in the *Morning Post* during the peace of Amiens. (Of this I was warned, directly, by Baron von Humboldt, the Prussian Plenipotentiary, who at that time was the minister of the Prussian court at Rome; and indirectly, through his secretary, by Cardinal Fesch[3] himself.) Nor do I lay any greater weight on the confirming fact that an order for my arrest was sent from Paris, from which danger I was rescued by the kindness of a noble Benedictine and the gracious connivance of that good old man, the present Pope. For the late tyrant's vindictive appetite was omnivorous, and preyed equally on a Duc d'Enghien[4] and

---

[1] [Coleridge seems to have finally ceased to write for the *Morning Post* in 1802, when it changed hands. Addington had succeeded Pitt as Prime Minister in 1801.]

[2] [William Cartwright (1611–43), *The Royall Slave* (1639), *Prologue to their Majesties, ll.* 7–10.]

[3] [An uncle of Napoleon and Archbishop of Lyons, then in Rome on a mission to Pope Pius VII. Coleridge left Rome hurriedly in the spring of 1806.]

[4] I seldom think of the murder of this illustrious Prince without recollecting the lines of Valerius Flaccus (*Argonaut.* Lib. I. 30):

> 'Super ipsius ingens
> instat fama viri virtusque haud laeta tyranno;
> ergo anteire metus juvenemque exstinguire pergit.'

the writer of a newspaper paragraph. Like a true vulture,[1] Napoleon, with an eye not less telescopic and with a taste equally coarse in his ravin, could descend from the most dazzling heights to pounce on the leveret in the brake, or even on the field-mouse amid the grass. But I do derive a gratification from the knowledge that my essays contributed to introduce the practice of placing the questions and events of the day in a moral point of view; in giving a dignity to particular measures by tracing their policy or impolicy to permanent principles, and an interest to principles by the application of them to individual measures. In Mr Burke's writings indeed the germs of almost all political truths may be found. But I dare assume to myself the merit of having first explicitly defined and analysed the nature of Jacobinism; and that in distinguishing the Jacobin from the republican, the democrat and the mere demagogue, I both rescued the word from remaining a mere term of abuse, and put on their guard many honest minds who even in their heat of zeal against Jacobinism admitted or supported principles from which the worst parts of that system may be legitimately deduced. That these are not necessary practical results of such principles we owe to that fortunate inconsequence of our nature which permits the heart to rectify the errors of the understanding. The detailed examination of the consular government and its pretended constitution and the proof given by me that it was a consummate despotism in masquerade extorted a recantation even from the *Morning Chronicle*, which had previously extolled this constitution as the perfection of a wise and regulated liberty. On every great occurrence I endeavoured to discover in past history the event that most nearly resembled it. I procured, wherever it was possible, the contemporary historians, memorialists and pamphleteers. Then fairly subtracting the points of difference from those of likeness, as the balance favored the former or the latter, I conjectured that the result would be the same or different. In the series of essays [2] entitled 'A comparison of France under Napoleon with Rome under the first Caesars,' and in those which followed 'On the probable final

---

[1] Θηρᾷ δὲ καὶ τὸν χῆνα, καὶ τὴν Δορκάδα,
Καὶ τὸν Λαγωὸν, καὶ τὸ τῶν ταύρων γένος.

PHILE de animal. propriet.

[Manuel Philes (*c.* 1275–1345), the Byzantine poet, *De animalium proprietate*, I. 12–13, *Of Eagles*: 'For he preys even upon the goose, and the antelope, and the hare, and the race of bulls.']

[2] A small selection from the numerous articles furnished by me to the *Morning Post* and *Courier*, chiefly as they regard the sources and effects of

restoration of the Bourbons,' I feel myself authorized to affirm, by the effect produced on many intelligent men, that were the dates wanting it might have been suspected that the essays had been written within the last twelve months.   The same plan I pursued at the commencement of the Spanish revolution, and with the same success, taking the war of the United Provinces with Philip 2nd as the ground work of the comparison.   I have mentioned this from no motives of vanity, nor even from motives of self-defence, which would justify a certain degree of egotism, especially if it be considered how often and grossly I have been attacked for sentiments which I had exerted my best powers to confute and expose, and how grievously these charges acted to my disadvantage while I was in Malta.   Or rather they would have done so, if my own feelings had not precluded the wish of a settled establishment in that island.   But I have mentioned it from the full persuasion that, armed with the two-fold know-ledge of history and the human mind, a man will scarcely err in his judgement concerning the sum total of any future national event, if he have been able to procure the original documents of the past together with authentic accounts of the present, and if he have a philosophic tact for what is truly important in facts, and in most instances therefore for such facts as the 'dignity of history' has excluded from the volumes of our modern compilers by the courtesy of the age entitled historians.

To have lived in vain must be a painful thought to any man, and especially so to him who has made literature his profession. I should therefore rather condole than be angry with the mind which could attribute to no worthier feelings than those of vanity of self-love the satisfaction which I acknowledge to have enjoyed from the republication of my political essays (either whole or as extracts) not only in many of our own provincial papers, but in the federal journals throughout America.   I regarded it as some proof of my not having labored altogether in vain that from the articles written by me shortly before and at the commencement of the late unhappy war with America, not only the sentiments were adopted, but in some instance the very language, in several of the Massachusetts state papers.

Jacobinism and the connection of certain systems of political economy with jacobinical despotism, will form part of *The Friend*, which I am now com-pleting and which will shortly be published, for I can scarcely say repub-lished, with the numbers arranged in Chapters according to their subjects.

Accipe principium rursus, corpusque coactum
Desere; mutata melior procede figura.

But no one of these motives, nor all conjointly, would have impelled me to a statement so uncomfortable to my own feelings, had not my character been repeatedly attacked by an unjustifiable intrusion on private life, as of a man incorrigibly idle and who, intrusted not only with ample talents but favored with unusual opportunities of improving them, had nevertheless suffered them to rust away without any efficient exertion either for his own good or that of his fellow-creatures. Even if the compositions which I have made public, and that too in a form the most certain of an extensive circulation though the least flattering to an author's self-love, had been published in books, they would have filled a respectable number of volumes, though every passage of merely temporary interest were omitted. My prose writings have been charged with a disproportionate demand on the attention; with an excess of refinement in the mode of arriving at truths; with beating the ground for that which might have been run down by the eye; with the length and laborious construction of my periods; in short with obscurity and the love of paradox. But my severest critics have not pretended to have found in my compositions triviality, or traces of a mind that shrunk from the toil of thinking. No one has charged me with tricking out in other words the thoughts of others, or with hashing up anew the *crambe jam decies coctam* [1] of English literature or philosophy. Seldom have I written that in a day, the acquisition or investigation of which had not cost me the previous labor of a month.

But are books the only channel through which the stream of intellectual usefulness can flow? Is the diffusion of truth to be estimated by publications; or publications by the truth which they diffuse or at least contain? I speak it in the excusable warmth of a mind stung by an accusation which has not only been advanced in reviews of the widest circulation, not only registered in the bulkiest works of periodical literature, but by frequency of repetition has become an admitted fact in private literary circles, and thoughtlessly repeated by too many who call themselves my friends and whose own recollections ought to have suggested a contrary testimony. Would that the criterion of a scholar's utility were the number and moral value of the truths which he has been the means of throwing into the general circulation; or the number and value of the minds whom, by his conversation or letters, he has excited into activity and supplied

---

[1] ['The mess warmed up ten times over.']

with the germs of their after-growth! A distinguished rank might not indeed, even then, be awarded to my exertions, but I should dare look forward with confidence to an honorable acquittal. I should dare appeal to the numerous and respectable audiences which at different times and in different places honored my lecture-rooms with their attendance, whether the points of view from which the subjects treated of were surveyed, whether the grounds of my reasoning were such as they had heard or read elsewhere, or have since found in previous publications. I can conscientiously declare, that the complete success of the *Remorse* on the first night of its representation [1] did not give me as great or as heart-felt a pleasure as the observation that the pit and boxes were crowded with faces familiar to me, though of individuals whose names I did not know, and of whom I knew nothing but that they had attended one or other of my courses of lectures. It is an excellent, though perhaps somewhat vulgar proverb, that there are cases where a man may be as well 'in for a pound as for a penny.' To those who from ignorance of the serious injury I have received from this rumour of having dreamt away my life to no purpose, injuries which I unwillingly remember at all, much less am disposed to record in a sketch of my literary life; or to those who from their own feelings, or the gratification they derive from thinking contemptuously of others, would like Job's comforters attribute these complaints, extorted from me by the sense of wrong, to self-conceit or presumptuous vanity, I have already furnished such ample materials that I shall gain nothing by withholding the remainder. I will not therefore hesitate to ask the consciences of those who from their long acquaintance with me and with the circumstances are best qualified to decide or be my judges, whether the restitution of the *suum cuique* would increase or detract from my literary reputation. In this exculpation I hope to be understood as speaking of myself comparatively, and in proportion to the claims which others are entitled to make on my time or my talents. By what I *have* effected am I to be judged by my fellow men; what I *could* have done is a question for my own conscience. On my own account I may perhaps have had sufficient reason to lament my deficiency in self-controul and the neglect of concentering my powers to the realization of some permanent work. But to verse rather than to prose, if to either, belongs the voice of mourning for

[1] [On 23 January 1813 at Drury Lane, where it ran successfully for twenty nights.]

Keen pangs of love, awakening as a babe
Turbulent, with an outcry in the heart,
And fears self-will'd that shunn'd the eye of hope,
And hope that scarce would know itself from fear;
Sense of past youth, and manhood come in vain,
And genius given and knowledge won in vain,
And all which I had cull'd in wood-walks wild
And all which patient toil had rear'd, and all,
Commune with thee had open'd out—but flowers
Strew'd on my corpse, and borne upon my bier
In the same coffin, for the self-same grave!

                                                                S. T. C.[1]

These will exist for the future, I trust, only in the poetic
strains which the feelings at the time called forth.   In those
only, gentle reader,

Affectus animi varios, bellumque sequacis
Perlegis invidiae; curasque revolvis inanes;
Quas humilis tenero stylus olim effudit in aevo.
Perlegis et lacrymas, et quod pharetratus acutâ
Ille puer puero fecit mihi cuspide vulnus.
Omnia paulatim consumit longior aetas
Vivendoque simul morimur, rapimurque manendo.
Ipse mihi collatus enim non ille videbor;
Frons alia est, moresque alii, nova mentis imago,
Vox aliudque sonat . . .   Jamque observatio vitae
Multa dedit:—lugere nihil, ferre omnia; jamque
Paulatim lacrymas rerum experientia tersit.[2]

[1] ['To William Wordsworth,' *ll.* 65–75.]
[2] [Petrarch, *Epistles*, Bk I (Barbato Sulmonensi), *ll.* 40–9, 54–6: 'You
read of the diverse passions of the soul, of war and its ensuing bitterness, and
in your mind you revolve those dead griefs which a humble pen once poured
forth in tender age.   You read of tears and of the wound given me as a boy by
that quivered boy with his sharp dart.   With age all things are gradually consumed, and in living we die and are snatched away while we are still here.
In that passing I shall not seem myself: another brow, other habits, a new
form of the mind, another voice sounding. . . . But now the study of life
offers much: to mourn for nothing, to bear all things.   And so, little by little,
experience wipes dry our tears.']

CHAPTER XI

An affectionate exhortation to those who in early life feel themselves disposed to become authors.

IT was a favorite remark of the late Mr Whitbread's [1] that no man does anything from a single motive. The separate motives, or rather moods of mind, which produced the preceding reflections and anecdotes have been laid open to the reader in each separate instance. But an interest in the welfare of those who at the present time may be in circumstances not dissimilar to my own at my first entrance into life has been the constant accompaniment and (as it were) the under-song of all my feelings. Whitehead,[2] exerting the prerogative of his laureateship, addressed to youthful poets a poetic *Charge* which is perhaps the best and certainly the most interesting of his works. With no other privilege than that of sympathy and sincere good wishes, I would address an affectionate exhortation to the youthful literati grounded on my own experience. It will be but short; for the beginning, middle and end converge to one charge: *never pursue literature ...s a trade.*[3] With the exception of one extraordinary man I have never known an individual, least of all an individual of genius, healthy or happy without a profession, i.e. some regular employment, which does not depend on the will of the moment, and which can be carried on so far mechanically that an average quantum only of health, spirits and intellectual exertion are requisite to its faithful discharge. Three hours of leisure, unannoyed by any alien anxiety and looked forward to with delight as a change and recreation, will suffice to realize in literature a larger product of what is truly genial than weeks of compulsion. Money and immediate

[1] [Samuel Whitbread (1758–1815), the Whig politician who organized the rebuilding of Drury Lane (1809–12).]

[2] [William Whitehead (1715–85), who was appointed laureate in 1757 after Gray's refusal of the post. His humorous poem *A Charge to the Poets* (1762) was in reply to attacks by Charles Churchill and other poets of the day.]

[3] ['O how often do I feel the wisdom of the advice which I have myself given in the Eleventh Chapter of my Literary Life' (letter to Tulk, 26 January 1818). Literature had been Coleridge's only career since January 1798 when he accepted the Wedgwoods' annuity and refused a career as a Unitarian minister.]

reputation form only an arbitrary and accidental end of literary labor. The hope of increasing them by any given exertion will often prove a stimulant to industry; but the necessity of acquiring them will in all works of genius convert the stimulant into a narcotic. Motives by excess reverse their very nature, and instead of exciting stun and stupefy the mind. For it is one contradistinction of genius from talent, that its predominant end is always comprized in the means; and this is one of the many points which establish an analogy between genius and virtue. Now though talents may exist without genius, yet as genius cannot exist, certainly not manifest itself, without talents, I would advise every scholar who feels the genial power working within him so far to make a division between the two, as that he should devote his talents to the acquirement of competence in some known trade or profession, and his genius to objects of his tranquil and unbiassed choice; while the consciousness of being actuated in both alike by the sincere desire to perform his duty will alike ennoble both. 'My dear young friend,' (I would say) 'suppose yourself established in any honourable occupation. From the manufactory or counting-house, from the law court, or from having visited your last patient, you return at evening,

> Dear tranquil time, when the sweet sense of home
> Is sweetest———— [1]

to your family, prepared for its social enjoyments, with the very countenances of your wife and children brightened, and their voice of welcome made doubly welcome by the knowledge that, as far as they are concerned, you have satisfied the demands of the day by the labor of the day. Then, when you retire into your study, in the books on your shelves you revisit so many venerable friends with whom you can converse. Your own spirit scarcely less free from personal anxieties than the great minds that in those books are still living for you! Even your writing desk with its blank paper and all its other implements will appear as a chain of flowers, capable of linking your feelings as well as thoughts to events and characters past or to come; not a chain of iron which binds you down to think of the future and the remote by recalling the claims and feelings of the peremptory present. But why should I say *retire*? The habits of active life and daily intercourse with the stir of the world will tend to give you such self-command that the presence of your family will be no

[1] ['To William Wordsworth,' *ll.* 92–3.]

interruption.   Nay, the social silence or undisturbing voices of a wife or sister will be like a restorative atmosphere or soft music which moulds a dream without becoming its object.   If facts are required to prove the possibility of combining weighty performances in literature with full and independent employment, the works of Cicero and Xenophon among the ancients; of Sir Thomas More, Bacon, Baxter, or to refer at once to later and contemporary instances, Darwin and Roscoe, are at once decisive of the question.

But all men may not dare promise themselves a sufficiency of self-controul for the imitation of those examples; though strict scrutiny should always be made, whether indolence, restlessness or a vanity impatient for immediate gratification, have not tampered with the judgement and assumed the vizard of humility for the purposes of self-delusion.   Still the church presents to every man of learning and genius a profession in which he may cherish a rational hope of being able to unite the widest schemes of literary utility with the strictest performance of professional duties.   Among the numerous blessings of Christianity, the introduction of an established church makes an especial claim on the gratitude of scholars and philosophers; in England at least, where the principles of Protestantism have conspired with the freedom of the government to double all its salutary powers by the removal of its abuses.'

That not only the maxims, but the grounds of a pure morality, the mere fragments of which

> —————— the lofty grave tragedians taught
> In chorus or iambic, teachers best
> Of moral prudence, with delight received
> In brief sententious precepts;
>
> *Paradise Regained.*[1]

and that the sublime truths of the divine unity and attributes which a Plato found most hard to learn, and deemed it still more difficult to reveal; that these should have become the almost hereditary property of childhood and poverty, of the hovel and the workshop; that even to the unlettered they sound as common-place, is a phenomenon which must withhold all but minds of the most vulgar cast from undervaluing the services even of the pulpit and the reading-desk.   Yet those who confine the efficiency of an established church to its public offices can hardly be placed in a much higher rank of intellect.   That to every

[1] [IV. 261–4.]

parish throughout the kingdom there is transplanted a germ of civilization; that in the remotest villages there is a nucleus round which the capabilities of the place may crystallize and brighten; a model sufficiently superior to excite, yet sufficiently near to encourage and facilitate imitation; this, the unobtrusive, continuous agency of a Protestant church establishment, this it is which the patriot and the philanthropist, who would fain unite the love of peace with the faith in the progressive amelioration of mankind, cannot estimate at too high a price. 'It cannot be valued with the gold of Ophir, with the precious onyx, or the sapphire. No mention shall be made of coral, or of pearls: for the price of wisdom is above rubies.' [1] The clergyman is with his parishioners and among them; he is neither in the cloistered cell, or in the wilderness, but a neighbour and a family man whose education and rank admit him to the mansion of the rich landholder, while his duties make him the frequent visitor of the farm-house and the cottage. He is, or he may become, connected with the families of his parish or its vicinity by marriage. And among the instances of the blindness, or at best the short-sightedness which it is the nature of cupidity to inflict, I know few more striking than the clamors of the farmers against church property. Whatever was not paid to the clergyman would inevitably at the next lease be paid to the landholder; while, as the case at present stands, the revenues of the church are in some sort the reversionary property of every family that may have a member educated for the church or a daughter that may marry a clergyman. Instead of being foreclosed and immovable, it is in fact the only species of landed property that is essentially moving and circulative. That there exist no inconveniences who will pretend to assert? But I have yet to expect the proof, that the inconveniences are greater in this than in any other species; or that either the farmers or the clergy would be benefited by forcing the latter to become either Trullibers [2] or salaried place-men. Nay, I do not hesitate to declare my firm persuasion that whatever reason of discontent the farmers may assign, the true cause is this: that they may cheat the parson, but cannot cheat the steward; and that they are disappointed if they should have been able to withhold only two pounds less than the legal claim, having expected to withhold five. At all events, considered relatively to the encouragement of learning and genius, the establishment presents a patronage at once so effective and unburthensome that

---

[1] [Job xxviii. 16, 18.]
[2] [Trulliber was the boorish curate in Fielding's *Joseph Andrews*, II. xiv.]

it would be impossible to afford the like or equal in any but a Christian and Protestant country.   There is scarce a department of human knowledge without some bearing on the various critical, historical, philosophical and moral truths in which the scholar must be interested as a clergyman; no one pursuit worthy of a man of genius which may not be followed without incongruity.   To give the history of the Bible as a book would be little less than to relate the origin or first excitement of all the literature and science that we now possess.   The very decorum which the profession imposes is favorable to the best purposes of genius and tends to counteract its most frequent defects. Finally, that man must be deficient in sensibility who would not find an incentive to emulation in the great and burning lights which in a long series have illustrated the church of England; who would not hear from within an echo to the voice from their sacred shrines:

Et pater Aeneas et avunculus excitat Hector.[1]

But whatever be the profession or trade chosen, the advantages are many and important compared with the state of a mere literary man, who in any degree depends on the sale of his works for the necessaries and comforts of life.   In the former a man lives in sympathy with the world in which he lives.   At least he acquires a better and quicker tact for the knowledge of that with which men in general can sympathize.   He learns to manage his genius more prudently and efficaciously.   His poweis and acquirements gain him likewise more real admiration; for they surpass the legitimate expectations of others.   He is something besides an author, and is not therefore considered merely as an author.   The hearts of men are open to him, as to one of their own class; and whether he exerts himself or not in the conversational circles of his acquaintance, his silence is not attributed to pride nor his communicativeness to vanity.   To these advantages I will venture to add a superior chance of happiness in domestic life, were it only that it is as natural for the man to be out of the circle of his household during the day, as it is meritorious for the woman to remain for the most part within it. But this subject involves points of consideration so numerous and so delicate, and would not only permit but require such ample documents from the biography of literary men, that I now merely allude to it *in transitu*.   When the same circumstance has

[1] [Aeneid, III. 343.]

occurred at very different times to very different persons, all of whom have some one thing in common, there is reason to suppose that such circumstance is not merely attributable to the persons concerned, but is in some measure occasioned by the one point in common to them all.   Instead of the vehement and almost slanderous dehortation from marriage which the *misogyne* Boccaccio[1] addresses to literary men, I would substitute the simple advice: be not *merely* a man of letters!   Let literature be an honourable augmentation to your arms, but not constitute the coat or fill the escutcheon!

To objections from conscience I can of course answer in no other way than by requesting the youthful objector (as I have already done on a former occasion) to ascertain with strict self-examination whether other influences may not be at work; whether spirits 'not of health' and with whispers 'not from heaven' may not be walking in the twilight of his consciousness. Let him catalogue his scruples and reduce them to a distinct intelligible form; let him be certain that he has read with a docile mind and favorable dispositions the best and most fundamental works on the subject; that he has had both mind and heart opened to the great and illustrious qualities of the many renowned characters who had doubted like himself, and whose researches had ended in the clear conviction that their doubts had been groundless, or at least in no proportion to the counterweight.   Happy will it be for such a man, if among his contemporaries elder than himself he should meet with one who, with similar powers and feelings as acute as his own, had entertained the same scruples; had acted upon them; and who by after-research (when the step was, alas! irretrievable, but for that very reason, his research undeniably disinterested) had discovered himself to have quarrelled with received opinions only to embrace errors, to have left the direction tracked out for him on the high road of honorable exertion only to deviate into a labyrinth where, when he had wandered till his head was giddy, his best good fortune was finally to have found his way out again, too late for prudence though not too late for conscience or for truth! Time spent in such delay is time won; for manhood in the meantime is advancing, and with it increase of knowledge, strength of judgement, and above all temperance of feelings.   And even if these should effect no change, yet the delay will at least prevent the final approval of the decision from being alloyed by the inward censure of the rashness and vanity by which it had been precipitated. It would be a sort of irreligion, and scarcely less than a libel on human nature, to believe that there is any established and reputable profession or employment in which a man may not continue to act with honesty and honor; and doubtless there is likewise none which may not at times present temptations to the contrary. But woefully will that man find himself mistaken who imagines that the profession of literature or (to speak more plainly) the trade of authorship besets its members with fewer or with less insidious temptations than the church, the law or the different branches of commerce. But I have treated sufficiently on this unpleasant subject in an early chapter of this volume.[1] I will conclude the present therefore with a short extract from Herder, whose name I might have added to the illustrious list of those who have combined the successful pursuit of the muses not only with the faithful discharge but with the highest honors and honorable emoluments of an established profession.[2] The translation the reader will find in a note below:[3] 'Am sorgfältigsten, meiden Sie die Autorschaft. Zu früh oder unmässig gebraucht, macht sie den Kopf wüste und das Herz leer, wenn sie auch sonst keine üble Folgen gäbe. Ein Mensch, der nur lieset um zu drücken, lieset wahrscheinlich übel, und wer jeden Gedanken, der ihm aufstösst, durch Feder und Presse versendet, hat sie in kurzer Zeit alle versandt, und wird bald ein blosser Diener der Druckerey, ein Buchstabensetzer werden.' Herder.

---

[1] [Ch. ii above, *Supposed irritability of men of genius.*]
[2] [Johann Gottfried Herder (1744–1803) held an appointment as court chaplain at Weimar from 1776.]
[3] [*Briefe, das Studium der Theologie betreffend* (1780–1), Letter 23. The third sentence actually reads: 'Ein Mensch, der die Bibel nur lieset, um sie zu erläutern, lieset sie wahrscheinlich übel . . .']

TRANSLATION

'With the greatest possible solicitude avoid authorship. Too early or immoderately employed, it makes the head waste and the heart empty, even were there no other worse consequences. A person who reads only to print in all probability reads amiss, and he who sends away through the pen and the press every thought the moment it occurs to him, will in a short time have sent all away, and will become a mere journeyman of the printing-office, a compositor.'

To which I may add from myself that what medical physiologists affirm of certain secretions applies equally to our thoughts; they too must be taken up again into the circulation, and be again and again re-secreted in order to ensure a healthful vigor, both to the mind and to its intellectual offspring.

CHAPTER XII

A chapter of requests and premonitions concerning the perusal or omission of the chapter that follows.

IN the perusal of philosophical works I have been greatly benefitted by a resolve which, in the antithetic form and with the allowed quaintness of an adage or maxim, I have been accustomed to word thus: 'Until you understand a writer's ignorance, presume yourself ignorant of his understanding.' This golden rule of mine does, I own, resemble those of Pythagoras in its obscurity rather than in its depth. If, however, the reader will permit me to be my own Hierocles,[1] I trust that he will find its meaning fully explained by the following instances. I have now before me a treatise of a religious fanatic, full of dreams and supernatural experiences. I see clearly the writer's grounds, and their hollowness. I have a complete insight into the causes which through the medium of his body had acted on his mind; and by application of received and ascertained laws I can satisfactorily explain to my own reason all the strange incidents which the writer records of himself. And this I can do without suspecting him of any intentional falsehood. As when in broad daylight a man tracks the steps of a traveller who had lost his way in a fog or by treacherous moonshine, even so, and with the same tranquil sense of certainty, can I follow the traces of this bewildered visionary. *I understand his ignorance.*

On the other hand, I have been re-perusing with the best energies of my mind the Timaeus of Plato. Whatever I comprehend impresses me with a reverential sense of the author's genius; but there is a considerable portion of the work to which I can attach no consistent meaning. In other treatises of the same philosopher intended for the average comprehensions of men, I have been delighted with the masterly good sense, with the perspicuity of the language and the aptness of the inductions. I recollect likewise that numerous passages in this author, which I thoroughly comprehend, were formerly no less unintelligible to me than the passages now in question. It would, I am aware, be quite fashionable to dismiss them at once as Platonic jargon.

[1] [Hierocles of Alexandria (fl. *c.* A.D. 430), a commentator of Pythagoras.]

134

But this I cannot do with satisfaction to my own mind, because I have sought in vain for causes adequate to the solution of the assumed inconsistency. I have no insight into the possibility of a man so eminently wise using words with such half-meanings to himself as must perforce pass into no-meaning to his readers. When, in addition to the motives thus suggested by my own reason, I bring into distinct remembrance the number and the series of great men who, after long and zealous study of these works, had joined in honoring the name of Plato with epithets that almost transcend humanity, I feel that a contemptuous verdict on my part might argue want of modesty, but would hardly be received by the judicious as evidence of superior penetration. Therefore, utterly baffled in all my attempts to understand the ignorance of Plato, *I conclude myself ignorant of his understanding.*

In lieu of the various requests which the anxiety of authorship addresses to the unknown reader I advance but this one: that he will either pass over the following chapter altogether or read the whole connectedly. The fairest part of the most beautiful body will appear deformed and monstrous if dissevered from its place in the organic whole. Nay, on delicate subjects, where a seemingly trifling difference of more or less may constitute a difference in kind, even a faithful display of the main and supporting ideas, if yet they are separated from the forms by which they are at once clothed and modified, may perchance present a skeleton indeed, but a skeleton to alarm and deter. Though I might find numerous precedents, I shall not desire the reader to strip his mind of all prejudices, not to keep all prior systems out of view during his examination of the present. For, in truth, such requests appear to me not much unlike the advice given to hypochondriacal patients in Dr Buchan's domestic medicine; *videlicet,* to preserve themselves uniformly tranquil and in good spirits. Till I had discovered the art of destroying the memory *a parte post,* without injury to its future operations, and without detriment to the judgement, I should suppress the request as premature; and, therefore, however much I may wish to be read with an unprejudiced mind, I do not presume to state it as a necessary condition.

The extent of my daring is to suggest one criterion by which it may be rationally conjectured beforehand whether or no a reader would lose his time, and perhaps his temper, in the perusal of this or any other treatise constructed on similar principles. But it would be cruelly misinterpreted as implying the least disrespect either for the moral or intellectual qualities of the individuals thereby precluded. The criterion is this: if a man receives as fundamental facts, and therefore of course indemonstrable and incapable of further analysis, the general notions of matter, spirit, soul, body, action, passiveness, time, space, cause and effect, consciousness, perception, memory and habit; if he feels his mind completely at rest concerning all these, and is satisfied if only he can analyse all other notions into some one or more of these supposed elements with plausible subordination and apt arrangement; to such a mind I would as courteously as possible convey the hint that for him the chapter was not written.

Vir bonus es, doctus, prudens! ast haud tibi spiro.

For these terms do in truth include all the difficulties which the human mind can propose for solution. Taking them therefore in mass, and unexamined, it requires only a decent apprenticeship in logic to draw forth their contents in all forms and colours, as the professors of legerdemain at our village fairs pull out ribbon after ribbon from their mouths. And not more difficult is it to reduce them back again to their different genera. But though this analysis is highly useful in rendering our knowledge more distinct, it does not really add to it. It does not increase, though it gives us a greater mastery over, the wealth which we before possessed. For forensic purposes, for all the established professions of society, this is sufficient. But for philosophy in its highest sense, as the science of ultimate truths and therefore *scientia scientiarum*, this mere analysis of terms is preparative only, though as a preparative discipline indispensable.

Still less dare a favorable perusal be anticipated from the proselytes of that compendious philosophy which, talking of mind but thinking of brick and mortar, or other images equally abstracted from body, contrives a theory of spirit by nicknaming matter, and in a few hours can qualify its dullest disciples to explain the *omne scibile* by reducing all things to impressions, ideas and sensations.

But it is time to tell the truth; though it requires some courage to avow it in an age and country in which disquisitions on all subjects not privileged to adopt technical terms or scientific symbols must be addressed to the public. I say then that it is neither possible or necessary for all men, or for many, to be philosophers. There is a philosophic (and inasmuch as it is actualized by an effort of freedom, an artificial) consciousness, which lies beneath or (as it were) behind the spontaneous consciousness natural to all reflecting beings. As the elder Romans distinguished their northern provinces into Cis-Alpine and Trans-Alpine, so may we divide all the objects of human knowledge into those on this side, and those on the other side of the spontaneous consciousness: citra et trans conscientiam communem. The latter is exclusively the domain of pure philosophy, which is therefore properly entitled transcendental, in order to discriminate it at once both from mere reflection and *re*-presentation on the one hand, and on the other from those flights of lawless speculation which, abandoned by all distinct consciousness because transgressing the bounds and purposes of our intellectual faculties, are justly condemned as transcendent.[1] The first range of hills that encircles the scanty vale of human life is the horizon for the majority of its inhabitants. On its ridges the common sun is born and departs. From them the stars rise, and touching them they vanish. By the many even this range, the natural limit and bulwark of the vale, is but imperfectly known. Its higher ascents are too often hidden by mists and clouds from uncultivated swamps which

[1] This distinction between transcendental and transcendent is observed by our elder divines and philosophers, whenever they express themselves scholastically. Dr Johnson indeed has confounded the two words; but his own authorities do not bear him out. Of this celebrated dictionary I will venture to remark once for all that I should suspect the man of a morose disposition who should speak of it without respect and gratitude as a most instructive and entertaining book, and hitherto, unfortunately, an indispensable book; but I confess, that I should be surprized at hearing from a philosophic and thorough scholar any but very qualified praises of it as a *dictionary*. I am not now alluding to the number of genuine words omitted; for this is (and perhaps to a greater extent) true, as Mr Wakefield has noticed, of our best Greek Lexicons, and this too after the successive labours of so many giants in learning. I refer at present both to omissions and commissions of a more important nature. What these are, *me saltem judice*, will be stated at full in *The Friend*, re-published and completed.

I had never heard of the correspondence between Wakefield and Fox till I saw the account of it this morning (16th September 1815) in the *Monthly Review*. I was not a little gratified at finding that Mr Wakefield had proposed to himself nearly the same plan for a Greek and English Dictionary which I had formed, and began to execute, now ten years ago. But far, far more grieved am I, that he did not live to compleat it. I cannot but think it a subject of most serious regret that the same heavy expenditure which is now employing in the republication of Stephanus augmented, had not been applied to a new Lexicon on a more philosophical plan, with the English, German and French synonimes as well as the Latin. In almost every instance the precise individual meaning might be given in an English or German word; whereas in Latin we must too often be contented with a mere general and inclusive term. How indeed can it be otherwise, when we attempt to render the most copious language of the world, the most admirable for the fineness of its distinctions, into one of the poorest and most vague languages? Especially, when we reflect on the comparative number of the works, still extant,

few have courage or curiosity to penetrate. To the multitude below these vapors appear, now as the dark haunts of terrific agents on which none may intrude with impunity; and now all a-glow with colors not their own, they are gazed at as the splendid palaces of happiness and power. But in all ages there have been a few who, measuring and sounding the rivers of the vale at the feet of their furthest inaccessible falls, have learnt that the sources must be far higher and far inward; a few who even in the level streams have detected elements which neither the vale itself nor the surrounding mountains contained or could supply. How and whence to these thoughts, these strong probabilities, the ascertaining vision, the intuitive knowledge, may finally supervene, can be learnt only by the fact. I might oppose to the question the words with which Plotinus [1] supposes nature to answer a similar difficulty: 'Should any one interrogate her, how she works, if graciously she vouchsafe to listen and speak, she will reply, it behoves thee not to disquiet me with interrogatories, but to understand in silence, even as I am silent, and work without words.'

Likewise in the fifth book of the fifth Ennead, speaking of the

---

written while the Greek and Latin were living languages. Were I asked what I deemed the greatest and most unmixed benefit which a wealthy individual or an association of wealthy individuals could bestow on their country and on mankind, I should not hesitate to answer, 'a philosophical English dictionary; with the Greek, Latin, German, French, Spanish and Italian synonimes, and with correspondent indexes.' That the learned languages might thereby be acquired, better, in half the time, is but a part, and not the most important part, of the advantages which would accrue from such a work. O! if it should be permitted by providence that without detriment to freedom and independence our government might be enabled to become more than a committee for war and revenue! There was a time, when every thing was to be done by government. Have we not flown off to the contrary extreme?

[1] Ennead, III. 1. 8. c. 3. The force of the Greek συνιέναι is imperfectly expressed by 'understand'; our own idiomatic phrase 'to go along with me' comes nearest to it. The passage that follows, full of profound sense, appears to me evidently corrupt; and in fact no writer more wants, better deserves, or is less likely to obtain, a new and more correct edition.—τί οὖν συνιέναι; ὅτι τὸ γενόμενον ἐστι θέαμα ἐμὸν, σιώπησις (mallem, θέαμα, ἐμοῦ σιωπωσῆς,) καὶ φύσει γενόμενον θεώρημα καὶ μοι γενομένη ἐκ θεωρίας τῆς ὡδί, τὴν φύσιν ἔχειν φιλαθεάμονα ὑπάρκει. (mallem, καὶ μοι ἡ γενομένη ἐκ θεωρίας αὐτῆς ὡδὶς.) 'What then are we to understand? That whatever is produced is an intuition, I silent; and that which is thus generated, is by its nature a theorem, or form of contemplation; and the birth which results to me from this contemplation attains to have a contemplative nature.' So Synesius; 'Ωδὶς ἱερά, Ἄρρητα γονά'. The after comparison of the process of the *natura naturans* with that of the geometrician is drawn from the very heart of philosophy.

highest and intuitive knowledge as distinguished from the discursive, or in the language of Wordsworth,

The vision and the faculty divine; [1]

he says: 'it is not lawful to inquire from whence it sprang, as if he were a thing subject to place and motion; for it neither approached hither, nor again departs from hence to some other place; but it either appears to us or it does not appear. So that we ought not to pursue it with a view of detecting its secret sources, but to watch in quiet till it suddenly shines upon us; preparing ourselves for the blessed spectacle as the eye waits patiently for the rising sun.' They and they only can acquire the philosophic imagination, the sacred power of self-intuition, who within themselves can interpret and understand the symbol that the wings of the air-sylph are forming within the skin of the caterpillar; these only who feel in their own spirits the same instinct which impels the chrysalis of the horned fly to leave room in its involucrum for antennae yet to come. They know and feel that the potential works in them, even as the actual works on them! In short, all the organs of sense are framed for a corresponding world of sense; and we have it. All the organs of spirit are framed for a correspondent world of spirit: tho' the latter organs are not developed in all alike. But they exist in all, and their first appearance discloses itself in the moral being. How else could it be that even worldlings not wholly debased will contemplate the man of simple and disinterested goodness with contradictory feelings of pity and respect? 'Poor man! he is not made for this world.' Oh! herein they utter a prophecy of universal fulfilment; for man must either rise or sink.

It is the essential mark of the true philosopher to rest satisfied with no imperfect light, as long as the impossibility of attaining a fuller knowledge has not been demonstrated. That the common consciousness itself will furnish proofs by its own direction, that it is connected with master-currents below the surface, I shall merely assume as a postulate *pro tempore*. This having been granted, though but in expectation of the argument, I can safely deduce from it the equal truth of my former assertion that philosophy cannot be intelligible to all, even of the most learned and cultivated classes. A system, the first principle of which it is to render the mind intuitive of the spiritual in man (i.e. of that which lies on the other side of our natural consciousness), must needs have a great obscurity for those who have

[1] [Wordsworth, *Excursion*, I. 79.]

never disciplined and strengthened this ulterior consciousness. It must in truth be a land of darkness, a perfect Anti-Goshen, for men to whom the noblest treasures of their own being are reported only through the imperfect translation of lifeless and sightless notions.   Perhaps, in great part, through words which are but the shadows of notions, even as the notional understanding itself is but the shadowy abstraction of living and actual truth.   On the immediate which dwells in every man, and on the original intuition or absolute affirmation of it (which is likewise in every man, but does not in every man rise into consciousness), all the certainty of our knowledge depends; and this becomes intelligible to no man by the ministry of mere words from without.   The medium by which spirits understand each other is not the surrounding air, but the freedom which they possess in common, as the common ethereal element of their being, the tremulous reciprocations of which propagate themselves even to the inmost of the soul.   Where the spirit of a man is not filled with the consciousness of freedom (were it only from its restlessness, as of one still struggling in bondage) all spiritual intercourse is interrupted, not only with others but even with himself.   No wonder then that he remains incomprehensible to himself as well as to others.   No wonder that in the fearful desert of his consciousness he wearies himself out with empty words to which no friendly echo answers, either from his own heart or the heart of a fellow-being, or bewilders himself in the pursuit of notional phantoms, the mere refractions from unseen and distant truths through the distorting medium of his own unenlivened and stagnant understanding!   To remain unintelligible to such a mind, exclaims Schelling on a like occasion, is honor and a good name before God and man.

The history of philosophy (the same writer observes) contains instances of systems which for successive generations have remained enigmatic.   Such he deems the system of Leibnitz, whom another writer (rashly, I think, and invidiously) extols as the only philosopher who was himself deeply convinced of his own doctrines.   As hitherto interpreted, however, they have not produced the effect which Leibnitz himself, in a most instructive passage,[1] describes as the criterion of a true philosophy;

[1] [*Trois lettres à Mr Remond de Montmort* (1714), iii: 'Si j'en avois le loisir, je comparerois mes dogmes avec ceux des Anciens et d'autres habiles hommes.   La vérité est plus répandue qu'on ne pense; mais elle est très souvent fardée et très souvent aussi enveloppée, et même affoiblie, mutilée, corrompue par des additions qui la gâtent ou la rendent moins utile.']

namely, that it would at once explain and collect the fragments of truth scattered through systems apparently the most incongruous. The truth, says he, is diffused more widely than is commonly believed; but it is often painted, yet oftener masked, and is sometimes mutilated, and sometimes, alas! in close alliance with mischievous errors. The deeper, however, we penetrate into the ground of things, the more truth we discover in the doctrines of the greater number of the philosophical sects. The want of substantial reality in the objects of the senses, according to the sceptics; the harmonies or numbers, the prototypes and ideas, to which the Pythagoreans and Platonists reduced all things; the *one* and *all* of Parmenides and Plotinus, without Spinozism; [1] the necessary connection of things, according to the Stoics, reconcileable with the spontaneity of the other schools; the vital-philosophy of the Cabalists and Hermetists, who assumed the universality of sensation; the substantial

---

[1] This is happily effected in three lines by Synesius in his Fourth Hymn:

$$'Εν καὶ Πάντα—(taken by itself) is Spinozism.$$
$$'Εν δ' 'Απάντων—a mere anima mundi.$$
$$'Εν τε πρὸ πάντων—is mechanical Theism.$$

But unite all three, and the result is the theism of Saint Paul and Christianity.

Synesius was censured for his doctrine of the pre-existence of the soul; but never, that I can find, arraigned or deemed heretical for his pantheism, tho' neither Giordano Bruno or Jacob Behmen ever avowed it more broadly.

$$Μύστας δὲ Νόος,$$
$$Τά τε καὶ τὰ λέγει$$
$$Βυθὸν ἄρρητον$$
$$'Αμφιχορεύων.$$
$$Σὺ τὸ τίκτον ἔφυς$$
$$Σὺ τὸ τικτόμενον·$$
$$Σὺ τὸ φωτίξαν,$$
$$Σὺ τὸ λαμπόμενον·$$
$$Σὺ τὸ φαινόμενον,$$
$$Σὺ τό κρυπτόμενον$$
$$'Ιδίαις αὐγαῖς,$$
$$"Εν καὶ πάντα,$$
$$"Εν καθ' έαυτό,$$
$$Καὶ διὰ πάντων.$$

Pantheism is therefore not necessarily irreligious or heretical; tho' it may be taught atheistically. Thus Spinoza would agree with Synesius in calling God Φύσις ἐν Νοεροῖς, the *Nature* in Intelligences; but he could not subscribe to the preceding Νοῦς καὶ Νοερὸς, i.e. Himself Intelligence and intelligent.

In this biographical sketch of my literary life I may be excused if I mention here that I had translated the eight Hymns of Synesius from the Greek into English anacreontics before my 15th year. [Synesius (*c.* A.D. 373–*c.* A.D. 414), a neoplatonist poet. The first quotation is in fact from Hymn III, *ll.* 180–2, and the second ibid. *ll.* 187–99.]

forms and entelechies of Aristotle and the schoolmen, together
with the mechanical solution of all particular phenomena
according to Democritus and the recent philosophers—all these
we shall find united in one perspective central point, which
shows regularity and a coincidence of all the parts in the very
object which from every other point of view must appear confused and distorted. The spirit of sectarianism has been
hitherto our fault and the cause of our failures. We have
imprisoned our own conceptions by the lines which we have
drawn, in order to exclude the conceptions of others. 'J'ai
trouvé que la plupart des sectes ont raison dans une bonne partie
de ce qu'elles avancent, mais non pas tant en ce qu'elles nient.' [1]

A system which aims to deduce the memory with all the other
functions of intelligence must of course place its first position
from beyond the memory and anterior to it, otherwise the
principle of solution would be itself a part of the problem to be
solved. Such a position, therefore, must in the first instance be
demanded, and the first question will be, by what right is it
demanded? On this account I think it expedient to make some
preliminary remarks on the introduction of postulates in philosophy. The word postulate is borrowed from the science of
mathematics.[2] In geometry the primary construction is not
demonstrated, but postulated. This first and most simple
construction in space is the point in motion, or the line. Whether
the point is moved in one and the same direction, or whether its
direction is continually changed, remains as yet undetermined.
But if the direction of the point have been determined, it is either
by a point without it, and then there arises the strait line which
incloses no space; or the direction of the point is not determined
by a point without it, and then it must flow back again on itself;
that is, there arises a cyclical line which does inclose a space.
If the straight line be assumed as the positive, the cyclical is then
the negation of the straight. It is a line which at no point
strikes out into the straight, but changes its direction continu-
ously. But if the primary line be conceived as undetermined,
and the strait line as determined throughout, then the cyclical is
the third compounded of both. It is at once undetermined and
determined; undetermined through any point without, and determined through itself. Geometry therefore supplies philosophy

---

[1] [Leibniz, *Trois lettres*, i: 'I have found that most sects are right in a good
part of what they assert, but not in what they deny.']
[2] See Schell., *Abhandl. zur Erläuter. des Id. der Wissenschaftslehre.* [Much
of the three ensuing paragraphs is based upon Schelling.]

with the example of a primary intuition, from which every science that lays claim to evidence must take its commencement. The mathematician does not begin with a demonstrable proposition but with an intuition, a practical idea.

But here an important distinction presents itself. Philosophy is employed on objects of the inner sense and cannot, like geometry, appropriate to every construction a correspondent outward intuition. Nevertheless philosophy, if it is to arrive at evidence, must proceed from the most original construction; and the question then is, what is the most original construction or first productive act for the inner sense? The answer to this question depends on the direction which is given to the inner sense. But in philosophy the inner sense cannot have its direction determined by any outward object. To the original construction of the line I can be compelled by a line drawn before me on the slate or on sand. The stroke thus drawn is indeed not the line itself, but only the image or picture of the line. It is not from it that we first learn to know the line; but, on the contrary, we bring this stroke to the original line generated by the act of the imagination, otherwise we could not define it as without breadth or thickness. Still however this stroke is the sensuous image of the original or ideal line, and an efficient mean to excite every imagination to the intuition of it.

It is demanded then whether there be found any means in philosophy to determine the direction of the inner sense, as in mathematics it is determinable by its specific image or outward picture. Now the inner sense has its direction determined for the greater part only by an act of freedom. One man's consciousness extends only to the pleasant or unpleasant sensations caused in him by external impressions; another enlarges his inner sense to a consciousness of forms and quantity; a third, in addition to the image, is conscious of the conception or notion of the thing; a fourth attains to a notion of his notions—he reflects on his own reflections; and thus we may say without impropriety that the one possesses more or less inner sense than the other. This more or less betrays already that philosophy in its first principles must have a practical or moral as well as a theoretical or speculative side. This difference in degree does not exist in mathematics. Socrates in Plato shows that an ignorant slave may be brought to understand and of himself to solve the most difficult geometrical problem. Socrates drew the figures for the slave in the sand. The disciples of the critical philosophy could likewise (as was indeed actually done by La Forge and some other

followers of Des Cartes) represent the origin of our representations in copper-plates; but no one has yet attempted it, and it
would be utterly useless.   To an Esquimaux or New Zealander
our most popular philosophy would be wholly unintelligible.
The sense, the inward organ for it, is not yet born in him.   So is
there many a one among us, yes, and some who think themselves
philosophers too, to whom the philosophic organ is entirely
wanting.   To such a man philosophy is a mere play of words and
notions, like a theory of music to the deaf, or like the geometry of
light to the blind.   The connection of the parts and their logical
dependencies may be seen and remembered; but the whole is
groundless and hollow, unsustained by living contact, unaccompanied with any realizing intuition which exists by and in the
act that affirms its existence, which is known because it is, and is
because it is known.   The words of Plotinus, in the assumed
person of Nature, hold true of the philosophic energy: $Τὸ$
$θεωροῦν$ $μοῦ$ $θεώρημα$ $ποιεῖ$, $ὥσπερ$ $οἱ$ $Γεωμέτραι$ $θεωροῦντες$
$γραφοῦσιν·$ $ἀλλ'$ $ἐμοῦ$ $μὴ$ $γραφούσης$, $θεωρούσης$ $δὲ$, $ὑφίστανται$ $αἱ$
$τῶν$ $σωμάτων$ $γραμμαί$.[1]   With me the act of contemplation
makes the thing contemplated, as the geometricians contemplating describe lines correspondent; but I not describing lines,
but simply contemplating, the representative forms of things
rise up into existence.
    The postulate of philosophy, and at the same time the test of
philosophic capacity, is no other than the heaven-descended *Know
thyself*! (E caelo descendit, $Γνῶθι$ $σεαυτόν$[2]).   And this at once
practically and speculatively.   For as philosophy is neither a
science of the reason or understanding only, nor merely a science
of morals, but the science of being altogether, its primary ground
can be neither merely speculative or merely practical, but both in
one.   All knowledge rests on the coincidence of an object with a
subject.[3]   (My readers have been warned in a former chapter that
for their convenience as well as the writer's the term *subject* is
used by me in its scholastic sense, as equivalent to mind or sentient being, and as the necessary correlative of object, or *quicquid
objicitur menti*.)   For we can *know* that only which is true; and
the truth is universally placed in the coincidence of the thought
with the thing, of the representation with the object represented.

---

[1] [*Ennead*, III. 8. 3: 'My contemplation creates what is contemplated, as
the geometricians draw figures as they contemplate.   But it is not in drawing
figures but in contemplating that the lines of the forms are settled.']
[2] [Juvenal, xi. 27: 'It came from heaven, Know yourself.']
[3] [The following discussion, apart from the mention of God, is based upon
Schelling.   Cf. Notebooks, 4265 and n.]

Now the sum of all that is merely objective we will henceforth call *nature*, confining the term to its passive and material sense, as comprising all the phaenomena by which its existence is made known to us. On the other hand, the sum of all that is subjective we may comprehend in the name of the *self* or *intelligence*. Both conceptions are in necessary antithesis. Intelligence is conceived of as exclusively representative, nature as exclusively represented; the one as conscious, the other as without consciousness. Now in all acts of positive knowledge there is required a reciprocal concurrence of both, namely of the conscious being and of that which is in itself unconscious. Our problem is to explain this concurrence, its possibility and its necessity.

During the act of knowledge itself, the objective and subjective are so instantly united that we cannot determine to which of the two the priority belongs. There is here no first and no second; both are coinstantaneous and one. While I am attempting to explain this intimate coalition, I must suppose it dissolved. I must necessarily set out from the one, to which therefore I give hypothetical antecedence, in order to arrive at the other. But as there are but two factors or elements in the problem, subject and object, and as it is left indeterminate from which of them I should commence, there are two cases equally possible.

1. EITHER THE OBJECTIVE IS TAKEN AS THE FIRST, AND THEN WE HAVE TO ACCOUNT FOR THE SUPERVENTION OF THE SUBJECTIVE WHICH COALESCES WITH IT.

The notion of the subjective is not contained in the notion of the objective. On the contrary, they mutually exclude each other. The subjective therefore must supervene to the objective. The conception of nature does not apparently involve the co-presence of the intelligence making an ideal duplicate of it, i.e. representing it. This desk for instance would (according to our natural notions) be, though there should exist no sentient being to look at it. This then is the problem of natural philosophy. It assumes the objective or unconscious nature as the first, and has therefore to explain how intelligence can supervene to it, or how itself can grow into intelligence. If it should appear that all enlightened naturalists, without having distinctly proposed the problem to themselves, have yet constantly moved in the line of its solution, it must afford a strong presumption that the problem itself is founded in nature. For if all knowledge has as it were two poles reciprocally required and pre-supposed, all sciences must proceed from the one or the other, and must tend towards the opposite as far as the equatorial point in which both are reconciled and become identical. The necessary tendence therefore of all natural philosophy is from nature to intelligence; and this, and no other, is the true ground and occasion of the instinctive striving to introduce theory into our views of natural phaenomena. The highest perfection of natural philosophy would consist in the perfect spiritualization of all the laws of nature into laws of intuition and intellect. The phaenomena (the material) must wholly disappear, and the laws alone (the formal) must remain. Thence it comes that in nature itself the more the principle of law breaks forth, the more does the husk drop off, the phaenomena themselves become more spiritual and at length cease altogether in our consciousness. The optical phaenomena are but a geometry, the lines of which are drawn by light, and the materiality of this light itself has already become matter of doubt. In the appearances of magnetism all trace of matter is lost, and of the phaenomena of gravitation, which not a few among the most illustrious Newtonians have declared no otherwise comprehensible than as an immediate spiritual influence, there remains nothing but its law, the execution of which on a vast scale is the mechanism of the heavenly motions. The theory of natural philosophy would then be completed when all nature was demonstrated to be identical in essence with that which in its highest known power exists in man as intelligence and self-consciousness; when the heavens and the earth shall declare not only the power of their maker but the glory and the presence of their God, even as he appeared to the great prophet during the vision of the mount in the skirts of his divinity.

This may suffice to show that even natural science, which commences with the material phaenomenon as the reality and substance of things existing, does yet, by the necessity of theorizing unconsciously, and as it were instinctively, end in nature as an intelligence; and by this tendency the science of nature becomes finally natural philosophy, the one of the two poles of fundamental science.

2. OR THE SUBJECTIVE IS TAKEN AS THE FIRST, AND THE PROBLEM THEN IS, HOW THERE SUPERVENES TO IT A COINCIDENT OBJECTIVE.

In the pursuit of these sciences, our success in each depends on an austere and faithful adherence to its own principles with a careful separation and exclusion of those which appertain to the opposite science. As the natural philosopher, who directs his views to the objective, avoids above all things the intermixture of the subjective in his knowledge, as for instance arbitrary suppositions or rather suffictions, occult qualities, spiritual agents and the substitution of final for efficient causes; so on the other hand the transcendental or intelligential philosopher is equally anxious to preclude all interpolation of the objective into the subjective principles of his science, as for instance the assumption of impresses or configurations in the brain, correspondent to miniature pictures on the retina painted by rays of light from supposed originals which are not the immediate and real objects of vision but deductions from it for the purposes of explanation. This purification of the mind is effected by an absolute and scientific scepticism to which the mind voluntarily determines itself for the specific purpose of future certainty. Des Cartes who (in his meditations) himself first, at least of the moderns, gave a beautiful example of this voluntary doubt, this self-determined indetermination, happily expresses its utter difference from the scepticism of vanity or irreligion: 'Nec tamen in eo scepticos imitabar, qui dubitant tantum ut dubitent, et praeter incertitudinem ipsam nihil quaerunt. Nam contra totus in eo eram ut aliquid certi reperirem'.[1] Nor is it less distinct in its motives and final aim than in its proper objects, which are not as in ordinary scepticism the prejudices of education and circumstance, but those original and innate prejudices which nature herself has planted in all men, and which to all but the philosopher are the first principles of knowledge and the final test of truth.

Now these essential prejudices are all reducible to the one fundamental presumption, that there exist things without us. As this on the one hand originates neither in grounds or arguments, and yet on the other hand remains proof against all attempts to remove it by grounds or arguments (*naturam furca expelles tamen usque recurret* [2]); on the one hand lays claim to immediate certainty as a position at once indemonstrable and irresistible, and yet on the other hand, inasmuch as it refers to something essentially different from ourselves, nay even in opposition to ourselves, leaves it inconceivable how it could possibly become a part of our immediate consciousness (in other

---

[1] Des Cartes, *De methodo*. [III: 'Not that I imitated the sceptics, who doubt as much as they may and who seek nothing beyond uncertainty itself. On the contrary, my whole object was to discover certainty.']

[2] [Horace, *Epistles*, I. x. 24: 'You may drive nature out with a pitchfork but she will always return.']

words, how that which *ex hypothesi* is and continues to be extrinsic and alien to our being should become a modification of our being); the philosopher therefore compels himself to treat this faith as nothing more than a prejudice, innate indeed and connatural, but still a prejudice.

The other position, which not only claims but necessitates the admission of its immediate certainty, equally for the scientific reason of the philosopher as for the common sense of mankind at large, namely *I Am*, cannot so properly be entitled a prejudice. It is groundless indeed; but then in the very idea it precludes all ground, and separated from the immediate consciousness loses its whole sense and import. It is groundless; but only because it is itself the ground of all other certainty. Now the apparent contradiction that the former position, namely the existence of things without us, which from its nature cannot be immediately certain, should be received as blindly and as independently of all grounds as the existence of our own being, the transcendental philosopher can solve only by the supposition that the former is unconsciously involved in the latter; that it is not only coherent but identical, and one and the same thing with our own immediate self-consciousness. To demonstrate this identity is the office and object of his philosophy.

If it be said that this is idealism, let it be remembered that it is only so far idealism as it is at the same time, and on that very account, the truest and most binding realism. For wherein does the realism of mankind properly consist? In the assertion that there exists a something without them, what, or how, or where they know not, which occasions the objects of their perception? Oh no! This is neither connatural or universal. It is what a few have taught and learnt in the schools, and which the many repeat without asking themselves concerning their own meaning. The realism common to all mankind is far elder and lies infinitely deeper than this hypothetical explanation of the origin of our perceptions, an explanation skimmed from the mere surface of mechanical philosophy. It is the table itself which the man of common sense believes himself to see, not the phantom of a table from which he may argumentatively deduce the reality of a table which he does not see. If to destroy the reality of all that we actually behold be idealism, what can be more egregiously so than the system of modern metaphysics which banishes us to a land of shadows, surrounds us with apparitions and distinguishes truth from illusion only by the majority of those who dream the same dream? 'I asserted that the world was mad,' exclaimed poor Lee,[1] 'and the world said that I was mad, and confound them, they outvoted me.'

It is to the true and original realism that I would direct the attention. This believes and requires neither more nor less than that the object which it beholds or presents to itself is the real and very object. In this sense, however much we may strive against it, we are all collectively born idealists, and therefore and only therefore are we at the same time realists. But of this the philosophers of the schools know nothing, or despise the faith as the prejudice of the ignorant vulgar, because they live and move in a crowd of phrases and notions from which human nature has long ago vanished. Oh, ye that reverence yourselves, and walk humbly with the divinity in your own hearts, ye are worthy of a better philosophy! Let the dead bury the dead, but do you preserve your human nature, the depth of which was never yet fathomed by a philosophy made up of notions and mere logical entities.

In the third treatise of my *Logosophia*, announced at the end of this volume,[2] I shall give (*deo volente*) the demonstrations and constructions of the Dynamic Philosophy scientifically arranged. It is, according to my conviction, no other than the system of Pythagoras and of Plato revived and purified from impure mixtures. *Doctrina per tot manus tradita tandem in vappam desiit!* [3] The science of arithmetic furnishes instances that a rule may be useful in practical application, and for the particular purpose may be sufficiently authenticated by the result, before it has itself been fully demonstrated. It is enough, if only it be rendered intelligible. This will, I trust, have been effected in the following Theses for those of my readers who are willing to accompany me through the following chapter, in which the results will be applied to the deduction of the imagination, and with it the principles of production and of genial criticism in the fine arts.

THESIS I

Truth is correlative to being. Knowledge without a correspondent reality is no knowledge; if we know, there must be

---

[1] [Nathaniel Lee (1649?-92), the Restoration dramatist, who was confined to Bedlam for five years in 1684. Coleridge may be thinking of Lee's portrayal of insanity in his tragedy *Caesar Borgia* (1680), v. i:

'He reasons well; his eyes their wildness lose,
And vows the keepers his wrong'd sense abuse.']

[2] [This announcement was never made.]

[3] ['A doctrine passed down through so many hands ends as flat wine.' Quotation untraced.]

somewhat known by us.   To know is in its very essence a verb active.

Thesis II

All truth is either mediate, that is, derived from some other truth or truths; or immediate and original.   The latter is absolute, and its formula A. A.; the former is of dependent or conditional certainty, and represented in the formula B. A.   The certainty which inheres in A. is attributable to B.

Scholium.   A chain without a staple from which all the links derived their stability, or a series without a first, has been not inaptly allegorized as a string of blind men each holding the skirt of the man before him, reaching far out of sight but all moving without the least deviation in one strait line.   It would be naturally taken for granted that there was a guide at the head of the file: what if it were answered, No! Sir, the men are without number, and infinite blindness supplies the place of sight?

Equally inconceivable is a cycle of equal truths without a common and central principle, which prescribes to each its proper sphere in the system of science.   That the absurdity does not so immediately strike us, that it does not seem equally unimaginable, is owing to a surreptitious act of the imagination which, instinctively and without our noticing the same, not only fills at the intervening spaces and contemplates the cycle (of B. C. D. E. F., etc.) as a continuous circle (A.) giving to all collectively the unity of their common orbit; but likewise supplies by a sort of *subintelligitur* the one central power which renders the movement harmonious and cyclical.

Thesis III

We are to seek therefore for some absolute truth capable of communicating to other positions a certainty which it has not itself borrowed; a truth self-grounded, unconditional and known by its own light.   In short, we have to find a somewhat which *is*, simply because it *is*.   In order to be such it must be one which is its own predicate, so far at least that all other nominal predicates must be modes and repetitions of itself.   Its existence too must be such as to preclude the possibility of requiring a cause or antecedent without an absurdity.

Thesis IV

That there can be but one such principle may be proved *a priori*; for were there two or more, each must refer to some other by which its equality is affirmed; consequently neither would be self-established, as the hypothesis demands. And *a posteriori*, it will be proved by the principle itself when it is discovered as involving universal antecedents in its very conception.

SCHOLIUM. If we affirm of a board that it is blue, the predicate (blue) is accidental, and not implied in the subject, board. If we affirm of a circle that it is equi-radial, the predicate indeed is implied in the definition of the subject; but the existence of the subject itself is contingent, and supposes both a cause and a percipient. The same reasoning will apply to the indefinite number of supposed indemonstrable truths exempted from the prophane approach of philosophic investigation by the amiable Beattie and other less eloquent and not more profound inaugurators of common sense on the throne of philosophy; a fruitless attempt, were it only that it is the two-fold function of philosophy to reconcile reason with common sense and to elevate common sense into reason.

THESIS V

Such a principle cannot be any thing or object. Each thing is what it is in consequence of some other thing. An infinite, independent [1] thing is no less a contradiction than an infinite circle or a sideless triangle. Besides a thing is that which is capable of being an object of which itself is not the sole percipient. But an object is inconceivable without a subject as its antithesis. Omne perceptum percipientem supponit.

But neither can the principle be found in a subject as a subject, contra-distinguished from an object: for unicuique percipienti aliquid objicitur perceptum. It is to be found therefore neither in object nor subject taken separately, and consequently, as no other third is conceivable, it must be found in that which is neither subject nor object exclusively, but which is the identity of both.[2]

THESIS VI

This principle, and so characterized, manifests itself in the SUM or I AM, which I shall hereafter indiscriminately express by the words spirit, self and self-consciousness. In this, and in this

[1] The impossibility of an absolute thing (*substantia unica*) as neither genus, species, nor individuum, as well as its utter unfitness for the fundamental position of a philosophic system, will be demonstrated in the critique on Spinozism in the fifth treatise of my Logosophia.

[2] [Cf. *Notebooks*, 921.]

alone, object and subject, being and knowing, are identical, each involving and supposing the other. In other words, it is a subject which becomes a subject by the act of constructing itself objectively to itself; but which never is an object except for itself, and only so far as by the very same act it becomes a subject. It may be described therefore as a perpetual self-duplication of one and the same power into object and subject, which pre-suppose each other, and can exist only as antitheses.

SCHOLIUM. If a man be asked how he *knows* that he is, he can only answer, sum quia sum. But if (the absoluteness of this certainly having been admitted) he be again asked how he, the individual person, came to be, then in relation to the ground of his existence, not to the ground of his knowledge of that existence, he might reply, sum quia deus est, or still more philosophically, sum quia in deo sum.

But if we elevate our conception to the absolute self, the great eternal I AM, then the principle of being, and of knowledge, of idea, and of reality, the ground of existence, and the ground of the knowledge of existence, are absolutely identical. Sum quia sum;[1] I am, because I affirm myself to be; I affirm myself to be, because I am.

---

[1] It is most worthy of notice, that in the first revelation of himself, not confined to individuals, indeed in the very first revelation of his absolute being, Jehovah at the same time revealed the fundamental truth of all philosophy, which must either commence with the absolute, or have no fixed commencement; i.e. cease to be philosophy. I cannot but express my regret, that in the equivocal use of the word *that*, for *in that*, or *because*, our admirable version has rendered the passage susceptible of a degraded interpretation in the mind of common readers or hearers, as if it were a mere reproof to an impertinent question, I am what I am, which might be equally affirmed of himself by any existent being.

The Cartesian *Cogito ergo sum* is objectionable, because either the *Cogito* is used *extra gradum*, and then it is involved in the *sum* and is tautological, or it is taken as a particular mode or dignity, and then it is subordinated to the *sum* as the species to the genus, or rather as a particular modification to the subject modified; and not pre-ordinated as the arguments seem to require. For *Cogita* is *Sum Cogitans*. This is clear by the inevidence of the converse. *Cogitat ergo est* is true, because it is a mere application of the logical rule: *Quicquid in genere est, est et in specie. Est (cogitans) ergo est.* It is a cherry tree; therefore it is a tree. But *est ergo cogitat* is illogical; for *quod est in specie, non necessario in genere est.* It may be true. I hold it to be true, that *quicquid vere est, est per veram sui affirmationem*; but it is a derivative, not an immediate truth. Here then we have, by anticipation, the distinction between the conditional finite I (which as known in distinct consciousness by occasion of experience is called by Kant's followers the empirical I) and the absolute I AM, and likewise the dependence or rather the inherence of the former in the latter; in whom 'we live, and move, and have our being,' as St Paul divinely asserts, differing widely from the theists of the mechanic school (as Sir I. Newton, Locke, etc.) who must say from whom we *had* our being, and with it life and the powers of life.

THESIS VII

If then I know myself only through myself, it is contradictory to require any other predicate of self but that of self-consciousness. Only in the self-consciousness of a spirit is there the required identity of object and of representation; for herein consists the essence of a spirit, that it is self-representative. If therefore this be the one only immediate truth in the certainty of which the reality of our collective knowledge is grounded, it must follow that the spirit in all the objects which it views, views only itself. If this could be proved, the immediate reality of all intuitive knowledge would be assured. It has been shown that a spirit is that which is its own object, yet not originally an object, but an absolute subject for which all, itself included, may become an object. It must therefore be an act; for every object is, as an object, dead, fixed, incapable in itself of any action, and necessarily finite. Again, the spirit (originally the identity of object and subject) must in some sense dissolve this identity, in order to be conscious of it: fit alter et idem. But this implies an act, and it follows therefore that intelligence or self-consciousness is impossible, except by and in a will. The self-conscious spirit therefore is a will; and freedom must be assumed as a *ground* of philosophy, and can never be deduced from it.

THESIS VIII

Whatever in its origin is objective is likewise as such necessarily finite. Therefore, since the spirit is not originally an object, and as the subject exists in antithesis to an object, the spirit cannot originally be finite. But neither can it be a subject without becoming an object, and as it is originally the identity of both it can be conceived neither as infinite nor finite exclusively, but as the most original union of both. In the existence, in the reconciling and the recurrence of this contradiction consists the process and mystery of production and life.[1]

THESIS IX

This *principium commune essendi et cognoscendi*, as subsisting in a will or primary act of self-duplication, is the mediate or indirect principle of every science; but it is the immediate and direct principle of the ultimate science alone, i.e. of transcendental philosophy alone. For it must be remembered, that all these Theses refer solely to one of the two Polar Sciences, namely, to

[1] [Cf. *Notebooks*, 921n., where Sara Coleridge's attribution of this passage to Schelling is questioned].

that which commences with and rigidly confines itself within the subjective, leaving the objective (as far as it is exclusively objective) to natural philosophy, which is its opposite pole. In its very idea therefore as a systematic knowledge of our collective knowing (*scientia scientiae*), it involves the necessity of some one highest principle of knowing, as at once the source and the accompanying form in all particular acts of intellect and perception. This, it has been shown, can be found only in the act and evolution of self-consciousness. We are not investigating an absolute *principium essendi*; for then, I admit, many valid objections might be started against our theory; but an absolute *principium cognoscendi*. The result of both the sciences, or their equatorial point, would be the principle of a total and undivided philosophy, as for prudential reasons I have chosen to anticipate in the Scholium to Thesis VI and the note subjoined. In other words, philosophy would pass into religion, and religion become inclusive of philosophy. We begin with the I KNOW MYSELF, in order to end with the absolute I AM. We proceed from the self, in order to lose and find all self in GOD.

THESIS X

The transcendental philosopher does not inquire what ultimate ground of our knowledge there may lie out of our knowing, but what is the last in our knowing itself, beyond which we cannot pass. The principle of our knowing is sought within the sphere of our knowing. It must be something therefore which can itself be known. It is asserted only that the act of self-consciousness is for us the source and principle of all our possible knowledge. Whether abstracted from us there exists anything higher and beyond this primary self-knowing, which is for us the form of all our knowing, must be decided by the result.

That the self-consciousness is the fixt point to which for us all is morticed and annexed needs no further proof. But that the self-consciousness may be the modification of a higher form of being, perhaps of a higher consciousness, and this again of a yet higher, and so on in an infinite regressus; in short, that self-consciousness may be itself something explicable into something which must lie beyond the possibility of our knowledge, because the whole synthesis of our intelligence is first formed in and through the self-consciousness, does not at all concern us as transcendental philosophers. For to us the self-consciousness is not a kind of *being*, but a kind of *knowing*, and that too the highest and farthest that exists for us. It may however be shown, and has in part already been shown in pages 115–16,[1] that even when the objective is assumed as the first, we yet can never pass beyond the principle of self-consciousness. Should we attempt it, we must be driven back from ground to ground, each of which would cease to be a ground the moment we pressed on it. We must be whirl'd down the gulf of an infinite series. But this would make our reason baffle the end and purpose of all reason, namely unity and system. Or we must break off the series arbitrarily, and affirm an absolute something that is in and of itself at once cause and effect (*causa sui*), subject and object, or rather the absolute identity of both. But as this is inconceivable, except in a self-consciousness, it follows that even as natural philosophers we must arrive at the same principle from which as transcendental philosophers we set out; that is, in a self-consciousness in which the *principium essendi* does not stand to the *principium cognoscendi* in the relation of cause to effect, but both the one and the other are co-inherent and identical. Thus the true system of natural philosophy places the sole reality of things in an absolute which is at once *causa sui et effectus* πατὴρ αὐτοπάτωρ, Υἱὸς ἑαυτοῦ—in the absolute identity of subject and object, which it calls nature, and which in its highest power is nothing else but self-conscious will or intelligence. In this sense the position of Malebranche,[2] that we see all things in God, is a strict philosophical truth; and equally true is the assertion of Hobbes, of Hartley and of their masters in ancient Greece, that all real knowledge supposes a prior sensation. For sensation itself is but vision nascent, not the cause of intelligence but intelligence itself revealed as an earlier power in the process of self-construction.

> Μάκαρ, ἵλαθί μοι!
> Πάτερ, ἵλαθί μοι
> Εἰ παρὰ κόσμον,
> Εἰ παρὰ μοῖραν
> Τῶν σῶν ἔθιγον![3]

Bearing then this in mind, that intelligence is a self-development, not a quality supervening to a substance, we may abstract

---

[1] [pp. 66–7 above.]

[2] [*De la recherche de la vérité* (1674), III. ii. ch. vi, entitled 'Que nous voyons toutes choses en Dieu.']

[3] [Synesius, Hymn iii, 113–17: 'Blessed one, be gracious to me! Father, be gracious if contrary to the world and to fate I have touched the One.']

from all degree, and for the purpose of philosophic construction reduce it to kind, under the idea of an indestructible power with two opposite and counteracting forces which, by a metaphor borrowed from astronomy, we may call the centrifugal and centripedal forces. The intelligence in the one tends to objectize itself, and in the other to know itself in the object. It will be hereafter my business to construct by a series of intuitions the progressive schemes that must follow from such a power with such forces, till I arrive at the fulness of the human intelligence. For my present purpose I assume such a power as my principle in order to deduce from it a faculty, the generation, agency and application of which form the contents of the ensuing chapter.

In a preceding page [1] I have justified the use of technical terms in philosophy, whenever they tend to preclude confusion of thought and when they assist the memory by the exclusive singleness of their meaning more than they may, for a short time, bewilder the attention by their strangeness. I trust that I have not extended this privilege beyond the grounds on which I have claimed it; namely, the conveniency of the scholastic phrase to distinguish the kind from all degrees, or rather to express the kind with the abstraction of degree, as for instance *multeity* instead of *multitude*; or secondly, for the sake of correspondence in sound in interdependent or antithetical terms, as *subject* and *object*; or lastly, to avoid the wearying recurrence of circumlocutions and definitions. Thus I shall venture to use *potence* in order to express a specific degree of a power, in imitation of the algebraists. I have even hazarded the new verb *potenziate* with its derivatives in order to express the combination or transfer of powers. It is with new or unusual terms as with privileges in courts of justice or legislature; there can be no legitimate privilege where there already exists a positive law adequate to the purpose; and when there is no law in existence the privilege is to be justified by its accordance with the end, or final cause, of all law. Unusual and new coined words are doubtless an evil; but vagueness, confusion and imperfect conveyance of our thoughts are a far greater. Every system which is under the necessity of using terms not familiarized by the metaphysics in fashion will be described as written in an unintelligible style, and the author must expect the charge of having substituted learned jargon for clear conception; while, according to the creed of our modern philosophers, nothing is deemed a clear conception but what

[1] [p. 91 above.]

is representable by a distinct image. Thus the conceivable is reduced within the bounds of the picturable. 'Hinc patet, quî fiat ut, *cum irrepraesentabile* et *impossibile* vulgo ejusdem significatus habeantur, conceptus tam *continui*, quam *infiniti* a plurimis rejiciantur, quippe quorum, *secundum leges cognitionis intuitivae*, repraesentatio est impossibilis. Quanquam autem harum e non paucis scholis explosarum notionum, praesertim prioris causam hic non gero, maximi tamen momenti erit monuisse: gravissimo illos errore labi, qui tam perversa argumentandi ratione utuntur. Quicquid enim *repugnat* legibus intellectus et rationis, utique est impossibile; quod autem, cum rationis purae sit objectum, legibus cognitionis intuitivae tantummodo *non subest*, non item. Nam hic dissensus inter facultatem *sensitivam* et *intellectualem*, (quarum indolem mox exponam) nihil indigitat, nisi, *quas mens ab intellectu acceptas fert ideas abstractas, illas in concreto exsequi et in intuitus commutare saepenumero non posse.* Haec autem reluctantia *subjectiva* mentitur, ut plurimum, repugnantiam aliquam *objectivam*, et incautos facile fallit, limitibus, quibus *mens humana* circumscribitur, pro iis habitis, quibus *ipsa rerum essentia* continetur.[1]

---

[1] Kant, *De mundi sensibilis atque intelligibilis forma et principiis*, 1770 [I. i.].

TRANSLATION

'Hence it is clear from what cause many reject the notion of the continuous and the infinite. They take namely the words irrepresentable and impossible in one and the same meaning; and, according to the forms of sensuous evidence, the notion of the continuous and the infinite is doubtless impossible. I am not now pleading the cause of these laws, which not a few schools have thought proper to explode, especially the former (the law of continuity). But it is of the highest importance to admonish the reader that those who adopt so perverted a mode of reasoning are under a grievous error. Whatever opposes the formal principles of the understanding and the reason is confessedly impossible; but not therefore that which is therefore not amenable to the forms of sensuous evidence, because it is exclusively an object of pure intellect. For this non-coincidence of the sensuous and the intellectual (the nature of which I shall presently lay open) proves nothing more but that the mind cannot always adequately represent in the concrete and transform into distinct images abstract notions derived from the pure intellect. But this contradiction, which is in itself merely subjective (i.e. an incapacity in the nature of man) too often passes for an incongruity or impossibility in the object (i.e. the notions themselves) and seduces the incautious to mistake the limitations of the human faculties for the limits of things as they really exist.'

I take this occasion to observe that here and elsewhere Kant uses the terms intuition, and the verb active (*intueri, germanice anschauen*) for which we have unfortunately no correspondent word, exclusively for that which can be represented in space and time. He therefore consistently and rightly denies the possibility of intellectual intuitions. But as I see no adequate reason for this exclusive sense of the term, I have reverted to its wider signification authorized by our elder theologians and metaphysicians, according to whom the term comprehends all truths known to us without a medium.

Critics, who are most ready to bring this charge of pedantry and unintelligibility, are the most apt to overlook the important fact that besides the language of words there is a language of spirits (*sermo interior*), and that the former is only the vehicle of the latter. Consequently their assurance that they do not understand the philosophic writer, instead of proving anything against the philosophy, may furnish an equal and (*caeteris paribus*) even a stronger presumption against their own philosophic talent.

Great indeed are the obstacles which an English metaphysician has to encounter. Amongst his most respectable and intelligent judges there will be many who have devoted their attention exclusively to the concerns and interests of human life and who bring with them to the perusal of a philosophic system an habitual aversion to all speculations, the utility and application of which are not evident and immediate. To these I would in the first instance merely oppose an authority which they themselves hold venerable, that of Lord Bacon: 'non inutiles scientiae existimandae sunt, quarum in se nullus est usus, si ingenia acuant et ordinent.'[1]

There are others whose prejudices are still more formidable, inasmuch as they are grounded in their moral feelings and religious principles, which had been alarmed and shocked by the impious and pernicious tenets defended by Hume, Priestley and the French fatalists or necessitarians; some of whom had perverted metaphysical reasonings to the denial of the mysteries and indeed of all the peculiar doctrines of Christianity; and others even to the subversion of all distinction between right and wrong. I would request such men to consider what an eminent and successful defender of the Christian faith has observed, that true metaphysics are nothing else but true divinity, and that in fact the writers who have given them such just offence were sophists, who had taken advantage of the general neglect into which the science of logic has unhappily fallen, rather than metaphysicians, a name indeed which those writers were the first to explode as unmeaning. Secondly, I would remind them that as long as there are men in the world to whom the Γνῶθι σεαυτὸν is an instinct and a command from their own nature, so long will there be metaphysicians and metaphysical speculations; that false metaphysics can be effectually counteracted by true metaphysics alone; and that if the reasoning be clear, solid and pertinent, the truth deduced can never be the less valuable on account of the depth from which it may have been drawn.

---

[1] [*De augmentis scientiarum* (1623), VI. 3: 'Sciences which are of no use in themselves do not exist uselessly if they sharpen and discipline the wits.']

A third class profess themselves friendly to metaphysics and believe that they are themselves metaphysicians. They have no objection to system or terminology, provided it be the method and the nomenclature to which they have been familiarized in the writings of Locke, Hume, Hartley, Condillac, or perhaps Dr Reid and Professor Stewart. To objections from this cause it is a sufficient answer that one main object of my attempt was to demonstrate the vagueness or insufficiency of the terms used in the metaphysical schools of France and Great Britain since the revolution, and that the errors which I propose to attack cannot subsist except as they are concealed behind the mask of a plausible and indefinite nomenclature.

But the worst and widest impediment still remains. It is the predominance of a popular philosophy, at once the counterfeit and the mortal enemy of all true and manly metaphysical research. It is that corruption, introduced by certain immethodical aphorisming Eclectics who, dismissing not only all system but all logical connection, pick and choose whatever is most plausible and showy; who select whatever words can have some semblance of sense attached to them without the least expenditure of thought, in short whatever may enable men to talk of what they do not understand with a careful avoidance of everything that might awaken them to a moment's suspicion of their ignorance. This, alas! is an irremediable disease, for it brings with it not so much an indisposition to any particular system, but an utter loss of taste and faculty for all system and for all philosophy. Like echoes that beget each other amongst the mountains, the praise or blame of such men rolls in volleys long after the report from the original blunderbuss. 'Sequacitas est potius et coitio quam consensus; et tamen (quod pessimum est) pusillanimitas ista non sine arrogantia et fastidio se offert.'[1]

I shall now proceed to the nature and genesis of the imagination; but I must first take leave to notice that after a more accurate perusal of Mr Wordsworth's remarks on the imagination in his preface to the new edition of his poems,[2] I find that my conclusions are not so consentient with his as, I confess, I had taken for granted. In an article contributed by me to Mr Southey's *Omniana* on the soul and its organs of sense are the

---

[1] *Novum Organum*, [I. 77 and 88: 'They follow after and lie with rather than concur; and what is worst of all this littleness of spirit is not without its air of arrogance and superiority.' Cf. *Notebooks*, 913.]

[2] [*Poems, with a New Preface*, 2 vols., 1815, in which Wordsworth had challenged Coleridge's distinction between fancy and imagination as stated in the *Omniana*. His objection is quoted below.]

following sentences: 'These (the human faculties) I would arrange under the different senses and powers; as the eye, the ear, the touch, etc.; the imitative power, voluntary and automatic; the imagination, or shaping or modifying power; the fancy, or the aggregative and associative power: the understanding, or the regulative, substantiating and realizing power; the speculative reason—*vis theoretica et scientifica*, or the power by which we produce, or aim to produce, unity, necessity and universality in all our knowledge by means of principles *a priori*; [1] the will, or practical reason; the faculty of choice (*germanice*, Willkühr) and (distinct both from the moral will and the choice) the sensation of volition, which I have found reason to include under the head of single and double touch.' [2]   To this, as far as it relates to the subject in question, namely the words (the aggregative and associative power), Mr Wordsworth's 'only objection is that the definition is too general.   To aggregate and to associate, to evoke and combine, belong as well to the imagination as to the fancy.'   I reply that if by the power of evoking and combining Mr W. means the same as, and no more than, I meant by the aggregative and associative, I continue to deny that it belongs at all to the imagination; and I am disposed to conjecture that he has mistaken the co-presence of fancy with imagination for the operation of the latter singly.   A man may work with two very different tools at the same moment; each has its share in the work, but the work effected by each is distinct and different.   But it will probably appear in the next Chapter that deeming it necessary to go back much further than Mr Wordsworth's subject required or permitted, I have attached a meaning to both fancy and imagination which he had not in view, at least while he was writing that preface.   He will judge. Would to heaven I might meet with many such readers.   I will conclude with the words of Bishop Jeremy Taylor: 'he to whom all things are one, who draweth all things to one, and seeth all things in one, may enjoy true peace and rest of spirit.' [3]

---

[1] This phrase *a priori* is in common most grossly misunderstood, and an absurdity burthened on it which it does not deserve!   By knowledge *a priori*, we do not mean that we can know anything previously to experience, which would be a contradiction in terms; but that having once known it by occasion of experience (i.e. something acting upon us from without), we then know that it must have pre-existed, or the experience itself would have been impossible.   By experience only I know that I have eyes; but then my reason convinces me that I must have had eyes in order to [have] the experience.

[2] [*Omniana* (1812), No. 174, pp. 13–14 and n.]

[3] J. Taylor's *Via Pacis* [in the *Golden Grove* (1651), *Sunday*, I. 8.]

CHAPTER XIII

On the imagination, or esemplastic power

O Adam! one Almighty is, from whom
All things proceed, and up to him return,
If not depraved from good; created all
Such to perfection, one first matter all,
Indued with various forms, various degrees
Of substance, and in things that live, of life;
But more refin'd, more spiritous and pure,
As nearer to him placed or nearer tending,
Each in their several active spheres assign'd,
Till body up to spirit work, in bounds
Proportion'd to each kind.   So from the root
Springs lighter the green stalk: from thence the leaves
More airy: last, the bright consummate flower
Spirits odorous breathes.   Flowers and their fruit,
Man's nourishment, by gradual scale sublim'd,
To vital spirits aspire: to animal:
To intellectual!—give both life and sense,
Fancy and understanding: whence the soul
Reason receives, and reason is her being,
Discursive, or intuitive.

Par. Lost, b.v.[1]

'Sane si res corporales nil nisi materiale continerent, verissime dicerentur in fluxu consistere neque habere substantiale quicquam, quemadmodum et Platonici olim recte agnovêre.—Hinc igitur, praeter purè mathematica et phantasiae subjecta, collegi quaedam metaphysica solâque mente perceptibilia, esse admittenda: et massae materiali principium quoddam superius et, ut sic dicam, formale addendum: quandoquidem omnes veritates rerum corporearum ex solis axiomatibus logisticis et geometricis, nempe de magno et parvo, toto et parte, figurâ et situ, colligi non possint: sed alia de causâ et effectu, actioneque et passione, accedere debeant, quibus ordinis rerum rationes solventur.   Id principium rerum, an ἐντελέχειαν an vim appellemus, non refert, modo meminerimus, per solam virium notionem intelligibiliter explicari.'

LEIBNITZ: Op. T. II. P. II. p. 53.—T. III. p. 321.[2]

---

[1] [*Paradise Lost,* v. 469–88.]

[2] [*De ipsa natura,* 8, and *Specimen dynamicum;* but Coleridge has substituted 'phantasiae' for 'imaginationi' in the second sentence: 'If indeed corporeal things contained nothing but matter they might truly be said to exist in flux and to have no substance, as the Platonists once rightly recognized. . . .   And so, apart from the purely mathematical and what is subject to the fancy I have collected certain metaphysical elements perceptible to the mind alone

161

Σέβομαι Νοερῶν
Κρυφίαν τάξιν
Χωρει ΤΙ ΜΕΣΟΝ
Οὐ καταχυθέν.

SYNESII, *Hymn* III. *l.* 231.[1]

DES CARTES, speaking as a naturalist and in imitation of Archimedes, said, Give me matter and motion and I will construct you the universe. We must of course understand him to have meant, I will render the construction of the universe intelligible. In the same sense the transcendental philosopher says: Grant me a nature having two contrary forces, the one of which tends to expand infinitely, while the other strives to apprehend or find itself in this infinity, and I will cause the world of intelligences with the whole system of their representations to rise up before you. Every other science pre-supposes intelligence as already existing and complete: the philosopher contemplates it in its growth, and as it were represents its history to the mind from its birth to its maturity.

The venerable Sage of Koenigsberg has preceded the march of this master-thought as an effective pioneer in his essay on the introduction of negative quantities into philosophy, published 1763.[2]   In this he has shown that instead of assailing the science of mathematics by metaphysics, as Berkeley did in his *Analyst*, or of sophisticating it, as Wolf did, by the vain attempt of deducing the first principles of geometry from supposed deeper grounds of ontology, it behoved the metaphysician rather to examine whether the only province of knowledge which man has succeeded in erecting into a pure science might not furnish materials or at least hints for establishing and pacifying the unsettled, warring and embroiled domain of philosophy. An imitation of the mathematical method has indeed been attempted with no better success than attended the essay of David to wear

---

which should be admitted; and some principle, being superior to material mass, must so to speak be formally added since all the truth about corporal things cannot be collected from logistic and geometric axioms alone, whether they concern great and small, whole and part, or shape and position. Others must be added on cause and effect, action and reaction, to explain the reasons for the order of the universe.   This principle of things, which we may call either an 'essence' or a power, is not, we should remember, to be explained only by the idea of powers.']

[1] ['I worship the hidden order of intellectual things. The Mean dances and is not still.']

[2] [Kant, *Versuch, den Begriff der negativen Grössen in die Weltweisheit einzuführen*.]

the armour of Saul.   Another use however is possible and of far greater promise, namely the actual application of the positions which had so wonderfully enlarged the discoveries of geometry, *mutatis mutandis*, to philosophical subjects.   Kant having briefly illustrated the utility of such an attempt in the questions of space, motion and infinitely small quantities, as employed by the mathematician, proceeds to the idea of negative quantities and the transfer of them to metaphysical investigation.   Opposites, he well observes, are of two kinds, either logical, i.e. such as are absolutely incompatible; or real without being contradictory.   The former he denominates *nihil negativum irrepraesentabile*, the connection of which produces nonsense.   A body in motion is something—*aliquid cogitabile*; but a body at one and the same time in motion and not in motion is nothing, or at most air articulated into nonsense.   But a motory force of a body in one direction, and an equal force of the same body in an opposite direction, is not incompatible, and the result, namely rest, is real and representable.   For the purposes of mathematical calculus it is indifferent which force we term negative, and which positive, and consequently we appropriate the latter to that which happens to be the principal object in our thoughts. Thus if a man's capital be ten and his debts eight, the subtraction will be the same, whether we call the capital negative debt or the debt negative capital.   But inasmuch as the latter stands practically in reference to the former, we of course represent the sum as 10—8.   It is equally clear that two equal forces acting in opposite directions, both being finite and each distinguished from the other by its direction only, must neutralize or reduce each other to inaction.   Now the transcendental philosophy demands: first, that two forces should be conceived which counteract each other by their essential nature, not only not in consequence of the accidental direction of each, but as prior to all direction, nay, as the primary forces from which the conditions of all possible directions are derivative and deducible; secondly, that these forces should be assumed to be both alike infinite, both alike indestructible.   The problem will then be to discover the result or product of two such forces, as distinguished from the result of those forces, which are finite, and derive their difference solely from the circumstance of their direction. When we have formed a scheme or outline of these two different kinds of force and of their different results by the process of discursive reasoning, it will then remain for us to elevate the Thesis from notional to actual by contemplating intuitively this one power with its two inherent indestructible yet counteracting forces, and the results or generations to which their inter-penetration gives existence in the living principle and in the process of our own self-consciousness. By what instrument this is possible the solution itself will discover, at the same time that it will reveal to and for whom it is possible. Non omnia possumus omnes. There is a philosophic, no less than a poetic genius, which is differenced from the highest perfection of talent not by degree but by kind.

The counteraction then of the two assumed forces does not depend on their meeting from opposite directions; the power which acts in them is indestructible; it is therefore inexhaustibly re-ebullient; and as something must be the result of these two forces, both alike infinite and both alike indestructible; and as rest or neutralization cannot be this result; no other conception is possible but that the product must be a *tertium aliquid*, or finite generation. Consequently this conception is necessary. Now this *tertium aliquid* can be no other than an inter-penetration of the counteracting powers, partaking of both

. . . . . .

Thus far had the work been transcribed for the press, when I received the following letter from a friend [1] whose practical judgment I have had ample reason to estimate and revere, and whose taste and sensibility preclude all the excuses which my self-love might possibly have prompted me to set up in plea against the decision of advisers of equal good sense, but with less tact and feeling.

Dear C.,

You ask my opinion concerning your Chapter on the Imagination, both as to the impressions it made on myself and as to those which I think it will make on the public, *i.e. that part of the public who, from the title of the work and from its forming a sort of introduction to a volume of poems, are likely to constitute the great majority of your readers.*

As to myself, and stating in the first place the effect on my understanding, *your opinions and method of argument were not only so new to me, but so directly the reverse of all I had ever been accustomed to consider as truth, that even if I had comprehended your premises sufficiently to have admitted them and had seen the necessity*

---

[1] [The 'friend' was Coleridge himself, as he explained in a letter to his publisher Curtis (29 April 1817).]

of your conclusions, I should still have been in that state of mind, which in your note, p. 75, 76,[1] you have so ingeniously evolved as the antithesis to that in which a man is when he makes a bull. In your own words, I should have felt as if I had been standing on my head.

The effect on my feelings, *on the other hand, I cannot better represent than by supposing myself to have known only our light airy modern chapels of ease, and then for the first time to have been placed, and left alone, in one of our largest Gothic cathedrals in a gusty moonlight night of autumn. 'Now in glimmer, and now in gloom'; often in palpable darkness not without a chilly sensation of terror; then suddenly emerging into broad yet visionary lights with coloured shadows, of fantastic shapes, yet all decked with holy insignia and mystic symbols; and ever and anon coming out full upon pictures and stone-work images of great men, with whose names I was familiar but which looked upon me with countenances and an expression, the most dissimilar to all I had been in the habit of connecting with those names. Those whom I had been taught to venerate as almost super-human in magnitude of intellect I found perched in little fret-work niches, as grotesque dwarfs; while the grotesques, in my hitherto belief, stood guarding the high altar with all the characters of Apotheosis. In short, what I had supposed substances were thinned away into shadows, while everywhere shadows were deepened into substances:*

> If substance may be call'd that shadow seem'd,
> For each seem'd either!
>
> MILTON.[2]

Yet after all, I could not but repeat the lines which you had quoted from a MS. poem of your own in The Friend *and applied to a work of Mr Wordsworth's, though with a few of the words altered:*

> ————————An orphic tale indeed,
> A tale *obscure* of high and passionate thoughts
> To a *strange* music chaunted! [3]

Be assured, however, that I look forward anxiously to your great book on the Constructive Philosophy *which you have promised and announced: and that I will do my best to understand it. Only I will not promise to descend into the dark cave of Trophonius with*

---

[1] [p. 43n. above.]
[2] [*Paradise Lost*, II. 669–70 ('Or substance might be call'd . . .')].
[3] [From *To William Wordsworth*, ll. 45–7:
　　　　'An Orphic song indeed,
　　A song divine of high and passionate thoughts
　　To their own music chaunted!']

you, there to rub my own eyes in order to make *the sparks and figured flashes which I am required to see.*

So much for myself. But as for the public, I do not hesitate a moment in advising and urging you to withdraw the Chapter from the present work, and to reserve it for your announced treatise on the Logos or communicative intellect in Man and Deity. First, because imperfectly as I understand the present Chapter, I see clearly that you have done too much, and yet not enough. You have been obliged to omit so many links from the necessity of compression, that what remains looks (if I may recur to my former illustration) like the fragments of the winding steps of an old ruined tower. Secondly, a still stronger argument (at least one that I am sure will be more forcible with you) is that your readers will have both right and reason to complain of you. This Chapter, which cannot, when it is printed, amount to so little as an hundred pages, will of necessity greatly increase the expense of the work; and every reader who, like myself, is neither prepared or perhaps calculated for the study of so abstruse a subject so abstrusely treated, will, as I have before hinted, be almost entitled to accuse you of a sort of imposition on him. For who, he might truly observe, could from your title-page, viz. My Literary Life and Opinions, *published too as introductory to a volume of miscellaneous poems, have anticipated, or even conjectured, a long treatise on ideal Realism, which holds the same relation in abstruseness to Plotinus, as Plotinus does to Plato. It will be well, if already you have not too much of metaphysical disquisition in your work, though as the larger part of the disquisition is historical, it will doubtless be both interesting and instructive to many to whose* unprepared *minds your speculations on the esemplastic power would be utterly unintelligible. Be assured, if you do publish this chapter in the present work, you will be reminded of Bishop Berkeley's Siris, announced as an* Essay on Tar-water, *which beginning with Tar ends with the Trinity, the omne scibile forming the interspace. I say in the* present *work. In that greater work to which you have devoted so many years, and study so intense and various, it will be in its proper place. Your prospectus will have described and announced both its contents and their nature; and if any persons purchase it who feel no interest in the subjects of which it treats, they will have themselves only to blame.*

I could add to these arguments one derived from pecuniary motives, and particularly from the probable effects on the sale *of your present publication; but they would weigh little with you compared with the preceding. Besides, I have long observed that arguments drawn from your own personal interests more often act on you as narcotics than as stimulants, and that in money concerns you have some small portion of pig-nature in your moral idiosyncracy, and like these amiable creatures must occasionally be pulled backward from the boat in order to make you enter it. All success attend you, for if hard thinking and hard reading are merits you have deserved it.*

Your affectionate, etc.

In consequence of this very judicious letter, which produced complete conviction on my mind, I shall content myself for the present with stating the main result of the chapter, which I have reserved for that future publication, a detailed prospectus of which the reader will find at the close of the second volume.[1]

The imagination then I consider either as primary, or secondary. The primary imagination I hold to be the living power and prime agent of all human perception, and as a repetition in the finite mind of the eternal act of creation in the infinite I AM. The secondary I consider as an echo of the former, co-existing with the conscious will, yet still as identical with the primary in the kind of its agency, and differing only in degree, and in the mode of its operation. It dissolves, diffuses, dissipates, in order to re-create; or where this process is rendered impossible, yet still, at all events, it struggles to idealize and to unify. It is essentially *vital*, even as all objects (as objects) are essentially fixed and dead.

Fancy, on the contrary, has no other counters to play with but fixities and definites. The fancy is indeed no other than a mode of memory emancipated from the order of time and space; and blended with, and modified by that empirical phaenomenon of the will which we express by the word *choice*. But equally with the ordinary memory it must receive all its materials ready made from the law of association.

Whatever more than this I shall think it fit to declare concerning the powers and privileges of the imagination in the present work will be found in the critical essay [2] on the uses of the supernatural in poetry and the principles that regulate its introduction: which the reader will find prefixed to the poem of *The Ancient Mariner.*

---

[1] [This prospectus was never published.]

[2] [Coleridge originally contemplated, as well as the metaphysical *Biographia* which ends with this chapter, a companion essay on the supernatural in poetry. But the study of the critical ideas of the 1800 Preface which follows unexpectedly absorbed his energies and the essay on the supernatural was never written.]

CHAPTER XIV

Occasion of the *Lyrical Ballads*, and the objects originally proposed—Preface to the second edition—The ensuing controversy, its causes and acrimony—Philosophic definitions of a poem and poetry with scholia.

DURING the first year that Mr Wordsworth and I were neighbours our conversations turned frequently on the two cardinal points of poetry, the power of exciting the sympathy of the reader by a faithful adherence to the truth of nature, and the power of giving the interest of novelty by the modifying colours of imagination. The sudden charm which accidents of light and shade, which moonlight or sunset diffused over a known and familiar landscape, appeared to represent the practicability of combining both. These are the poetry of nature. The thought suggested itself (to which of us I do not recollect) that a series of poems might be composed of two sorts. In the one, the incidents and agents were to be, in part at least, supernatural; and the excellence aimed at was to consist in the interesting of the affections by the dramatic truth of such emotions as would naturally accompany such situations, supposing them real. And real in this sense they have been to every human being who, from whatever source of delusion, has at any time believed himself under supernatural agency. For the second class, subjects were to be chosen from ordinary life; the characters and incidents were to be such as will be found in every village and its vicinity where there is a meditative and feeling mind to seek after them, or to notice them when they present themselves.

In this idea originated the plan of the *Lyrical Ballads*; [1] in which it was agreed that my endeavours should be directed to persons and characters supernatural, or at least romantic; yet so as to transfer from our inward nature a human interest and a

---

[1] [In Miss Fenwick's note to *We Are Seven* (*Poetical Works*, 1857) Wordsworth's account of the genesis of the book is reported as the joint composition of the 'Ancient Mariner' by the two poets on a walking tour to Lynton in November 1797, 'till it became too important for our first object, which was limited to our expectation of five pounds; and we began to talk of a volume which was to consist, as Mr Coleridge has told the world, of poems chiefly on natural subjects taken from common life but looked at, as much as might be, through an imaginative medium.' When we remember that nineteen of the twenty-three poems in the first collection of 1798 were Wordsworth's this account does not appear inconsistent with the above.]

168

semblance of truth sufficient to procure for these shadows of imagination that willing suspension of disbelief for the moment, which constitutes poetic faith.   Mr Wordsworth, on the other hand, was to propose to himself as his object to give the charm of novelty to things of every day, and to excite a feeling analogous to the supernatural, by awakening the mind's attention from the lethargy of custom and directing it to the loveliness and the wonders of the world before us; an inexhaustible treasure, but for which, in consequence of the film of familiarity [1] and selfish solicitude, we have eyes yet see not, ears that hear not, and hearts that neither feel nor understand.

With this view I wrote the 'Ancient Mariner,' and was preparing, among other poems, the 'Dark Ladie,' and the 'Christabel,' [2] in which I should have more nearly realized my ideal than I had done in my first attempt.   But Mr Wordsworth's industry had proved so much more successful and the number of his poems so much greater, that my compositions, instead of forming a balance, appeared rather an interpolation of heterogeneous matter.[3]   Mr Wordsworth added two or three poems written in his own character, in the impassioned, lofty and sustained diction which is characteristic of his genius.   In this form the *Lyrical Ballads* were published; and were presented by him, as an experiment, whether subjects which from their nature rejected the usual ornaments and extra-colloquial style of poems in general might not be so managed in the language of ordinary life as to produce the pleasurable interest which it is the peculiar business of poetry to impart.   To the second edition he added a preface of considerable length; in which, notwithstanding some passages of apparently a contrary import, he was understood to contend for the extension of this style to poetry of all kinds, and to reject as vicious and indefensible all phrases and forms of style that were not included in what he (unfortunately, I think, adopting an equivocal expression) called the language of *real* life.

---

[1] [A phrase borrowed by Shelley towards the end of *A Defence of Poetry* (comp. 1821): 'Poetry . . . reproduces the common universe of which we are portions, and it purges from our inward sight the film of familiarity which obscures from us the wonder of our being.'   Shelley read the *Biographia* as soon as it appeared, before the end of 1817 (*Mary Shelley's Journal*, ed. F. L. Jones (1947), p. 90).]

[2] [The two parts of 'Christabel' were composed in 1797 (1798?) and 1800, but Coleridge failed to complete the poem in time for the second edition of the *Lyrical Ballads* (1800) and the fragment was not published till 1816. 'The Dark Ladie' (first published 1834) was an expansion of the ballad 'Love,' which did appear in 1800.]

[3] [Only four of the twenty-three poems in the first edition were by Coleridge.]

From this preface, prefixed to poems in which it was impossible to deny the presence of original genius, however mistaken its direction might be deemed, arose the whole long continued controversy. For from the conjunction of perceived power with supposed heresy I explain the inveteracy and in some instances, I grieve to say, the acrimonious passions with which the controversy has been conducted by the assailants.

Had Mr Wordsworth's poems been the silly, the childish things which they were for a long time described as being; had they been really distinguished from the compositions of other poets merely by meanness of language and inanity of thought; had they indeed contained nothing more than what is found in the parodies and pretended imitations of them; they must have sunk at once, a dead weight, into the slough of oblivion, and have dragged the preface along with them. But year after year increased the number of Mr Wordsworth's admirers. They were found too not in the lower classes of the reading public, but chiefly among young men of strong sensibility and meditative minds; and their admiration (inflamed perhaps in some degree by opposition) was distinguished by its intensity, I might almost say, by its religious fervour. These facts, and the intellectual energy of the author, which was more or less consciously felt where it was outwardly and even boisterously denied, meeting with sentiments of aversion to his opinions and of alarm at their consequences, produced an eddy of criticism which would of itself have borne up the poems by the violence with which it whirled them round and round. With many parts of this preface, in the sense attributed to them and which the words undoubtedly seem to authorize, I never concurred; but, on the contrary objected to them as erroneous in principle, and as contradictory (in appearance at least) both to other parts of the same preface and to the author's own practice in the greater number of the poems themselves. Mr Wordsworth in his recent collection [1] has, I find, degraded this prefatory disquisition to the end of his second volume, to be read or not at the reader's choice. But he has not, as far as I can discover, announced any change in his poetic creed. At all events, considering it as the source of a controversy in which I have been honored more than I deserve by the frequent conjunction of my name with his, I think it expedient to declare once for all in what points I coincide with his opinions, and in what points I altogether differ. But in

---

[1] [Poems, including Lyrical Ballads and Miscellaneous Pieces, with Additional Poems, a New Preface and a Supplementary Essay, 2 vols. (1815).]

order to render myself intelligible I must previously, in as few
words as possible, explain my ideas, first, of a poem; and
secondly, of poetry itself, in kind and in essence.

The office of philosophical disquisition consists in just distinction; while it is the privilege of the philosopher to preserve
himself constantly aware that distinction is not division.   In
order to obtain adequate notions of any truth, we must intellectually separate its distinguishable parts; and this is the technical *process* of philosophy.   But having so done, we must then
restore them in our conceptions to the unity in which they
actually co-exist; and this is the *result* of philosophy.   A poem
contains the same elements as a prose composition; the difference
therefore must consist in a different combination of them, in
consequence of a different object proposed.   According to the
difference of the object will be the difference of the combination.
It is possible that the object may be merely to facilitate the
recollection of any given facts or observations by artificial
arrangement; and the composition will be a poem, merely
because it is distinguished from prose by metre, or by rhyme, or
by both conjointly.   In this, the lowest sense, a man might
attribute the name of a poem to the well-known enumeration of
the days in the several months:

> Thirty days hath September
> April, June, and November, etc.

and others of the same class and purpose.   And as a particular
pleasure is found in anticipating the recurrence of sounds and
quantities, all compositions that have this charm superadded,
whatever be their contents, *may* be entitled poems.

So much for the superficial form.   A difference of object and
contents supplies an additional ground of distinction.   The immediate purpose may be the communication of truths; either of
truth absolute and demonstrable, as in works of science; or of
facts experienced and recorded, as in history.   Pleasure, and that
of the highest and most permanent kind, may result from the
attainment of the end; but it is not itself the immediate end.   In
other works the communication of pleasure may be the immediate purpose; and though truth, either moral or intellectual, ought
to be the ultimate end, yet this will distinguish the character of
the author, not the class to which the work belongs.   Blest
indeed is that state of society in which the immediate purpose
would be baffled by the perversion of the proper ultimate end;
in which no charm of diction or imagery could exempt the

Bathyllus even of an Anacreon, or the Alexis of Virgil, from disgust and aversion! [1]

But the communication of pleasure may be the immediate object of a work not metrically composed; and that object may have been in a high degree attained, as in novels and romances. Would then the mere superaddition of metre, with or without rhyme, entitle these to the name of poems? The answer is that nothing can permanently please which does not contain in itself the reason why it is so, and not otherwise. If metre be super-added, all other parts must be made consonant with it. They must be such as to justify the perpetual and distinct attention to each part which an exact correspondent recurrence of accent and sound are calculated to excite. The final definition then, so deduced, may be thus worded. A poem is that species of com-position which is opposed to works of science by proposing for its *immediate* object pleasure, not truth; and from all other species (having this object in common with it) it is discriminated by proposing to itself such delight from the whole as is com-patible with a distinct gratification from each component part.

Controversy is not seldom excited in consequence of the dis-putants attaching each a different meaning to the same word; and in few instances has this been more striking than in disputes concerning the present subject. If a man chooses to call every composition a poem which is rhyme, or measure, or both, I must leave his opinion uncontroverted. The distinction is at least competent to characterize the writer's intention. If it were sub-joined that the whole is likewise entertaining or affecting as a tale or as a series of interesting reflections, I of course admit this as another fit ingredient of a poem and an additional merit. But if the definition sought for be that of a legitimate poem, I answer it must be one the parts of which mutually support and explain each other; all in their proportion harmonizing with, and supporting the purpose and known influences of metrical arrangement. The philosophic critics of all ages coincide with the ultimate judgment of all countries in equally denying the praises of a just poem on the one hand to a series of striking lines or distichs, each of which absorbing the whole attention of the reader to itself disjoins it from its context and makes it a separate whole, instead of a harmonizing part; and on the other hand, to an unsustained composition, from which the reader collects

---

[1] [Bathyllus was the beautiful youth of Samos celebrated by Anacreon in his twenty-ninth ode, Alexis a youth wooed by the shepherd Corydon in Virgil's second Eclogue.]

rapidly the general result unattracted by the component parts. The reader should be carried forward, not merely or chiefly by the mechanical impulse of curiosity, or by a restless desire to arrive at the final solution; but by the pleasurable activity of mind excited by the attractions of the journey itself. Like the motion of a serpent, which the Egyptians made the emblem of intellectual power; or like the path of sound through the air; at every step he pauses and half recedes, and from the retrogressive movement collects the force which again carries him onward. 'Praecipitandus est liber spiritus,' says Petronius Arbiter most happily.[1] The epithet *liber* here balances the preceding verb; and it is not easy to conceive more meaning condensed in fewer words.

But if this should be admitted as a satisfactory character of a poem, we have still to seek for a definition of poetry. The writings of Plato, and Bishop Taylor, and the *Theoria Sacra* of Burnet, furnish undeniable proofs that poetry of the highest kind may exist without metre, and even without the contradistinguishing objects of a poem. The first chapter of Isaiah (indeed a very large proportion of the whole book) is poetry in the most emphatic sense; yet it would be not less irrational than strange to assert that pleasure, and not truth, was the immediate object of the prophet. In short, whatever specific import we attach to the word poetry, there will be found involved in it, as a necessary consequence, that a poem of any length neither can be, nor ought to be, all poetry. Yet if a harmonious whole is to be produced, the remaining parts must be preserved *in keeping* with the poetry; and this can be no otherwise effected than by such a studied selection and artificial arrangement as will partake of one, though not a peculiar, property of poetry. And this again can be no other than the property of exciting a more continuous and equal attention than the language of prose aims at, whether colloquial or written.

My own conclusions on the nature of poetry, in the strictest use of the word, have been in part anticipated in the preceding disquisition on the fancy and imagination. What is poetry? is so nearly the same question with, what is a poet? that the answer to the one is involved in the solution of the other. For it is a distinction resulting from the poetic genius itself, which sustains and modifies the images, thoughts and emotions of the poet's own mind. The poet, described in ideal perfection, brings the whole soul of man into activity, with the subordination of its

---

[1] [*Satyricon*, 118: 'The free spirit (of the epic poet) must be hurried onwards (through digressions, etc.).']

faculties to each other, according to their relative worth and
dignity. He diffuses a tone and spirit of unity that blends and
(as it were) fuses, each into each, by that synthetic and magical
power to which we have exclusively appropriated the name of
imagination. This power, first put in action by the will and
understanding and retained under their irremissive, though
gentle and unnoticed, controul (*laxis effertur habenis*[1]) reveals
itself in the balance or reconciliation of opposite or discordant
qualities: of sameness, with difference; of the general, with the
concrete; the idea, with the image; the individual, with the
representative; the sense of novelty and freshness, with old and
familiar objects; a more than usual state of emotion, with more
than usual order; judgement ever awake and steady self-possession, with enthusiasm and feeling profound or vehement; and
while it blends and harmonizes the natural and the artificial, still
subordinates art to nature; the manner to the matter; and
our admiration of the poet to our sympathy with the poetry.
'Doubtless,' as Sir John Davies observes of the soul (and his
words may with slight alteration be applied, and even more
appropriately, to the poetic imagination):

> Doubtless this could not be, but that she turns
> Bodies to spirit by sublimation strange,
> As fire converts to fire the things it burns,
> As we our food into our nature change.
>
> From their gross matter she abstracts their forms,
> And draws a kind of quintessence from things;
> Which to her proper nature she transforms
> To bear them light on her celestial wings.
>
> Thus does she, when from individual states
> She doth abstract the universal kinds;
> Which then re-clothed in divers names and fates
> Steal access through our senses to our minds.[2]

Finally, good sense is the body of poetic genius, fancy its,
drapery, motion its life, and imagination the soul that is every
where, and in each; and forms all into one graceful and intelligent whole.

---

[1] ['is borne onwards with loose reins.' From Virgil, *Georgics*, II. 364:
'laxis . . . immissus habenis.']

[2] [*Nosce Teipsum* (1599), p. 24, spelling modernized, with 'food' for
'meates' in *l.* 4.   The third stanza should read:

> This doth she, when from things particular
> She doth abstract the universall kinds,
> Which bodilesse and immateriall are,
> And can be lodg'd but onely in our minds.]

CHAPTER XV

The specific symptoms of poetic power elucidated in a critical analysis of Shakespeare's *Venus and Adonis* and *Lucrece*.[1]

IN the application of these principles to purposes of practical criticism as employed in the appraisal of works more or less imperfect, I have endeavoured to discover what the qualities in a poem are which may be deemed promises and specific symptoms of poetic power, as distinguished from general talent determined to poetic composition by accidental motives, by an act of the will, rather than by the inspiration of a genial and productive nature. In this investigation I could not, I thought, do better than keep before me the earliest work of the greatest genius, that perhaps human nature has yet produced, our *myriad-minded* [2] Shakespeare. I mean the *Venus and Adonis*, and the *Lucrece*; works which give at once strong promises of the strength, and yet obvious proofs of the immaturity of his genius. From these I abstracted the following marks, as characteristics of original poetic genius in general.

1. In the *Venus and Adonis* the first and most obvious excellence is the perfect sweetness of the versification; its adaptation to the subject; and the power displayed in varying the march of the words without passing into a loftier and more majestic rhythm than was demanded by the thoughts, or permitted by the propriety of preserving a sense of melody predominant. The delight in richness and sweetness of sound, even to a faulty excess, if it be evidently original and not the result of an easily imitable mechanism, I regard as a highly favorable promise in the compositions of a young man. 'The man that hath not music in his soul' [3] can indeed never be a

---

[1] [Coleridge had delivered a lecture of similar content to this chapter in his course on Shakespeare and Milton held near Fetter Lane from November 1811 to January 1812.]

[2] ᾿Ανὴρ μυριόνους, a phrase which I have borrowed from a Greek monk, who applies it to a Patriarch of Constantinople. I might have said that I have reclaimed rather than borrowed it: for it seems to belong to Shakespeare *de jure singulari, et ex privilegio naturae*. [The borrowing is from William Cave, *Scriptorum ecclesiasticorum historia literaria* (1688) where the phrase occurs in the article on Naucratius as part of his eulogy of his dead master Theodorus Studites (759–826), who was abbot of the Studium monastery in Constantinople but never Patriarch. Cf. *Notebooks*, 1070 and n., 3285 and n.]

[3] [From *Merchant of Venice*, v. i. 83: 'The man that hath no music in himself . . .']

175

genuine poet.   Imagery (even taken from nature, much more
when transplanted from books, as travels, voyages and works of
natural history); affecting incidents; just thoughts; interesting
personal or domestic feelings; and with these the art of their
combination or intertexture in the form of a poem, may all by
incessant effort be acquired as a trade, by a man of talents and
much reading who, as I once before observed,[1] has mistaken an
intense desire of poetic reputation for a natural poetic genius; the
love of the arbitrary end for a possession of the peculiar means.
But the sense of musical delight, with the power of producing it,
is a gift of imagination; and this, together with the power of
reducing multitude into unity of effect, and modifying a series of
thoughts by some one predominant thought or feeling, may be
cultivated and improved, but can never be learnt.   It is in these
that 'Poeta nascitur non fit.'

2. A second promise of genius is the choice of subjects very
remote from the private interests and circumstances of the writer
himself.   At least I have found that where the subject is taken
immediately from the author's personal sensations and experiences, the excellence of a particular poem is but an equivocal
mark, and often a fallacious pledge, of genuine poetic power.
We may perhaps remember the tale of the statuary, who had
acquired considerable reputation for the legs of his goddesses,
though the rest of the statue accorded but indifferently with ideal
beauty; till his wife, elated by her husband's praises, modestly
acknowledged that she herself had been his constant model.
In the *Venus and Adonis* this proof of poetic power exists even to
excess.   It is throughout as if a superior spirit, more intuitive,
more intimately conscious even than the characters themselves,
not only of every outward look and act but of the flux and reflux
of the mind in all its subtlest thoughts and feelings, were placing
the whole before our view; himself meanwhile unparticipating in
the passions, and actuated only by that pleasurable excitement
which had resulted from the energetic fervor of his own spirit,
in so vividly exhibiting what it had so accurately and profoundly
contemplated.   I think I should have conjectured from these
poems that even then the great instinct which impelled the poet
to the drama was secretly working in him, prompting him by a
series and never-broken chain of imagery, always vivid and,
because unbroken, often minute; by the highest effort of the
picturesque in words of which words are capable, higher perhaps

<hr>

[1] [p. 20 above.]

than was ever realized by any other poet, even Dante not ex-
cepted; to provide a substitute for that visual language, that
constant intervention and running comment by tone, look and
gesture, which in his dramatic works he was entitled to expect
from the players.   His Venus and Adonis seem at once the
characters themselves, and the whole representation of those
characters by the most consummate actors.   You seem to be
told nothing, but to see and hear everything.   Hence it is, that
from the perpetual activity of attention required on the part of
the reader; from the rapid flow, the quick change and the playful
nature of the thoughts and images; and, above all, from the
alienation and, if I may hazard such an expression, the utter
aloofness of the poet's own feelings from those of which he is at
once the painter and the analyst; that though the very subject
cannot but detract from the pleasure of a delicate mind, yet never
was poem less dangerous on a moral account.   Instead of doing
as Ariosto and as, still more offensively, Wieland has done;
instead of degrading and deforming passion into appetite, the
trials of love into the struggles of concupiscence, Shakespeare has
here represented the animal impulse itself so as to preclude all
sympathy with it, by dissipating the reader's notice among the
thousand outward images and now beautiful, now fanciful
circumstances, which form its dresses and its scenery; or by
diverting our attention from the main subject by those frequent
witty or profound reflections which the poet's ever active mind
has deduced from, or connected with, the imagery and the incidents.   The reader is forced into too much action to sympathize
with the merely passive of our nature.   As little can a mind thus
roused and awakened be brooded on by mean and instinct
emotion as the low, lazy mist can creep upon the surface of a lake
while a strong gale is driving it onward in waves and billows.

3. It has been before observed that images, however beautiful,
though faithfully copied from nature, and as accurately represented in words, do not of themselves characterize the poet.
They become proofs of original genius only as far as they are
modified by a predominant passion; or by associated thoughts or
images awakened by that passion; or when they have the effect
of reducing multitude to unity, or succession to an instant; or
lastly, when a human and intellectual life is transferred to them
from the poet's own spirit,

Which shoots its being through earth, sea and air.[1]

---

[1] [From *France: an Ode*, *l.* 100: 'And shot my being thro' earth, sea
and air.']

In the two following lines, for instance, there is nothing objectionable, nothing which would preclude them from forming, in their proper place, part of a descriptive poem:

> Behold yon row of pines, that shorn and bow'd
> Bend from the sea-blast, seen at twilight eve.

But with the small alteration of rhythm, the same words would be equally in their place in a book of topography, or in a descriptive tour.   The same image will rise into a semblance of poetry if thus conveyed:

> Yon row of bleak and visionary pines,
> By twilight-glimpse discerned, mark! how they flee
> From the fierce sea-blast, all their tresses wild
> Streaming before them.

I have given this as an illustration, by no means as an instance, of that particular excellence which I had in view and in which Shakespeare, even in his earliest as in his latest works, surpasses all other poets.   It is by this that he still gives a dignity and a passion to the objects which he presents.   Unaided by any previous excitement, they burst upon us at once in life and in power.

> Full many a glorious morning have I seen
> *Flatter* the mountain-tops with sovereign eye.
>
> > Shakespeare's Sonnet 33rd.

> Not mine own fears, nor the prophetic soul
> Of the wide world dreaming on things to come—
>
> *   *   *   *   *
> *   *   *   *   *
>
> The mortal moon hath her eclipse endur'd,
> And the sad augurs mock their own presage:
> Incertainties now crown themselves assur'd,
> And peace proclaims olives of endless age.
> Now with the drops of this most balmy time
> My love looks fresh, and Death to me subscribes,
> Since, spite of him, I'll live in this poor rime,
> While he insults o'er dull and speechless tribes.
> And thou in this shalt find thy monument,
> When tyrants' crests, and tombs of brass are spent.
>
> > Sonnet 107.

As of higher worth, so doubtless still more characteristic of poetic genius does the imagery become when it moulds and colors itself to the circumstances, passion or character present and foremost in the mind.   For unrivalled instances of this excellence the reader's own memory will refer him to the *Lear*,

Othello, in short to which not of the 'great, ever living, dead man's dramatic works? Inopem me copia fecit.[1] How true it is to nature, he has himself finely expressed in the instance of love in Sonnet 98:

> From you have I been absent in the spring,
> When proud-pied April drest in all his trim
> Hath put a spirit of youth in every thing;
> That heavy Saturn laugh'd and leap'd with him.
> Yet nor the lays of birds, nor the sweet smell
> Of different flowers in odour and in hue,
> Could make me any summer's story tell,
> Or from their proud lap pluck them where they grew:
> Nor did I wonder at the lily's white,
> Nor praise the deep vermilion in the rose;
> They were, but sweet, but figures of delight,
> Drawn after you, you pattern of all those.
> Yet seem'd it winter still, and you away,
> *As with your shadow I with these did play!*

Scarcely less sure, or if a less valuable, not less indispensable mark

> Γόνιμον μὲν Ποιητοῦ————————
> ————————ὅστις ῥῆμα γενναῖον λάκοι,[2]

will the imagery supply when, with more than the power of the painter, the poet gives us the liveliest image of succession with the feeling of simultaneousness!

> With this he breaketh from the sweet embrace
> Of those fair arms which bound him to her breast,
> And homeward through the dark laund runs apace; . . .
> *Look, how a bright star shooteth from the sky,*
> *So glides he in the night from Venus' eye.*[3]

4. The last character I shall mention, which would prove indeed but little except as taken conjointly with the former, yet without which the former could scarce exist in a high degree and (even if this were possible) would give promises only of transitory flashes and a meteoric power, is depth and energy of thought. No man was ever yet a great poet, without being at the same time a profound philosopher. For poetry is the blossom and the fragrancy of all human knowledge, human thoughts, human passions, emotions, language. In Shakespeare's poems, the creative power and the intellectual energy wrestle as in a war

---

[1] [Ovid, *Metamorphoses*, III, 466: 'Plenty has made me poor.']
[2] [From Aristophanes, *Frogs*, 96–7: 'You'll never find a true poet to utter notable things.']
[3] [*Venus and Adonis*, ll. 811–13 and 815–16.]

embrace. Each in its excess of strength seems to threaten the extinction of the other. At length in the drama they were reconciled, and fought each with its shield before the breast of the other. Or like two rapid streams that at their first meeting within narrow and rocky banks mutually strive to repel each other, and intermix reluctantly and in tumult, but soon finding a wider channel and more yielding shores, blend and dilate, and flow on in one current and with one voice. The *Venus and Adonis* did not perhaps allow the display of the deeper passions. But the story of Lucretia seems to favor, and even demand, their intensest workings. And yet we find in Shakespeare's management of the tale neither pathos nor any other dramatic quality. There is the same minute and faithful imagery as in the former poem, in the same vivid colours, inspirited by the same impetuous vigour of thought, and diverging and contracting with the same activity of the assimilative and of the modifying faculties; and with a yet larger display, a yet wider range of knowledge and reflection; and lastly, with the same perfect dominion, often domination, over the whole world of language. What then shall we say? Even this: that Shakespeare, no mere child of nature; no automaton of genius; no passive vehicle of inspiration possessed by the spirit, not possessing it; first studied patiently, meditated deeply, understood minutely, till knowledge become habitual and intuitive wedded itself to his habitual feelings, and at length gave birth to that stupendous power by which he stands alone, with no equal or second in his own class; to that power which seated him on one of the two glory-smitten summits of the poetic mountain, with Milton as his compeer not rival. While the former darts himself forth, and passes into all the forms of human character and passion, the one Proteus of the fire and the flood; the other attracts all forms and things to himself, into the unity of his own ideal. All things and modes of action shape themselves anew in the being of Milton; while Shakespeare becomes all things, yet for ever remaining himself. O what great men hast thou not produced, England! my country! Truly indeed,

> Must *we* be free or die, who speak the tongue,
> Which Shakespeare spake; the faith and morals hold,
> Which Milton held. In every thing we are sprung
> Of Earth's first blood, have titles manifold!

WORDSWORTH.[1]

---

[1] [From Sonnet ('It is not to be thought of . . .') (1803):
> 'We must be free or die, who speak the tongue
> That Shakespeare spake . . .']

CHAPTER XVI

CHRISTENDOM, from its first settlement on feudal rights, has been so far one great body, however imperfectly organized, that a similar spirit will be found in each period to have been acting in all its members. The study of Shakespeare's poems (I do not include his dramatic works, eminently as they too deserve that title) led me to a more careful examination of the contemporary poets both in this and in other countries. But my attention was especially fixed on those of Italy, from the birth to the death of Shakespeare; that being the country in which the fine arts had been most sedulously, and hitherto most successfully cultivated. Abstracted from the degrees and peculiarities of individual genius, the properties common to the good writers of each period seem to establish one striking point of difference between the poetry of the fifteenth and sixteenth centuries and that of the present age. The remark may perhaps be extended to the sister art of painting. At least the latter will serve to illustrate the former. In the present age the poet (I would wish to be understood as speaking generally, and without allusion to individual names) seems to propose to himself as his main object, and as that which is the most characteristic of his art, new and striking images; with incidents that interest the affections or excite the curiosity. Both his characters and his descriptions he renders, as much as possible, specific and individual, even to a degree of portraiture. In his diction and metre, on the other hand, he is comparatively careless. The measure is either constructed on no previous system and acknowledges no justifying principle but that of the writer's convenience; or else some mechanical movement is adopted, of which one couplet or stanza is so far an adequate specimen, as that the occasional differences appear evidently to arise from accident or the qualities of the language itself, not from meditation and an intelligent purpose. And the language from Pope's translation of Homer to Darwin's 'Temple of Nature' may, notwithstanding some illustrious exceptions, be too faithfully characterized as claiming to be poetical for no better reason than that it would be intolerable in conversation or

181

in prose. Though, alas! even our prose writings, nay, even the
stile of our more set discourses, strive to be in the fashion, and
trick themselves out in the soiled and over-worn finery of the
meretricious muse.   It is true that of late a great improvement in
this respect is observable in our most popular writers.   But it
is equally true that this recurrence to plain sense and genuine
mother English is far from being general; and that the composition of our novels, magazines, public harangues, etc., is commonly as trivial in thought, and yet enigmatic in expression, as
if Echo and Sphinx had laid their heads together to construct it.
Nay, even of those who have most rescued themselves from this
contagion, I should plead inwardly guilty to the charge of
duplicity or cowardice if I withheld my conviction that few have
guarded the purity of their native tongue with that jealous care
which the sublime Dante, in his tract 'De la nobile volgare
eloquenza,'[1] declares to be the first duty of a poet.   For language is the armoury of the human mind; and at once contains
the trophies of its past, and the weapons of its future conquests.
'Animadverte quam sit ab improprietate verborum pronum
hominibus prolabi in errores circa res!'[2] 'Sat vero, in hac
vitae brevitate et naturae obscuritate rerum est, quibus cognos-
cendis tempus impendatur, ut confusis et multivocis sermonibus
intelligendis illud consumere non opus est. Eheu! quantas
strages paravere verba nubila, quae tot dicunt, ut nihil dicunt—
nubes potius, e quibus et in rebus politicis et in ecclesiâ turbines
et tonitrua erumpunt!   Et proinde recte dictum putamus a
Platone in Gorgia, ὃς ἂν τὰ ὀνόματα εἰδεῖ, εἴσεται καὶ τὰ ηράγματα:
et ab Epicteto, ἀρχὴ παιδεύσεως ἡ τῶν ὀνομάτων ἐπίσκεψις; et
prudentissime Galenus scribit, ἡ τῶν ὀνομάτων χρῆσις παραχθεῖσα
καὶ τὴν τῶν πραγμάτων ἐπιταράττει γνῶσιν... Egregie vero J.
C. Scaliger, in Lib. I. De plantis: Est primum, inquit, sapientis
officium, bene sentire, ut sibi vivat: proximum, bene loqui,
ut patriae vivat.' Sennertus, De puls. differentia.[3]

---

[1] [De vulgari eloquentia, in which Dante urges the use of the vernacular by
Italian poets.   But he nowhere makes the precise claim attributed to him
here.]
[2] Hobbes, Exam. et emend. hod. math. [Examinatio et emendatio mathe-
maticae hodiernae (1660), p. 52 (Dialogue ii): 'See how easily men fall from
the wrong use of words into errors about things themselves' (circa ipsas res).]
[3] [Daniel Sennert (1572–1637), the German physician and philosopher,
Tractatus de consensu Galenicorum cum chymicis (1619), v (with minor inaccuracies and disturbed sentence order): 'There are certainly plenty of things
in this short life and dark world which are worth time to study, so that we
need not spend time in trying to understand confused and many-sided dis-
cussions. Alas, cloudy words are so many failures, they say so much that
they say nothing—clouds, rather, from which hurricanes burst, both in

Something analogous to the materials and structure of modern poetry I seem to have noticed (but here I beg to be understood as speaking with the utmost diffidence) in our common landscape painters. Their foregrounds and intermediate distances are comparatively unattractive; while the main interest of the landscape is thrown into the background, where mountains and torrents and castles forbid the eye to proceed, and nothing tempts it to trace its way back again. But in the works of the great Italian and Flemish masters, the front and middle objects of the landscape are the most obvious and determinate, the interest gradually dies away in the background, and the charm and peculiar worth of the picture consists not so much in the specific objects which it conveys to the understanding in a visual language formed by the substitution of figures for words as in the beauty and harmony of the colours, lines and expression with which the objects are represented. Hence novelty of subject was rather avoided than sought for. Superior excellence in the manner of treating the same subjects was the trial and test of the artist's merit.

Not otherwise is it with the more polished poets of the fifteenth and sixteenth centuries, especially with those of Italy. The imagery is almost always general: sun, moon, flowers, breezes, murmuring streams, warbling songsters, delicious shades, lovely damsels, cruel as fair, nymphs, naiads and goddesses are the materials which are common to all, and which each shaped and arranged according to his judgement or fancy, little solicitous to add or to particularize. If we make an honorable exception in favor of some English poets, the thoughts too are as little novel as the images; and the fable of their narrative poems, for the most part drawn from mythology or sources of equal notoriety, derive their chief attractions from the manner of treating them; from impassioned flow or picturesque arrangement. In opposition to the present age, and perhaps in as faulty an extreme, they placed the essence of poetry in the *art*. The excellence at which they aimed consisted in the exquisite polish of the diction combined with perfect simplicity.

---

church and state! What Plato has said in the Gorgias is indeed true: "Anyone who knows words will know things too"; and as Epictetus says, "the study of words is the beginning of education"; and Galen wrote most wisely, "Confusion in our knowledge of words makes confusion in our knowledge of things." J. C. Scaliger has indeed said excellently, in Book I of his *Plants*: "A wise man's first duty (he says), is to think well so that he can live for himself; the next is to speak well so that he can live for his country."' The Plato quotation is in fact from *Cratylus*, 436A. Cf. *Notebooks*, 1000C.]

This, their prime object, they attained by the avoidance of every
word which a gentleman would not use in dignified conversation,
and of every word and phrase which none but a learned man
would use; by the studied position of words and phrases, so that
not only each part should be melodious in itself, but contribute
to the harmony of the whole, each note referring and conducing
to the melody of all the foregoing and following words of the
same period or stanza; and lastly, with equal labour, the greater
because unbetrayed, by the variation and various harmonies of
their metrical movement.   Their measures, however, were not
indebted for their variety to the introduction of new metres, such
as have been attempted of late in the 'Alonzo and Imogen' [1]
and others borrowed from the German, having in their very
mechanism a specific overpowering tune, to which the generous
reader humours his voice and emphasis, with more indulgence to
the author than attention to the meaning or quantity of the
words, but which, to an ear familiar with the numerous sounds
of the Greek and Roman poets, has an effect not unlike that of
galloping over a paved road in a German stage-waggon without
springs.   On the contrary the elder bards, both of Italy and
England, produced a far greater as well as more charming variety,
by countless modifications and subtle balances of sound in the
common metres of their country.   A lasting and enviable
reputation awaits that man of genius who should attempt and
realize a union; who should recall the high finish, the appropriateness, the facility, the delicate proportion, and above all the
perfusive and omnipresent grace which have preserved, as in
a shrine of precious amber, the 'Sparrow' of Catullus, the
'Swallow,' the 'Grasshopper' and all the other little loves of
Anacreon; and which, with bright though diminished glories,
revisited the youth and early manhood of Christian Europe in
the vales of Arno,[2] and the groves of Isis and of Cam; and who

---

[1] ['Alonzo and Imogene,' a ballad by 'Monk' Lewis (1775–1818), published
in *The Monk* (1796), which Coleridge had reviewed (cf. *Notebooks*, 1128 and
n.).   Its metre, which anticipates 'The Hunting of the Snark,' was certainly not of German origin.]

[2] These thoughts were suggested to me during the perusal of the Madrigals
of Giovambatista Strozzi published in Florence (nella Stamperia del Sermar-
telli) 1st May 1593, by his sons Lorenzo and Filippo Strozzi, with a dedication to their deceased paternal uncle, 'Signor Leone Strozzi, Generale delle
battaglie di Santa Chiesa.'   As I do not remember to have seen either the
poems or their author mentioned in any English work, or to have found them
in any of the common collections of Italian poetry; and as the little work is of
rare occurrence, I will transcribe a few specimens.   I have seldom met with
compositions that possessed, to my feelings, more of that satisfying entireness,
that complete adequateness of the manner to the matter which so charms us in
Anacreon, joined with the tenderness, and more than the delicacy of Catullus.

with these should combine the keener interest, deeper pathos, manlier reflection, and the fresher and more various imagery which give a value and a name that will not pass away to the poets who have done honor to our own times, and to those of our immediate predecessors.

Trifles as they are, they were probably elaborated with great care; yet in the perusal we refer them to a spontaneous energy rather than to voluntary effort. To a cultivated taste there is a delight in perfection for its own sake, independent of the material in which it is manifested, that none but a cultivated taste can understand or appreciate.

After what I have advanced, it would appear presumption to offer a translation; even if the attempt were not discouraged by the different genius of the English mind and language, which demands a denser body of thought as the condition of a high polish than the Italian. I cannot but deem it likewise an advantage in the Italian tongue, in many other respects inferior to our own, that the language of poetry is more distinct from that of prose than with us. From the earlier appearance and established primacy of the Tuscan poets, concurring with the number of independent states, and the diversity of written dialects, the Italians have gained a poetic idiom, as the Greeks before them had obtained from the same causes, with greater and more various discriminations—ex. gr. the ionic for their heroic verses; the attic for their iambic; and the two modes of the doric, the lyric or sacerdotal, and the pastoral, the distinctions of which were doubtless more obvious to the Greeks themselves than they are to us.

I will venture to add one other observation before I proceed to the transcription. I am aware that the sentiments which I have avowed concerning the points of difference between the poetry of the present age, and that of the period between 1500 and 1650 are the reverse of the opinion commonly entertained. I was conversing on this subject with a friend, when the servant, a worthy and sensible woman, coming in, I placed before her two engravings, the one a pinky-coloured plate of the day, the other a masterly etching by Salvator Rosa, from one of his own pictures. On pressing her to tell us which she preferred, after a little blushing and flutter of feeling, she replied— 'why, that, Sir! to be sure! (pointing to the ware from the Fleet-street print shops). It's so neat and elegant. T'other is such a scratchy slovenly thing.' An artist, whose writings are scarcely less valuable than his works, and to whose authority more deference will be willingly paid than I could even wish should be shown to mine, has told us, and from his own experience too, that good taste must be acquired, and like all other good things, is the result of thought and the submissive study of the best models. If it be asked, 'But what shall I deem such?' the answer is: 'Presume these to be the best, the reputation of which has been matured into fame by the consent of ages. For wisdom always has a final majority, if not by conviction, yet by acquiescence.' In addition to Sir J. Reynolds I may mention Harris of Salisbury, who in one of his philosophical disquisitions has written on the means of acquiring a just taste with the precision of Aristotle and the elegance of Quintillian.

MADRIGALE

Gelido suo ruscel chiaro, e tranquillo
M'insegnò Amor di state a mezzo'l giorno;
Ardean le selve, ardean le piagge, e i colli.
Ond 'io, ch' al più gran gielo ardo e sfavillo,
Subito corsi, ma si puro adorno
Girsene il vidi, che turbar no'l volli:
Sol mi specchiava, e'n dolce ombrosa sponda
Mi stava intento al mormorar dell' onda.

Continued

MADRIGALE

Aure dell' angoscioso viver mio
Refrigerio soave,
E dolce sì, che più non mi par grave
Ne'l arder, ne'l morir, anz' il desio;
Deh voi'l ghiaccio, e le nubi, e'l tempo rio
Discacciatene omai, che l'onda chiara,
E l'ombra non men cara
A scherzare, e cantar per suoi boschetti
E prati festa ed allegrezza alletti.

MADRIGALE

Pacifiche, ma spesso in amorosa
Guerra co'fiori, e l'erba
Alla stagione acerba
Verde insegne del giglio e della rosa
Movete, Aure pian pian; che tregua o posa
Se non pace, io ritrove:
E so ben dove—Oh vago, et mansueto
Sguardo, oh labbra d'ambrosia, oh rider lieto!

MADRIGALE

Hor come un scoglio stassi,
Hor come un rio se'n fugge,
Ed hor crud' orsa rugge,
Hor canta angelo pio: ma che non fassi
E che non fammi, O sassi,
O rivi, o belve, o Dii, questa mia vaga
Non so, se Ninfa, o Maga,
Non so, se Donna, o Dea,
Non so, se dolce o rea?

MADRIGALE

Piangendo mi baciaste,
E ridendo il negaste:
In doglia hebbivi pia,
In festa hebbivi ria:
Nacque gioia di pianti,
Dolor di riso: O amanti
Miseri, habbiate insieme
Ognor paura e speme.

MADRIGALE

Bel Fior, tu mi rimembri
La rugiadosa guancia del bel viso;
E si vera l'assembri,
Che'n te sovente, come in lei m'affiso:
Ed hor del vago riso,
Hor del sereno sguardo
Io, pur cieco riguardo.   Ma qual fugge,
O Rosa, il mattin lieve?
E chi te, come neve,
E'l mio cor teco, e la mia vita strugge?

MADRIGALE

Anna mia, Anna dolce, oh sempre nuovo
E più chiaro concento,
Quanta dolcezza sento
In sol Anna dicendo?   Io mi pur pruovo
Nè qui tra noi ritruovo,
Ne tra cieli armonia,
Che del bel nome suo più dolce sia:
Altro il Cielo, altro Amore.
Altro non suona l'Eco del mio core.

MADRIGALE

Hor che'l prato, e la selva si scolora,
Al tuo sereno ombroso
Muovine, alto Riposo!
Deh ch 'io riposi una sol notte, un hora!
Han le fere, e gli augelli, ognun talora
Ha qualche pace; io quando,
Lasso non vonne errando,
E non piango, e non grido? e qual pur forte?
Ma poichè non sent' egli, odine Morte.

MADRIGALE

Risi e piansi d'Amor; nè pero mai
Se non in fiamma, o 'n nda, o 'n vento scrissi;
Spesso mercè trovai
Crudel: sempre in me morto, in altri vissi!
Hor da 'più scuri Abissi al Ciel m'alzai,
Hor ne pur caddi giuso;
Stanco al fin qui son chiuso!

[In a long note, perhaps composed in the summer of 1805, Coleridge copied twenty-seven Strozzi poems (*Notebooks*, 2599 and n.), from which some ten years later he copied these nine. Much of the stylistic discussion on pp. 183–4 above is based on this note, which includes an explanation why Coleridge interested himself in this little-remembered Renaissance poet: the copies were made 'as mementos to myself, if ever I should once more be happy enough to resume poetic composition', in the hope of uniting an established perfection of style with modern romantic incident.   Coleridge has substituted 'Anna' for 'Filli' in the seventh madrigal.]

CHAPTER XVII

Examination of the tenets peculiar to Mr Wordsworth—Rustic life (above all, low and rustic life) especially unfavorable to the formation of a human diction—The best parts of language the products of philosophers, not of clowns or shepherds—Poetry essentially ideal and generic—The language of Milton as much the language of real life, yea, incomparably more so than that of the cottager.

As far then as Mr Wordsworth in his preface contended, and most ably contended, for a reformation in our poetic diction, as far as he has evinced the truth of passion, and the dramatic propriety of those figures and metaphors in the original poets which, stript of their justifying reasons and converted into mere artifices of connection or ornament, constitute the characteristic falsity in the poetic style of the moderns; and as far as he has, with equal acuteness and clearness, pointed out the process by which this change was effected and the resemblances between that state into which the reader's mind is thrown by the pleasurable confusion of thought from an unaccustomed train of words and images and that state which is induced by the natural language of impassioned feeling, he undertook a useful task and deserves all praise, both for the attempt and for the execution. The provocations to this remonstrance in behalf of truth and nature were still of perpetual recurrence before and after the publication of this preface. I cannot likewise but add that the comparison of such poems of merit as have been given to the public within the last ten or twelve years with the majority of those produced previously to the appearance of that preface leave no doubt on my mind that Mr Wordsworth is fully justified in believing his efforts to have been by no means ineffectual. Not only in the verses of those who have professed their admiration of his genius, but even of those who have distinguished themselves by hostility to his theory and depreciation of his writings, are the impressions of his principles plainly visible. It is possible that with these principles others may have been blended, which are not equally evident, and some which are unsteady and subvertible from the narrowness or imperfection of their basis. But it is more than possible that these errors of defect or exaggeration, by kindling and feeding the controversy, may have conduced not only to the wider propagation of the accompanying truths, but that, by their frequent presentation to the mind in an excited state they may have won for them a more permanent and practical result. A man will borrow a part from his opponent the more easily, if he feel himself justified in continuing to reject a part. While there remain important points in which he can still feel himself in the right, in which he still finds firm footing for continued resistance, he will gradually adopt those opinions which were the least remote from his own convictions as not less congruous with his own theory than with that which he reprobates. In like manner, with a kind of instinctive prudence, he will abandon by little and little his weakest posts, till at length he seems to forget that they had ever belonged to him, or affects to consider them at most as accidental and 'petty annexments' the removal of which leaves the citadel unhurt and unendangered.

My own differences from certain supposed parts of Mr Wordsworth's theory ground themselves on the assumption that his words had been rightly interpreted, as purporting that the proper diction for poetry in general consists altogether in a language taken, with due exceptions, from the mouths of men in real life, a language which actually constitutes the natural conversation of men under the influence of natural feelings.[1] My objection is, first, that in any sense this rule is applicable only to certain classes of poetry; secondly, that even to these classes it is not applicable, except in such a sense as hath never by any one (as far as I know or have read) been denied or doubted; and, lastly, that as far as, and in that degree in which it is practicable, it is yet as a *rule* useless, if not injurious, and therefore either need not or ought not to be practised. The poet informs his reader that he had generally chosen low and rustic life, but not *as* low and rustic, or in order to repeat that pleasure of doubtful moral effect which persons of elevated rank and of superior refinement oftentimes derive from a happy imitation of the rude unpolished manners and discourse of their inferiors. For the pleasure so derived may be traced to three exciting causes. The first is the naturalness, in fact, of the things represented. The second is the

---

[1] ['A selection of the real language of men in a state of vivid sensation' (Preface to *Lyrical Ballads*, 1800, 1802). Wordsworth's original wording, in the Advertisement to the first edition (1798), had been 'the language of conversation in the middle and lower classes of society.']

apparent naturalness of the representation, as raised and qualified by an imperceptible infusion of the author's own knowledge and talent, which infusion does indeed constitute it an imitation, as distinguished from a mere copy. The third cause may be found in the reader's conscious feeling of his superiority, awakened by the contrast presented to him; even as for the same purpose the kings and great barons of yore retained sometimes actual clowns and fools, but more frequently shrewd and witty fellows in that character. These, however, were not Mr Wordsworth's objects. *He* chose low and rustic life, 'because in that condition the essential passions of the heart find a better soil in which they can attain their maturity, are less under restraint, and speak a plainer and more emphatic language; because in that condition of life our elementary feelings co-exist in a state of greater simplicity and consequently may be more accurately contemplated and more forcibly communicated; because the manners of rural life germinate from those elementary feelings, and from the necessary character of rural occupations are more easily comprehended and are more durable; and lastly, because in that condition the passions of men are incorporated with the beautiful and permanent forms of nature.' [1]

Now it is clear to me that in the most interesting of the poems in which the author is more or less dramatic, as the 'Brothers,' 'Michael,' 'Ruth,' the 'Mad Mother,' etc., the persons introduced are by no means taken from low or rustic life in the common acceptation of those words; and it is not less clear that the sentiments and language, as far as they can be conceived to have been really transferred from the minds and conversation of such persons, are attributable to causes and circumstances not necessarily connected with 'their occupations and abode.' The thoughts, feelings, language and manners of the shepherd-farmers in the vales of Cumberland and Westmoreland, as far as they are actually adopted in those poems, may be accounted for from causes which will and do produce the same results in every state of life, whether in town or country. As the two principal I rank that independence which raises a man above servitude or daily toil for the profit of others, yet not above the necessity of industry and a frugal simplicity of domestic life, and the accompanying unambitious, but solid and religious education which has rendered few books familiar but the bible and the liturgy or hymn book. To this latter cause indeed, which is so far

---

[1] [Preface, op. cit., text of 1802.]

accidental that it is the blessing of particular countries and a
particular age, not the product of particular places or employ-
ments, the poet owes the show of probability that his personages
might really feel, think and talk with any tolerable resemblance
to his representation.   It is an excellent remark of Dr Henry
More's,[1] that 'a man of confined education, but of good parts,
by constant reading of the bible, will naturally form a more
winning and commanding rhetoric than those that are learned,
the intermixture of tongues and of artificial phrases debasing
their style.'

It is, moreover, to be considered that to the formation of
healthy feelings and a reflecting mind, negations involve impedi-
ments not less formidable than sophistication and vicious intermixture.   I am convinced that for the human soul to prosper in
rustic life, a certain vantage-ground is pre-requisite.   It is not
every man that is likely to be improved by a country life or by
country labours.   Education, or original sensibility, or both,
must pre-exist if the changes, forms and incidents of nature are
to prove a sufficient stimulant.   And where these are not sufficient, the mind contracts and hardens by want of stimulants, and
the man becomes selfish, sensual, gross and hard-hearted.   Let
the management of the Poor Laws in Liverpool, Manchester or
Bristol be compared with the ordinary dispensation of the poor
rates in agricultural villages, where the farmers are the overseers
and guardians of the poor.   If my own experience has not been
particularly unfortunate, as well as that of the many respectable
country clergymen with whom I have conversed on the subject,
the result would engender more than scepticism concerning the
desirable influences of low and rustic life in and for itself.   Whatever may be concluded on the other side, from the stronger local
attachments and enterprising spirit of the Swiss and other
mountaineers, applies to a particular mode of pastoral life under
forms of property that permit and beget manners truly republican, not to rustic life in general or to the absence of artificial
cultivation.   On the contrary the mountaineers, whose manners
have been so often eulogized, are in general better educated and
greater readers than men of equal rank elsewhere.   But where
this is not the case, as among the peasantry of North Wales, the
ancient mountains, with all their terrors and all their glories, are
pictures to the blind and music to the deaf.

---

[1] *Enthusiasmus triumphatus*, Sec. xxxv, [1656.   The original begins: 'For
a man illiterate, as he was, but of good parts, by constant reading of the Bible
will naturally contract a more winning and commanding Rhetorick . . .']

I should not have entered so much into detail upon this passage, but here seems to be the point to which all the lines of difference converge as to their source and centre. (I mean, as far as and in whatever respect my poetic creed *does* differ from the doctrines promulgated in this preface.) I adopt with full faith the principle of Aristotle that poetry as poetry is essentially ideal,[1] that it avoids and excludes all accident; that its apparent individualities of rank, character or occupation must be representative of a class; and that the persons of poetry must be clothed with generic attributes, with the common attributes of the class; not with such as one gifted individual might possibly possess, but such as from his situation it is most probably beforehand that he would possess.[2] If my premises are right and my deductions legitimate, it follows that there can be no poetic medium between the swains of Theocritus and those of an imaginary golden age.

The characters of the vicar and the shepherd-mariner in the poem of the 'Brothers,' those of the Shepherd of Green-head Gill in the 'Michael,' have all the verisimilitude and representative quality that the purposes of poetry can require. They are persons of a known and abiding class, and their manners and

---

[1] Say not that I am recommending abstractions, for these class-characteristics which constitute the instructiveness of a character are so modified and particularized in each person of the Shakespearian drama that life itself does not excite more distinctly that sense of individuality which belongs to real existence. Paradoxical as it may sound, one of the essential properties of geometry is not less essential to dramatic excellence; and Aristotle has accordingly required of the poet an involution of the universal in the individual. The chief differences are that in geometry it is the universal truth which is uppermost in the consciousness; in poetry the individual form in which truth is clothed. With the ancients, and not less with the elder dramatists of England and France, both comedy and tragedy were considered as kinds of poetry. They neither sought in comedy to make us laugh merely; much less to make us laugh by wry faces, accidents of jargon, slang phrases for the day or the clothing of common-place morals in metaphors drawn from the shops or mechanic occupations of their characters. Nor did they condescend in tragedy to wheedle away the applause of the spectators by representing before them facsimiles of their own mean selves in all their existing meanness, or to work on their sluggish sympathies by a pathos not a whit more respectable than the maudlin tears of drunkenness. Their tragic scenes were meant to *affect* us indeed; but yet within the bounds of pleasure, and in union with the activity both of our understanding and imagination. They wished to transport the mind to a sense of its possible greatness, and to implant the germs of that greatness, during the temporary oblivion of the worthless 'thing we are' and of the peculiar state in which each man happens to be, suspending our individual recollections and lulling them to sleep amid the music of nobler thoughts. *The Friend*, pp. 251, 252.

[2] [*Poetics*, ix: 'Poetry tends to represent the universal, history the particular. By the universal I mean how a person of a certain type will on occasion speak or act, according to the law of probability or necessity.']

sentiments the natural product of circumstances common to the
class.   Take 'Michael' for instance:

> An old man, stout of heart, and strong of limb;
> His bodily frame had been from youth to age
> Of an unusual strength: his mind was keen,
> Intense, and frugal, apt for all affairs,
> And in his shepherd's calling he was prompt
> And watchful more than ordinary men.
> Hence he had learnt the meaning of all winds,
> Of blasts of every tone; and oftentimes,
> When others heeded not, he heard the South
> Make subterraneous music, like the noise
> Of bagpipers on distant Highland hills.
> The shepherd, at such warning, of his flock
> Bethought him, and he to himself would say,
> 'The winds are now devising work for me!'
> And truly, at all times, the storm, that drives
> The traveller to a shelter, summoned him
> Up to the mountains: he had been alone
> Amid the heart of many thousand mists,
> That came to him and left him, on the heights.
> So lived he till his eightieth year was passed.
> And grossly that man errs, who should suppose
> That the green valleys, and the streams and rocks,
> Were things indifferent to the shepherd's thoughts.
> Fields, where with cheerful spirits he had breathed
> The common air; the hills, which he so oft
> Had climbed with vigorous steps; which had impressed
> So many incidents upon his mind
> Of hardship, skill or courage, joy or fear;
> Which like a book preserved the memory
> Of the dumb animals, whom he had saved,
> Had fed or sheltered, linking to such acts,
> So grateful in themselves, the certainty
> Of honourable gain; these fields, these hills
> Which were his living being, even more
> Than his own blood—what could they less?—had laid
> Strong hold on his affections, were to him
> A pleasurable feeling of blind love,
> The pleasure which there is in life itself.[1]

On the other hand, in the poems which are pitched at a lower
note, as the 'Harry Gill,' 'Idiot Boy,' etc., the feelings are those
of human nature in general; though the poet has judiciously laid
the scene in the country, in order to place himself in the vicinity
of interesting images without the necessity of ascribing a sentimental perception of their beauty to the persons of his drama.
In the 'Idiot Boy,' indeed, the mother's character is not so much

[1] ['Michael' (1800), ll. 42–77.]

a real and native product of a 'situation where the essential
passions of the heart find a better soil, in which they can attain
their maturity and speak a plainer and more emphatic language,'[1]
as it is an impersonation of an instinct abandoned by judgement.
Hence the two following charges seem to me not wholly groundless; at least, they are the only plausible objections which I have
heard to that fine poem.   The one is that the author has not, in
the poem itself, taken sufficient care to preclude from the reader's
fancy the disgusting images of ordinary, morbid idiocy, which
yet it was by no means his intention to represent.   He has even
by the 'burr, burr, burr,' uncounteracted by any preceding
description of the boy's beauty, assisted in recalling them.   The
other is that the idiocy of the boy is so evenly balanced by the
folly of the mother as to present to the general reader rather a
laughable burlesque on the blindness of anile dotage than an
analytic display of maternal affection in its ordinary workings.

In the 'Thorn,' the poet himself acknowledges in a note the
necessity of an introductory poem in which he should have pour-
trayed the character of the person from whom the words of the
poem are supposed to proceed: a superstitious man moderately
imaginative, of slow faculties and deep feelings, 'a captain of a
small trading vessel, for example, who, being past the middle age
of life, had retired upon an annuity, or small independent income,
to some village or country town of which he was not a native, or
in which he had not been accustomed to live.   Such men, having
nothing to do, become credulous and talkative from indolence.'
But in a poem, still more in a lyric poem (and the Nurse in
Shakespeare's *Romeo and Juliet* alone prevents me from
extending the remark even to dramatic poetry, if indeed the
Nurse itself can be deemed altogether a case in point), it is not
possible to imitate truly a dull and garrulous discourser without
repeating the effects of dulness and garrulity.   However this
may be, I dare assert that the parts (and these form the far
larger portion of the whole) which might as well or still better
have proceeded from the poet's own imagination, and have been
spoken in his own character, are those which have given, and
which will continue to give, universal delight; and that the
passages exclusively appropriate to the supposed narrator, such
as the last couplet of the third stanza,[2] the seven last lines of the

---

[1] [From Preface, op. cit., text of 1800 (with omissions).]

[2] I've measured it from side to side;
     'Tis three feet long, and two feet wide.

tenth,[1] and the five following stanzas, with the exception of the
four admirable lines at the commencement of the fourteenth, are
felt by many unprejudiced and unsophisticated hearts as sudden
and unpleasant sinkings from the height to which the poet had
previously lifted them, and to which he again re-elevates both
himself and his reader.

If then I am compelled to doubt the theory by which the
choice of characters was to be directed, not only *a priori*, from
grounds of reason, but both from the few instances in which the
poet himself need be supposed to have been governed by it, and
from the comparative inferiority of those instances; still more
must I hesitate in my assent to the sentence which immediately
follows the former citation, and which I can neither admit as
particular fact or as general rule.   'The language too of these
men is adopted (purified indeed from what appear to be its real
defects, from all lasting and rational causes of dislike or disgust)
because such men hourly communicate with the best objects
from which the best part of language is originally derived; and
because, from their rank in society and the sameness and narrow

---

[1] Nay, rack your brain—'tis all in vain,
I'll tell you every thing I know;
But to the Thorn, and to the Pond
Which is a little step beyond,
I wish that you would go:
Perhaps when you are at the place,
You something of her tale may trace.

I'll give you the best help I can:
Before you up the mountain go,
Up to the dreary mountain-top,
I'll tell you all I know.
'Tis now some two-and-twenty years
Since she (her name is Martha Ray)
Gave, with a maiden's true good will,
Her company to Stephen Hill;
And she was blithe and gay,
And she was happy, happy still
Whene'er she thought of Stephen Hill.

And they had fixed the wedding-day,
The morning that must wed them both;
But Stephen to another maid
Had sworn another oath;
And with this other maid to church
Unthinking Stephen went—
Poor Martha! on that woeful day
A pang of pitiless dismay
Into her soul was sent;
A fire was kindled in her breast,
Which might not burn itself to rest.

circle of their intercourse, being less under the action of social
vanity they convey their feelings and notions in simple and
unelaborated expressions.' [1]   To this I reply: that a rustic's
language, purified from all provincialism and grossness, and so
far re-constructed as to be made consistent with the rules of
grammar (which are in essence no other than the laws of universal logic applied to psychological materials), will not differ
from the language of any other man of common-sense, however
learned or refined he may be, except as far as the notions which
the rustic has to convey are fewer and more indiscriminate.
This will become still clearer if we add the consideration (equally
important though less obvious) that the rustic, from the more
imperfect development of his faculties and from the lower state
of their cultivation, aims almost solely to convey insulated facts,
either those of his scanty experience or his traditional belief;
while the educated man chiefly seeks to discover and express
those connections of things, or those relative bearings of fact to

---

They say, full six months after this,
While yet the summer leaves were green
She to the mountain-top would go,
And there was often seen.
'Tis said, a child was in her womb,
As now to any eye was plain;
She was with child, and she was mad;
Yet often she was sober sad
From her exceeding pain.
Oh me! ten thousand times I'd rather
That he had died, that cruel father!

*   *   *   *

Last Christmas when we talked of this,
Old farmer Simpson did maintain,
That in her womb the infant wrought
About its mother's heart, and brought
Her senses back again:
And when at last her time drew near,
Her looks were calm, her senses clear.

No more I know, I wish I did,
And I would tell it all to you;
For what became of this poor child
There's none that ever knew:
And if a child was born or no,
There's no one that could ever tell:
And if 'twas born alive or dead,
There's no one knows, as I have said;
But some remember well,
That Martha Ray about this time
Would up the mountain often climb.

[1] [Preface, op. cit., text of 1800.]

fact, from which some more or less general law is deducible. For facts are valuable to a wise man chiefly as they lead to the discovery of the indwelling law which is the true being of things, the sole solution of their modes of existence and in the knowledge of which consists our dignity and our power.

As little can I agree with the assertion that from the objects with which the rustic hourly communicates the best part of language is formed. For first, if to communicate with an object implies such an acquaintance with it as renders it capable of being discriminately reflected on, the distinct knowledge of an uneducated rustic would furnish a very scanty vocabulary. The few things and modes of action requisite for his bodily conveniences would alone be individualized; while all the rest of nature would be expressed by a small number of confused general terms. Secondly, I deny that the words and combinations of words derived from the objects with which the rustic is familiar, whether with distinct or confused knowledge, can be justly said to form the best part of language. It is more than probable that many classes of the brute creation possess discriminating sounds by which they can convey to each other notices of such objects as concern their food, shelter or safety. Yet we hesitate to call the aggregate of such sounds a language otherwise than metaphorically. The best part of human language, properly so called, is derived from reflections on the acts of the mind itself. It is formed by a voluntary appropriation of fixed symbols to internal acts, to processes and results of imagination, the greater part of which have no place in the consciousness of uneducated man; though in civilized society, by imitation and passive remembrance of what they hear from their religious instructors and other superiors, the most uneducated share in the harvest which they neither sowed or reaped. If the history of the phrases in hourly currency among our peasants were traced, a person not previously aware of the fact would be surprized at finding so large a number which three or four centuries ago were the exclusive property of the universities and the schools, and at the commencement of the Reformation had been transferred from the school to the pulpit, and thus gradually passed into common life. The extreme difficulty, and often the impossibility, of finding words for the simplest moral and intellectual processes in the languages of uncivilized tribes has proved perhaps the weightiest obstacle to the progress of our most zealous and adroit missionaries. Yet these tribes are surrounded by the same nature as our peasants are; but in still more impressive forms; and they are, moreover, obliged to particularize many more of them. When therefore Mr Wordsworth adds, 'accordingly such a language' (meaning, as before, the language of rustic life purified from provincialism), 'arising out of repeated experience and regular feelings is a more permanent and a far more philosophical language than that which is frequently substituted for it by poets, who think they are conferring honor upon themselves and their art in proportion as they indulge in arbitrary and capricious habits of expression'; [1] it may be answered that the language which he has in view can be attributed to rustics with no greater right than the style of Hooker or Bacon to Tom Brown or Sir Roger L'Estrange. Doubtless, if what is peculiar to each were omitted in each, the result must needs be the same. Further, that the poet who uses an illogical diction, or a style fitted to excite only the low and changeable pleasure of wonder by means of groundless novelty, substitutes a language of folly and vanity, not for that of the rustic, but for that of good sense and natural feeling.

Here let me be permitted to remind the reader that the positions which I controvert are contained in the sentences—'a selection of the real language of men';—'the language of these men (i.e. men in low and rustic life) I propose to myself to imitate, and as far as possible to adopt the very language of men.' 'Between the language of prose and that of metrical composition there neither is, nor can be any essential difference.' It is against these exclusively that my opposition is directed.

I object, in the very first instance, to an equivocation in the use of the word 'real.' Every man's language varies according to the extent of his knowledge, the activity of his faculties and the depth or quickness of his feelings. Every man's language has, first, its individualities; secondly, the common properties of the class to which he belongs; and thirdly, words and phrases of universal use. The language of Hooker, Bacon, Bishop Taylor and Burke differs from the common language of the learned class only by the superior number and novelty of the thoughts and relations which they had to convey. The language of Algernon Sidney [2] differs not at all from that which every well educated gentleman would wish to write, and (with due allowances for the undeliberateness and less connected train of thinking natural and proper to conversation) such as he would

---

[1] [Preface, op. cit., with omissions.]
[2] [The republican statesman (1622–83) whose *Discourses concerning Government* appeared after his death in 1698.]

wish to talk.   Neither one or the other differ half as much from
the general language of cultivated society as the language of Mr
Wordsworth's homeliest composition differs from that of a
common peasant.   For 'real' therefore we must substitute
ordinary, or *lingua communis*.   And this, we have proved, is no
more to be found in the phraseology of low and rustic life than in
that of any other class.   Omit the peculiarities of each, and the
result of course must be common to all.   And assuredly the
omissions and changes to be made in the language of rustics
before it could be transferred to any species of poem, except the
drama or other professed imitation, are at least as numerous and
weighty as would be required in adapting to the same purpose the
ordinary language of tradesmen and manufacturers.   Not to
mention that the language so highly extolled by Mr Wordsworth
varies in every county, nay in every village, according to the
accidental character of the clergyman, the existence or non-
existence of schools; or even, perhaps, as the exciseman, publican
or barber happen to be, or not to be, zealous politicians and
readers of the weekly newspaper *pro bono publico*.   Anterior to
cultivation the *lingua communis* of every country, as Dante [1] has
well observed, exists everywhere in parts and nowhere as a whole.

Neither is the case rendered at all more tenable by the addition
of the words 'in a state of excitement.' [2]   For the nature of a
man's words, when he is strongly affected by joy, grief or anger,
must necessarily depend on the number and quality of the
general truths, conceptions and images, and of the words
expressing them, with which his mind had been previously
stored.   For the property of passion is not to *create*, but to set
in increased activity.   At least, whatever new connections of
thoughts or images, or (which is equally, if not more than equally,
the appropriate effect of strong excitement) whatever generalizations of truth or experience the heat of passion may produce, yet
the terms of their conveyance must have pre-existed in his
former conversations, and are only collected and crowded
together by the unusual stimulation.   It is indeed very possible
to adopt in a poem the unmeaning repetitions, habitual phrases
and other blank counters which an unfurnished or confused
understanding interposes at short intervals in order to keep hold

---

[1] [*De vulgari eloquentia*, I. xvi: 'We affirm that the vernacular language
in Italy—illustrious, cardinal, courtly and curial—is that which belongs to all
the Italian cities but not obviously to any one of them.']

[2] [Wordsworth's actual expression in the Preface is 'in a state of vivid
sensation.']

of his subject which is still slipping from him, and to give him
time for recollection; or in mere aid of vacancy, as in the scanty
companies of a country stage the same player pops backwards
and forwards, in order to prevent the appearance of empty
spaces, in the procession of *Macbeth* or *Henry VIIIth*. But
what assistance to the poet or ornament to the poem these can
supply, I am at a loss to conjecture. Nothing assuredly can
differ either in origin or in mode more widely from the apparent
tautologies of intense and turbulent feeling in which the passion
is greater and of longer endurance than to be exhausted or satisfied by a single representation of the image or incident exciting
it. Such repetitions I admit to be a beauty of the highest kind;
as illustrated by Mr Wordsworth himself from the song of
Deborah. 'At her feet he bowed, he fell, he lay down: at her
feet he bowed, he fell: where he bowed, there he fell down
dead.' [1]

[1] [Judges v. 27, quoted by Wordsworth in a note to 'The Thorn' (edd.
1800–5) to show that 'repetition and apparent tautology are frequently
beauties of the highest kind.']

CHAPTER XVIII

Language of metrical composition, why and wherein essentially different from
that of prose—Origin and elements of metre—Its necessary consequences,
and the conditions thereby imposed on the metrical writer in the choice of
his diction.

I CONCLUDE therefore that the attempt is impracticable; and
that, were it not impracticable, it would still be useless. For
the very power of making the selection implies the previous possession of the language selected. Or where can the poet have
lived? And by what rules could he direct his choice which
would not have enabled him to select and arrange his words by
the light of his own judgement? We do not adopt the language
of a class by the mere adoption of such words exclusively as that
class would use, or at least understand; but likewise by following
the order in which the words of such men are wont to succeed
each other. Now this order, in the intercourse of uneducated
men, is distinguished from the diction of their superiors in
knowledge and power by the greater disjunction and separation
in the component parts of that, whatever it be, which they wish
to communicate. There is a want of that prospectiveness of
mind, that *surview*, which enables a man to foresee the whole of
what he is to convey, appertaining to any one point; and by this
means so to subordinate and arrange the different parts according
to their relative importance as to convey it at once and as an
organized whole.

Now I will take the first stanza on which I have chanced to
open in the *Lyrical Ballads*. It is one the most simple and the
least peculiar in its language:

> In distant countries I have been,
> And yet I have not often seen
> A healthy man, a man full grown,
> Weep in the public roads, alone.
> But such a one, on English ground,
> And in the broad highway, I met;
> Along the broad highway he came,
> His cheeks with tears were wet.
> Sturdy he seemed, though he was sad,
> And in his arms a lamb he had.[1]

[1] ['The Last of the Flock' (1798), *ll.* 1–10.]

The words here are doubtless such as are current in all ranks of life: and of course not less so in the hamlet and cottage than in the shop, manufactory, college or palace. But is this the order in which the rustic would have placed the words? I am grievously deceived if the following less compact mode of commencing the same tale be not a far more faithful copy. 'I have been in a many parts far and near, and I don't know that I ever saw before a man crying by himself in the public road; a grown man I mean, that was neither sick nor hurt,' etc. etc. But when I turn to the following stanza in 'The Thorn':

> At all times of the day and night
> This wretched woman thither goes,
> And she is known to every star
> And every wind that blows:
> And there beside the Thorn she sits,
> When the blue day-light's in the skies,
> And when the whirlwind's on the hill,
> Or frosty air is keen and still,
> And to herself she cries,
> 'Oh misery! Oh misery!
> Oh woe is me! Oh misery!' [1]

and compare this with the language of ordinary men, or with that which I can conceive at all likely to proceed, in real life, from such a narrator as is supposed in the note to the poem, compare it either in the succession of the images or of the sentences, I am reminded of the sublime prayer and hymn of praise [2] which Milton, in opposition to an established liturgy, presents as a fair specimen of common extemporary devotion and such as we might expect to hear from every self-inspired minister of a conventicle! And I reflect with delight how little a mere theory, though of his own workmanship, interferes with the processes of genuine imagination in a man of true poetic genius who possesses, as Mr Wordsworth, if ever man did, most assuredly does possess,

> The vision and the faculty divine. [3]

One point then alone remains, but that the most important;

---

[1] ['The Thorn' (1798), *ll*. 67–77.]
[2] [*Paradise Lost*, v. 144 ff.:
> Lowly they bowd adoring, and began
> Thir Orisons, each Morning duly paid
> In various stile, for neither various stile
> Nor holy rapture wanted they to praise
> Thir Maker . . .]
[3] [*Excursion*, I. 79.]

its examination having been, indeed, my chief inducement for the preceding inquisition. 'There neither is or can be any essential difference between the language of prose and metrical composition.' Such is Mr Wordsworth's assertion. Now prose itself, at least in all argumentative and consecutive works, differs, and ought to differ, from the language of conversation; even as reading [1] ought to differ from talking. Unless therefore the difference denied be that of the mere words, as materials common to all styles of writing, and not of the style itself in the universally admitted sense of the term, it might be naturally presumed that there must exist a still greater between the ordonnance of poetic composition and that of prose than is expected to distinguish prose from ordinary conversation.

There are not, indeed, examples wanting in the history of literature of apparent paradoxes that have summoned the public wonder as new and startling truths but which on examination have shrunk into tame and harmless truisms; as the eyes of a cat, seen in the dark, have been mistaken for flames of fire. But Mr Wordsworth is among the last men to whom a delusion of this kind would be attributed by any one who had enjoyed the slightest opportunity of understanding his mind and character. Where an objection has been anticipated by such an author as natural, his answer to it must needs be interpreted in some sense

[1] It is no less an error in teachers than a torment to the poor children to enforce the necessity of reading as they would talk. In order to cure them of singing, as it is called, that is, of too great a difference, the child is made to repeat the words with his eyes from off the book; and then, indeed, his tones resemble talking, as far as his fears, tears and trembling will permit. But as soon as the eye is again directed to the printed page the spell begins anew; for an instinctive sense tells the child's feelings that to utter its own momentary thoughts, and to recite the written thoughts of another, as of another and a far wiser than himself, are two widely different things; and as the two acts are accompanied with widely different feelings, so must they justify different modes of enunciation. Joseph Lancaster, among his other sophistications of the excellent Dr Bell's invaluable system, cures this fault of singing by hanging fetters and chains on the child, to the music of which one of his school-fellows, who walks before, dolefully chants out the child's last speech and confession, birth, parentage and education. And this soul-benumbing ignominy, this unholy and heart-hardening burlesque on the last fearful infliction of outraged law, in pronouncing the sentence to which the stern and familiarized judge not seldom bursts into tears, has been extolled as a happy and ingenious method of remedying—what? and how?—why, one extreme in order to introduce another, scarce less distant from good sense and certainly likely to have worse moral effects, by enforcing a semblance of petulant ease and self-sufficiency, in repression, and possible after-perversion of the natural feelings. I have to beg Dr Bell's pardon for this connection of the two names, but he knows that contrast is no less powerful a cause of association than likeness. [Lancaster, a Quaker, was a rival educationalist to Coleridge's friend Andrew Bell (1753–1832), who invented the 'Madras' system of mutual instruction among schoolchildren.]

which either is, or has been, or is capable of being controverted. My object then must be to discover some other meaning for the term 'essential difference' in this place, exclusive of the indistinction and community of the words themselves. For whether there ought to exist a class of words in the English in any degree resembling the poetic dialect of the Greek and Italian is a question of very subordinate importance. The number of such words would be small indeed in our language; and even in the Italian and Greek they consist not so much of different words as of slight differences in the forms of declining and conjugating the same words; forms, doubtless, which having been, at some period more or less remote, the common grammatic flexions of some tribe or province, had been accidentally appropriated to poetry by the general admiration of certain master intellects, the first established lights of inspiration, to whom that dialect happened to be native.

Essence, in its primary signification, means the principle of individuation, the inmost principle of the possibility of any thing as that particular thing. It is equivalent to the idea of a thing, whenever we use the word *idea* with philosophic precision. Existence, on the other hand, is distinguished from essence by the superinduction of reality. Thus we speak of the essence and essential properties of a circle; but we do not therefore assert that any thing which really exists is mathematically circular. Thus too, without any tautology, we contend for the existence of the Supreme Being; that is, for a reality correspondent to the idea. There is, next, a secondary use of the word essence, in which it signifies the point or ground of contradistinction between two modifications of the same substance or subject. Thus we should be allowed to say that the style of architecture of Westminster Abbey is essentially different from that of Saint Paul's, even though both had been built with blocks cut into the same form and from the same quarry. Only in this latter sense of the term must it have been denied by Mr Wordsworth (for in this sense alone is it affirmed by the general opinion) that the language of poetry (i.e. the formal construction, or architecture, of the words and phrases) is essentially different from that of prose. Now the burthen of the proof lies with the oppugner, not with the supporters of the common belief. Mr Wordsworth, in consequence, assigns as the proof of his position 'that not only the language of a large portion of every good poem, even of the most elevated character, must necessarily, except with reference to the metre, in no respect differ from that of good prose, but likewise that some of the most interesting parts of the best poems will be found to be strictly the language of prose when prose is well written. The truth of this assertion might be demonstrated by innumerable passages from almost all the poetical writings, even of Milton himself.' He then quotes Gray's sonnet—

> In vain to me the smiling mornings shine,
> And reddening Phoebus lifts his golden fire;
> The birds in vain their amorous descant join
> Or cheerful fields resume their green attire;
> These ears, alas! for other notes repine;
> *A different object do these eyes require;*
> *My lonely anguish melts no heart but mine.*
> *And in my breast the imperfect joys expire!*
> Yet morning smiles the busy race to cheer,
> And new-born pleasure brings to happier men;
> The fields to all their wonted tribute bear,
> To warm their little loves the birds complain.
> *I fruitless mourn to him who cannot hear,*
> *And weep the more because I weep in vain;*

and adds the following remark: 'It will easily be perceived that the only part of this Sonnet which is of any value is the lines printed in italics. It is equally obvious that except in the rhyme, and in the use of the single word "fruitless" for fruitlessly, which is so far a defect, the language of these lines does in no respect differ from that of prose.'

An idealist defending his system by the fact that when asleep we often believe ourselves awake, was well answered by his plain neighbour, 'Ah! but when awake do we ever believe ourselves asleep?' Things identical must be convertible. The preceding passage seems to rest on a similar sophism. For the question is not whether there may not occur in prose an order of words which would be equally proper in a poem; nor whether there are not beautiful lines and sentences of frequent occurrence in good poems which would be equally becoming as well as beautiful in good prose; for neither the one or the other has ever been either denied or doubted by any one. The true question must be whether there are not modes of expression, a construction and an order of sentences, which are in their fit and natural place in a serious prose composition but would be disproportionate and heterogeneous in metrical poetry; and, vice versa, whether in the language of a serious poem there may not be an arrangement both of words and sentences and a use and selection of (what are called) figures of speech, both as to their kind, their frequency and their occasions, which on a subject of equal weight would be vicious and alien in correct and manly prose.   I contend that in both cases this unfitness of each for the place of the other frequently will and ought to exist.

And, first, from the origin of metre.   This I would trace to the balance in the mind effected by that spontaneous effort which strives to hold in check the workings of passion.   It might be easily explained likewise in what manner this salutary antagonism is assisted by the very state which it counteracts; and how this balance of antagonists became organized into metre (in the usual acceptation of that term) by a supervening act of the will and judgement, consciously and for the foreseen purpose of pleasure. Assuming these principles as the data of our argument, we deduce from them two legitimate conditions which the critic is entitled to expect in every metrical work.   First, that as the elements of metre owe their existence to a state of increased excitement, so the metre itself should be accompanied by the natural language of excitement.   Secondly, that as these elements are formed into metre artificially, by a voluntary act, with the design and for the purpose of blending delight with emotion, so the traces of present volition should throughout the metrical language be proportionally discernible.   Now these two conditions must be reconciled and co-present.   There must be not only a partnership, but a union; an interpenetration of passion and of will, of spontaneous impulse and of voluntary purpose.   Again, this union can be manifested only in a frequency of forms and figures of speech (originally the offspring of passion, but now the adopted children of power) greater than would be desired or endured where the emotion is not voluntarily encouraged and kept up for the sake of that pleasure which such emotion so tempered and mastered by the will is found capable of communicating.   It not only dictates, but of itself tends to produce, a more frequent employment of picturesque and vivifying language than would be natural in any other case in which there did not exist, as there does in the present, a previous and well understood, though tacit, compact between the poet and his reader, that the latter is entitled to expect and the former bound to supply this species and degree of pleasurable excitement.   We may in some measure apply to this union the answer of Polixenes, in the Winter's Tale, to Perdita's neglect of the streaked gilly-flowers, because she had heard it said,

> There is an art which in their piedness shares
> With great creating nature.
> *Pol.*   Say there be.
> Yet nature is made better by no mean
> But nature makes that mean.   So over that art,
> Which you say adds to nature, is an art
> That nature makes!   You see, sweet maid, we marry
> A gentler scion to the wildest stock:
> And make conceive a bark of baser kind
> By bud of nobler race.   This is an art,
> Which does mend nature—change it rather; but
> The art itself is nature. [1]

Secondly, I argue from the effects of metre.   As far as metre acts in and for itself, it tends to increase the vivacity and susceptibility both of the general feelings and of the attention.   This effect it produces by the continued excitement of surprize, and by the quick reciprocations of curiosity still gratified and still re-excited, which are too slight indeed to be at any one moment objects of distinct consciousness, yet become considerable in their aggregate influence.   As a medicated atmosphere, or as wine during animated conversation, they act powerfully, though themselves unnoticed.   Where, therefore, correspondent food and appropriate matter are not provided for the attention and feelings thus roused, there must needs be a disappointment felt; like that of leaping in the dark from the last step of a staircase, when we had prepared our muscles for a leap of three or four.

The discussion on the powers of metre in the preface is highly ingenious and touches at all points on truth.   But I cannot find any statement of its powers considered abstractly and separately. On the contrary, Mr Wordsworth seems always to estimate metre by the powers which it exerts during (and, as I think, in consequence of) its combination with other elements of poetry.   Thus the previous difficulty is left unanswered, what the elements are with which it must be combined in order to produce its own effects to any pleasurable purpose.   Double and trisyllable rhymes, indeed, form a lower species of wit and attended to exclusively for their own sake may become a source of momentary amusement; as in poor Smart's distich to the Welch 'Squire who had promised him a hare:

> 'Tell me, thou son of great Cadwallader!
> Hast sent the hare? or hast thou swallow'd her?' [2]

---

[1] [*Winter's Tale*, IV. 4. 87–97.]
[2] [From Christopher Smart, *To the Rev. Mr P[owel]l* (1752), *ll.* 13–14:
    'Thou valiant son of great Cadwallader,
    Hast thou a Hare, or hast thou swallow'd her?']

But for any poetic purposes, metre resembles (if the aptness of the simile may excuse its meanness) yeast, worthless or disagreeable by itself, but giving vivacity and spirit to the liquor with which it is proportionally combined.

The reference to the 'Children in the Wood'[1] by no means satisfies my judgement. We all willingly throw ourselves back for awhile into the feelings of our childhood. This ballad, therefore, we read under such recollections of our own childish feelings as would equally endear to us poems which Mr Wordsworth himself would regard as faulty in the opposite extreme of gaudy and technical ornament. Before the invention of printing, and in a still greater degree before the introduction of writing, metre, especially alliterative metre (whether alliterative at the beginning of the words, as in 'Pierce Plouman,' or at the end as in rhymes), possessed an independent value as assisting the recollection, and consequently the preservation of *any* series of truths or incidents. But I am not convinced by the collation of facts that the 'Children in the Wood' owes either its preservation, or its popularity, to its metrical form. Mr Marshal's repository[2] affords a number of tales in prose inferior in pathos and general merit, some of as old a date, and many as widely popular. Tom Hickathrift, Jack the Giant-killer, Goody Two-shoes and Little Red Riding Hood are formidable rivals. And that they have continued in prose cannot be fairly explained by the assumption that the comparative meanness of their thoughts and images precluded even the humblest forms of metre. The scene of Goody Two-shoes in the church is perfectly susceptible of metrical narration; and among the $\theta a \dot{\nu} \mu a \tau a$ $\theta a \nu \mu a \sigma \tau \acute{o} \tau a \tau a$[3] even of the present age I do not recollect a more astonishing image than that of the 'whole rookery that flew out of the giant's beard,' scared by the tremendous voice with which this monster answered the challenge of the heroic Tom Hickathrift!

If from these we turn to compositions universally and independently of all early associations beloved and admired, would

---

[1] ['Babes in the Wood,' a stanza of which is contrasted by Wordsworth in the Preface with Johnson's quatrain (p. 214 below):

These pretty Babes with hand in hand
Went wandering up and down;
But never more they saw the Man
Approaching from the Town.]

[2] [Probably the bookshop of John Marshall in Aldermary Churchyard, where many books for children were published in the 1780's.]

[3] [i.e. marvels most marvellous.]

the Maria, the Monk or the Poor Man's Ass of Sterne [1] be read with more delight, or have a better chance of immortality, had they without any change in the diction been composed in rhyme, than in their present state? If I am not grossly mistaken, the general reply would be in the negative. Nay, I will confess that in Mr Wordsworth's own volumes, the 'Anecdote for Fathers,' 'Simon Lee,' 'Alice Fell,' the 'Beggars,' and the 'Sailor's Mother,' notwithstanding the beauties which are to be found in each of them where the poet interposes the music of his own thoughts, would have been more delightful to me in prose, told and managed as by Mr Wordsworth they would have been in a moral essay or pedestrian tour.

Metre in itself is simply a stimulant of the attention, and therefore excites the question: Why is the attention to be thus stimulated? Now the question cannot be answered by the pleasure of the metre itself; for this we have shown to be conditional and dependent on the appropriateness of the thoughts and expressions to which the metrical form is superadded. Neither can I conceive any other answer that can be rationally given, short of this: I write in metre because I am about to use a language different from that of prose. Besides, where the language is not such, how interesting soever the reflections are that are capable of being drawn by a philosophic mind from the thoughts or incidents of the poem, the metre itself must often become feeble. Take the three last stanzas of the 'Sailor's Mother,' for instance. If I could for a moment abstract from the effect produced on the author's feelings, as a man, by the incident at the time of its real occurrence, I would dare appeal to his own judgement, whether in the metre itself he found sufficient reason for their being written metrically?

> And thus continuing, she said,
> 'I had a son, who many a day
> Sailed on the seas, but he is dead;
> In Denmark he was cast away:
> And I have travelled far as Hull, to see
> What clothes he might have left, or other property.

> 'The bird and cage they both were his;
> 'Twas my son's bird; and neat and trim
> He kept it: many voyages
> This singing bird hath gone with him;
> When last he sailed, he left the bird behind;
> As it might be, perhaps, from bodings of his mind.

[1] [Stories from Sterne's *A Sentimental Journey through France and Italy* (1768).]

'He to a fellow-lodger's care
Had left it, to be watched and fed,
Till he came back again; and there
I found it when my son was dead;
And now, God help me for my little wit!
I trail it with me, Sir! he took so much delight in it.'[1]

If disproportioning the emphasis we read these stanzas so as
to make the rhymes perceptible, even trisyllable rhymes could
scarcely produce an equal sense of oddity and strangeness as we
feel here in finding rhymes at all in sentences so exclusively colloquial. I would further ask whether, but for that visionary
state into which the figure of the woman and the susceptibility of
his own genius had placed the poet's imagination (a state which
spreads its influence and coloring over all that co-exists with
the exciting cause and in which

The simplest and the most familiar things
Gain a strange power of spreading awe around them [2])—

I would ask the poet whether he would not have felt an abrupt
down-fall in these verses from the preceding stanza?

The ancient spirit is not dead;
Old times, thought I, are breathing there!
Proud was I, that my country bred
Such strength, a dignity so fair!
She begged an alms, like one in poor estate;
I looked at her again, nor did my pride abate.[3]

[1] [The 'Sailor's Mother' (comp. 1802, publ. 1807), *ll.* 19–36, text of 1815
(revised for 1820).]
[2] Altered from the description of Night-Mair in the *Remorse*:
'Oh Heaven! 'twas frightful! Now run down and stared at,
By hideous shapes that cannot be remembered;
Now seeing nothing and imagining nothing,
But only being afraid—stifled with fear!
While every goodly or familiar form
Had a strange power of spreading terror round me.'
N.B. Though Shakespeare has for his own all-justifying purposes intro-
duced the Night-*Mare* with her own foals, yet Mair means a Sister, or
perhaps a Hag.
[From *Remorse*, IV. i:
'O sleep of horrors! Now run down and stared at . . .'
Edgar's charm in *Lear*, III. iv. 124 begins:
'Swithold footed thrice the old;
He met the night-mare, and her nine-fold.'
'Nine-fold' probably means 'company of nine,' but Tyrwhitt interpreted
it as 'put, for the sake of rhyme, instead of *nine-foals*.']
[3] [The 'Sailor's Mother,' *ll.* 7–12.]

It must not be omitted, and is besides worthy of notice, that those stanzas furnish the only fair instance that I have been able to discover in all Mr Wordsworth's writings of an actual adoption, or true imitation, of the real and very language of low and rustic life, freed from provincialisms.

Thirdly, I deduce the position from all the causes elsewhere assigned which render metre the proper form of poetry, and poetry imperfect and defective without metre. Metre therefore having been connected with poetry most often and by a peculiar fitness, whatever else is combined with metre must, though it be not itself essentially poetic, have nevertheless some property in common with poetry as an intermedium of affinity, a sort (if I may dare borrow a well-known phrase from technical chemistry) of *mordaunt* [1] between it and the superadded metre. Now poetry, Mr Wordsworth truly affirms, does always imply passion; [2] which word must be here understood in its most general sense, as an excited state of the feelings and faculties. And as every passion has its proper pulse, so will it likewise have its characteristic modes of expression. But where there exists that degree of genius and talent which entitles a writer to aim at the honors of a poet, the very act of poetic composition itself is, and is allowed to imply and to produce, an unusual state of excitement, which of course justifies and demands a correspondent difference of language as truly, though not perhaps in as marked a degree, as the excitement of love, fear, rage or jealousy. The vividness of the descriptions or declamations in Donne, or Dryden, is as much and as often derived from the force and fervour of the describer as from the reflections, forms or incidents which constitute their subject and materials. The wheels take fire from the mere rapidity of their motion. To what extent, and under what modifications, this may be admitted to act, I shall attempt to define in an after remark on Mr Wordsworth's reply to this objection, or rather on his objection to this reply as already anticipated in his preface.

Fourthly, and as intimately connected with this, if not the same argument in a more general form, I adduce the high spiritual instinct of the human being impelling us to seek unity by harmonious adjustment, and thus establishing the principle that all the parts of an organized whole must be assimilated to the more important and essential parts. This and the preceding

[1] [A substance used to prepare stuffs for dyeing in order to fix the colour.]
[2] [Preface, op. cit.: 'All good poetry is the spontaneous overflow of powerful feelings.']

arguments may be strengthened by the reflection that the composition of a poem is among the imitative arts; and that imitation, as opposed to copying, consists either in the interfusion of the same throughout the radically different, or of the different throughout a base radically the same.

Lastly, I appeal to the practice of the best poets of all countries and in all ages as authorizing the opinion (deduced from all the foregoing) that in every import of the word *essential* which would not here involve a mere truism, there may be, is and ought to be, an essential difference between the language of prose and of metrical composition.

In Mr Wordsworth's criticism of Gray's Sonnet, the reader's sympathy with his praise or blame of the different parts is taken for granted rather perhaps too easily. He has not, at least, attempted to win or compel it by argumentative analysis. In *my* conception at least, the lines rejected as of no value do, with the exception of the two first, differ as much and as little from the language of common life as those which he has printed in italics as possessing genuine excellence. Of the five lines thus honorably distinguished, two of them differ from prose even more widely than the lines which either precede or follow in the position of the words:

> *A different object do these eyes require;*
> My lonely anguish melts no heart but mine;
> *And in my breast the imperfect joys expire.*

But were it otherwise, what would this prove but a truth of which no man ever doubted? Videlicet, that there are sentences which would be equally in their place both in verse and prose. Assuredly it does not prove the point which alone requires proof: namely, that there are not passages which would suit the one and not suit the other. The first line of this sonnet is distinguished from the ordinary language of men by the epithet to morning. (For we will set aside, at present, the consideration, that the particular word *smiling* is hackneyed and— as it involves a sort of personification—not quite congruous with the common and material attribute of *shining*.) And, doubtless, this adjunction of epithets for the purpose of additional description where no particular attention is demanded for the quality of the thing, would be noticed as giving a poetic cast to a man's conversation. Should the sportsman exclaim, 'Come boys! the rosy morning calls you up,' he will be supposed to have some song in his head. But no one suspects this when he says, 'A

wet morning shall not confine us to our beds.' This then is
either a defect in poetry, or it is not.   Whoever should decide in
the affirmative, I would request him to re-peruse any one poem
of any confessedly great poet from Homer to Milton, or from
Eschylus to Shakespeare; and to strike out (in thought, I mean)
every instance of this kind. If the number of these fancied
erasures did not startle him, or if he continued to deem the work
improved by their total omission, he must advance reasons of
no ordinary strength and evidence, reasons grounded in the
essence of human nature.   Otherwise I should not hesitate to
consider him as a man not so much proof against all authority
as dead to it.

The second line,

>And reddening Phoebus lifts his golden fire,

has indeed almost as many faults as words.   But then it is a bad
line not because the language is distinct from that of prose, but
because it conveys incongruous images, because it confounds the
cause and the effect, the real thing with the personified representative of the thing; in short, because it differs from the
language of good sense!   That the 'Phoebus' is hackneyed, and
a schoolboy image, is an accidental fault, dependent on the age in
which the author wrote and not deduced from the nature of the
thing.   That it is part of an exploded mythology is an objection
more deeply grounded.   Yet when the torch of ancient learning
was rekindled, so cheering were its beams that our eldest poets,
cut off by Christianity from all accredited machinery, and
deprived of all acknowledged guardians and symbols of the
great objects of nature, were naturally induced to adopt as a
poetic language those fabulous personages, those forms of the
supernatural [1] in nature, which had given them such dear
delight in the poems of their great masters. Nay, even at
this day what scholar of genial taste will not so far sympathize
with them as to read with pleasure in Petrarch, Chaucer or
Spenser what he would perhaps condemn as puerile in a
modern poet?

I remember no poet whose writings would safelier stand the
test of Mr Wordsworth's theory than Spenser. Yet will Mr
Wordsworth say that the style of the following stanzas is either

---

[1] But still more by the mechanical system of philosophy which has need-
lessly infected our theological opinions, and teaching us to consider the world
in its relation to God as of a building to its mason, leaves the idea of omni-
presence a mere abstract notice in the state-room of our reason.

undistinguished from prose and the language of ordinary life? Or that it is vicious, and that the stanzas are blots in the *Faery Queen*?

> By this the northerne wagoner had set
> His sevenfold teme behind the stedfast starre,
> That was in ocean waves yet never wet,
> But firme is fixt, and sendeth light from farre
> To all, that in the wild deepe wandring arre:
> And chearefull Chauntliclere with his note shrill
> Had warned once, that Phoebus fiery carre
> In hast was climbing up the easterne hill,
> Full envious that night so long his roome did fill.
>
> Bk I, Can. 2, St. 2.[1]

> At last the golden orientall gate
> Of greatest heaven gan to open faire,
> And Phoebus fresh, as bridegrome to his mate,
> Came dauncing forth, shaking his deawie haire,
> And hurld his glistring beames through gloomy aire
> Which when the wakeful elfe perceiv'd, streight way
> He started up, and did him selfe prepaire,
> In sun-bright armes, and battailous array:
> For with that pagan proud he combat will that day.
>
> Bk I, Can. 5, St. 2.

On the contrary, to how many passages, both in hymn books and in blank verse poems, could I (were it not invidious) direct the reader's attention, the style of which is most unpoetic because, and only because, it is the style of prose? He will not suppose me capable of having in my mind such verses as

> I put my hat upon my head
> And walked into the Strand;
> And there I met another man
> Whose hat was in his hand.[2]

To such specimens it would indeed be a fair and full reply that these lines are not bad because they are unpoetic, but because they are empty of all sense and feeling; and that it were an idle attempt to prove that an ape is not a Newton, when it is evident

---

[1] [*Faerie Queene*, I. ii. 1.]

[2] [A parody by Samuel Johnson of the metre of Thomas Percy's 'The Hermit of Warkworth: a Northumberland Ballad' (1771), first published in *St James's Chronicle*, 13 January 1785. Wordsworth quoted it in the Preface in contrast to a stanza from 'Babes in the Wood' (p. 208n. above); he had probably seen it quoted in Sir John Hawkins's *Life of Johnson* (1787).]

that he is not a man.[1]   But the sense shall be good and weighty,
the language correct and dignified, the subject interesting and
treated with feeling; and yet the style shall, notwithstanding all
these merits, be justly blameable as prosaic, and solely because
the words and the order of the words would find their appropriate place in prose but are not suitable to metrical composition.
The *Civil Wars* of Daniel is an instructive and even interesting
work; but take the following stanzas (and from the hundred
instances which abound I might probably have selected others
far more striking):

> And to the end we may with better ease
> Discern the true discourse, vouchsafe to shew
> What were the times foregoing near to these,
> That these we may with better profit know:
> Tell how the world fell into this disease,
> And how so great distemperature did grow.
> So shall we see with what degrees it came,
> How things at full do soon wax out of frame.
>
> Ten kings had from the Norman Conqueror reign'd
> With intermixt and variable fate,
> When England to her greatest height attain'd
> Of power, dominion, glory, wealth, and state;
> After it had with much ado sustain'd
> The violence of princes with debate
> For titles, and the often mutinies
> Of nobles for their ancient liberties.
>
> For first the Norman, conqu'ring all by might,
> By might was forced to keep what he had got;
> Mixing our customs and the form of right
> With foreign constitutions, he had brought:
> Mastering the mighty, humbling the poorer wight,
> By all severest means that could be wrought;
> And making the succession doubtful, rent
> His new-got state, and left it turbulent.
>
> Bk I, st. vii, viii & ix.[2]

Will it be contended, on the one side, that these lines are mean
and senseless?   Or on the other, that they are not prosaic, and

---

[1] [A paraphrase of Wordsworth's own comment in the Preface: 'The
proper method . . . is not to say this is a bad kind of poetry, or this is not
poetry, but this wants sense; it is neither interesting in itself, nor can lead to
anything interesting; the images neither originate in that sane state of feeling
which arises out of thought, nor can excite thought or feeling in the reader.
This is the only sensible manner of dealing with such verses: why trouble
yourself about the species till you have previously decided upon the genus?
Why take pains to prove that an ape is not a Newton when it is self-evident
that he is not a man?']

[2] [*Civile Wars* (1595), I, st. 7–9 (spelling modernized).]

for that reason unpoetic? This poet's well-merited epithet is that of the 'well-languaged Daniel'; [1] but likewise and by the consent of his contemporaries no less than of all succeeding critics, the 'prosaic Daniel.' Yet those who thus designate this wise and amiable writer from the frequent incorrespondency of his diction to his metre in the majority of his compositions not only deem them valuable and interesting in other accounts, but willingly admit that there are to be found throughout his poems, and especially in his *Epistles* and in his *Hymen's Triumph*, many and exquisite specimens of that style which, as the neutral ground of prose and verse, is common to both. A fine and almost faultless extract, eminent as for other beauties so for its perfection in this species of diction, may be seen in Lamb's *Dramatic Specimens*, [2] etc., a work of various interest from the nature of the selections themselves (all from the plays of Shakespeare's contemporaries), and deriving a high additional value from the notes, which are full of just and original criticism, expressed with all the freshness of originality.

Among the possible effects of practical adherence to a theory that aims to identify the style of prose and verse (if it does not indeed claim for the latter a yet nearer resemblance to the average style of men in the *viva voce* intercourse of real life) we might anticipate the following as not the least likely to occur. It will happen, as I have indeed before observed, that the metre itself, the sole acknowledged difference, will occasionally become metre to the eye only. The existence of prosaisms, and that they detract from the merits of a poem, must at length be conceded when a number of successive lines can be rendered, even to the most delicate ear, unrecognizable as verse, or as having even been intended for verse, by simply transcribing them as prose: when if the poem be in blank verse, this can be effected without any alteration, or at most by merely restoring one or two words to their proper places from which they had been transplanted [3]

---

[1] [So called by William Browne (1590?–1645?), *Britannia's Pastorals* (1613–16), II. ii. 303.]

[2] [*Specimens of English Dramatic Poets*, ed. Charles Lamb (1808), I. 266–71, where 'Hymens Triumph' (1615), *ll.* 83–98, 115–38, and 1476–1631 (with omissions) is quoted by Lamb without comment. The last-named extract, the story of Isulia, is probably referred to here.]

[3] As the ingenious gentleman under the influence of the Tragic Muse contrived to dislocate, 'I wish you a good morning, Sir! Thank you, Sir, and I wish you the same,' into two blank-verse heroics:

'To you a morning good, good Sir! I wish,
You, Sir! I thank: to you the same wish I.'

In those parts of Mr Wordsworth's works which I have thoroughly studied

for no assignable cause or reason but that of the author's convenience; but if it be in rhyme, by the mere exchange of the final word of each line for some other of the same meaning, equally appropriate, dignified and euphonic.

The answer or objection in the preface to the anticipated remark 'that metre paves the way to other distinctions,' is contained in the following words: 'The distinction of rhyme and metre is voluntary and uniform, and not like that produced by (what is called) poetic diction, arbitrary and subject to infinite caprices upon which no calculation whatever can be made. In the one case the reader is utterly at the mercy of the poet respecting what imagery or diction he may choose to connect with the passion.'[1] But is this a poet of whom a poet is speaking? No, surely! rather of a fool or madman: or at best of a vain or ignorant phantast! And might not brains so wild and so deficient make just the same havock with rhymes and metres as they are supposed to effect with modes and figures of speech? How is the reader at the mercy of such men? If he continue to read their nonsense, is it not his own fault? The ultimate end of criticism is much more to establish the principles of writing than to furnish rules how to pass judgement on what has been written by others; if indeed it were possible that the two could be separated. But if it be asked by what principles the poet is to regulate his own style, if he do not adhere closely to the sort and

---

I find fewer instances in which this would be practicable than I have met in many poems where an approximation of prose has been sedulously and on system guarded against. Indeed, excepting the stanzas already quoted from the 'Sailor's Mother,' I can recollect but one instance: viz. a short passage of four or five lines in 'The Brothers,' that model of English pastoral, which I never yet read with unclouded eye: 'James, pointing to its summit, over which they had all purposed to return together, informed them that he would wait for them there. They parted, and his comrades passed that way some two hours after, but they did not find him at the appointed place, *a circumstance of which they took no heed*: but one of them going by chance into the house, which at this time was James's house, learnt there that nobody had seen him all that day.' The only change which has been made is in the position of the little word 'there' in two instances, the position in the original being clearly such as is not adopted in ordinary conversation. The other words printed in italics were so marked because, though good and genuine English, they are not the phraseology of common conversation either in the word put in apposition, or in the connection by the genitive pronoun. Men in general would have said, 'but that was a circumstance they paid no attention to, or took no notice of,' and the language is, on the theory of the preface, justified only by the narrator's being the Vicar. Yet if any ear could suspect that these sentences were ever printed as metre, on those very words alone could the suspicion have been grounded. ['The Brothers' (1800). But the poem had already been revised, especially with regard to this passage, for the third edition of the *Lyrical Ballads* (1802).]

[1] [Preface, op. cit., text of 1802.]

order of words which he hears in the market, wake, high-road or plough-field? I reply: by principles, the ignorance or neglect of which would convict him of being no poet, but a silly or presumptuous usurper of the name! By the principles of grammar, logic, psychology! In one word, by such a knowledge of the facts, material and spiritual, that most appertain to his art as, if it have been governed and applied by good sense and rendered instinctive by habit, becomes the representative and reward of our past conscious reasonings, insights and conclusions, and acquires the name of taste. By what rule that does not leave the reader at the poet's mercy, and the poet at his own, is the latter to distinguish between the language suitable to suppressed, and the language which is characteristic of indulged, anger? Or between that of rage and that of jealousy? Is it obtained by wandering about in search of angry or jealous people in uncultivated society, in order to copy their words? Or not far rather by the power of imagination proceeding upon the *all in each* of human nature? By meditation, rather than by observation? And by the latter in consequence only of the former? As eyes, for which the former has pre-determined their field of vision and to which, as to its organ, it communicates a microscopic power? There is not, I firmly believe, a man now living who has from his own inward experience a clearer intuition than Mr Wordsworth himself that the last mentioned are the true sources of genial discrimination. Through the same process and by the same creative agency will the poet distinguish the degree and kind of the excitement produced by the very act of poetic composition. As intuitively will he know what differences of style it at once inspires and justifies; what intermixture of conscious volition is natural to that state; and in what instances such figures and colors of speech degenerate into mere creatures of an arbitrary purpose, cold technical artifices of ornament or connection. For even as truth is its own light and evidence, discovering at once itself and falsehood, so is it the prerogative of poetic genius to distinguish by parental instinct its proper offspring from the changelings which the gnomes of vanity or the fairies of fashion may have laid in its cradle or called by its names. Could a rule be given from without poetry would cease to be poetry and sink into a mechanical art. It would be $\mu\acute{o}\rho\phi\omega\sigma\iota\varsigma$ not $\pi o\acute{\iota}\eta\sigma\iota\varsigma$.[1] The rules of the imagination are themselves the very powers of growth and production. The words to which

---

[1] [i.e. a fashioning, not a creation.]

they are reducible present only the outlines and external appearance of the fruit. A deceptive counterfeit of the superficial form and colors may be elaborated; but the marble peach feels cold and heavy, and children only put it to their mouths. We find no difficulty in admitting as excellent, and the legitimate language of poetic fervor self-impassioned, Donne's apostrophe to the Sun in the second stanza of his 'Progress of the Soul':

> Thee, eye of heaven! this great soul envies not:
> By thy male force is all we have begot.
> In the first East thou now beginn'st to shine,
> Suck'st early balm and island spices there;
> And wilt anon in thy loose-rein'd career
> At Tagus, Po, Seine, Thames, and Danow dine,
> And see at night this western world of mine:
> Yet hast thou not more nations seen than she,
> Who before thee one day began to be,
> And thy frail light being quenched, shall long, long outlive thee?

Or the next stanza but one:

> Great Destiny, the commissary of God,
> That hast marked out a path and period
> For ev'ry thing! Who, where we offspring took,
> Our ways and ends see'st at one instant: thou
> Knot of all causes! Thou, whose changeless brow
> Ne'er smiles or frowns! O! vouchsafe thou to look,
> And shew my story in thy eternal book, etc.

As little difficulty do we find in excluding from the honors of unaffected warmth and elevation the madness prepense of pseudo-poesy, or the startling hysteric of weakness over-exerting itself which bursts on the unprepared reader in sundry odes and apostrophes to abstract terms. Such are the Odes to Jealousy, to Hope, to Oblivion and the like, in Dodsley's collection [1] and the magazines of that day, which seldom fail to remind me of an Oxford copy of verses on the two Suttons,[2] commencing with:

> Inoculation, heavenly maid! descend!

It is not to be denied that men of undoubted talents, and even poets of true though not of first-rate genius, have from a mistaken theory deluded both themselves and others in the opposite

[1] [*A Collection of Poems*, ed. Robert Dodsley (1748, etc.).]

[2] [Daniel and Robert Sutton, who about 1760 popularized the process of inoculation. The poem on Lady Mary Wortley Montagu, first published in the *Gentleman's Mag.* (Oct. 1783), and later revised and shortened for *Oxford Prize Poems* (1807), runs:
> Inoculation, heaven-instructed maid,
> She woo'd from Turkey's shores to Britain's aid.
'She,' of course, refers to Lady Mary, and Coleridge is therefore mistaken in supposing that inoculation is personified.]

extreme. I once read to a company of sensible and well-edu-
cated women the introductory period of Cowley's preface to his
'Pindaric odes, written in imitation of the style and manner of the
odes of Pindar.' 'If (says Cowley) a man should undertake to
translate Pindar word for word, it would be thought that one mad
man had translated another; as may appear when he that understands not the original reads the verbal traduction of him into
Latin prose, than which nothing seems more raving.' I then proceeded with his own free version of the second Olympic, composed
for the charitable purpose of rationalizing the Theban Eagle:

> Queen of all harmonious things,
> Dancing words and speaking strings,
> What God, what hero wilt thou sing?
> What happy man to equal glories bring?
> Begin, begin thy noble choice,
> And let the hills around reflect the image of thy voice.
> Pisa does to Jove belong,
> Jove and Pisa claim thy song.
> The fair first-fruits of war, th' Olympic games,
> Alcides offer'd up to Jove;
> Alcides too thy strings may move;
> But oh! what man to join with these can worthy prove!
> Join Theron boldly to their sacred names;
> Theron the next honour claims;
> Theron to no man gives place;
> Is first in Pisa's, and in Virtue's race;
> Theron there, and he alone,
> Ev'n his own swift forefathers has outgone.

One of the company exclaimed, with the full assent of the rest,
that if the original were madder than this it must be incurably
mad.   I then translated the ode from the Greek, and as nearly as
possible word for word; and the impression was that in the
general movement of the periods, in the form of the connections
and transitions, and in the sober majesty of lofty sense, it
appeared to them to approach more nearly than any other poetry
they had heard to the style of our bible in the prophetic books.
The first strophe will suffice as a specimen:

> Ye harp-controlling hymns! (or) ye hymns the sovereigns of harps!
> What God? what Hero?
> What Man shall we celebrate?
> Truly Pisa indeed is of Jove,
> But the Olympiad (or the Olympic games) did Hercules establish,
> The first-fruits of the spoils of war.
> But Theron for the four-horsed car,
> That bore victory to him,

It behoves us now to voice aloud:
The Just, the Hospitable,
The Bulwark of Agrigentum,
Of renowned fathers
The Flower, even him
Who preserves his native city erect and safe.

But are such rhetorical caprices condemnable only for their deviation from the language of real life? and are they by no other means to be precluded, but by the rejection of all distinctions between prose and verse save that of metre?   Surely good sense and a moderate insight into the constitution of the human mind would be amply sufficient to prove that such language and such combinations are the native produce neither of the fancy nor of the imagination; that their operation consists in the excitement of surprize by the juxtaposition and apparent reconciliation of widely different or incompatible things.   As when, for instance, the hills are made to reflect the image of a voice.   Surely no unusual taste is requisite to see clearly that this compulsory juxtaposition is not produced by the presentation of impressive or delightful forms to the inward vision, nor by any sympathy with the modifying powers with which the genius of the poet had united and inspirited all the objects of his thought; that it is therefore a species of wit, a pure work of the will, and implies a leisure and self-possession both of thought and of feeling, incompatible with the steady fervour of a mind possessed and filled with the grandeur of its subject.   To sum up the whole in one sentence: when a poem, or a part of a poem, shall be adduced which is evidently vicious in the figures and contexture of its style, yet for the condemnation of which no reason can be assigned except that it differs from the style in which men actually converse, then, and not till then, can I hold this theory to be either plausible, or practicable, or capable of furnishing either rule, guidance or precaution that might not, more easily and more safely, as well as more naturally, have been deduced in the author's own mind from considerations of grammar, logic and the truth and nature of things, confirmed by the authority of works whose fame is not of one country nor of one age.

CHAPTER XIX

Continuation—Concerning the real object which, it is probable, Mr Wordsworth had before him in his critical preface—Elucidation and application of this—The neutral style, or that common to prose and poetry, exemplified by specimens from Chaucer, Herbert, etc.[1]

IT might appear from some passages in the former part of Mr Wordsworth's preface that he meant to confine his theory of style, and the necessity of a close accordance with the actual language of men, to those particular subjects from low and rustic life which by way of experiment he had purposed to naturalize as a new species in our English poetry. But from the train of argument that follows, from the reference to Milton and from the spirit of his critique on Gray's sonnet, those sentences appear to have been rather courtesies of modesty than actual limitations of his system. Yet so groundless does this system appear on a close examination, and so strange and overwhelming [2] in its consequences, that I cannot, and I do not, believe that the poet did ever himself adopt it in the unqualified sense in which his expressions have been understood by others and which indeed according to all the common laws of interpretation they seem to bear. What then did he mean? I apprehend that in the clear perception, not unaccompanied with disgust or contempt, of the gaudy affectations of a style which passed too current with too many for poetic diction (though in truth it had as little pretensions to poetry as to logic or common sense), he narrowed his view for the time; and feeling a justifiable preference for the language of nature and of good sense, even in its humblest and least ornamented forms, he suffered himself to express, in terms at once too large and too exclusive, his predilection for a style the

---

[1] [By some oversight the last part of this argument was originally printed at the head of ch. xx.]

[2] I had in my mind the striking but untranslatable epithet which the celebrated Mendelssohn applied to the great founder of the Critical Philosophy, 'Der alleszermalmende KANT,' i.e. the all-becrushing or rather the *all-to-nothing-crushing* KANT. In the facility and force of compound epithets, the German from the number of its cases and inflections approaches to the Greek, that language so

Bless'd in the happy marriage of sweet words.

It is in the woeful harshness of its sounds alone that the German need shrink from the comparison.

most remote possible from the false and showy splendor which he wished to explode. It is possible that this predilection, at first merely comparative, deviated for a time into direct partiality. But the real object which he had in view was, I doubt not, a species of excellence which had been long before most happily characterized by the judicious and amiable Garve, whose works are so justly beloved and esteemed by the Germans, in his remarks on Gellert,[1] from which the following is literally translated: 'The talent that is required in order to make excellent verses is perhaps greater than the philosopher is ready to admit, or would find it in his power to acquire; the talent to seek only the apt expression of the thought, and yet to find at the same time with it the rhyme and the metre. Gellert possessed this happy gift, if ever any one of our poets possessed it; and nothing perhaps contributed more to the great and universal impression which his fables made on their first publication or conduces more to their continued popularity. It was a strange and curious phenomenon, and such as in Germany had been previously unheard of, to read verses in which every thing was expressed just as one would wish to talk, and yet all dignified, attractive and interesting; and all at the same time perfectly correct as to the measure of the syllables and the rhyme. It is certain that poetry when it has attained this excellence makes a far greater impression than prose. So much so indeed, that even the gratification which the very rhymes afford becomes then no longer a contemptible or trifling gratification.'

However novel this phenomenon may have been in Germany at the time of Gellert, it is by no means new nor yet of recent existence in our language. Spite of the licentiousness with which Spenser occasionally compels the orthography of his words into a subservience to his rhymes, the whole *Faery Queen* is an almost continued instance of this beauty. Waller's song 'Go, lovely Rose, etc.,' is doubtless familiar to most of my readers; but if I had happened to have had by me the poems of Cotton,[2] more but far less deservedly celebrated as the author of the Virgil travestied, I should have indulged myself, and I think have gratified many who are not acquainted with his serious

---

[1] See *Sammlung einiger Abhandlungen von Christian Garve* [(1779), pp 233–4. Garve (1742–98) was Gellert's successor as professor of philosophy at Leipzig in 1770. The *Fabeln und Erzählungen* of Christian Gellert (1715–1769) had appeared in 1746–8 and attracted wide popularity. Cf. *Notebooks*, 1702n.].

[2] [Charles Cotton (1630–87), whose *Scarronides: or Virgile Travestie* appeared in 1664–5. His original verse which Coleridge praises here appeared posthumously in 1689 as *Poems on Several Occasions*.]

works, by selecting some admirable specimens of this style.
There are not a few poems in that volume, replete with every
excellence of thought, image and passion which we expect or
desire in the poetry of the milder muse; and yet so worded that
the reader sees no one reason either in the selection or the order
of the words why he might not have said the very same in an
appropriate conversation and cannot conceive how indeed he
could have expressed such thoughts otherwise, without loss or
injury to his meaning.

But in truth our language is, and from the first dawn of poetry
ever has been, particularly rich in compositions distinguished by
this excellence. The final *e*, which is now mute, in Chaucer's
age was either sounded or dropt indifferently. We ourselves
still use either *beloved* or *belov'd* according as the rhyme, or
measure, or the purpose of more or less solemnity may require.
Let the reader then only adopt the pronunciation of the poet and
of the court at which he lived, both with respect to the final *e* and
to the accentuation of the last syllable: I would then venture to
ask what even in the colloquial language of elegant and unaffected
women (who are the peculiar mistresses of 'pure English and
undefiled'), what could we·hear more natural, or seemingly more
unstudied, than the following stanzas from Chaucer's *Troilus
and Creseide*:

> And after this forth to the gate he went,
> Ther as Creseide out rode a ful gode paas:
> And up and doun there made he many a wente,
> And to himselfe ful oft he said, Alas!
> Fro hennis rode my blisse and my solas:
> As wouldè blisful God now for his joie,
> I might her sene agen come in to Troie!

> And to the yondir hil I gan her guide,
> Alas! and there I toke of her my leave:
> And yond I saw her to her fathir ride;
> For sorrow of whiche mine hearte shall to-cleve;
> And hithir home I came whan it was eve;
> And here I dwel; out-cast from allè joie.
> And shall, til I maie sene her efte in Troie.

> And of himselfe imaginid he ofte
> To ben defaitid, pale and waxen lesse
> Than he was wonte, and that men saidin softe,
> What may it be? who can the sothè guess,
> Why Troilus hath al this heviness?
> And al this n' as but his melancolie,
> That he had of himselfe suche fantasie.

Anothir time imaginin he would
That every wight that past him by the wey
Had of him routhe, and that thei saien should,
I am right sorry, Troilus wol die!
And thus he drove a daie yet forth or twey
As ye have herde: such life gan he to lede
As he that stode betwixin hope and drede:

For which him likid in his songis shewe
Th' encheson of his wo as he best might,
And made a songe of wordis but a fewe.
Somwhat his woeful herte for to light,
And when he was from every mann is sight
With softé voice he of his lady dere,
That absent was, gan sing as ye may here:

＊　　　＊　　　＊　　　＊　　　＊

This song when he thus songin had, ful sone
He fel agen into his sighis olde:
And every night, as was his wonte to done,
He stodè the bright moonè to beholde
And all his sorowe to the moone he tolde,
And said: I wis, whan thou art hornid newe,
I shall be glad, if al the world be trewe! [1]

Another exquisite master of this species of style where the
scholar and the poet supplies the material, but the perfect well-
bred gentleman the expressions and the arrangement, is George
Herbert. As from the nature of the subject and the too frequent
quaintness of the thoughts, his *Temple*,[2] or *Sacred Poems and
Private Ejaculations* are comparatively but little known, I shall
extract two poems. The first is a Sonnet, equally admirable for
the weight, number and expression of the thoughts, and for the
simple dignity of the language (unless indeed a fastidious taste
should object to the latter half of the sixth line). The second is a
poem of greater length, which I have chosen not only for the
present purpose, but likewise as a striking example and illustration of an assertion hazarded in a former page of these sketches:
namely that the characteristic fault of our elder poets is the

---

[1] [*Troilus and Criseyde*, v. 603–37 and 645–51.]
[2] [The *Temple* (1633) of George Herbert (1593–1633) remained unprinted
from 1709 to 1799, apart from a selection by John Wesley (1773). Except as
Wesleyan hymns the poems were largely unknown to eighteenth-century
readers, though Cowper read them with delight. The revival of his reputation begins with this passage in the *Biographia*. Coleridge's own admiration for Herbert came late; the *Temple*, 'which I used to read to amuse myself
with his quaintness, in short only to laugh at' (letter to W. Collins, December
1818), he came to prize above all English verse since Milton. Some notes by
Coleridge were included by William Pickering at the end of his edition of
Herbert's *Works* (1835–6).]

reverse of that which distinguishes too many of our more recent
versifiers; the one conveying the most fantastic thoughts in the
most correct and natural language; the other in the most
fantastic language conveying the most trivial thoughts.[1] The
latter is a riddle of words; the former an enigma of thoughts.
The one reminds me of an odd passage in Drayton's *Ideas*:

SONNET IX

As other men, so I myself do muse,
Why in this sort I wrest invention so;
And why these giddy metaphors I use,
Leaving the path the greater part do go;
I will resolve you: I am lunatic![2]

The other recalls a still odder passage in the 'Synagogue, or the
Shadow of the Temple,' a connected series of poems in imitation
of Herbert's *Temple* and in some editions annexed to it:

O how my mind
Is gravell'd!
Not a thought,
That I can find,
But's ravell'd
All to nought.
Short ends of threds,
And narrow shreds
Of lists,
Knot's snarled ruffs,
Loose broken tufts
Of twists,
Are my torn meditation's ragged cloathing.
Which, wound and woven, shape a sute for nothing:
One while I think, and then I am in pain
To think how to unthink that thought again.[3]

Immediately after these burlesque passages I cannot proceed to
the extracts promised without changing the ludicrous tone of feeling
by the interposition of the three following stanzas of Herbert's:

VIRTUE

Sweet day, so cool, so calm, so bright,
The bridal of the earth and sky:
The dew shall weep thy fall to-night,
For thou must die!

---

[1] [Cf. Dryden, *Essay of Dramatic Poesy* (1668), preferring Donne's satires
to Cleveland's: 'the one gives us deep thoughts in common language, though
rough cadence; the other gives us common thoughts in abstruse words.']
[2] ['Ideas Mirrour' (1594; 1619), No. 9 in the final version.]
[3] [Christopher Harvey (1597–1663), 'The Synagogue' (1640), which was
bound up with the sixth edition of Herbert's *Temple* and many later
editions. The quotation is from Harvey's 'Confusion,' *ll.* 1–16.]

Sweet rose, whose hue angry and brave
Bids the rash gazer wipe his eye:
Thy root is ever in its grave,
  And thou must die!

Sweet spring, full of sweet days and rose
A nest where sweets compacted lie:
My musick shows ye have your closes,
  And all must die!

THE BOSOM SIN:

A SONNET BY GEORGE HERBERT

Lord, with what care hast thou begirt us round!
Parents first season us; then schoolmasters
Deliver us to laws: they send us bound
To rules of reason, holy messengers,
Pulpits and Sundays, sorrow dogging sin,
Afflictions sorted, anguish of all sizes,
Fine nets and stratagems to catch us in,
Bibles laid open, millions of surprizes;
Blessings beforehand, ties of gratefulness,
The sound of glory ringing in our ears:
Without, our shame; within, our consciences;
Angels and grace, eternal hopes and fears!
 Yet all these fences, and their whole array
 One cunning bosom-sin blows quite away.

LOVE UNKNOWN

Dear friend, sit down, the tale is long and sad:
And in my faintings, I presume, your love
Will more comply than help.   A Lord I had,
And have, of whom some grounds, which may improve,
I hold for two lives, and both lives in me.
To him I brought a dish of fruit one day
And in the middle placed my heart.   But he
     (I sigh to say)
Lookt on a servant who did know his eye
Better than you know me, or (which is one)
Than I myself.   The servant instantly
Quitting the fruit, seiz'd on my heart alone,
And threw it in a font, wherein did fall
A stream of blood, which issued from the side
Of a great rock: I well remember all,
And have good cause: there it was dipt and dy'd,
And washt, and wrung! the very wringing yet
Enforceth tears.   *Your heart was foul, I fear.*
Indeed 'tis true.   I did and do commit
Many a fault, more than my lease will bear;
Yet still ask'd pardon, and was not deny'd.
But you shall hear.   After my heart was well,
And clean and fair, as I one eventide
     (I sigh to tell)

Walkt by myself abroad, I saw a large
And spacious furnace flaming, and thereon
A boiling caldron, round about whose verge
Was in great letters set AFFLICTION.
The greatness shew'd the owner.   So I went
To fetch a sacrifice out of my fold,
Thinking with that which I did thus present,
To warm his love which, I did fear, grew cold.
But as my heart did tender it, the man
Who was to take it from me, slipt his hand,
And threw my heart into the scalding pan;
My heart that brought it (do you understand?)
The offerer's heart.   *Your heart was hard, I fear.*
Indeed 'tis true.   I found a callous matter
Began to spread and to expatiate there:
But with a richer drug than scalding water
I bath'd it often, ev'n with holy blood,
Which at a board, while many drank bare wine,
A friend did steal into my cup for good,
Ev'n taken inwardly, and most divine
To supple hardnesses.   But at the length
Out of the caldron getting, soon I fled
Unto my house, where to repair the strength
Which I had lost, I hasted to my bed;
But when I thought to sleep out all these faults
                              (I sigh to speak)
I found that some had stuff'd the bed with thoughts,
I would say *thorns*.   Dear, could my heart not break
When with my pleasures ev'n my rest was gone?
Full well I understood who had been there:
For I had given the key to none but one:
It must be he.   *Your heart was dull, I fear.*
Indeed a slack and sleepy state of mind
Did oft possess me, so that when I pray'd,
Though my lips went, my heart did stay behind.
But all my scores were by another paid,
Who took the debt upon him.   *Truly friend,*
For ought I hear, your master shows to you
More favour than you wot of.   Mark the end!
The font did only what was old renew:
The caldron suppled what was grown too hard:
The thorns did quicken what was grown too dull:
All did but strive to mend what you had marr'd.
Wherefore be cheer'd, and praise him to the full
Each day, each hour, each moment of the week,
Who fain would have you be new, tender, quick! [1]

---

[1] ['Vertue' (last stanza omitted), 'Sinne,' and 'Love Unknown.' In 'Vertue,' *l*. 10, Coleridge has substituted 'nest' for the 'box' of the original, apparently as a deliberate 'improvement' since the suggestion is repeated in his notes on Herbert in the Pickering edition (op. cit.).]

CHAPTER XX

The former subject continued

I HAVE no fear in declaring my conviction that the excellence defined and exemplified in the preceding chapter is not the characteristic excellence of Mr Wordsworth's style; because I can add, with equal sincerity, that it is precluded by higher powers. The praise of uniform adherence to genuine, logical English is undoubtedly his; nay, laying the main emphasis on the word *uniform*, I will dare add that, of all contemporary poets, it is his alone. For in a less absolute sense of the word, I should certainly include Mr Bowles, Lord Byron, and, as to all his later writings, Mr Southey, the exceptions in their works being so few and unimportant. But of the specific excellence described in the quotation from Garve, I appear to find more and more undoubted specimens in the works of others; for instance, among the minor poems of Mr Thomas Moore, and of our illustrious Laureate.[1] To me it will always remain a singular and noticeable fact that a theory which would establish this *lingua communis*, not only as the best, but as the only commendable style, should have proceeded from a poet whose diction, next to that of Shakespeare and Milton, appears to me of all others the most individualized and characteristic. And let it be remembered too that I am now interpreting the controverted passages of Mr W.'s critical preface by the purpose and object which he may be supposed to have intended rather than by the sense which the words themselves must convey if they are taken without this allowance.

A person of any taste who had but studied three or four of Shakespeare's principal plays would without the name affixed scarcely fail to recognize as Shakespeare's a quotation from any other play, though but of a few lines. A similar peculiarity, though in a less degree, attends Mr Wordsworth's style whenever he speaks in his own person; or whenever, though under a feigned name, it is clear that he himself is still speaking, as in

---

[1] [Robert Southey.]

229

the different *dramatis personae* of the *Recluse*.[1] Even in the
other poems in which he purposes to be most dramatic there are
few in which it does not occasionally burst forth.   The reader
might often address the poet in his own words with reference to
persons introduced:

> It seems, as I retrace the ballad line by line,
> That but half of it is theirs, and the better half is thine.[2]

Who, having been previously acquainted with any considerable portion of Mr Wordsworth's publications and having
studied them with a full feeling of the author's genius, would not
at once claim as Wordsworthian the little poem on the rainbow?

> The child is father of the man, etc.[3]

Or in the Lucy Gray?

> No mate, no comrade Lucy knew:
> She dwelt on a wide moor;
> *The sweetest thing that ever grew*
> *Beside a human door.*[4]

Or in the 'Idle Shepherd-Boys'?

> Along the river's stony marge
> The sand-lark chants a joyous song;
> The thrush is busy in the wood,
> And carols loud and strong.
> A thousand lambs are on the rocks
> All newly born! both earth and sky
> Keep jubilee, and more than all,
> Those boys with their green coronal;
> They never hear the cry,
> That plaintive cry! which up the hill
> Comes from the depths of Dungeon-Ghyll.[5]

Need I mention the exquisite description of the Sea Loch in
the 'Blind Highland Boy'?   Who but a poet tells a tale in such
language to the little ones by the fire-side as—

[1] [The 'long and laborious work' in three parts, never accomplished, of
which the *Excursion* was to be the second and the *Prelude* the 'ante-chapel.'
In his Preface to the *Excursion* (1814) Wordsworth had announced that there
'the intervention of characters speaking is employed, and something of a
dramatic form adopted,' whereas the unwritten Parts I and III were to
'consist chiefly of meditations in the author's own person.']

[2] [From the 'Pet-Lamb' (1800), *ll*. 63–4:
> 'And it seemed, as I retraced the ballad line by line,
> That but half of it was hers, and one half of it was mine.']

[3] ['My heart leaps up . . .' (comp. 1802, publ. 1807), *l*. 7.]

[4] ['Lucy Gray' (comp. 1799, publ. 1800), *ll*. 5–8.]

[5] ['The Idle Shepherd-Boys' (1800), *ll*. 23–33.]

Yet had he many a restless dream,
Both when he heard the eagle's scream,
And when he heard the torrents roar,
And heard the water beat the shore
    Near where their cottage stood.

Beside a lake their cottage stood,
Not small like ours, a peaceful flood;
But one of mighty size, and strange;
That rough or smooth is full of change,
    And stirring in its bed.

For to this lake by night and day,
The great sea-water finds its way
Through long, long windings of the hills,
And drinks up all the pretty rills
    And rivers large and strong:

Then hurries back the road it came—
Returns on errand still the same;
This did it when the earth was new;
And this for evermore will do,
    As long as earth shall last.

And, with the coming of the tide,
Come boats and ships that sweetly ride,
Between the woods and lofty rocks;
And to the shepherds with their flocks
    Bring tales of distant lands.[1]

I might quote almost the whole of his 'Ruth,' but take the following stanzas:

But as you have before been told,
This stripling, sportive, gay, and bold,
And with his dancing crest,
So beautiful, through savage lands
Had roamed about with vagrant bands
    Of Indians in the West.

The wind, the tempest roaring high,
The tumult of a tropic sky,
Might well be dangerous food
For him, a youth to whom was given
So much of earth, so much of heaven,
    And such impetuous blood.

[1] ['The Blind Highland Boy' (comp. 1806, publ. 1807), *ll.* 46-70.]

Whatever in those climes he found
Irregular in sight or sound,
Did to his mind impart
A kindred impulse, seemed allied
To his own powers, and justified
          The workings of his heart.

Nor less to feed voluptuous thought
The beauteous forms of nature wrought
Fair trees and lovely flowers;
The breezes their own languor lent;
The stars had feelings, which they sent
          Into those magic bowers.

Yet in his worst pursuits, I ween,
That sometimes there did intervene
Pure hopes of high intent:
For passions linked to forms so fair
And stately, needs must have their share
          Of noble sentiment.[1]

But from Mr Wordsworth's more elevated compositions, which already form three-fourths of his works and will, I trust, constitute hereafter a still greater proportion—from these, whether in rhyme or in blank verse, it would be difficult and almost superfluous to select instances of a diction peculiarly his own, of a style which cannot be imitated without being at once recognized as originating in Mr Wordsworth. It would not be easy to open on any one of his loftier strains that does not contain examples of this; and more in proportion as the lines are more excellent and most like the author. For those who may happen to be less familiar with his writings I will give three specimens taken with little choice. The first from the lines on the 'Boy of Winander-Mere,' who

Blew mimic hootings to the silent owls,
That they might answer him. And they would shout,
Across the watery vale and shout again
With long halloos, and screams, and echoes loud
Redoubled and redoubled, concourse wild
Of mirth and jocund din! And when it chanced,
That pauses of deep silence mock'd his skill,
Then sometimes in that silence, while he hung
Listening, a gentle shock of mild surprise
Has carried far into his heart the voice

[1] ['Ruth' (comp. 1799, publ. 1800), *ll.* 115–44, text of 1800–5.]

Of mountain torrents: or the visible scene [1]
Would enter unawares into his mind
With all its solemn imagery, its rocks,
Its woods, and that uncertain heaven, received
Into the bosom of the steady lake.[2]

The second shall be that noble imitation of Drayton [3] (if it was
not rather a coincidence) in the 'Joanna':

When I had gazed perhaps two minutes' space,
Joanna, looking in my eyes, beheld
That ravishment of mind, and laughed aloud.

[1] Mr Wordsworth's having judiciously adopted 'concourse wild' in this
passage for 'a wild scene' as it stood in the former edition, encourages me to
hazard a remark which I certainly should not have made in the works of a
poet less austerely accurate in the use of words than he is, to his own great
honor.   It respects the propriety of the word 'scene' even in the sentence in
which it is retained.   Dryden, and he only in his more careless verses, was the
first, as far as my researches have discovered, who for the convenience of
rhyme used this word in the vague sense which has been since too current
even in our best writers and which (unfortunately, I think) is given as its first
explanation in Dr Johnson's Dictionary, and therefore would be taken by an
incautious reader as its proper sense.   In Shakespeare and Milton the word
is never used without some clear reference, proper or metaphorical, to the
theatre.   Thus Milton:

'Cedar and pine, and fir and branching palm
A sylvan *scene*; and as the ranks ascend
Shade above shade, a woody *theatre*
Of stateliest view.'

I object to any extension of its meaning, because the word is already more
equivocal than might be wished; inasmuch as in the limited use which I
recommend it may still signify two different things; namely the scenery, and
the characters and actions presented on the stage during the presence of
particular scenes.   It can therefore be preserved from obscurity only by
keeping the original signification full in the mind.   Thus Milton again:

'Prepare thee for another scene.'

[Wordsworth made the change for the fourth edition of the *Lyrical
Ballads* (1805).   Coleridge is mistaken in supposing that Johnson listed the
'vague' sense of the word first; in fact he entered 'the stage' as the first
sense and quoted the two passages from Milton reproduced (*Paradise
Lost*, iv. 139–42 and xi. 633) as examples of the second.   It was undoubtedly
Dryden's use of the word in the extended sense that led to its abuse by Pope,
Cowper and other eighteenth-century poets.]
[2] [From 'There was a Boy' (comp. 1798, publ. 1800), *ll*. 10–12, 14–25,
later incorporated into the *Prelude*, v. 373 ff.]
[3] 'Which Copland scarce had spoke, but quickly every hill
Upon her verge that stands, the neighbouring vallies fill;
Helvillon from his height, it through the mountains threw,
From whom as soon again, the sound Dunbalrase drew,
From whose stone-trophied head, it on the Wendross went,
Which, tow'rds the sea again, resounded it to Dent.
That Brodwater, therewith within her banks astound,
In sailing to the sea told it to Egremound,
Whose buildings, walks and streets, with echoes loud and long,
Did mightily commend old Copland for her song!'
                          DRAYTON's *Polyolbion*: Song XXX.

The rock, like something starting from a sleep,
Took up the lady's voice, and laughed again!
That ancient woman seated on Helm-crag
Was ready with her cavern!   Hammar-scar,
And the tall steep of Silver-How sent forth
A noise of laughter: southern Loughrigg heard,
And Fairfield answered with a mountain tone.
Helvellyn far into the clear blue sky
Carried the lady's voice!—old Skiddaw blew
His speaking trumpet!—back out of the clouds
From Glaramara southward came the voice:
And Kirkstone tossed it from his misty head! [1]

The third, which is in rhyme, I take from the 'Song at the
Feast of Brougham Castle, upon the restoration of Lord Clifford
the shepherd to the estates of his ancestors':

Now another day is come,
Fitter hope, and nobler doom:
He hath thrown aside his crook,
And hath buried deep his book;
Armour rusting in the halls
On the blood of Clifford calls;
Quell the Scot, exclaims the lance!
Bear me to the heart of France,
Is the longing of the shield—
Tell thy name, thou trembling field!
Field of death, where'er thou be,
Groan thou with our victory!
Happy day, and mighty hour,
When our shepherd in his power,
Mailed and horsed, with lance and sword,
To his ancestors restored
Like a re-appearing star,
Like a glory from afar,
First shall head the flock of war!

Alas! the fervent harper did not know
That for a tranquil soul the lay was framed,
Who, long compelled in humble walks to go,
Was softened into feeling, soothed, and tamed.

Love had he found in huts where poor men lie:
His daily teachers had been woods and rills,
The silence that is in the starry sky,
The sleep that is among the lonely hills. [2]

The words themselves in the foregoing extracts are, no doubt,
sufficiently common for the greater part.   (But in what poem are

[1] ['To Joanna' (1800), *ll.* 51–65.]
[2] ['Song at the Feast of Brougham Castle' (1807), *ll.* 138–64.]

they not so? if we except a few misadventurous attempts to translate the arts and sciences into verse?)   In the *Excursion* the
number of polysyllabic (or what the common people call
dictionary) words is more than usually great.   And so must it
needs be, in proportion to the number and variety of an author's
conceptions and his solicitude to express them with precision.
But are those words in those places commonly employed in real
life to express the same thought or outward thing?   Are they the
style used in the ordinary intercourse of spoken words?   No!
nor are the modes of connections: and still less the breaks and
transitions.   Would any but a poet—at least could any one
without being conscious that he had expressed himself with
noticeable vivacity—have described a bird singing loud by 'The
thrush is *busy* in the wood'?   Or have spoken of boys with a
string of club-moss round their rusty hats, as the boys 'with
their green coronal'?   Or have translated a beautiful May-day
into 'Both earth and sky keep jubilee'?   Or have brought all the
different marks and circumstances of a sea-loch before the mind,
as the actions of a living and acting power?   Or have represented
the reflection of the sky in the water as 'That uncertain heaven
received into the bosom of the steady lake'?   Even the gram-
matical construction is not unfrequently peculiar; as 'The
wind, the tempest roaring high, the tumult of a tropic sky, might
well be *dangerous food to him*, a youth to whom was given,' etc.
There is a peculiarity in the frequent use of the ἀσυνάρτητον (i.e.
the omission of the connective particle before the last of several
words, or several sentences used grammatically as single words,
all being in the same case and governing or governed by the same
verb), and not less in the construction of words by apposition
(*to him, a youth*).   In short, were there excluded from Mr
Wordsworth's poetic compositions all that a literal adherence to
the theory of his preface would exclude, two-thirds at least of the
marked beauties of his poetry must be erased.   For a far greater
number of lines would be sacrificed than in any other recent poet;
because the pleasure received from Wordsworth's poems being
less derived either from excitement of curiosity or the rapid
flow of narration, the striking passages form a larger proportion
of their value.   I do not adduce it as a fair criterion of comparative excellence, nor do I even think it such; but merely as
matter of fact.   I affirm that from no contemporary writer could
so many lines be quoted without reference to the poem in which
they are found, for their own independent weight or beauty.
From the sphere of my own experience I can bring to my

recollection three persons, of no every-day powers and acquirements, who had read the poems of others with more and more
unallayed pleasure, and had thought more highly of their authors
as poets; who yet have confessed to me, that from no modern
work had so many passages started up anew in their minds at
different times, and as different occasions had awakened a
meditative mood.

CHAPTER XXI

Remarks on the present mode of conducting critical journals.

LONG have I wished to see a fair and philosophical inquisition into the character of Wordsworth as a poet, on the evidence of his published works; and a positive, not a comparative, appreciation of their characteristic excellences, deficiences and defects. I know no claim that the mere opinion of any individual can have to weigh down the opinion of the author himself; against the probability of whose parental partiality we ought to set that of his having thought longer and more deeply on the subject. But I should call that investigation fair and philosophical in which the critic announces and endeavors to establish the principles which he holds for the foundation of poetry in general, with the specification of these in their application to the different classes of poetry. Having thus prepared his canons of criticism for praise and condemnation, we would proceed to particularize the most striking passages to which he deems them applicable, faithfully noticing the frequent or infrequent recurrence of similar merits or defects, and as faithfully distinguishing what is characteristic from what is accidental, or a mere flagging of the wing. Then if his premises be rational, his deductions legitimate and his conclusions justly applied, the reader, and possibly the poet himself, may adopt his judgement in the light of judgement and in the independence of free agency. If he has erred, he presents his errors in a definite place and tangible form, and holds the torch and guides the way to their detection.

I most willingly admit, and estimate at a high value, the services which the *Edinburgh Review*,[1] and others formed afterwards on the same plan, have rendered to society in the diffusion of knowledge. I think the commencement of the *Edinburgh Review* an important epoch in periodical criticism; and that it has a claim upon the gratitude of the literary republic, and indeed of the reading public at large, for having originated the scheme of reviewing those books only which are susceptible and deserving

[1] [The *Edinburgh Review* (1802–1929) was founded in Edinburgh in October 1802 by Francis Jeffrey, Sydney Smith and others, and was soon followed by the *Literary Journal* (1803–6), the *Monthly Repository* (1806–37), the *London Review* (1809), the *Quarterly Review* (1809–) and many others.]

of argumentative criticism.   Not less meritorious, and far more
faithfully and in general far more ably executed, is their plan of
supplying the vacant place of the trash or mediocrity wisely left
to sink into oblivion by their own weight with original essays on
the most interesting subjects of the time, religious or political;
in which the titles of the books or pamphlets prefixed furnish
only the name and occasion of the disquisition.   I do not arraign
the keenness or asperity of its damnatory style in and for itself,
as long as the author is addressed or treated as the mere impersonation of the work then under trial.   I have no quarrel
with them on this account, as long as no personal allusions are
admitted, and no re-commitment (for new trial) of juvenile
performances that were published, perhaps forgotten, many
years before the commencement of the review; [1] since for the
forcing back of such works to public notice no motives are easily
assignable but such as are furnished to the critic by his own
personal malignity; or what is still worse, by a habit of malignity
in the form of mere wantonness.

> No private grudge they need, no personal spite:
> The *viva sectio* is its own delight!
> All enmity, all envy, they disclaim,
> Disinterested thieves of our good name:
> Cool, sober murderers of their neighbour's fame!
>
>   S. T. C. [2]

Every censure, every sarcasm respecting a publication which
the critic, with the criticized work before him, can make good is
the critic's right.   The writer is authorized to reply, but not to
complain.   Neither can any one prescribe to the critic how soft
or how hard, how friendly or how bitter, shall be the phrases
which he is to select for the expression of such reprehension or
ridicule.   The critic must know what effect it is his object to
produce; and with a view to this effect must he weigh his words.
But as soon as the critic betrays that he knows more of his
author than the author's publications could have told him, as
soon as from this more intimate knowledge, elsewhere obtained,
he avails himself of the slightest trait against the author, his

---

[1] [Seven years before Coleridge had written to Jeffrey (23 May 1808),
protesting he had 'frequently introduced my name when I had never brought
any publication within your court.   With one slight exception, a shilling
pamphlet that never obtained the least notice, I have not published anything
with my name, or known to be mine, for thirteen years.']

[2] [This epigram appears here for the first time and may have been written
for this context.]

censure instantly becomes personal injury, his sarcasms personal insults. He ceases to be a critic and takes on him the most contemptible character to which a rational creature can be degraded, that of a gossip, backbiter and pasquillant: but with this heavy aggravation, that he steals the unquiet, the deforming passions of the world into the museum; into the very place which, next to the chapel and oratory, should be our sanctuary and secure place of refuge; offers abominations on the altar of the muses; and makes its sacred paling the very circle in which he conjures up the lying and prophane spirit.

This determination of unlicensed personality and of permitted and legitimate censure (which I owe in part to the illustrious Lessing,[1] himself a model of acute, spirited, sometimes stinging, but always argumentative and honorable criticism) is beyond controversy the true one; and though I would not myself exercise all the rights of the latter, yet, let but the former be excluded, I submit myself to its exercise in the hands of others, without complaint and without resentment.

Let a communication be formed between any number of learned men in the various branches of science and literature; and whether the president or central committee be in London, or Edinburgh, if only they previously lay aside their individuality and pledge themselves inwardly, as well as ostensibly, to administer judgement according to a constitution and code of laws; and if by grounding this code on the two-fold basis of universal morals and philosophic reason, independent of all foreseen application to particular works and authors, they obtain the right to speak each as the representative of their body corporate; they shall have honor and good wishes from me, and I shall accord to them their fair dignities, though self-assumed, not less chearfully than if I could inquire concerning them in the herald's office, or turn to them in the book of peerage. However loud may be the outcries for prevented or subverted

---

[1] [*Briefe antiquarischen Inhalts* (1768–9), Letter 57, from which most of the preceding paragraph is a direct translation: 'Jeder Tadel, jeder Spott, den der Kunstrichter mit dem kritisierten Buch in der Hand gut machen kann, ist dem Kunstrichter erlaubt. Auch kann ihm niemand vorschreiben, wie sanft oder wie hart, wie lieblich oder wie bitter er die Ausdrücke eines solchen Tadels oder Spottes wählen soll. Er muss wissen, welche Wirkung er damit hervorbringen will, und es ist nothwendig, dass er seine Worte nach dieser Wirkung abwägt. Aber sobald der Kunstrichter verrät, dass er von seinem Autor mehr weiss, als ihm die Schriften desselben sagen können; sobald er sich aus dieser nähern Kenntnis des geringsten nachteiligen Zuges wider ihn bedienet, sogleich wird sein Tadel persönliche Beleidigung. Er höret auf, Kunstrichter zu sein, und wird—das Verächtlichste, was ein vernünftiges Geschöpf werden kann—Klätscher, Anschwärzer, Pasquillant.']

reputation, however numerous and impatient the complaints of merciless severity and insupportable despotism, I shall neither feel nor utter aught but to the defence and justification of the critical machine. Should any literary Quixote find himself provoked by its sounds and regular movements, I should admonish him, with Sancho Panza, that it is no giant but a windmill; there it stands on its own place and its own hillock, never goes out of the way to attack any one, and to none and from none either gives or asks assistance. When the public press has poured in any part of its produce between its mill-stones, it grinds it off, one man's sack the same as another, and with whatever wind may then happen to be blowing. All the two and thirty winds are alike its friends. Of the whole wide atmosphere it does not desire a single finger-breadth more than what is necessary for its sails to turn round in. But this space must be left free and unimpeded. Gnats, beetles, wasps, butter-flies and the whole tribe of ephemerals and insignificants may flit in and out and between; may hum, and buzz, and jar; may shrill their tiny pipes, and wind their puny horns, unchastised and unnoticed. But idlers and bravadoes of larger size and prouder show must beware how they place themselves within its sweep. Much less may they presume to lay hands on the sails, the strength of which is neither greater or less than as the wind is which drives them round. Whomsoever the remorseless arm slings aloft, or whirls along with it in the air, he has himself alone to blame; though when the same arm throws him from it, it will more often double than break the force of his fall.

Putting aside the too manifest and too frequent interference of national party, and even personal predilection or aversion, and reserving for deeper feelings those worse and more criminal intrusions into the sacredness of private life which not seldom merit legal rather than literary chastisement, the two principal objects and occasions which I find for blame and regret in the conduct of the review in question are: first, its unfaithfulness to its own announced and excellent plan,[1] but subjecting to criticism works neither indecent or immoral, yet of such trifling importance even in point of size and, according to the critic's own verdict, so devoid of all merit as must excite in the most candid mind the suspicion either that dislike or vindictive

---

[1] [In their Advertisement to the first number (October 1802) the editors announced 'that it forms no part of their object to take note of every pro-duction that issues from the press: and that they wish their journal to be distinguished rather for the selection than for the number of articles.']

feelings were at work; or that there was a cold prudential pre-determination to increase the sale of the review by flattering the malignant passions of human nature. That I may not myself become subject to the charge which I am bringing against others by an accusation without proof, I refer to the article on Dr Rennell's sermon [1] in the very first number of the *Edinburgh Review* as an illustration of my meaning. If in looking through all the succeeding volumes the reader should find this a solitary instance, I must submit to that painful forfeiture of esteem which awaits a groundless or exaggerated charge.

The second point of objection belongs to this review only in common with all other works of periodical criticism; at least, it applies in common to the general system of all, whatever exception there may be in favor of particular articles. Or if it attaches to the *Edinburgh Review*, and to its only co-rival (the *Quarterly*) with any peculiar force, this results from the superiority of talent, acquirement and information which both have so undeniably displayed, and which doubtless deepens the regret though not the blame. I am referring to the substitution of assertion for argument; to the frequency of arbitrary and sometimes petulant verdicts, not seldom unsupported even by a single quotation from the work condemned, which might at least have explained the critic's meaning if it did not prove the justice of his sentence. Even where this is not the case the extracts are too often made without reference to any general grounds or rules from which the faultiness or inadmissibility of the qualities attributed may be deduced, and without any attempt to show that the qualities *are* attributable to the passage extracted. I have met with such extracts from Mr Wordsworth's poems annexed to such assertions as lead me to imagine that the reviewer, having written his critique before he had read the work, had been pricked with a pin for passages wherewith to illustrate the various branches of his preconceived opinions. By what principle of rational choice can we suppose a critic to have been directed (at least in a Christian country, and himself, we hope, a Christian) who gives the following lines, portraying the fervor of solitary devotion excited by the magnificent display of the Almighty's works, as a proof and example of an author's tendency to downright ravings and absolute unintelligibility?

> O then what soul was his, when on the tops
> Of the high mountains he beheld the sun

[1] [Thomas Rennell, *Discourses on Various Subjects* (1801).]

Rise up, and bathe the world in light! He looked—
Ocean and earth, the solid frame of earth,
And ocean's liquid mass, beneath him lay
In gladness and deep joy.   The clouds were touched,
And in their silent faces did he read
Unutterable love!   Sound needed none,
Nor any voice of joy: his spirit drank
The spectacle! sensation, soul, and form,
All melted into him.   They swallowed up
His animal being: in them did he live,
And by them did he live: they were his life.

$$\hspace{8cm}(Excursion.)\text{ }^1$$

Can it be expected that either the author or his admirers should
be induced to pay any serious attention to decisions which prove
nothing but the pitiable state of the critic's own taste and sensibility?   On opening the review they see a favorite passage, of
the force and truth of which they had an intuitive certainty in
their own inward experience confirmed, if confirmation it could
receive, by the sympathy of their most enlightened friends; some
of whom perhaps, even in the world's opinion, hold a higher intellectual rank than the critic himself would presume to claim.
And this very passage they find selected as the characteristic
effusion of a mind deserted by reason; as furnishing evidence
that the writer was raving, or he could not have thus strung
words together without sense or purpose!   No diversity of taste
seems capable of explaining such a contrast in judgement.

That I had over-rated the merit of a passage or poem, that I
had erred concerning the degree of its excellence, I might be
easily induced to believe or apprehend.   But that lines, the sense
of which I had analysed and found consonant with all the best
convictions of my understanding, and the imagery and diction
of which had collected round those convictions my noblest as
well as my most delightful feelings; that I should admit such
lines to be mere nonsense or lunacy, is too much for the most
ingenious arguments to effect.   But that such a revolution of
taste should be brought about by a few broad assertions seems
little less than impossible.   On the contrary, it would require
an effort of charity not to dismiss the criticism with the aphorism
of the wise man, 'in animam malevolam sapientia haud intrare
potest.' ²

---

¹ [I. 198–210. The *Excursion* was reviewed and damned by Jeffrey in
November 1814.]
² [From the apocryphal Wisdom of Solomon, I. 4: 'Wisdom cannot enter
into a malevolent soul.' (The Vulgate reads: 'In malevolam animam non
introibit sapientia.')]

What then if this very critic should have cited a large number of single lines and even of long paragraphs which he himself acknowledges to possess eminent and original beauty? What if he himself has owned that beauties as great are scattered in abundance throughout the whole book? And yet, though under this impression, should have commenced his critique in vulgar exaltation with a prophecy meant to secure its own fulfilment? With a 'This won't do!'[1] What if after such acknowledgements extorted from his own judgement he should proceed from charge to charge of tameness and raving, flights and flatness, and at length, consigning the author to the house of incurables, should conclude with a strain of rudest contempt evidently grounded in the distempered state of his own moral associations? Suppose too all this done without a single leading principle established or even announced, and without any one attempt at argumentative deduction, though the poet had presented a more than usual opportunity for it by having previously made public his own principles of judgement in poetry and supported them by a connected train of reasoning!

The office and duty of the poet is to select the most dignified as well as

> The happiest, gayest attitude of things.[2]

The reverse, for in all cases a reverse is possible, is the appropriate business of burlesque and travesty, a predominant taste for which has been always deemed a mark of a low and degraded mind. When I was at Rome, among many other visits to the tomb of Julius II I went thither once with a Prussian artist, a man of genius and great vivacity of feeling. As we were gazing on Michael Angelo's Moses, our conversation turned on the horns and beard of that stupendous statue; of the necessity of each to support the other; of the superhuman effect of the former and the necessity of the existence of both to give a harmony and integrity both to the image and the feeling excited by it. Conceive them removed, and the statue would become un-natural, without being super-natural. We called to mind the horns of

---

[1] [Jeffrey's review (op. cit.) begins: 'This will never do! It bears no doubt the stamp of the author's heart and fancy, but unfortunately not half so visibly as that of his particular system. . . . It is longer, weaker and tamer than any of Mr Wordsworth's other productions. . . . The case of Mr Wordsworth, we perceive, is now manifestly hopeless; and we give him up as altogether incurable and beyond the power of criticism.' Severe as Jeffrey's strictures were, Coleridge has here exaggerated their severity.]

[2] [Mark Akenside (1721-70), The Pleasures of Imagination (1744), I. 30:
'The gayest, happiest attitude of things.']

the rising sun, and I repeated the noble passage from Taylor's *Holy Dying*.[1] That horns were the emblem of power and sovereignty among the Eastern nations, and are still retained as such in Abyssinia; the Achelous of the ancient Greeks; and the probable ideas and feelings that originally suggested the mixture of the human and the brute form in the figure by which they realized the idea of their mysterious Pan, as representing intelligence blended with a darker power, deeper, mightier and more universal than the conscious intellect of man, than intelligence: all these thoughts and recollections passed in procession before our minds. My companion, who possessed more than his share of the hatred which his countrymen bore to the French, had just observed to me, 'A Frenchman, Sir! is the only animal in the human shape that by no possibility can lift itself up to religion or poetry'; when, lo! two French officers of distinction and rank entered the church! 'Mark you,' whispered the Prussian, 'the first thing which those scoundrels will notice (for they will begin by instantly noticing the statue in parts, without one moment's pause of admiration impressed by the whole) will be the horns and the beard. And the associations which they will immediately connect with them will be those of a he-goat and a cuckold.' Never did man guess more luckily. Had he inherited a portion of the great legislator's prophetic powers whose statue we had been contemplating he could scarcely have uttered words more coincident with the result; for even as he had said, so it came to pass.

In the *Excursion* the poet has introduced an old man, born in humble but not abject circumstances, who had enjoyed more than usual advantages of education, both from books and from the more awful discipline of nature. This person he represents as having been driven by the restlessness of fervid feelings and from a craving intellect to an itinerant life, and as having in consequence passed the larger portion of his time from earliest manhood in villages and hamlets from door to door,

A vagrant merchant bent beneath his load.[2]

[1] [*Holy Dying* (1651), I. iii. 2: 'For the life of a man comes upon him slowly and insensibly. But as when the sun approaches towards the gates of the morning he first opens a little eye of Heaven, and sends away the spirits of darknesse, and gives light to a cock, and calls up the lark to mattins, and by and by gilds the fringes of a cloud and peeps over the eastern hills, thrusting out his golden horns like those which decked the browes of Moses when he was forced to wear a vail because himself had seen the face of God . . .' Cf. Exodus, xxxiv. 33–5.]
[2] [*Excursion*, I. 324.]

Now whether this be a character appropriate to a lofty didactick poem is perhaps questionable.　It presents a fair subject for controversy; and the question is to be determined by the congruity or incongruity of such a character with what shall be proved to be the essential constituents of poetry.　But surely the critic who, passing by all the opportunities which such a mode of life would present to such a man; all the advantages of the liberty of nature, of solitude and of solitary thought; all the varieties of places and seasons through which his track had lain, with all the varying imagery they bring with them; and lastly, all the observations of men,

> Their manners, their enjoyments and pursuits,
> Their passions and their feelings [1]

which the memory of these yearly journies must have given and recalled to such a mind—the critic, I say, who from the multitude of possible associations should pass by all these in order to fix his attention exclusively on the pin-papers and stay-tapes which *might* have been among the wares of his pack: this critic in my opinion cannot be thought to possess a much higher or much healthier state of moral feeling than the Frenchmen above recorded.

[Ibid., i. 342–3.]

CHAPTER XXII

The characteristic defects of Wordsworth's poetry, with the principles from which the judgement that they are defects is deduced—Their proportion to the beauties—For the greatest part characteristic of his theory only.

IF Mr Wordsworth has set forth principles of poetry which his arguments are insufficient to support, let him and those who have adopted his sentiments be set right by the confutation of those arguments and by the substitution of more philosophical principles. And still let the due credit be given to the portion and importance of the truths which are blended with his theory: truths, the too exclusive attention to which had occasioned its errors by tempting him to carry those truths beyond their proper limits. If his mistaken theory has at all influenced his poetic compositions, let the effects be pointed out and the instances given. But let it likewise be shown how far the influence has acted; whether diffusively, or only by starts; whether the number and importance of the poems and passages thus infected be great or trifling compared with the sound portion; and lastly, whether they are inwoven into the texture of his works, or are loose and separable. The result of such a trial would evince beyond a doubt what it is high time to announce decisively and aloud, that the supposed characteristics of Mr Wordsworth's poetry, whether admired or reprobated; whether they are simplicity or simpleness; faithful adherence to essential nature or wilful selections from human nature of its meanest forms and under the least attractive associations: are as little the real characteristics of his poetry at large as of his genius and the constitution of his mind.

In a comparatively small number of poems he chose to try an experiment; and this experiment we will suppose to have failed. Yet even in these poems it is impossible not to perceive that the natural tendency of the poet's mind is to great objects and elevated conceptions. The poem entitled 'Fidelity' is for the greater part written in language as unraised and naked as any perhaps in the two volumes. Yet take the following stanza and compare it with the preceding stanzas of the same poem:

> There sometimes does a leaping fish
> Send through the tarn a lonely cheer;

> The crags repeat the raven's croak
> In symphony austere;
> Thither the rainbow comes—the cloud,
> And mists that spread the flying shroud;
> And sunbeams; and the sounding blast,
> That if it could would hurry past,
> But that enormous barrier holds it fast.[1]

Or compare the four last lines of the concluding stanza with the former half:

> Yes, proof was plain that since the day
> On which the traveller thus had died,
> The dog had watched about the spot,
> Or by his master's side:
> *How nourished here for such long time*
> *He knows who gave that love sublime,*
> *And gave that strength of feeling, great*
> *Above all human estimate.*

Can any candid and intelligent mind hesitate in determining which of these best represents the tendency and native character of the poet's genius? Will he not decide that the one was written because the poet *would* so write, and the other because he could not so entirely repress the force and grandeur of his mind, but that he must in some part or other of every composition write otherwise? In short, that his only disease is the being out of his element; like the swan, that having amused himself for a while with crushing the weeds on the river's bank soon returns to his own majestic movements on its reflecting and sustaining surface. Let it be observed that I am here supposing the imagined judge to whom I appeal to have already decided against the poet's theory, as far as it is different from the principles of the art generally acknowledged.

I cannot here enter into a detailed examination of Mr Wordsworth's works; but I will attempt to give the main results of my own judgement after an acquaintance of many years and repeated perusals. And though to appreciate the defects of a great mind it is necessary to understand previously its characteristic excellences, yet I have already expressed myself with sufficient fulness to preclude most of the ill effects that might arise from my pursuing a contrary arrangement. I will therefore commence with what I deem the prominent defects of his poems hitherto published.

----

[1] ['Fidelity' (comp. 1805, publ. 1807), *ll.* 25–33. Many of the passages criticized in this chapter were later revised or suppressed by Wordsworth.]

The first characteristic, though only occasional defect, which I appear to myself to find in these poems is the inconstancy of the style.   Under this name I refer to the sudden and unprepared transitions from lines or sentences of peculiar felicity (at all events striking and original) to a style not only unimpassioned but undistinguished.   He sinks too often and too abruptly to that style which I should place in the second division of language, dividing it into the three species: first, that which is peculiar to poetry; second, that which is only proper in prose; and third, the neutral or common to both.   There have been works, such as Cowley's essay on Cromwell,[1] in which prose and verse are intermixed (not as in the Consolation of Boetius, or the Argenis of Barclay, by the insertion of poems supposed to have been spoken or composed on occasions previously related in prose, but) the poet passing from one to the other as the nature of the thoughts or his own feelings dictated.   Yet this mode of composition does not satisfy a cultivated taste.   There is something unpleasant in the being thus obliged to alternate states of feeling so dissimilar, and this too in a species of writing the pleasure from which is in part derived from the preparation and previous expectation of the reader.   A portion of that awkwardness is felt which hangs upon the introduction of songs in our modern comic operas; and to prevent which the judicious Metastasio [2] (as to whose exquisite taste there can be no hesitation, whatever doubts may be entertained as to his poetic genius) uniformly placed the aria at the end of the scene, at the same time that he almost always raises and impassions the style of the recitative immediately preceding.   Even in real life the difference is great and evident between words used as the arbitrary marks of thought, our smooth market-coin of intercourse with the image and superscription worn out by currency, and those which convey pictures either borrowed from one outward object to enliven and particularize some other; or used allegorically to body forth the inward state of the person speaking; or such as are at least the exponents of his peculiar turn and unusual extent of faculty.   So much so indeed, that in the social circles of private life we often find a striking use of the latter put a stop to the general flow of conversation, and by the excitement arising from concentered attention produce a sort of damp and interruption for some minutes after. But in the perusal of works of literary art we *prepare* ourselves

---

[1] [*A Vision concerning the late Pretended Highness Cromwell the Wicked* (1661).]

[2] [Pietro Metastasio (1698–1782), an Italian dramatist and librettist.]

for such language; and the business of the writer, like that of a painter whose subject requires unusual splendor and prominence, is so to raise the lower and neutral tints, that what in a different style would be the commanding colors are here used as the means of that gentle degradation requisite in order to produce the effect of a whole.   Where this is not atchieved in a poem, the metre merely reminds the reader of his claims in order to disappoint them; and where this defect occurs frequently, his feelings are alternately started by anticlimax and hyperclimax.

I refer the reader to the exquisite stanzas cited for another purpose from 'The Blind Highland Boy'; and then annex as being in my opinion instances of this disharmony in style the two following:

> And one, the rarest, was a shell
> Which he, poor child, had studied well:
> The shell of a green turtle, thin
> And hollow; you might sit therein,
>   It was so wide, and deep.

> Our Highland Boy oft visited
> The house which held this prize, and led
> By choice or chance did thither come
> One day, when no one was at home,
>   And found the door unbarred.

Or page 172, vol. i:

> 'Tis gone, forgotten, *let me do*
> *My best*.   There was a smile or two—
> I can remember them, I see
> The smiles worth all the world to me.
> Dear Baby, I must lay thee down.
> Thou troublest me with strange alarms!
> Smiles hast thou, sweet ones of thine own;
> I cannot keep thee in my arms,
> For they confound me: *as it is,*
> I have forgot those smiles of his! [1]

Or page 269, vol. i:

> Thou hast a nest for thy love and thy rest,
> And though little troubled with sloth,
> Drunken lark! thou would'st be loth
> To be such a traveller as I.
>   Happy, happy liver!
> *With a soul as strong as a mountain river,*
> *Pouring out praise to th' almighty giver,*

---

[1] ['The Emigrant Mother' (comp. 1802, publ. 1807), *ll.* 55–64.]

> Joy and jollity be with us both!
> Hearing thee or else some other,
>   As merry a brother,
> I on the earth will go plodding on
> By myself chearfully till the day is done.[1]

The incongruity which I appear to find in this passage is that of the two noble lines in italics with the preceding and following. So vol. ii, page 30:

> Close by a pond, upon the further side,
> He stood alone: a minute's space I guess
> I watched him, he continuing motionless;
> To the pool's further margin then I drew;
> He being all the while before me full in view.[2]

Compare this with the repetition of the same image, in the next stanza but two:

> And still as I drew near with gentle pace,
> Beside the little pond or moorish flood
> Motionless as a cloud the old man stood:
> That heareth not the loud winds as they call,
> And moveth altogether, if it move at all.

Or lastly, the second of the three following stanzas, compared both with the first and the third:

> My former thoughts returned: the fear that kills;
> And hope that is unwilling to be fed;
> Cold, pain, and labour, and all fleshly ills;
> And mighty poets in their misery dead.
> But now, perplex'd by what the old man had said,
> My question eagerly did I renew,
> 'How is it that you live, and what is it you do?'

> He with a smile did then his tale repeat;
> And said, that, gathering leeches far and wide,
> He travelled: stirring thus about his feet
> The waters of the ponds where they abide.
> 'Once I could meet with them on every side,
> But they have dwindled long by slow decay;
> Yet still I persevere, and find them where I may.'

> While he was talking thus, the lonely place,
> The old man's shape, and speech, all troubled me:
> In my mind's eye I seemed to see him pace
> About the weary moors continually,
> Wandering about alone and silently.

---

[1] ['To a Skylark' (comp. 1802?, publ. 1807), *ll*. 18–25, 28–31.]
[2] ['Resolution and Independence' (comp. 1802, publ. 1807).]

Indeed, this fine poem is especially characteristic of the author. There is scarce a defect or excellence in his writings of which it would not present a specimen. But it would be unjust not to repeat that this defect is only occasional. From a careful reperusal of the two volumes of poems I doubt whether the objectionable passages would amount in the whole to one hundred lines; not the eighth part of the number of pages. In the *Excursion* the feeling of incongruity is seldom excited by the diction of any passage considered in itself, but by the sudden superiority of some other passage forming the context.

The second defect I could generalize with tolerable accuracy if the reader will pardon an uncouth and new coined word. There is, I should say, not seldom a *matter-of-factness* in certain poems. This may be divided into, first, a laborious minuteness and fidelity in the representation of objects and their positions as they appeared to the poet himself; secondly, the insertion of accidental circumstances, in order to the full explanation of his living characters, their dispositions and actions: which circumstances might be necessary to establish the probability of a statement in real life, where nothing is taken for granted by the hearer, but appear superfluous in poetry, where the reader is willing to believe for his own sake. To this accidentality I object, as contravening the essence of poetry, which Aristotle pronounces to be σπουδαιότατον καὶ φιλοσοφώτατον γένος,[1] the most intense, weighty and philosophical product of human art; adding, as the reason, that it is the most catholic and abstract. The following passage from Davenant's prefatory letter to Hobbes well expresses this truth: ' When I considered the actions which I meant to describe (those inferring the persons) I was again persuaded rather to choose those of a former age than the present; and in a century so far removed as might preserve me from their improper examinations who know not the requisites of a poem, nor how much pleasure they lose (and even the pleasures of heroic poesy are not unprofitable) who take away the liberty of a poet, and fetter his feet in the shackles of an historian. For why should a poet doubt in story to mend the intrigues of fortune by more delightful conveyances of probable fictions, because austere historians have entered into bond to truth; an obligation which were in poets as foolish and unnecessary as is the bondage of false martyrs, who lie in chains for a mistaken

---

[1] [Altered from the *Poetics*, IX. 3: 'Poetry is a more philosophical and a higher thing than history: for poetry tends to express the universal, history the particular.' Wordsworth commits the same mistake in the 1800 Preface.]

opinion. *But by this I would imply, that truth, narrative and past is the idol of historians (who worship a dead thing), and truth operative, and by effects continually alive, is the mistress of poets, who hath not her existence in matter, but in reason.'* [1]

For this minute accuracy in the painting of local imagery, the lines in the *Excursion*, pp. 96, 97 and 98 [2] may be taken, if not as a striking instance, yet as an illustration of my meaning. It must be some strong motive (as, for instance, that the description was necessary to the intelligibility of the tale) which could induce me to describe in a number of verses what a draftsman could present to the eye with incomparably greater satisfaction by half a dozen strokes of his pencil, or the painter with as many touches of his brush. Such descriptions too often occasion in the mind of a reader who is determined to understand his author a feeling of labour, not very dissimilar to that with which he would construct a diagram, line by line, for a long geometrical proposition. It seems to be like taking the pieces of a dissected map out of its box. We first look at one part, and then at another, then join and dove-tail them; and when the successive acts of attention have been completed, there is a retrogressive effort of mind to behold it as a whole. The poet should paint to the imagination, not to the fancy; and I know no happier case to exemplify the distinction between these two faculties. Masterpieces of the former mode of poetic painting abound in the writings of Milton, ex. gr.

> The fig-tree, not that kind for fruit renown'd,
> But such as at this day to Indians known
> In Malabar or Decan spreads her arms
> Branching so broad and long, that in the ground
> The bended twigs take root, *and daughters grow*
> *About the mother-tree, a pillar'd shade*
> *High over-arched, and* ECHOING WALKS BETWEEN:
> *There oft the Indian Herdsman shunning heat*
> *Shelters in cool, and tends his pasturing herds*
> *At loopholes cut through thickest shade.*
>   MILTON, *P.L.* 9, 1100.[3]

This is creation rather than painting, or if painting, yet such, and with such co-presence of the whole picture flash'd at once upon the eye, as the sun paints in a camera obscura. But the poet must likewise understand and command what Bacon calls

---

[1] [William Davenant (1606–68), *Gondibert* (1651), *Preface to Mr Hobs*, pp. 13–14.]
[2] [III. 50–73.]
[3] [*Paradise Lost*, IX. 1101–10.]

the *vestigia communia* of the senses, the latency of all in each, and more especially as by a magical *penna duplex*, the excitement of vision by sound and the exponents of sound. Thus, 'the echoing walks between' may be almost said to reverse the fable in tradition of the head of Memnon in the Egyptian statue.[1] Such may be deservedly entitled the *creative words* in the world of imagination.

The second division respects an apparent minute adherence to matter-of-fact in character and incidents; a biographical attention to probability, and an anxiety of explanation and retrospect. Under this head I shall deliver, with no feigned diffidence, the results of my best reflection on the great point of controversy between Mr Wordsworth and his objectors; namely, on the choice of his characters. I have already declared, and I trust justified, my utter dissent from the mode of argument which his critics have hitherto employed. To their question, why did you chuse such a character, or a character from such a rank of life? the poet might, in my opinion, fairly retort: why with the conception of my character did you make wilful choice of mean or ludicrous associations not furnished by me but supplied from your own sickly and fastidious feelings? How was it indeed probable that such arguments could have any weight with an author whose plan, whose guiding principle and main object it was to attack and subdue that state of association which leads us to place the chief value on those things on which man differs from man, and to forget or disregard the high dignities which belong to human nature, the sense and the feeling which may be, and ought to be, found in all ranks? The feelings with which, as Christians, we contemplate a mixed congregation rising or kneeling before their common maker, Mr Wordsworth would have us entertain at all times, as men and as readers; and by the excitement of this lofty yet prideless impartiality in poetry, he might hope to have encouraged its continuance in real life. The praise of good men be his! In real life and, I trust, even in my imagination, I honor a virtuous and wise man, without reference to the presence or absence of artificial advantages. Whether in the person of an armed baron, a laurel'd bard, etc., or of an old pedlar, or still older leach-gatherer, the same qualities of head and heart must claim the same reverence. And even in poetry I am not conscious that I have ever suffered my feelings to be

---

[1] [A statue on the Nile said to utter a musical sound when first struck by the sun. So the vision is prompted by the line of Milton, but in reverse, sound prompting sight.]

disturbed or offended by any thoughts or images which the poet himself has not presented.

But yet I object nevertheless, and for the following reasons. First, because the object in view, as an immediate object, belongs to the moral philosopher, and would be pursued not only more appropriately, but in my opinion with far greater probability of success, in sermons or moral essays than in an elevated poem. It seems, indeed, to destroy the main fundamental distinction, not only between a poem and prose, but even between philosophy and works of fiction, inasmuch as it proposes truth for its immediate object instead of pleasure.   Now till the blessed time shall come when truth itself shall be pleasure, and both [1] shall be so united as to be distinguishable in words only, not in feeling, it will remain the poet's office to proceed upon that state of association which actually exists as general; instead of attempting first to make it what it ought to be, and then to let the pleasure follow. But here is unfortunately a small *hysteron-proteron*.[2]   For the communication of pleasure is the introductory means by which alone the poet must expect to moralize his readers.   Secondly: though I were to admit, for a moment, this argument to be groundless; yet how is the moral effect to be produced by merely attaching the name of some low profession to powers which are least likely, and to qualities which are assuredly not more likely, to be found in it?   The poet, speaking in his own person, may at once delight and improve us by sentiments which teach us the independence of goodness, of wisdom, and even of genius, on the favors of fortune.   And having made a due reverence before the throne of Antonine, he may bow with equal awe before Epictetus among his fellow-slaves— [3]

——————————————— and rejoice
In the plain presence of his dignity.[4]

Who is not at once delighted and improved, when the *poet* Wordsworth himself exclaims,

O many are the poets that are sown
By Nature; men endowed with highest gifts,
The vision and the faculty divine,
Yet wanting the accomplishment of verse,

[1] [At this point in *1817* (II. 144) the sheets printed in Bristol come to an end; the rest of the book was printed in London.   The remainder of the chapter was probably padded by Coleridge late in 1816.]
[2] [A 'latter-former,' putting the cart before the horse.]
[3] [Of the two philosophers Marcus Aurelius Antoninus (121–80) was an emperor, Epictetus (*c.* 50–120) a slave.]
[4] [*Excursion,* I. 75–6.]

> Nor having e'er, as life advanced, been led
> By circumstance to take unto the height
> The measure of themselves, these favoured beings,
> All but a scattered few, live out their time,
> Husbanding that which they possess within,
> And go to the grave unthought of.   Strongest minds
> Are often those of whom the noisy world
> Hears least.
>
> *Excursion*, B.I.[1]

To use a colloquial phrase, such sentiments, in such language, do one's heart good; though I for my part have not the fullest faith in the *truth* of the observation.   On the contrary I believe the instances to be exceedingly rare; and should feel almost as strong an objection to introduce such a character in a poetic fiction as a pair of black swans on a lake, in a fancy-landscape. When I think how many and how much better books than Homer, or even than Herodotus, Pindar or Eschylus, could have read, are in the power of almost every man, in a country where almost every man is instructed to read and write; and how restless, how difficultly hidden, the powers of genius are, and yet find even in situations the most favorable, according to Mr Wordsworth, for the formation of a pure and poetic language, in situations which ensure familiarity with the grandest objects of the imagination, but one Burns among the shepherds of Scotland, and not a single poet of humble life among those of *English* lakes and mountains; I conclude that Poetic Genius is not only a very delicate but a very rare plant.

But be this as it may, the feelings with which

> I think of Chatterton, the marvellous boy,
> The sleepless soul that perish'd in his pride:
> Of Burns, that walk'd in glory and in joy
> Behind his plough upon the mountain-side,[2]

are widely different from those with which I should read a poem where the author, having occasion for the character of a poet and a philosopher in the fable of his narration, had chosen to make him a chimney-sweeper; and then, in order to remove all doubts on the subject, had invented an account of his birth, parentage and education, with all the strange and fortunate accidents which

---

[1] [Ibid., I. 77–80, 86–93.]

[2] [From 'Resolution and Independence' (op. cit.), *ll.* 43–6, text of 1815:

> I thought of Chatterton, the marvellous boy,
> The sleepless soul that perished in his pride;
> Of him who walked in glory and in joy
> Behind his plough, along the mountain-side.]

had concurred in making him at once poet, philosopher and
sweep! Nothing but biography can justify this. If it be admis-
sible even in a novel, it must be one in the manner of De Foe's,
that were meant to pass for histories, not in the manner of
Fielding's: in the life of Moll Flanders, or Colonel Jack, not in a
Tom Jones or even a Joseph Andrews. Much less then can it
be legitimately introduced in a poem, the characters of which,
amid the strongest individualization, must still remain representative. The precepts of Horace,[1] on this point, are grounded
on the nature both of poetry and of the human mind. They are
not more peremptory than wise and prudent. For in the first
place a deviation from them perplexes the reader's feelings, and
all the circumstances which are feigned in order to make such
accidents less improbable divide and disquiet his faith, rather
than aid and support it. Spite of all attempts, the fiction will
appear, and unfortunately not as fictitious but as false. The
reader not only knows that the sentiments and the language are
the poet's own, and his own too in his artificial character, as
poet; but by the fruitless endeavours to make him think the
contrary he is not even suffered to forget it. The effect is
similar to that produced by an epic poet when the fable and
characters are derived from Scripture history, as in the *Messiah*
of Klopstock, or in Cumberland's *Calvary*:[2] and not merely
suggested by it as in the *Paradise Lost* of Milton. That illusion,
contradistinguished from delusion, that *negative* faith[3] which
simply permits the images presented to work by their own force,
without either denial or affirmation of their real existence by the
judgement, is rendered impossible by their immediate neighbourhood to words and facts of known and absolute truth. A

---

[1] [*Ars poetica, ll.* 114 ff.]

[2] [Klopstock's *Messias* (1748–73), a German epic on Christ's passion and
resurrection for which Coleridge had a hearty contempt; Richard Cumberland (1732–1811), a dramatist and poet whose *Calvary*, a blank-verse epic,
appeared in 1792.]

[3] [Perhaps it was this expression, linked with the name of Coleridge, that
lay at the back of Keats's mind when he made his more famous pronounce-
ment on 'negative capability' in a letter to his brothers George and Thomas
written five months after the appearance of the *Biographia* (21 December
1817): 'It struck me what quality went to form a man of achievement, especially in literature, and which Shakespeare possessed so enormously—I mean
Negative Capability, that is, when a man is capable of being in uncertainties,
mysteries, doubts, without any irritable reaching after fact and reason—
Coleridge, for instance, would let go by a fine isolated verisimilitude caught
from the Penetralium of mystery, from being incapable of remaining content
with half knowledge.' There is no evidence that Keats ever read the
Biographia, though in the previous month (November 1817) he had written
to Dilke for a copy of *Sibylline Leaves*.]

faith which transcends even historic belief must absolutely put
out this mere poetic analogon of faith, as the summer sun is said
to extinguish our household fires when it shines full upon them.
What would otherwise have been yielded to as pleasing fiction
is repelled as revolting falsehood.   The effect produced in this
latter case by the solemn belief of the reader is in a less degree
brought about in the instances to which I have been objecting,
by the baffled attempts of the author to *make* him believe.

Add to all the foregoing the seeming uselessness both of the
project and of the anecdotes from which it is to derive support.
Is there one word, for instance, attributed to the pedlar in the
Excursion characteristic of a pedlar?   One sentiment that might
not more plausibly, even without the aid of any previous explanation, have proceeded from any wise and beneficent old man of a
rank or profession in which the language of learning and refinement are natural and to be expected?   Need the rank have been at
all particularized, where nothing follows which the knowledge
of that rank is to explain or illustrate?   When on the contrary
this information renders the man's language, feelings, sentiments
and information a riddle which must itself be solved by episodes
of anecdote?   Finally when this, and this alone, could have
induced a genuine poet to inweave in a poem of the loftiest style,
and on subjects the loftiest and of the most universal interest
such minute matters of fact, not unlike those furnished for the
obituary of a magazine by the friends of some obscure *ornament
of society lately deceased* in some obscure town, as

> Among the hills of Athol he was born.
> There on a small hereditary farm,
> An unproductive slip of rugged ground,
> His father dwelt; and died in poverty:
> While he, whose lowly fortune I retrace,
> The youngest of three sons, was yet a babe,
> A little one—unconscious of their loss.
> But ere he had outgrown his infant days
> His widowed mother, for a second mate,
> Espoused the teacher of the village school;
> Who on her offspring zealously bestowed
> Needful instruction.
>
> From his sixth year, the boy of whom I speak,
> In summer tended cattle on the hills;
> But through the inclement and the perilous days
> Of long-continuing winter, he repaired
> To his step-father's school, etc.[1]

[1] [*Excursion*, I. 108 ff.]

For all the admirable passages interposed in this narration might, with trifling alterations, have been far more appropriately and with far greater verisimilitude told of a poet in the character of a poet; and without incurring another defect which I shall now mention, and a sufficient illustration of which will have been here anticipated.

Third: an undue predilection for the dramatic form in certain poems, from which one or other of two evils result. Either the thoughts and diction are different from that of the poet, and then there arises an incongruity of style; or they are the same and indistinguishable, and then it presents a species of ventriloquism, where two are represented as talking while in truth one man only speaks.

The fourth class of defects is closely connected with the former; but yet are such as arise likewise from an intensity of feeling disproportionate to such knowledge and value of the objects described as can be fairly anticipated of men in general, even of the most cultivated classes; and with which therefore few only, and those few particularly circumstanced, can be supposed to sympathize: in this class I comprize occasional prolixity, repetition and an eddying instead of progression of thought. As instances, see pages 27, 28 and 62 of the *Poems*, vol. i,[1] and the first eighty lines of the Sixth Book of the *Excursion*.

Fifth and last: thoughts and images too great for the subject. This is an approximation to what might be called *mental* bombast, as distinguished from verbal; for as in the latter there is a disproportion of the expressions to the thoughts, so in this there is a disproportion of thought to the circumstance and occasion. This, by the bye, is a fault of which none but a man of genius is capable. It is the awkwardness and strength of Hercules with the distaff of Omphale.[2]

It is a well-known fact that bright colours in motion both make and leave the strongest impressions on the eye. Nothing is more likely too than that a vivid image or visual spectrum thus originated may become the link of association in recalling the feelings and images that had accompanied the original impression. But if we describe this in such lines, as

---

[1] [*Poems*, 2 vols. (1815), vol. i, pp. 27–8, contain the 'Anecdote for Fathers,' st. 4–13; p. 62 is a blank. Sara Coleridge suggested that the reference intended was to vol. ii, p. 62, i.e. 'Song at the Feast of Brougham Castle,' *ll.* 78–101.]

[2] [A queen of Lydia who bought Hercules as a slave and put him to woman's work. Cf. Ovid, *Heroides*, ix. 52 ff.]

> They flash upon that inward eye,
> Which is the bliss of solitude! [1]

in what words shall we describe the joy of retrospection when the images and virtuous actions of a whole well-spent life pass before that conscience which is indeed the inward eye: which is indeed 'the bliss of solitude'? Assuredly we seem to sink most abruptly, not to say burlesquely and almost as in a medley, from this couplet to

> And then my heart with pleasure fills,
> And dances with the *daffodils*.
>
> Vol. i. p. 320.

The second instance is from vol. ii., page 12, where the poet having gone out for a day's tour of pleasure meets early in the morning with a knot of gipsies, who had pitched their blanket-tents and straw beds, together with their children and asses, in some field by the road-side.   At the close of the day on his return our tourist found them in the same place.   'Twelve hours,' says he,

> Twelve hours, twelve bounteous hours are gone, while I
> Have been a traveller under open sky,
> Much witnessing of change and cheer,
> Yet as I left I find them here! [2]

Whereat the poet, without seeming to reflect that the poor tawny wanderers might probably have been tramping for weeks together through road and lane, over moor and mountain, and consequently must have been right glad to rest themselves, their children and cattle for one whole day; and overlooking the obvious truth that such repose might be quite as necessary for them as a walk of the same continuance was pleasing or healthful for the more fortunate poet; expresses his indignation in a series of lines, the diction and imagery of which would have been rather above than below the mark, had they been applied to the immense empire of China improgressive for thirty centuries:

> The weary Sun betook himself to rest,—
> Then issued Vesper from the fulgent west,
> Outshining like a visible God,
> The glorious path in which he trod!
> And now ascending, after one dark hour,
> And one night's dimunution of her power,

---

[1] ['I wandered lonely as a cloud' (comp. 1804, publ. 1807), *ll*. 21–2.]
[2] ['Gipsies' (1807), *ll*. 9–12.]

> Behold the mighty Moon! this way
> She looks as if at them—but they
> Regard not her:—oh, better wrong and strife,
> Better vain deed or evil than such life!
> The silent Heavens have goings-on:
> The stars have tasks!—but these have none!

The last instance of this defect (for I know no other than these already cited), is from the 'Ode,' page 351, vol. ii, where, speaking of a child, 'a six years' darling of a pigmy size,' he thus addresses him:

> Thou best philosopher, who yet dost keep
> Thy heritage!   Thou eye among the blind,
> That, deaf and silent, read'st the eternal deep—
> Haunted for ever by the eternal mind—
> Mighty Prophet!   Seer blest!
> On whom those truths do rest,
> Which we are toiling all our lives to find!
> Thou, over whom thy immortality
> Broods like the day, a master o'er the slave,
> A presence which is not to be put by![1]

Now here, not to stop at the daring spirit of metaphor which connects the epithets 'deaf and silent' with the apostrophized eye: or (if we are to refer it to the preceding word *philosopher*) the faulty and equivocal syntax of the passage; and without examining the propriety of making a 'master *brood* o'er a slave,' or the day brood at all; we will merely ask, what does all this mean?   In what sense is a child of that age a philosopher?   In what sense does he read 'the eternal deep'?   In what sense is he declared to be 'for ever haunted' by the Supreme Being? or so inspired as to deserve the splendid titles of a mighty prophet, a blessed seer?   By reflection? by knowledge? by conscious intuition? or by any form or modification of consciousness? These would be tidings indeed; but such as would pre-suppose an immediate revelation to the inspired communicator and require miracles to authenticate his inspiration.   Children at this age give us no such information of themselves; and at what time were we dipt in the Lethe, which has produced such utter oblivion of a state so godlike?   There are many of us that still possess some remembrances, more or less distinct, respecting themselves at six years old; pity that the worthless straws only should float while treasures, compared with which all the mines

[1] ['Intimations of Immortality' (comp. 1802–4, publ. 1807), *ll.* 111–17, 119–21.]

of Golconda and Mexico were but straws, should be absorbed by
some unknown gulf into some unknown abyss.

But if this be too wild and exorbitant to be suspected as having
been the poet's meaning; if these mysterious gifts, faculties and
operations are not accompanied with consciousness; who else is
conscious of them? or how can it be called the child, if it be no
part of the child's conscious being?   For aught I know, the
thinking spirit within me may be substantially one with the
principle of life and of vital operation.   For aught I know, it may
be employed as a secondary agent in the marvellous organization
and organic movements of my body.   But surely it would be
strange language to say that I construct my heart! or that I
propel the finer influences through my nerves! or that I compress
my brain, and draw the curtains of sleep round my own eyes!
Spinoza and Behmen were on different systems both Pantheists;
and among the ancients there were philosophers, teachers of the
EN KAI ΠΑΝ, who not only taught that God was All, but that this
All constituted God.   Yet not even these would confound the
part, as a part, with the Whole, as the whole.   Nay, in no system
is the distinction between the individual and God, between the
modification and the one only substance, more sharply drawn
than in that of Spinoza.   Jacobi indeed relates of Lessing that
after a conversation with him at the house of the poet Gleim (the
Tyrtaeus and Anacreon of the German Parnassus)[1] in which
conversation L. had avowed privately to Jacobi his reluctance to
admit any personal existence of the Supreme Being, or the
possibility of personality except in a finite Intellect, and while
they were sitting at table a shower of rain came on unexpectedly.
Gleim expressed his regret at the circumstance, because they had
meant to drink their wine in the garden: upon which Lessing, in
one of his half-earnest, half-joking moods, nodded to Jacobi
and said, 'It is I, perhaps, that am doing that,' i.e. raining! and
J. answered, 'Or perhaps I'; Gleim contented himself with
staring at them both, without asking for any explanation.[2]

So with regard to this passage.   In what sense can the magnificent attributes above quoted be appropriated to a child, which
would not make them equally suitable to a bee, or a dog, or a

[1] [Johann Gleim (1719–1803), whose *Kriegslieder von einem preussischen
Grenadier* (1758) are at once patriotic like Tyrtaeus and wine-loving like
Anacreon.]

[2] [Coleridge has much expanded the story from the work of the German
philosopher and controversialist F. H. Jacobi (1743–1819), *Wider Mendels-
sohns Beschuldingungen betreffend die Briefe über Spinoza* (1786), p. 60:
'Über Tische, bey einfallendem Regen: "Jacobi, das thue ich vielleicht."']

field of corn; or even to a ship, or to the wind and waves that propel it? The omnipresent Spirit works equally in them as in the child; and the child is equally unconscious of it as they. It cannot surely be that the four lines immediately following are to contain the explanation?

> To whom the grave
> Is but a lonely bed without the sense or sight
> Of day or the warm light,
> A place of thought where we in waiting lie.[1]

Surely, it cannot be that this wonder-rousing apostrophe is but a comment on the little poem of 'We are Seven'? that the whole meaning of the passage is reducible to the assertion that a child, who by the bye at six years old would have been better instructed in most Christian families, has no other notion of death than that of lying in a dark, cold place? And still, I hope, not as in a place of thought! not the frightful notion of lying awake in his grave! The analogy between death and sleep is too simple, too natural, to render so horrible a belief possible for children; even had they not been in the habit, as all Christian children are, of hearing the latter term used to express the former. But if the child's belief be only that 'he is not dead, but sleepeth,' wherein does it differ from that of his father and mother, or any other adult and instructed person? To form an idea of a thing's becoming nothing, or of nothing becoming a thing, is impossible to all finite beings alike, of whatever age and however educated or uneducated. Thus it is with splendid paradoxes in general. If the words are taken in the common sense, they convey an absurdity; and if, in contempt of dictionaries and custom, they are so interpreted as to avoid the absurdity, the meaning dwindles into some bald truism. Thus you must at once understand the words contrary to their common import, in order to arrive at any sense; and according to their common import, if you are to receive from them any feeling of sublimity or admiration.

Though the instances of this defect in Mr Wordsworth's poems are so few that for themselves it would have been scarcely just to attract the reader's attention toward them, yet I have dwelt on it, and perhaps the more for this very reason. For being so very few, they cannot sensibly detract from the repu-

---

[1] ['Intimations of Immortality' (op. cit.), *ll.* 122 ff. (later suppressed by Wordsworth).]

tation of an author who is even characterized by the number of profound truths in his writings which will stand the severest analysis; and yet few as they are, they are exactly those passages which his blind admirers would be most likely, and best able, to imitate. But Wordsworth, where he is indeed Wordsworth, may be mimicked by copyists, he may be plundered by plagiarists; but he cannot be imitated except by those who are not born to be imitators. For without his depth of feeling and his imaginative power his sense would want its vital warmth and peculiarity; and without his strong sense, his mysticism would become sickly—mere fog and dimness!

To these defects which, as appears by the extracts, are only occasional I may oppose with far less fear of encountering the dissent of any candid and intelligent reader the following (for the most part correspondent) excellencies. First, an austere purity of language both grammatically and logically; in short a perfect appropriateness of the words to the meaning. Of how high value I deem this, and how particularly estimable I hold the example at the present day, has been already stated: and in part too the reasons on which I ground both the moral and intellectual importance of habituating ourselves to a strict accuracy of expression. It is noticeable, how limited an acquaintance with the masterpieces of art will suffice to form a correct and even a sensitive taste, where none but masterpieces have been seen and admired: while on the other hand, the most correct notions, and the widest acquaintance with the works of excellence of all ages and countries will not perfectly secure us against the contagious familiarity with the far more numerous offspring of tastelessness or of a perverted taste. If this be the case, as it notoriously is, with the arts of music and painting, much more difficult will it be to avoid the infection of multiplied and daily examples in the practice of an art which uses words, and words only, as its instruments. In poetry, in which every line, every phrase, may pass the ordeal of deliberation and deliberate choice, it is possible, and barely possible, to attain that ultimatum which I have ventured to propose as the infallible test of a blameless style, namely its untranslatableness in words of the same language without injury to the meaning. Be it observed, however, that I include in the meaning of a word not only its correspondent object, but likewise all the associations which it recalls. For language is framed to convey not the object alone, but likewise the character, mood and intentions of the person who is representing it. In poetry it is practicable to preserve the diction uncorrupted by the affectations and misappropriations which promiscuous authorship, and reading not promiscuous only because it is disproportionally most conversant with the compositions of the day, have rendered general.   Yet even to the poet, composing in his own province, it is an arduous work: and as the result and pledge of a watchful good sense, of fine and luminous distinction, and of complete self-possession, may justly claim all the honor which belongs to an attainment equally difficult and valuable, and the more valuable for being rare.   It is at all times the proper food of the understanding; but in an age of corrupt eloquence it is both food and antidote.

In prose I doubt whether it be even possible to preserve our style wholly unalloyed by the vicious phraseology which meets us every where, from the sermon to the newspaper, from the harangue of the legislator to the speech from the convivial chair announcing a toast or sentiment.   Our chains rattle even while we are complaining of them.   The poems of Boetius rise high in our estimation when we compare them with those of his contemporaries, as Sidonius Apollinaris, etc.   They might even be referred to a purer age but that the prose in which they are set, as jewels in a crown of lead or iron, betrays the true age of the writer.   Much however may be effected by education.   I believe not only from grounds of reason, but from having in great measure assured myself of the fact by actual though limited experience, that to a youth led from his first boyhood to investigate the meaning of every word and the reason of its choice and position, logic presents itself as an old acquaintance under new names.

On some future occasion more especially demanding such disquisition, I shall attempt to prove the close connection between veracity and habits of mental accuracy; the beneficial aftereffects of verbal precision in the preclusion of fanaticism, which masters the feelings more especially by indistinct watch-words; and to display the advantages which language alone, at least which language with incomparably greater ease and certainty than any other means, presents to the instructor of impressing modes of intellectual energy so constantly, so imperceptibly and as it were by such elements and atoms as to secure in due time the formation of a second nature.   When we reflect that the cultivation of the judgement is a positive command of the moral law, since the reason can give the principle alone, and the conscience bears witness only to the motive, while the application and effects must depend on the judgement; when we consider that the greater part of our success and comfort in life depends on distinguishing the similar from the same, that which is peculiar in each thing from that which it has in common with others, so as still to select the most probable, instead of the merely possible or positively unfit, we shall learn to value earnestly and with a practical seriousness a mean, already prepared for us by nature and society, of teaching the young mind to think well and wisely by the same unremembered process and with the same never forgotten results as those by which it is taught to speak and converse.   Now how much warmer the interest is, how much more genial the feelings of reality and practicability and thence how much stronger the impulses to imitation are which a contemporary writer, and especially a contemporary poet, excites in youth and commencing manhood has been treated of in the earlier pages of these sketches.   I have only to add that all the praise which is due to the exertion of such influence for a purpose so important, joined with that which must be claimed for the infrequency of the same excellence in the same perfection, belongs in full right to Mr Wordsworth.   I am far however from denying that we have poets whose general style possesses the same excellence, as Mr Moore, Lord Byron, Mr Bowles and in all his later and more important works our laurel-honoring Laureate.   But there are none in whose works I do not appear to myself to find more exceptions than in those of Wordsworth. Quotations or specimens would here be wholly out of place, and must be left for the critic who doubts and would invalidate the justice of this eulogy so applied.

The second characteristic excellence of Mr W.'s works is: a correspondent weight and sanity of the thoughts and sentiments —won, not from books, but—from the poet's own meditative observation.   They are fresh and have the dew upon them. His muse, at least when in her strength of wing and when she hovers aloft in her proper element,

> Makes audible a linked lay of truth,
> Of truth profound a sweet continuous lay,
> Not learnt, but native, her own natural notes! [1]
>
> S.T.C.

Even throughout his smaller poems there is scarcely one which is not rendered valuable by some just and original reflection.

[1] ['To William Wordsworth,' *ll.* 58–60.]

See page 25, vol. 2nd;[1] or the two following passages in one of his humblest compositions:

> O Reader! had you in your mind
> Such stores as silent thought can bring,
> O gentle Reader! you would find
> A tale in every thing.

and

> I have heard of hearts unkind, kind deeds
> With coldness still returning:
> Alas! the gratitude of men
> Has oftener left me mourning.[2]

Or in a still higher strain the six beautiful quatrains, page 134:

> Thus fares it still in our decay:
> And yet the wiser mind
> Mourns less for what age takes away
> Than what it leaves behind.
>
> The blackbird in the summer trees,
> The lark upon the hill,
> Let loose their carols when they please,
> Are quiet when they will.
>
> With Nature never do *they* wage
> A foolish strife: they see
> A happy youth, and their old age
> Is beautiful and free!
>
> But we are pressed by heavy laws
> And often, glad no more,
> We wear a face of joy, because
> We have been glad of yore.
>
> If there is one, who need bemoan
> His kindred laid in earth,
> The household hearts that were his own
> It is the man of mirth.
>
> My days, my Friend, are almost gone,
> My life has been approved,
> And many love me; but by none
> Am I enough beloved;[3]

---

[1] ['Star-Gazers' (comp. 1806, publ. 1807), st. 3–6.]
[2] ['Simon Lee' (1798), *ll*. 65–8, 93–6.]
[3] ['The Fountain' (comp. 1799, publ. 1800), *ll*. 33–56.]

or the Sonnet on Buonaparte, page 202, vol. 2;[1] or finally (for a volume would scarce suffice to exhaust the instances), the last stanza of the poem on the withered Celandine, vol. 2, p. 212:

> To be a prodigal's favorite—then, worse truth,
> A miser's pensioner—behold our lot!
> O man! that from thy fair and shining youth
> Age might but take the things youth needed not.[2]

Both in respect of this and of the former excellence, Mr Wordsworth strikingly resembles Samuel Daniel,[3] one of the golden writers of our golden Elizabethan age, now most causelessly neglected: Samuel Daniel, whose diction bears no mark of time, no distinction of age, which has been and, as long as our language shall last, will be so far the language of the to-day and for ever, as that it is more intelligible to us than the transitory fashions of our own particular age.   A similar praise is due to his sentiments.   No frequency of perusal can deprive them of their freshness.   For though they are brought into the full daylight of every reader's comprehension, yet are they drawn up from depths which few in any age are priviledged to visit, into which few in any age have courage or inclination to descend.   If Mr Wordsworth is not equally with Daniel alike intelligible to all readers of average understanding in all passages of his works, the comparative difficulty does not arise from the greater impurity of the ore but from the nature and uses of the metal.   A poem is not necessarily obscure because it does not aim to be popular.   It is enough if a work be perspicuous to those for whom it is written, and

> Fit audience find, though few.[4]

To the 'Ode on the Intimation of Immortality from Recollections of early Childhood' the poet might have prefixed the lines which Dante addresses to one of his own Canzoni—

> Canzone, io credo, che saranno radi
> Che tua ragione intendan bene:
> Tanto lor sei faticoso ed alto.[5]

[1] ['I grieved for Buonaparte . . .' (1802).]
[2] ['The Small Celandine' (comp. 1804, publ. 1807), *ll*. 21–4.]
[3] [Wordsworth's own sense of kinship with Daniel is demonstrated by the fact that he more than once quoted from him in his poems.   Cf. Sonnet 'It is not to be thought of,' and *Excursion*, IV. 324–31.]
[4] [*Paradise Lost*, VII. 31.]
[5] ['Convivio,' II, Ode I, *ll*. 53–5.]

O lyric song, there will be few, think I,
Who may thy import understand aright:
Thou art for them so arduous and so high!

But the ode was intended for such readers only as had been
accustomed to watch the flux and reflux of their inmost nature,[1]
to venture at times into the twilight realms of consciousness and
to feel a deep interest in modes of inmost being to which they
know that the attributes of time and space are inapplicable and
alien, but which yet cannot be conveyed save in symbols of time
and space. For such readers the sense is sufficiently plain, and
they will be as little disposed to charge Mr Wordsworth with
believing the platonic pre-existence in the ordinary interpretation of the words, as I am to believe that Plato himself ever
meant or taught it.

> Πολλά οἱ ὑπ' ἀγκῶ
> -νος ὠκέα βέλη
> Ἔνδον ἐντὶ φαρέτρας
> Φωνᾶντα συνετοῖσιν· ἐς
> Δὲ τὸ πᾶν ἑρμηνέων
> Χατίζει. Σοφὸς ὁ πολ-
> -λὰ εἰδὼς φυᾷ
> Μαθόντες δὲ λάβροι
> Παγγλωσσίᾳ, κόρακες ὣς
> Ἄκραντα γαρύετον
> Διὸς πρὸς ὄρνιχα θεῖον.[2]

Third (and wherein he soars far above Daniel) the sinewy
strength and originality of single lines and paragraphs: the frequent *curiosa felicitas* of his diction of which I need not here
give specimens, having anticipated them in a preceding page.
This beauty, and as eminently characteristic of Wordsworth's
poetry, his rudest assailants have felt themselves compelled to
acknowledge and admire.

Fourth: the perfect truth of nature in his images and descriptions as taken immediately from nature, and proving a long and
genial intimacy with the very spirit which gives the physiognomic
expression to all the works of nature. Like a green field

---

[1] [An echo from Wordsworth's Preface (op. cit.): ['The purpose of these
poems] is to follow the fluxes and refluxes of the mind when agitated by the
great and simple affections of our nature.']

[2] [Pindar, *Olympiad*, II. 149–59: 'I have many a swift arrow in the quiver
beneath my arm to sing for those with understanding. But the masses need
interpreters. The true poet is he who knows much by the light of nature,
but those who have only learnt verse as a craft and are violent and im-
moderate in their speech waste their breath in screeching like crows against
the divine bird of Zeus.']

reflected in a calm and perfectly transparent lake, the image is distinguished from the reality only by its greater softness and lustre. Like the moisture or the polish on a pebble, genius neither distorts nor false-colours its objects; but on the contrary brings out many a vein and many a tint which escape the eye of common observation, thus raising to the rank of gems what had been often kicked away by the hurrying foot of the traveller on the dusty highroad of custom.

Let me refer to the whole description of skating, vol. i., page 42 to 47, especially to the lines

> So through the darkness and the cold we flew,
> And not a voice was idle: with the din
> Meanwhile the precipices rang aloud;
> The leafless trees and every icy crag
> Tinkled like iron; while the distant hills
> Into the tumult sent an alien sound
> Of melancholy, not unnoticed while the stars
> Eastward were sparkling clear, and in the west
> The orange sky of evening died away.[1]

Or to the poem on the green linnet, vol. i, p. 244. What can be more accurate yet more lovely than the two concluding stanzas?

> Upon yon tuft of hazel trees,
> That twinkle to the gusty breeze,
> Behold him perched in ecstasies,
>   Yet seeming still to hover,
> There! where the flutter of his wings
> Upon his back and body flings
> Shadows and sunny glimmerings
>   That cover him all over.
>
> While thus before my eyes he gleams
> A brother of the leaves he seems:
> When in a moment forth he teems
>   His little song in gushes:
> As if it pleased him to disdain
> And mock the form which he did feign,
> While he was dancing with the train
>   Of leaves among the bushes.[2]

Or the description of the blue-cap, and of the noon-tide silence, p. 284;[3] or the poem to the cuckoo, p. 299;[4] or lastly, though I

---

[1] ['Influence of Natural Objects' (comp. 1798, publ. in *Friend*, 28 December 1809).   It had already been incorporated in the unpublished *Prelude*.]
[2] ['The Green Linnet' (comp. 1803, publ. 1807).]
[3] ['The Kitten and the Falling Leaves' (comp. 1804, publ. 1807).]
[4] ['To the Cuckoo,' 'O blithe new-comer . . .' (comp. 1802, publ. 1807).]

might multiply the references to ten times the number, to the
poem so completely Wordsworth's commencing

Three years she grew in sun and shower, etc.[1]

Fifth: a meditative pathos, a union of deep and subtle thought
with sensibility; a sympathy with man as man; the sympathy
indeed of a contemplator, rather than a fellow-sufferer or co-mate
(*spectator, haud particeps*), but of a contemplator from whose
view no difference of rank conceals the sameness of the nature;
no injuries of wind or weather, of toil or even of ignorance,
wholly disguise the human face divine. The superscription and
the image of the Creator still remain legible to him under the
dark lines with which guilt or calamity had cancelled or cross-
barred it. Here the man and the poet lose and find themselves
in each other, the one as glorified, the latter as substantiated.
In this mild and philosophic pathos Wordsworth appears to me
without a compeer. Such he is: so he writes. See vol. i, page
134 to 136,[2] or that most affecting composition, the 'Affliction of
Margaret —— of ——,'[3] page 165 to 168, which no mother, and
if I may judge by my own experience, no parent can read without
a tear. Or turn to that genuine lyric, in the former edition,
entitled the 'Mad Mother,' page 174 to 178, of which I cannot
refrain from quoting two of the stanzas, both of them for their
pathos, and the former for the fine transition in the two concluding lines of the stanza, so expressive of that deranged state
in which from the increased sensibility the sufferer's attention is
abruptly drawn off by every trifle and in the same instant
plucked back again by the one despotic thought, and bringing
home with it, by the blending, fusing power of imagination and
passion, the alien object to which it had been so abruptly
diverted, no longer an alien but an ally and an inmate:

> Suck, little babe, oh suck again!
> It cools my blood, it cools my brain:
> Thy lips, I feel them, baby! they
> Draw from my heart the pain away.
> Oh! press me with thy little hand;
> It loosens something at my chest;
> About that tight and deadly band
> I feel thy little fingers prest.
> The breeze I see is in the tree!
> It comes to cool my babe and me.

[1] [Comp. 1799, publ. 1800.]
[2] [''Tis said that some have died for love' (1807).]
[3] ['The Affliction of Margaret ——' (comp. 1801 ?, publ. 1807).]

> Thy father cares not for my breast,
> 'Tis thine, sweet baby, there to rest,
> 'Tis all thine own!—and, if its hue
> Be changed, that was so fair to view,
> 'Tis fair enough for thee, my dove!
> My beauty, little child, is flown,
> But thou wilt live with me in love,
> And what if my poor cheek be brown?
> 'Tis well for me, thou canst not see
> How pale and wan it else would be.[1]

Lastly, and pre-eminently, I challenge for this poet the gift of imagination in the highest and strictest sense of the word. In the play of fancy Wordsworth, to my feelings, is not always graceful, and sometimes recondite. The likeness is occasionally too strange, or demands too peculiar a point of view, or is such as appears the creature of predetermined research rather than spontaneous presentation. Indeed his fancy seldom displays itself as mere and unmodified fancy. But in imaginative power he stands nearest of all modern writers to Shakespeare and Milton; and yet in a kind perfectly unborrowed and his own. To employ his own words, which are at once an instance and an illustration, he does indeed to all thoughts and to all objects—

> add the gleam,
> The light that never was on sea or land.
> The consecration, and the poet's dream.[2]

I shall select a few examples as most obviously manifesting this faculty; but if I should ever be fortunate enough to render my analysis of imagination, its origin and characters, thoroughly intelligible to the reader, he will scarcely open on a page of this poet's works without recognizing, more or less, the presence and the influences of this faculty.

From the poem on the Yew Trees, vol. i. page 303, 304:

> But worthier still of note
> Are those fraternal four of Borrowdale,
> Joined in one solemn and capacious grove;
> Huge trunks! and each particular trunk a growth
> Of intertwisted fibres serpentine
> Up-coiling, and inveterately convolved;
> Not uninformed with phantasy, and looks
> That threaten the profane;—a pillared shade,
> Upon whose grassless floor of red-brown hue,
> By sheddings from the pining umbrage tinged

---

[1] ['Her eyes are wild' (1798), st. iv. and vii.]
[2] ['Elegiac Stanzas Suggested by a Picture of Peele Castle' (comp. 1805, publ. 1807), *ll.* 14–16.]

Perennially—beneath whose sable roof
Of boughs, as if for festal purpose decked
With unrejoicing berries—ghostly shapes
May meet at noontide; Fear and trembling Hope,
Silence and Foresight; Death, the skeleton,
And Time, the shadow;—there to celebrate,
As in a natural temple scattered o'er
With altars undisturbed of mossy stone,
United worship; or in mute repose
To lie, and listen to the mountain flood
Murmuring from Glaramara's inmost caves.[1]

The effect of the old man's figure in the poem of Resignation and Independence, vol. ii., page 33:

While he was talking thus, the lonely place,
The old man's shape, and speech, all troubled me:
In my mind's eye I seemed to see him pace
About the weary moors continually,
Wandering about alone and silently.[2]

Or the 8th, 9th, 19th, 26th, 31st and 33rd in the collection of miscellaneous sonnets—the sonnet on the subjugation of Switzerland, page 210,[3] or the last ode from which I especially select the two following stanzas or paragraphs, page 349 to 350:

Our birth is but a sleep and a forgetting:
The soul that rises with us, our life's star,
Hath had elsewhere its setting,
And cometh from afar.
Not in entire forgetfulness,
And not in utter nakedness,
But trailing clouds of glory do we come
From God, who is our home:
Heaven lies about us in our infancy!
Shades of the prison-house begin to close
Upon the growing boy;
But he beholds the light, and whence it flows,
He sees it in his joy!
The youth who daily further from the east
Must travel, still is nature's priest,
And by the vision splendid
Is on his way attended;
At length the man perceives it die away,
And fade into the light of common day.

---

[1] ['Yew-Trees' (comp. 1803?, publ. 1815), *ll.* 13–33.]
[2] ['Resolution and Independence' (op. cit.), *ll.* 127–31.]
[3] [The sonnets beginning 'Where lies the land,' 'Even as a dragon's eye,' 'O mountain stream,' 'Earth has not anything to shew more fair,' 'Methought I saw' and 'It is a beauteous evening.' The sonnet on Switzerland begins 'Two voices are there.' All but the second (which appeared in the 1815 collection for the first time) were first published in 1807.]

And page 352 to 354 of the same ode:

> O joy that in our embers
> Is something that doth live,
> That nature yet remembers
> What was so fugitive!
> The thought of our past years in me doth breed
> Perpetual benedictions: not indeed
> For that which is most worthy to be blest;
> Delight and liberty, the simple creed
> Of childhood, whether busy or at rest,
> With new-fledged hope still fluttering in his breast:—
> Not for these I raise
> The song of thanks and praise;
> But for those obstinate questionings
> Of sense and outward things,
> Fallings from us, vanishings;
> Blank misgivings of a creature
> Moving about in worlds not realized,
> High instincts, before which our mortal nature
> Did tremble like a guilty thing surprised!
> But for those first affections,
> Those shadowy recollections,
> Which, be they what they may,
> Are yet the fountain light of all our day,
> Are yet a master light of all our seeing;
> Uphold us—cherish—and have power to make
> Our noisy years seem moments in the being
> Of the eternal silence; truths that wake
> To perish never:
> Which neither listlessness, nor mad endeavour,
> Nor man nor boy,
> Nor all that is at enmity with joy
> Can utterly abolish or destroy!
> Hence, in a season of calm weather,
> Though inland far we be,
> Our souls have sight of that immortal sea
> Which brought us hither,
> Can in a moment travel thither—
> And see the children sport upon the shore,
> And hear the mighty waters rolling evermore.[1]

And since it would be unfair to conclude with an extract which though highly characteristic must yet from the nature of the thoughts and the subjects be interesting, or perhaps intelligible, to but a limited number of readers, I will add from the poet's last published work a passage equally Wordsworthian, of the beauty of which, and of the imaginative power displayed therein, there

---

[1] ['Intimations of Immortality' (op. cit.), st. v and ix.]

can be but one opinion and one feeling. See 'White Doe,'
page 5:

> Fast the church-yard fills;—anon
> Look again and they all are gone;
> The cluster round the porch, and the folk
> Who sate in the shade of the prior's oak!
> And scarcely have they disappeared
> Ere the prelusive hymn is heard:
> With one consent the people rejoice,
> Filling the church with a lofty voice!
> They sing a service which they feel
> For 'tis the sun-rise of their zeal
> And faith and hope are in their prime
> In great Eliza's golden time.
>
> A moment ends the fervent din
> And all is hushed without and within;
> For though the priest more tranquilly
> Recites the holy liturgy,
> The only voice which you can hear
> Is the river murmuring near.
> When soft!—the dusky trees between
> And down the path through the open green,
> Where is no living thing to be seen;
> And through yon gateway, where is found,
> Beneath the arch with ivy bound,
> Free entrance to the church-yard ground;
> And right across the verdant sod
> Towards the very house of God;
> Comes gliding in with lovely gleam,
> Comes gliding in serene and slow,
> Soft and silent as a dream,
> A solitary doe!
> White she is as lily of June,
> And beauteous as the silver moon
> When out of sight the clouds are driven
> And she is left alone in heaven!
> Or like a ship some gentle day
> In sunshine sailing far away—
> A glittering ship that hath the plain
> Of ocean for her own domain.
>
> *   *   *   *   *
>
> What harmonious pensive changes
> Wait upon her as she ranges
> Round and round this pile of state
> Overthrown and desolate!
> Now a step or two her way
> Is through space of open day,
> Where the enamoured sunny light
> Brightens her that was so bright:

> Now doth a delicate shadow fall,
> Falls upon her like a breath
> From some lofty arch or wall,
> As she passes underneath.[1]

The following analogy will, I am apprehensive, appear dim and fantastic, but in reading Bartram's *Travels* I could not help transcribing the following lines as a sort of allegory or connected simile and metaphor of Wordsworth's intellect and genius: 'The soil is a deep, rich, dark mould, on a deep stratum of tenacious clay, and that on a foundation of rocks which often break through both strata, lifting their backs above the surface. The trees which chiefly grow here are the gigantic black oak, magnolia magniflora, fraximus excelsior, platane and a few stately tulip trees.' [2]   What Mr Wordsworth *will* produce it is not for me to prophesy: but I could pronounce with the liveliest convictions what he is capable of producing. It is the FIRST GENUINE PHILOSOPHIC POEM.[3]

The preceding criticism will not, I am aware, avail to overcome the prejudices of those who have made it a business to attack and ridicule Mr Wordsworth's compositions.

Truth and prudence might be imaged as concentric circles. The poet may perhaps have passed beyond the latter, but he has confined himself far within the bounds of the former in designating these critics as too petulant to be passive to a genuine poet, and too feeble to grapple with him: 'men of palsied imaginations, in whose minds all healthy action is languid; who therefore feel as the many direct them, or with the many are greedy after vicious provocatives.' [4]

Let not Mr Wordsworth be charged with having expressed

---

[1] ['The White Doe of Rylstone' (comp. 1807–8, publ. 1815), *ll.* 31–66, 79–90.]

[2] [William Bartram, *Travels through Carolina*, etc. (1792), pp. 36 ff. Coleridge has telescoped several of Bartram's descriptions.]

[3] [The *Excursion* had already done something to disappoint this expectation, which in the event was never fulfilled. In a letter to Wordsworth (30 May 1815) expressing his disappointment with the poem at the moment when he was about to begin work on the *Biographia*, Coleridge wrote: 'In the very pride of confident hope I looked forward to the *Recluse* as the first and only true philosophical poem in existence' and proceeded to announce a vast plan to include 'the faculties of man in the abstract,' an affirmation of the Fall, an attack upon Mechanism, etc.]

[4] [Wordsworth, *Essay Supplementary to the Preface* (1815): '. . . critics too petulant to be passive to a genuine poet, and too feeble to grapple with him; . . . men of palsied imaginations and indurated hearts; in whose minds all healthy action is languid, who therefore feel as many direct them, or with the many are greedy after vicious provocatives!']

himself too indignantly till the wantonness and the systematic and malignant perseverance of the aggressions have been taken into fair consideration.[1] I myself heard the commander-in-chief [2] of this unmanly warfare make a boast of his private admiration of Wordsworth's genius. I have heard him declare that whoever came into his room would probably find the *Lyrical Ballads* lying open on his table, and that (speaking exclusively of those written by Mr Wordsworth himself) he could nearly repeat the whole of them by heart. But a Review, in order to be a saleable article, must be personal, sharp and pointed: and since then the poet has made himself, and with himself all who were, or were supposed to be, his friends and admirers, the object of the critic's revenge—how? by having spoken of a work so conducted in the terms which it deserved! I once heard a clergyman in boots and buckskin avow that he would cheat his own father in a horse. A moral system of a similar nature seems to have been adopted by too many anonymous critics. As we used to say at school, in reviewing they *make* being rogues: and he who complains is to be laughed at for his ignorance of the game. With the pen out of their hand they are honorable men. They exert indeed power (which is to that of the injured party who should attempt to expose their glaring perversions and mis-statements as twenty to one) to write down and (where the author's circumstances permit) to impoverish the man whose learning and genius they themselves in private have repeatedly admitted. They knowingly strive to make it impossible for the man even to publish [3] any future work without exposing himself to all the wretchedness of debt and embarrassment. But this is all in their vocation: and bating what they do in their vocation, 'who can say that black is the white of their eye?'

So much for the detractors from Wordsworth's merits. On the other hand, much as I might wish for their fuller sympathy,

---

[1] [This paragraph, with its footnote, was suppressed by Sara Coleridge in the second edition of the *Biographia* (1847): 'As those passages contain personal remarks, right or wrong, they were anomalies in my father's writings. unworthy of them and of him' (i. clviii).]

[2] [Jeffrey himself Cf. letter to Daniel Stuart (9 July 1825) and Crabb Robinson's *Diary*, 14 November 1810.]

[3] Not many months ago an eminent bookseller was asked what he thought of ——? The answer was: 'I have heard his powers very highly spoken of by some of our first-rate men; but I would not have a work of his if any one would give it me: for he is spoken but slightly of, or not at all, in the *Quarterly Review*: and the *Edinburgh*, you know, is decided to cut him up!'

I dare not flatter myself that the freedom with which I have
declared my opinions concerning both his theory and his defects,
most of which are more or less connected with his theory either
as cause or effect, will be satisfactory or pleasing to all the poet's
admirers and advocates.   More indiscriminate than mine their
admiration may be: deeper and more sincere it cannot be.   But
I have advanced no opinion either for praise or censure other
than as texts introductory to the reasons which compel me to
form it.   Above all, I was fully convinced that such a criticism
was not only wanted; but that, if executed with adequate ability,
it must conduce in no mean degree to Mr Wordsworth's reputation.   His fame belongs to another age, and can neither be
accelerated nor retarded.   How small the proportion of the
defects are to the beauties I have repeatedly declared; and that
no one of them originates in deficiency of poetic genius.   Had
they been more and greater, I should still, as a friend to his
literary character in the present age, consider an analytic display
of them as pure gain; if only it removed, as surely to all reflecting
minds even the foregoing analysis must have removed, the
strange mistake so slightly grounded yet so widely and indus-
triously propagated of Mr Wordsworth's turn for simplicity!
I am not half as much irritated by hearing his enemies abuse him
for vulgarity of style, subject and conception, as I am disgusted
with the gilded side of the same meaning, as displayed by some
affected admirers with whom he is, forsooth, a sweet, simple
poet! and so natural, that little master Charles and his younger
sister are so charmed with them, that they play at 'Goody
Blake,' or at 'Johnny and Betty Foy'!

Were the collection of poems published with these biographical sketches important enough (which I am not vain
enough to believe) to deserve such a distinction: even as I have
done, so would I be done unto.

For more than eighteen months have the volume of poems
entitled *Sibylline Leaves* and the present volumes up to this
page been printed and ready for publication.   But ere I speak of
myself in the tones which are alone natural to me under the circumstances of late years, I would fain present myself to the
reader as I was in the first dawn of my literary life:

> When Hope grew round me, like the climbing vine,
> And fruits, and foliage, not my own, seem'd mine.[1]

---

[1] ['Dejection: an Ode,' *ll.* 80–1.]

For this purpose I have selected from the letters which I wrote home from Germany those which appeared likely to be most interesting, and at the same time most pertinent to the title of this work.[1]

---

[1] [There follows in *1817* and in subsequent reprints three letters written during his stay in Germany (1798–9): 'Satyrane's Letters,' first published in *The Friend* (Nos. 14, 16 and 18) in 1809 and much revised; after which there follows as 'Chapter XXIII' a reprint from the *Courier* of an attack upon the tragedy *Bertram* by the Irish dramatist and novelist C. R. Maturin (1782–1824), which ran successfully at Drury Lane in May 1816 where it had been accepted in preference to Coleridge's own *Zapolya*. In the writing of this critique John Morgan, Coleridge's host at Calne, played a large but undefined part. See Introduction, pp. xv–xviii above.]

CONCLUSION

IT sometimes happens that we are punished for our faults by incidents in the causation of which these faults had no share: and this I have always felt the severest punishment. The wound indeed is of the same dimensions; but the edges are jagged, and there is a dull under-pain that survives the smart which it had aggravated. For there is always a consolatory feeling that accompanies the sense of a proportion between antecedents and consequents. The sense of Before and After becomes both intelligible and intellectual when, and only when, we contemplate the succession in the relations of Cause and Effect, which like the two poles of the magnet manifest the being and unity of the one power by relative opposites and give, as it were, a substratum of permanence, of identity and therefore of reality to the shadowy flux of Time. It is Eternity revealing itself in the phaenomena of Time: and the perception and acknowledgment of the proportionality and appropriateness of the Present to the Past prove to the afflicted Soul that it has not yet been deprived of the sight of God, that it can still recognize the effective presence of a Father, though through a darkened glass and a turbid atmosphere, though of a Father that is chastising it. And for this cause, doubtless, are we so framed in mind, and even so organized in brain and nerve, that all confusion is painful. It is within the experience of many medical practitioners that a patient with strange and unusual symptoms of disease has been more distressed in mind, more wretched, from the fact of being unintelligible to himself and others than from the pain or danger of the disease: nay, that the patient has received the most solid comfort, and resumed a genial and enduring chearfulness, from some new symptom or product that had at once determined the name and nature of his complaint and rendered it an intelligible effect of an intelligible cause; even though the discovery did at the same moment preclude all hope of restoration. Hence the mystic theologians, whose delusions we may more confidently hope to separate from their actual intuitions when we condescend to read their works without the presumption that whatever our fancy (always the ape, and too often the adulterator and counterfeit of our memory) has not made or cannot make a picture of, must be nonsense,—

279

hence I say, the mystics have joined in representing the state of
the reprobate spirits as a dreadful dream in which there is no
sense of reality, not even of the pangs they are enduring—an
eternity without time, and as it were below it—God present
without manifestation of his presence.   But these are depths
which we dare not linger over.   Let us turn to an instance more
on a level with the ordinary sympathies of mankind.   Here
then, and in this same healing influence of light and distinct
beholding, we may detect the final cause of that instinct which
in the great majority of instances leads and almost compels the
afflicted to communicate their sorrows.   Hence too flows the
alleviation that results from 'opening out our griefs': which are
thus presented in distinguishable forms instead of the mist
through which whatever is shapeless becomes magnified and
(literally) *enormous*.   Casimir, in the fifth Ode of his third Book,
has happily [1] expressed this thought:

> Me longus silendi
> Edit amor, facilesque luctus

> Hausit medullas.   Fugerit ocyus,
> Simul negantem visere jusseris
>   Aures amicorum, et loquacem
>   Questibus evacuaris iram.

> Olim querendo desinimus queri,
> Ipsoque fletu lacryma perditur,
>   Nec fortis aequè, si per omnes
>   Cura volat residetque ramos.

> Vires amicis perdit in auribus
> Minorque semper dividitur dolor,
>   Per multa permissus vagari
>   Pectora.

> *Id. Lib.* iii. Od. 5.[2]

---

[1] Classically too, as far as consists with the allegorizing fancy of the modern,
that still striving to project the inward contra-distinguishes itself from the
seeming ease with which the poetry of the ancients reflects the world without.
Casimir affords, perhaps, the most striking instance of this characteristic
difference.   For his style and diction are really classical: while Cowley, who
resembles Casimir in many respects, completely barbarizes his Latinity, and
even his metre, by the heterogeneous nature of his thoughts.   That Dr
Johnson should have passed a contrary judgement, and have even preferred
Cowley's Latin poems to Milton's, is a caprice that has, if I mistake not,
excited the surprise of all scholars.   I was much amused last summer with
the laughable affright with which an Italian poet perused a page of Cowley's
Davideis, contrasted with the enthusiasm with which he first ran through,
and then read aloud, Milton's 'Mansus' and 'Ad Patrem.'

[2] [Casimir Sarbiewski (1595–1640), the Polish Jesuit poet, *Odes* (1635),

I shall not make this an excuse, however, for troubling my readers with any complaints or explanations with which, as readers, they have little or no concern. It may suffice (for the present at least) to declare that the causes that have delayed the publication of these volumes for so long a period after they had been printed off were not connected with any neglect of my own; and that they would form an instructive comment on the chapter concerning authorship as a trade addressed to young men of genius in the first volume of this work.[1] I remember the ludicrous effect which the first sentence of an autobiography [produced], which happily for the writer was as meagre in incidents as it is well possible for the life of an individual to be—'the *eventful* life which I am about to record, from the hour in which I rose into existence on this planet, etc.' Yet when, notwithstanding this warning example of self-importance before me, I review my own life, I cannot refrain from applying the same epithet to it, and with more than ordinary emphasis—and no private feeling that affected myself only should prevent me from publishing the same (for write it I assuredly shall, should life and leisure be granted me [2]) if continued reflection should strengthen my present belief that my history would add its contingent to the enforcement of one important truth, viz. that we must not only love our neighbours as ourselves, but ourselves likewise as our neighbours; and that we can do neither unless we love God above both.

> Who lives, that's not
> Depraved or depraves? Who dies, *that bears*
> *Not one spurn to the grave—of their friends' gift?* [3]

Strange as the delusion may appear, yet it is most true that three

---

III. v. 11–24 ('*Te* longus silendi . . .'): 'The long love of keeping silent consumed me, and grief drew its soft marrows. It will fly swiftly as soon as you order it, against all refusal, to visit the ears of your friends and empty your anger in talk and lamentations. By complaining we cease to complain, a tear is lost in the very act of weeping, and sorrow grows less if it takes flight like a bird and sits on all the branches. Grief loses its strength in friendly ears and grows ever less when divided and sent to wander through many hearts.']

[1] [Chapter XI above.]

[2] [This projected autobiography was never written, but the fact that Coleridge promises it here shows how little he regarded the *Biographia* as autobiographical.]

[3] [*Timon of Athens*, I. ii. 147–9:
  'Who lives that's not depraved or depraves?
  Who dies that bears not one spurn to their graves
  Of their friend's gift?']

years ago I did not know or believe that I had an enemy in the
world: and now even my strongest sensations of gratitude are
mingled with fear, and I reproach myself for being too often
disposed to ask, Have I one friend? During the many years
which intervened between the composition and the publication
of the Christabel,[1] it became almost as well known among literary
men as if it had been on common sale; the same references were
made to it, and the same liberties taken with it, even to the very
names of the imaginary persons in the poem. From almost all of
our most celebrated poets, and from some with whom I had no
personal acquaintance, I either received or heard of expressions
of admiration that (I can truly say) appeared to myself utterly
disproportionate to a work that pretended to be nothing more
than a common faery tale. Many who had allowed no merit to
my other poems, whether printed or manuscript, and who have
frankly told me as much, uniformly made an exception in favour
of the Christabel and the poem entitled 'Love.'[2] Year after
year, and in societies of the most different kinds, I had been
entreated to recite it: and the result was still the same in all, and
altogether different in this respect from the effect produced by
the occasional recitation of any other poems I had composed.
This before the publication. And since then, with very few
exceptions, I have heard nothing but abuse, and this too in a
spirit of bitterness at least as disproportionate to the pretensions
of the poem, had it been the most pitiably below mediocrity,
as the previous eulogies, and far more inexplicable. In the
Edinburgh Review it was assailed with a malignity and a spirit of
personal hatred that ought to have injured only the work in
which such a tirade was suffered to appear; and this review was
generally attributed (whether rightly or no I know not) to a man
who both in my presence and in my absence has repeatedly

---

[1] [i.e. 1800–16, during which period the poem must have been passed
round in manuscript and often recited. Walter Scott certainly borrowed from
it, Byron may have done. Scott admitted in a letter to Mrs Hughes (11 November 1824) that he had been 'led to imitate the stile' of 'Christabel' in his
'Lay of the Last Minstrel' (1805); Byron, in a note to his 'Siege of Corinth,'
published like 'Christabel' in February 1816, admitted 'a close, though unin-
tentional resemblance' at *ll*. 521–32. In a letter to Coleridge (June 1815) he
admitted having heard Scott recite the poem but again denied plagiarism.
It is clear that Coleridge was in a strong position when he declared in his
Preface to 'Christabel' that 'the celebrated poets whose writings I might be
suspected of having imitated . . . would be among the first to vindicate me
from the charge.']

[2] [Published in the *Morning Post* (1799) and reprinted in the second edition
of the *Lyrical Ballads* (1800). It seems to have been a first draft of the longer
poem 'The Dark Ladie.']

pronounced it the finest poem of its kind in the language.[1] This may serve as a warning to authors that in their calculations on the probable reception of a poem they must subtract to a large amount from the panegyric which may have encouraged them to publish it, however unsuspicious and however various the sources of this panegyric may have been. And first, allowances must be made for private enmity, of the very existence of which they had perhaps entertained no suspicion—for personal enmity behind the mask of anonymous criticism: secondly, for the necessity of a certain proportion of abuse and ridicule in a review in order to make it saleable, in consequence of which, if they have no friends behind the scenes, the chance must needs be against them; but lastly and chiefly, for the excitement and temporary sympathy of feeling which the recitation of the poem by an admirer, especially if he be at once a warm admirer and a man of acknowledged celebrity, calls forth in the audience. For this is really a species of animal magnetism, in which the enkindling reciter, by perpetual comment of looks and tones, lends his own will and apprehensive faculty to his editors. They live for the time within the dilated sphere of his intellectual being. It is equally possible, though not equally common, that a reader left to himself should sink below the poem as that the poem left to itself should flag beneath the feelings of the reader. But in my own instance, I had the additional misfortune of having been gossipped about as devoted to metaphysics, and worse than all to a system incomparably nearer to the visionary flights of Plato, and even to the jargon of the mystics, than to the estab-lished tenets of Locke. Whatever therefore appeared with my name was condemned beforehand as predestined metaphysics. In a dramatic poem which had been submitted by me to a gentle-man of great influence in the theatrical world, occurred the following passage:

> O we are querulous creatures!   Little less
> Than all things can suffice to make us happy:
> And little more than nothing is enough
> To make us wretched.[2]

Aye, here now (exclaimed the critic)—here comes Coleridge's metaphysics!   And the very same motive (that is, not that the

---

[1] [i.e. Hazlitt. But the attribution of this review is uncertain and its manner uncharacteristic of Hazlitt. If his at all it must have been con-siderably retouched by Jeffrey.]

[2] [Zapolya, II. i. i. The fourth line reads 'To discontent us' in the original. The 'gentleman of great influence' was apparently Byron, in spite of whose sponsorship the play was not accepted for production.]

lines were unfit for the present state of our immense theatres,
but that they were metaphysics [1]) was assigned elsewhere for the
rejection of the two following passages.   The first is spoken in
answer to a usurper, who had rested his plea on the circumstance
that he had been chosen by the acclamations of the people:

> What people? How conven'd? Or if conven'd,
> Must not that magic power that charms together
> Millions of men in council, needs have power
> To win or wield them?   Rather, O far rather,
> Shout forth thy titles to yon circling mountains,
> And with a thousandfold reverberation
> Make the rocks flatter thee, and the volleying air,
> Unbribed, shout back to thee, King Emerick!
> By wholesome laws to embank the sovereign power;
> To deepen by restraint; and by prevention
> Of lawless will to amass and guide the flood
> In its majestic channel, is man's task
> And the true patriot's glory!   In all else,
> Men safelier trust to heaven than to themselves
> When least themselves: even in those whirling crowds
> When folly is contagious, and too oft
> Even wise men leave their better sense at home
> To chide and wonder at them when return'd.[2]

The second passage is in the mouth of an old and experienced
courtier, betrayed by the man in whom he had most trusted:

> And yet Sarolta, simple, inexperienced,
> Could see him as he was and oft has warn'd me.
> Whence learnt she this? O she was innocent!
> And to be innocent is Nature's wisdom.
> The fledge-dove knows the prowlers of the air,
> Fear'd soon as seen, and flutters back to shelter!
> And the young steed recoils upon his haunches,
> The never-yet-seen adder's hiss first heard!
> Ah! surer than suspicion's hundred eyes
> Is that fine sense, which to the pure in heart
> By mere oppugnancy of their own goodness
> Reveals the approach of evil![3]

As therefore my character as a writer could not easily be more
injured by an overt act than it was already in consequence of the

---

[1] Poor unlucky metaphysics! and what are they? A single sentence
expresses the object and thereby the contents of this science.   Γνῶθι σεαυτόν:
et Deum quantum licet et in Deo omnia scibis.   Know thyself: and so shalt
thou know God, as far as is permitted to a creature, and in God all things.
Surely, there is a strange—nay, rather a too natural—aversion in many to
know themselves.

[2] [Zapolya, I. i. i. (with minor inaccuracies).]

[3] [Ibid., II. iv. i.]

report, I published a work a large portion of which was professedly metaphysical.[1] A long delay occurred between its first annunciation and its appearance; it was reviewed therefore by anticipation with a malignity so avowedly and exclusively personal as is, I believe, unprecedented even in the present contempt of all common humanity that disgraces and endangers the liberty of the press. After its appearance, the author of this lampoon was chosen to review it in the *Edinburgh Review*: [2] and under the single condition that he should have written what he himself really thought, and have criticized the work as he would have done had its author been indifferent to him, I should have chosen that man myself, both from the vigour and the originality of his mind and from his particular acuteness in speculative reasoning, before all others. I remembered Catullus's lines:

> Desine de quoquam quicquam bene velle mereri,
>   aut aliquem fieri posse putare pium.
> omnia sunt ingrata, nihil fecisse benigne est,
>   immo etiam taedet, taedet obestque magis;
> ut mihi, quem nemo gravius nec acerbius urget
>   quam modo qui me unum atque unicum amicum habuit.[3]

But I can truly say that the grief with which I read this rhapsody of predetermined insult had the rhapsodist himself for its whole and sole object: and that the indignant contempt which it excited in me was as exclusively confined to his employer and suborner. I refer to this review at present in consequence of information having been given me that the innuendo of my 'potential infidelity,' grounded on one passage of my first Lay Sermon, has been received and propagated with a degree of credence of which I can safely acquit the originator of the calumny. I give the sentences as they stand in the sermon, premising only that I was speaking exclusively of miracles worked for the outward senses of men. 'It was only to overthrow the usurpation exercised in and through the senses that

---

[1] [The *Statesman's Manual* (1816), first of the two *Lay Sermons*.]

[2] [The complaint is again directed against Hazlitt, who had 'reviewed' the work unseen on the appearance of its advertisement, attacking Coleridge for his obscurity (*Examiner*, 8 September 1816), and later reviewed the work itself both in the *Examiner* and in the *Edinburgh Review* (December 1816).]

[3] [*Carmina*, lxxiii: 'Cease wanting to deserve well or think well of anyone. The world is ungrateful, kindness goes for nothing and even irritates and impedes. As for me, no one has treated me more severely and cruelly than one who held me for his one and only friend.' *ll.* 3–4 should read:
'nihil fecisse benigne
prodest, immo etiam taedet obestque magis.']

the senses were miraculously appealed to. REASON AND
RELIGION ARE THEIR OWN EVIDENCE. The natural sun is in this
respect a symbol of the spiritual. Ere he is fully arisen, and
while his glories are still under veil, he calls up the breeze to
chase away the usurping vapours of the night-season, and thus
converts the air itself into the minister of its own purification:
not surely in proof or elucidation of the light from heaven, but to
prevent its interception.

'Wherever, therefore, similar circumstances co-exist with the
same moral causes, the principles revealed and the examples
recorded in the inspired writings render miracles superfluous:
and if we neglect to apply truths in expectation of wonders, or
under pretext of the cessation of the latter, we tempt God, and
merit the same reply which our Lord gave to the Pharisees on a
like occasion.'

In the sermon and the notes both the historical truth and the
necessity of the miracles are strongly and frequently asserted.
'The testimony of books of history (i.e. relatively to the signs and
wonders, with which Christ came) is one of the strong and
stately pillars of the church; but it is not the foundation!'
Instead, therefore, of defending myself, which I could easily
effect by a series of passages expressing the same opinion from
the Fathers and the most eminent Protestant divines from the
Reformation to the Revolution, I shall merely state what my
belief is concerning the true evidences of Christianity. 1. Its
consistency with right reason I consider as the outer court of
the temple—the common area within which it stands. 2. The
miracles with and through which the religion was first revealed
and attested I regard as the steps, the vestibule and the portal
of the temple. 3. The sense, the inward feeling, in the soul of
each believer of its exceeding desirableness—the experience that
he needs something, joined with the strong foretokening that the
redemption and the graces propounded to us in Christ are what
he needs—this I hold to be the true foundation of the spiritual
èdifice. With the strong *a priori* probability that flows in from
1 and 3 on the correspondent historical evidence of 2, no man can
refuse or neglect to make the experiment without guilt. But 4,
it is the experience derived from a practical conformity to the
conditions of the Gospel—it is the opening eye; the dawning
light; the terrors and the promises of spiritual growth; the
blessedness of loving God as God, the nascent sense of sin hated
as sin, and of the incapability of attaining to either without
Christ; it is the sorrow that still rises up from beneath and the

consolation that meets it from above; the bosom treacheries of the principal in the warfare and the exceeding faithfulness and long-suffering of the uninterested ally; in a word, it is the actual trial of the faith in Christ, with its accompaniments and results, that must form the arched roof, and the faith itself is the completing key-stone. In order to an efficient belief in Christianity a man must have been a Christian, and this is the seeming *argumentum in circulo* incident to all spiritual truths, to every subject not presentable under the forms of time and space, as long as we attempt to master by the reflex acts of the understanding what we can only know by the act of becoming. 'Do the will of my father, and ye shall know whether I am of God.' [1] These four evidences I believe to have been and still to be for the world, for the whole church, all necessary, all equally necessary; but that at present, and for the majority of Christians born in Christian countries, I believe the third and the fourth evidences to be the most operative, not as superseding, but as involving a glad undoubting faith in the two former. *Credidi, indeóque intellexi* [2] appears to me the dictate equally of philosophy and religion, even as I believe redemption to be the antecedent of sanctification and not its consequent. All spiritual predicates may be construed indifferently as modes of action or as states of being. Thus holiness and blessedness are the same idea, now seen in relation to act and now to existence. The ready belief which has been yielded to the slander of my 'potential infidelity' I attribute in part to the openness with which I have avowed my doubts whether the heavy interdict under which the name of Benedict Spinoza lies is merited on the whole or to the whole extent. Be this as it may, I wish however that I could find in the books of philosophy, theoretical or moral, which are alone recommended to the present students of theology in our established schools, a few passages as thoroughly Pauline, as completely accordant with the doctrines of the established Church, as the following sentences in the concluding page of Spinoza's Ethics: 'Deinde quo mens hoc amore divino seu beatitudine magis gaudet, eo plus intelligit, eo majorem in affectus habet potentiam, et eó minus ab affectibus, qui mali sunt, patitur: atque adeo ex eo, quód mens hoc amore divino seu beatitudine gaudet, potestatem habet libidines coercendi, . . . nemo beatitudine

---

[1] [From John vii. 17: 'If any man will do his will, he shall know of the doctrine, whether it be of God, or whether I speak of myself.']

[2] ['I believed, and so I understood.' From Augustine, *Tractatus* xxix. 6: 'Noli quaerere intelligere ut credas, sed crede ut intelligas.']

gaudet quia affectus coercuit; sed contra potestas libidines coercendi ex ipsa beatitudine oritur.'[1]

With regard to the Unitarians, it has been shamelessly asserted that I have denied them to be Christians. God forbid! For how should I know what the piety of the heart may be, or what quantum of error in the understanding may consist with a saving faith in the intentions and actual dispositions of the whole moral being in any one individual? Never will God reject a soul that sincerely loves him, be his speculative opinions what they may: and whether in any given instance certain opinions, be they unbelief or misbelief, are compatible with a sincere love of God, God only can know. But this I have said, and shall continue to say: that if the doctrines, the sum of which I believe to constitute the truth in Christ, be Christianity, then Unitarianism is not, and vice versa: and that in speaking theologically and impersonally, i.e. of Psilanthropism and Theanthropism as schemes of belief, without reference to individuals who profess either the one or the other, it will be absurd to use a different language as long as it is the dictate of common sense that two opposites cannot properly be called by the same name. I should feel no offence if a Unitarian applied the same to me, any more than if he were to say that 2 and 2 being 4, 4 and 4 must be 8.

> ἀλλὰ βροτῶν
> τὸν μὲν κενεόφρονες αὖχαι
> ἐξ ἀγαθῶν ἔβαλον.
> τὸν δ' αὖ καταμεμφθέντ' ἄγαν
> ἰσχὺν οἰκείων παρέσφαλεν καλῶν,
> χειρὸς ἕλκων ὀπίσσω, θυμός ἄτολμος ἐών.

> PINDAR, Nem. Ode XI.[2]

This has been my object, and this alone can be my defence—and O! that with this my personal as well as my LITERARY LIFE might conclude! the unquenched desire I mean, not without the consciousness of having earnestly endeavoured to kindle young minds and to guard them against the temptations of scorners by

---

[1] [*Ethics*, V. 42: 'And then, the more the mind delights in this divine love or blessedness, the more it understands, the greater its power over its instincts and the less it suffers from instincts that are evil. And so it is because the mind delights in this divine love or blessedness that it has the power to restrain lusts. . . . No one delights in blessedness because he has restrained his instincts, but on the contrary the power of restraining lusts arises from the blessedness itself.']

[2] [Ode xi, *ll.* 29–32: 'But one among mortals is cast down from the height of joy by empty-headed conceit; another through too little confidence in his strength loses the honour of victory, because timidity snatched his hand and drew it back.']

showing that the scheme of Christianity, as taught in the liturgy and homilies of our Church, though not discoverable by human reason, is yet in accordance with it; that link follows link by necessary consequence; that religion passes out of the ken of reason only where the eye of reason has reached its own horizon; and that faith is then but its continuation: even as the day softens away into the sweet twilight, and twilight, hushed and breathless, steals into the darkness. It is night, sacred night! the upraised eye views only the starry heaven which manifests itself alone: and the outward beholding is fixed on the sparks twinkling in the aweful depth, though suns of other worlds, only to preserve the soul steady and collected in its pure act of inward adoration to the great I AM, and to the filial WORD that re-affirmeth it from eternity to eternity, whose choral echo is the universe.

$$\Theta E\Omega\iota \ MON\Omega\iota \ \Delta O\Xi A.^1$$

FINIS

---

1 ['Glory to God alone'—from John v. 44.]

INDEX